CONTINUING GERMAN
A Bridge to Literature

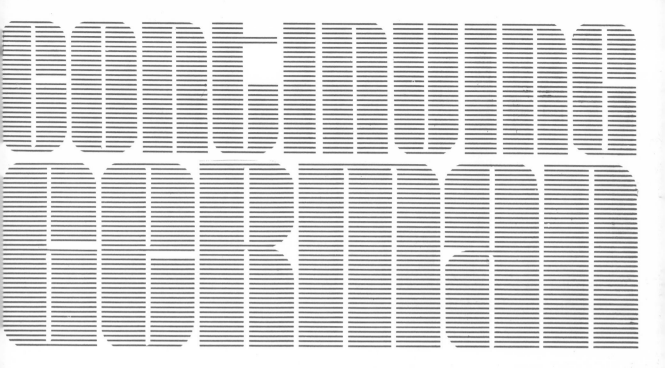

CONTINUING GERMAN

A Bridge to Literature

Albert M. Reh

Department of German   University of Massachusetts

McGRAW-HILL BOOK COMPANY

New York   St. Louis   San Francisco   Düsseldorf
London   Mexico   Panama   Sydney   Toronto

WOLFGANG BORCHERT: An diesem Dienstag,
Nachts schlafen die Ratten doch,

From *Gesamtwerk*, Rowohlt Verlag, GmbH, Hamburg, © 1949

HEINRICH BÖLL: Die ungezählte Geliebte (original title: An der Brücke)

From *1947 bis 1951*, 4. Auflage, Friedrich Middelhauve Verlag, Köln, © 1965   © 1965

HERBERT MALECHA: Die Probe,

From *die Probe, Kurzgeschichten verschiedener Autoren*, Marion von Schröder Verlag, Hamburg, © 1955

BERTOLT BRECHT: Wenn die Haifische Menschen wären,
Der Augsburger Kreidekreis,

From *Kalendergeschichten*, Gebrüder Weiss Verlag, Berlin, © 1953

FRANZ KAFKA: Der Türhüter,
Eine Kaiserliche Botschaft,
Aus dem Nachlass,

From *Parabeln und Paradoxe*, Schocken Books Inc., New York, © 1946, 1953, 1958

FRANZ KAFKA: Section No. 54, Part II ("Mit stärkstem Licht...") of Betrachtungen über Sünde...,

From *Hochzeitsvorbereitungen auf dem Lande*, Schocken Books Inc., New York, © 1953

FRANZ KAFKA: Der Schlag ans Hoftor,
Der Steuermann,
Gibs Auf!
Nachts,

From *Beschreibungen eines Kampfes*, Schocken Books Inc., New York, © 1946

CONTINUING GERMAN: A Bridge to Literature

Library of Congress Catalog Card Number 77-103910
51698

1 2 3 4 5 6 7 8 9 0 VHVH 7 9 8 7 6 5 4 3 2 1 0

This book was set in Baskerville and News Gothic by Monotype
Composition Company, Inc., and printed on permanent paper and
bound by Von Hoffmann Press, Inc. The designer was Elliot Epstein.
The editors were Samuel B. Bossard and Madelaine Eichberg. Les
Kaplan supervised production.

PREFACE

"Continuing German: A Bridge to Literature" is designed to help student and teacher to accomplish the most difficult step in language learning and language teaching: the transition from elementary lessons in grammar to reading and discussing literary texts. In most colleges this is the goal of the intermediate class, that is, the second-year college language course. It is at this level that we find ourselves presented with acute problems, and it is to those problems that this text is addressed.

Because students enter the intermediate course from a wide variety of language backgrounds and have not all been taught by the same methods, the teacher has little idea of what they really know. These students must somehow be brought to a common level of knowledge. One way of trying to achieve this is to use a review grammar along with reading material. But it usually turns out that there is no relation at all between the reading material, on the one hand, and the review grammar on the other. Students discover in their literary reader a new world of vocabulary, grammar, and meaning but when they turn to their review grammar they find a second—and largely unrelated—world of vocabulary, grammar, and meaning.

The main feature of this textbook is direct coordination of grammar review with the reading of literature. Only by close coordination can we hope to avoid teaching grammar in a vacuum and at the same time ease the transition to literature.

The Grammar Review

1. The grammar is based on Schulz-Griesbach, *Grammatik der deutschen Sprache*, especially the presentation of the noun and adjective declensions, the modal verbs (objective and subjective use), and the syntax (Vorfeld, Satzfeld, Nachfeld).

2. The presentation of the grammatical problems as well as the drills follow the principles of programmed learning consistently, that is, each problem is dealt with separately, and each step forward follows upon the preceding steps. A typical sequence of drills consists of a drill for each problem, followed by a drill combining the problems. The very purpose of the combination drills is to test each new step. For the teacher this means that he may concentrate on the combination drills in checking the grammatical assignments, thus holding the drill work in class to a minimum. He is thus also provided with the grammatical material for the chapter quizzes and the tests of the course. For the student it means that, in his homework as well as during the work in the language laboratory, he has a reliable means for checking his knowledge of grammar, especially when he reviews earlier chapters.

3. The grammar review at this stage should be intermediate in nature. The basic type of exercise selected by the author is the pattern drill, because only the pattern drill can be practiced with-

out the book or any other printed material, thus developing the student's listening comprehension as well as his ability to *speak independently of any written guide.* The pattern drill also makes possible a close coordination of the work in the language laboratory with that in the classroom, so that the language laboratory functions as an extension of the classroom and the student can do the bulk of his oral homework in the language laboratory. Therefore the tape script for the language laboratory repeats the drills of the book.

The pattern drill, however, must be more sophisticated than at the elementary level. In place of the typical "cue" or "formal grammar drill," in which the student concentrates only on producing the correct *form,* the *comprehension drill* is used, which stresses with varied and sophisticated vocabulary not only form but also *meaning and use.* Such drills show a real *dialogue constellation* in which the student answers or asks a question, agrees or disagrees, responds logically, or expresses given statements in some other manner using the grammatical form to be mastered. In this way the student is trained throughout the grammar review to *concentrate on meaning as well as form* and to practice the natural and logical application of the particular grammatical problem. Thus grammar review leads directly to classroom work with the literature itself.

4. The grammar review is closely tied to the literary pieces being read and discussed; its function is to give the student confidence and competence in active approach to his reading.

But literature does not—and should not—lend itself to the review of mere problems of form, that is, of mere morphological problems. It is the experience of the author (and probably of most teachers) that a student should not begin to read literature in a foreign language until he has achieved basic control of declension and conjugation. Therefore a general introductory chapter (Chapter 1) accompanies the intensive review of these basic matters. Only problems of syntax and style, in the broadest sense of these words (the use and function of main and subordinate clauses, modals, the subjunctive, the passive voice, etc.) are presented along with the reading of literature. The entire vocabulary of the grammar review consists of words and expressions taken from the literary pieces as well as of abstract words and expressions needed in discussing them. The student is thus greatly assisted in building his knowledge of vocabulary—the crux of intermediate courses.

The Literature

The literature itself presents (*a*) vocabulary and (*b*) grammatical and stylistic problems that take the student beyond any basic review of grammar.

a. The vocabulary is given on left-hand pages, facing the text, and is divided into two columns: The right-hand column shows the active vocabulary needed in discussing the text, and the left-hand column shows the passive vocabulary.

b. Idiomatic expressions that occur in the text and should be learned for active use follow the text; they are then practiced in drill sections. The principle of continuous re-entry of vocabulary is followed, and expressions learned in previous chapters are reintroduced and reviewed until the student has mastered them and can control their usage. The first chapters also contain special vocabulary-building exercises which are designed to teach the student to build derivatives and to understand their use and meaning.

2. The ultimate goal of an approach to literature in a language course is classroom discussion of the literary work and a probing into its value and style. One device traditionally used to attain at least part of this goal is the set of questions that so often accompany literary texts—those familiar "end of chapter" questions. The main weakness of such questions is that they offer the student no linguistic aids for formulating his answers; about all he can do is to memorize blindly the exact wording of the text. This can be highly frustrating. It can also lead him to use highly literary phrases in answers that are otherwise conversational in style. One solution to this dilemma would be to abandon questions altogether and to try to replace them with other devices. The author has instead introduced new patterns of question and response called *questionnaires*.

The questionnaires are divided into three groups: The first, the A-questions, deal with points of fact. They test the student's ability to retell the plot. In trying to help the student formulate his answers, the author has found two devices particularly useful. First, each A-question is followed by a series of English key words, so-called dehydrated sentences. By using these key words the student need not rely on memory but can concentrate on the necessary grammar to formulate his answer. The key words are given in English to help the student build up his active vocabulary. Second, the author of the literary piece usually writes his story in the narrative past. In retelling a story, however, we shift to the present and perfect tenses—the present-time system—if we are relating single details. Therefore all A-questions are asked, and are to be answered, in the present-time system (if not otherwise indicated). Special instructions ask the student to use syntactical forms which he has already practiced in the parallel grammatical chapter. By retelling the story in this way the student not only avoids memorizing but also gains valuable practice in the manipulation of grammar.

The student is now able to handle *the C-questions*. They will provide opportunity to discuss the ideas and problems of the story. As these questions require free composition and discussion, the C-question should be prepared first in writing, later orally. At this stage a free discussion of the meaning, idea, and value of the literary work should be no longer a linguistic problem because all previous work leads to this goal.

The Teacher's Manual

Every teacher using the text may obtain and should use the Teacher's Manual which offers suggestions on how to teach individual parts of this text, quiz and test samples for all the chapters, and a suggested syllabus as a guide to planning the lessons.

Acknowledgements

I wish to thank Miss Carol T. Washburn who developed the vocabulary and participated in the design and formulation of the exercises and questionnaires.

My particular thanks go to Professor Victor A. Oswald of UCLA who was my severest critic and my most thorough adviser. He not only worked as a critic but also contributed his own ideas. The quick-response principle of the questionnaires and the use of the tenses in them are his suggestions.

I am indebted to Miss Madelaine Eichberg of McGraw-Hill Book Company for her excellent work in organizing and copy editing the manuscript and to Elliot Epstein for designing the book.

My debt and gratitude are also due to the instructors and teaching assistants who have taught and to all the students who have been taught with the manuscript for the last four years, to the members of the language laboratories and duplicating offices of the University of Massachusetts and Smith College, and to Mrs. K. Butler and Mrs. Mary Greenwood of Amherst who typed the manuscript.

Albert M. Reh

CONTENTS

CONTINUING GERMAN
A Bridge to Literature

CHAPTER

THE NOUN

The two characteristic features of the German noun that cause difficulty to the English-speaking student are the *plural forms* and the *genders*.

I. THE PLURAL FORMS OF THE NOUN

Whereas the great majority of English nouns form their plural by adding *–s* or *–es, German nouns* form their *plural* in *five different ways.*

A. Five Different Ways of Forming the Plural of Nouns

	Singular	*Plural*	*Plural form*	*Ending*	*English*
1	der Dichter	die Dichter		–	poet
	das Fenster	die Fenster			window
	der Vater	die Väter	with umlaut	··	father
	die Mutter	die Mütter			mother
2	der Freund	die Freunde		–e	friend
	das Jahr	die Jahre			year
	die Kenntnis	die Kenntnisse			knowledge
	der Satz	die Sätze	with umlaut	··e	sentence
	die Stadt	die Städte			city, town
3	das Kind	die Kinder		–er	child
	der Mann	die Männer	with umlaut	··er	man
	das Wort	die Wörter			word
4	der Mensch	die Menschen		–(e)n	human being
	das Bett	die Betten			bed
	die Tafel	die Tafeln			blackboard
	die Erzählung	die Erzählungen			story, narration
5	der Chef	die Chefs		–s	boss
	das Auto	die Autos			automobile
	die Bar	die Bars			bar

B. Plural Forms of Some Special Words of Non-German Origin

das Individuum	die Individuen	individual
das Kriterium	die Kriterien	criterion
das Prinzip	die Prinzipien	principle
das Datum	die Daten	date
der Typus	die Typen	type
der Rhythmus	die Rhythmen	rhythm
das Epos	die Epen	epic (poem)
das Drama	die Dramen	drama
das Thema	die Themen (die Themata)	theme, topic, subject
das Schema	die Schemata	scheme
der Charakter	die Charaktere	character
der Dialog	die Dialoge	dialogue
das Problem	die Probleme	problem
der Kontrast	die Kontraste	contrast
die Kritik	die Kritiken	criticism

C. The Plural Form of the Basic Word –mann

The basic word **–mann** compounded with nouns is often changed to **–leute** in the plural:

Hier kommt der Haupt**mann**.	Here comes the captain.
Hier kommen die Haupt**leute**.	Here come the captains.

der Kauf**mann**	die Kauf**leute**	dealer, businessman
der Fach**mann**	die Fach**leute**	specialist, expert
der Schutz**mann**	die Schutz**leute**	policeman
der Lands**mann**	die Lands**leute**	fellow countryman

▸ **Always learn the nouns with their articles and plural forms!**

D. Some Rules of Thumb for Forming the Plural

1. Masculine nouns

The *majority* of the *masculine nouns,* especially the *monosyllabic nouns,* have the *plural ending* **–e:**

Das ist der Krieg.	(war)	Das sind die Krieg**e**.
Das ist der Arzt.	(doctor)	Das sind die Ärzt**e**.
Das ist der Inhalt.	(contents)	Das sind die Inhalt**e**.

A small *minority* of *masculine nouns* have the *plural ending* **–en:**

Das ist der Mensch.	(human being)	Das sind die Mensch**en**.
Das ist der Staat.	(state)	Das sind die Staat**en**.

2. Neuter nouns

The *majority* of the *neuter nouns* have either the *plural ending* **–e** or the *plural ending* **–er:**

Das ist das Jahr.	(year)	Das sind die Jahr**e**.
Das ist das Vorbild.	(example, standard)	Das sind die Vorbild**er**.

Many monosyllabic neuter nouns with the *plural ending* **–er** are *umlauted* in the *plural:*

Das ist das Grab.	(grave)	Das sind die Gräb**er**.
Das ist das Wort.	(word)	Das sind die Wört**er**.
Das ist das Buch.	(book)	Das sind die Büch**er**.

3. Feminine nouns

The *vast majority* of the *feminine nouns* have the *plural ending* **–(e)n:**

Das ist die Grube.	(ditch)	Das sind die Grub**en**.
Das ist die Sache.	(matter, thing)	Das sind die Sach**en**.
Das ist die Person.	(person)	Das sind die Person**en**.

Vocabulary for Drills 1 and 2

sehen	to see	**kennen**	to know, to be acquainted with
lesen	to read	**verstehen**	to understand
fragen	to ask	**lernen**	to learn

Drill 1 *Give the plural of the nouns.*

Wir sehen das Fenster.
Wir sehen die Fenster.

Wir lesen den Satz.
Wir lesen die Sätz**e**.

Wir fragen den Mann.
Wir fragen die Männ**er**.

Wir sehen die Tafel.
Wir sehen die Tafel**n**.

Wir kennen den Chef.
Wir kennen die Chef**s**.

Wir lernen das Wort.
Wir verstehen den Satz.
Wir lesen die Erzählung.
Wir kennen den Dichter.
Wir fragen den Freund.
Wir sehen das Kind.
Wir fragen den Vater.
Wir kennen die Mutter.
Wir sehen das Auto.
Wir kennen die Stadt.
Wir sehen die Bar.

Drill 2 *Give the plural of the nouns.*

Wir verstehen das Prinzip.
Wir verstehen die Prinzip**ien**.

Wir kennen das Thema.
Wir kennen die Them**en**.

Wir verstehen den Charakter.
Wir verstehen die Charaktere.

Wir fragen den Hauptmann.
Wir fragen die Hauptleute.

Wir verstehen das Kriterium.
Wir kennen den Typus.
Wir lesen das Drama.
Wir verstehen den Dialog.

Wir lesen das Epos.
Wir kennen das Problem.
Wir lernen den Rhythmus.
Wir kennen den Charakter.
Wir verstehen das Schema.
Wir kennen den Schutzmann.
Wir lesen die Kritik.
Wir sehen den Kontrast.

Drill 3   *Combination Drill*   *Give the plural of the nouns.*

Wir lernen das Wort.
Wir verstehen den Satz.
Wir lesen das Drama.
Wir verstehen den Charakter.
Wir lernen den Rhythmus.
Wir lesen den Dialog.
Wir kennen den Typus.

Wir verstehen das Problem.
Wir sehen den Kontrast.
Wir kennen das Prinzip.
Wir fragen den Freund.
Wir kennen den Schutzmann.
Wir sehen das Auto.
Wir kennen das Kind.

Wir sehen die Tafel.
Wir fragen den Vater.
Wir sehen die Mutter.
Wir verstehen das Kriterium.
Wir lesen die Kritik.

II. THE GENDERS AND DECLENSION FORMS OF THE NOUN

		Masculine I	*Masculine II*	*Neuter*	*Feminine*
Sing.	*Nom.*	der Satz	der Mensch	das Wort	die Sache
	Acc.	den Satz	den Menschen	das Wort	die Sache
	Dat.	dem Satz	dem Menschen	dem Wort	der Sache
	Gen.	des Satzes	des Menschen	des Wortes	der Sache
Plur.	*Nom.*	die Sätze	die Menschen	die Wörter	die Sachen
	Acc.	die Sätze	die Menschen	die Wörter	die Sachen
	Dat.	den Sätzen	den Menschen	den Wörtern	den Sachen
	Gen.	der Sätze	der Menschen	der Wörter	der Sachen

There are three classes of nouns in German: masculine, feminine, and neuter. These are linguistic, not biological, terms. Note that the masculine gender has two declension forms, called masculine I (MI) and masculine II (MII). Most masculine nouns follow the masculine I pattern. Only few masculine nouns follow the masculine II pattern.

The masculine II declension

Sing.	*Nom.*	Das ist der Student.
	Acc.	Ich kenne den Studenten.
	Dat.	Ich antworte dem Studenten.
	Gen.	Das ist das Buch des Studenten.

The *majority* of *masculine nouns* with the *plural ending* **–(e)n** form *all endings* with **–(e)n**, *except* in the *nominative singular*.

Nom. sing.	All other sing. and plur. forms		Nom. sing.	All other sing. and plur. forms	
der Philosoph	–en	philosopher	der Franzose	–n	Frenchman
der Student	–en	student	der Russe	–n	Russian
der Präsident	–en	president	der Gehilfe	–n	help
der Automat	–en	automat	der Scharfschütze	–n	sharpshooter
der Soldat	–en	soldier	der Bote	–n	messenger
der Held	–en	hero	der Löwe	–n	lion
der Untertan	–en	subject (to a king)	der Junge	–n	boy

Note that in *colloquial German* all *plural forms* of **der Junge** *may add an* **–ns: die Jungens.**

As you see from the foregoing examples, *many* of these *masculine II nouns end in* **–t** or **–ph**, having a Latin or Greek root, and designate in most cases *a man's profession, status,* or *activity:*

der Poet	poet		der Philosoph	philosopher
der Kandidat	candidate		der Geograph	geographer

Masculine II nouns *ending in* **–e** signify in many cases a man's *nationality* or an *animal's name.*

der Russe	Russian		der Franzose	Frenchman
der Tscheche	Czech		der Hase	hare, rabbit

Distinguish carefully between the following groups of nouns designating *a man's nationality:*

Masculine I ending in –er			Masculine II ending in –e		
der Amerikaner	–	American	der Russe	–n	Russian
der Engländer	–	Englishman	der Tscheche	–n	Czech
der Österreicher	–	Austrian	der Franzose	–n	Frenchman
der Schweizer	–	Swiss	der Grieche	–n	Greek
der Inder	–	Indian	der Pole	–n	Pole
der Indianer	–	American Indian	der Chinese	–n	Chinese

One denotes *the woman's nationality* in the following way:

die Amerikanerin, –nen	die Russin, –nen
die Engländerin, –nen	die Tschechin, –nen

The declension of der Herr

	Singular	*Plural*
Nom.	Das ist der Herr.	Das sind die Herren.
Acc.	Wir kennen den Herrn.	Wir kennen die Herren.
Dat.	Wir antworten dem Herrn.	Wir antworten den Herren.
Gen.	Wir kommen wegen des Herrn.	Wir kommen wegen der Herren.

Herr *together with a name* **(Herr Meier)** *is always* *declined* according to *its use in the sentence:*

Das ist Herr Meier.	That is Mr. Meier.
Wir kennen Herrn Meier.	We know Mr. Meier.
Wir antworten Herrn Meier.	We answer Mr. Meier.
Das ist Herrn Meiers Haus.	That is Mr. Meier's house.

Special masculine II nouns

Sing. Nom.	Das ist der Buchstabe.
Acc.	Ich schreibe den Buchstaben.
Dat.	Das steht vor dem Buchstaben.
Gen.	Das ist die Form des Buchstabens.

The following masculine II nouns have an **–s** in the genitive singular only:

Nom. sing.	*Gen. sing.*	*All other sing. and plur. forms*	
der Buchstabe	des Buchstabens	–n	letter
der Friede	des Friedens	–n	peace
der Gedanke	des Gedankens	–n	thought, idea
der Glaube	des Glaubens	–n	belief
der Name	des Namens	–n	name
der Wille	des Willens	–n	will

Note the *declension* of the *neuter noun* **das Herz** (heart).

Sing. Acc.	Ich höre das Herz.
Dat.	Das kommt vom Herzen.
Gen.	Das ist die Form des Herzens.

Vocabulary for Drills 4 and 5 **danken** + dative to thank   **kommen wegen** + genitive to come because of   **antworten** + dative to answer

Drill 4 *Form sentences using the cues as shown in the following examples.*

Pattern   *Cues*

Wir sehen **den** Präsident**en**.   wir antworten
Wir antworten **dem** Präsident**en**.   der Philosoph
Wir antworten **dem** Philosoph**en**.   wir kommen wegen
Wir kommen wegen **des** Philosoph**en**.   der Student

_____   wir fragen
_____   der Junge
_____   wir antworten
_____   der Bote
_____   wir kommen wegen
_____   der Gehilfe
_____   wir verstehen
_____   der Russe
_____   wir antworten
_____   der Franzose
_____   wir kommen wegen
_____   der Held
_____   wir verstehen
_____   der Mensch
_____   wir danken
_____   der Soldat
_____   wir kommen wegen
_____   der Scharfschütze
_____   wir fragen
_____   Herr Meier
_____   wir antworten
_____   der Untertan
_____   wir kommen wegen
_____   der Automat
_____   wir sehen
_____   der Buchstabe
_____   wir verstehen
_____   der Gedanke
_____

Drill 5 *Combination Drill*   *Give the singular of the nouns.*

Wir kennen die Dichter.

Wir kennen die Studenten.

Wir antworten den Amerikanern.

Wir antworten den Russen.

Wir fragen die Schutzleute.

Wir fragen die Jungens.

Wir hören die Rhythmen.

Wir hören die Musikautomaten.

Wir kennen die Charaktere.

Wir kennen die Untertanen.

Wir verstehen die Prinzipien.

Wir verstehen die Buchstaben.

Wir danken den Müttern.

Wir danken den Soldaten.

Wir kennen die Probleme.

Wir kennen die Menschen.

Wir fragen die Schriftsteller.

Wir verstehen die Gedanken.

Wir kennen die Romane.

Wir sehen die Scharfschützen.

A. The Cases of the Noun

1. The nominative case

	Masculine I	*Masculine II*	*Neuter*	*Feminine*
Sing. Nom.	**der** Satz **ein** Satz	**der** Mensch **ein** Mensch	**das** Wort **ein** Wort	**die** Frau **eine** Frau
Plur. Nom.	**die** Sätze Sätze	**die** Menschen Menschen	**die** Wörter Wörter	**die** Frauen Frauen

The *interrogative pronouns* for the *subject:*

Wer ist beliebt? Der Schriftsteller.

Was ist das? Der neue Roman.

Was ist das? Ein abstrakter Begriff.

Who is popular? The writer.

What is that? The new novel.

What is that? An abstract concept.

The *nominative* of the *interrogative* is (*a*) **Wer?** for *persons* and (*b*) **Was?** for *things* or *concepts.*

The *nominative case* is used (*a*) for the *subject of a sentence;* (*b*) for the *predicate noun;* and (*c*) in *direct address.*

Der Schriftsteller ist beliebt.

Das ist **der neue Roman.**

Herr Meier, kennen Sie den Roman?

The writer is popular.

That is the new novel.

Mr. Meier, do you know the novel?

2. The accusative case

		Masculine I		Masculine II	Neuter	Feminine
Sing. Nom.	der	Satz	der	Mensch	das Wort	die Frau
	ein	Satz	ein	Mensch	ein Wort	eine Frau
Acc.	den	Satz	den	Menschen	das Wort	die Frau
	einen	Satz	einen	Menschen	ein Wort	eine Frau
Plur. Nom.	die	Sätze	die	Menschen	die Wörter	die Frauen
		Sätze		Menschen	Wörter	Frauen
Acc.	die	Sätze	die	Menschen	die Wörter	die Frauen
		Sätze		Menschen	Wörter	Frauen

▶ Note that there are *recognizable accusative articles only* in the *singular masculine!*

The *interrogative pronouns* for the *accusative object:*

Wen kennen Sie? Den Schriftsteller.　　Whom do you know? The writer.
Was schreiben Sie? Einen Brief.　　What are you writing? A letter.
Was besprechen Sie? Ein Problem.　　What are you discussing? A problem.

The *accusative* of the *interrogative* is (a) **Wen?** for *persons* and (b) **Was?** for *things* and *concepts.*

(a) The accusative object as the direct object

In German the *majority of the verbs* have an *accusative object* which is the counterpart of the *direct object* in English.

Verb + accusative object　　　　*Verb + direct object*

Ich kenne **den** Schriftsteller.　　I know the writer.
Ich schreibe **einen** Brief.　　I am writing a letter.
Ich bespreche **ein** Problem.　　I am discussing a problem.

(b) Special uses of the accusative

Es gibt takes the accusative case. Note that **es gibt** is more limited than its English counterpart *there is.* **Es gibt** expresses only *general* existence or condition, and is *never used* in the sense of *to be present.* (See also page 38.)

Es gibt hier nur **einen** Arzt.　　　　There is only one doctor here.

Without a preposition the *accusative case* expresses *definite time* or *duration of time:*

Näch**sten** Herbst geht er auf die Universität.	Next fall he'll go to the university.
Die**sen** Sommer arbeiten wir.	We shall work this summer.
Er arbeitet **den** gan**zen** Monat.	He works the whole month.

The *accusative case* is also used in time constructions expressing *periodic repetition* or *fixed intervals:*

Er kommt jed**en** Tag.	He comes every day.
Er kommt alle drei Woch**en**.	He comes every three weeks.

3. The dative case

	Masculine I		Masculine II		Neuter		Feminine	
Sing. dat.	**dem**	Krieg(e)	**dem**	Studenten	**dem**	Haus(e)	**der**	Frau
	einem	Krieg(e)	**einem**	Studenten	**einem**	Haus(e)	**einer**	Frau
Plur. dat.	**den**	Kriegen	**den**	Studenten	**den**	Häusern	**den**	Frauen
		Kriegen		Studenten		Häusern		Frauen

Monosyllabic masculine and *neuter nouns* in the dative singular *sometimes* end in **–e.** The use of this **–e** is a *question of style* and not of grammar!

Sie kommen aus **dem** Krieg**e**.	They come from the war.
Sie sind auf **dem** Weg**e**.	They are on the way.

All nouns in the *dative plural* end in **–n,** *except* the *nouns* with the *plural ending* **–s:**

Sie schreiben von Trümmer**n**.	They write about ruins.
Sie antworten mit Beispiel**en**.	They answer with examples.
Er spricht mit **den** Chef**s**.	He speaks with the bosses.
Er geht zu **den** Park**s**.	He goes to the parks.

The *interrogative pronoun* for the *dative object:*

Wem gibt er ein Buch? Dem Jungen.	To whom does he give a book? To the boy.
Wem erklärt er das Problem? Dem Studenten.	To whom does he explain the problem? To the student.
Wem antwortet er? Dem Mann.	Whom does he answer? The man.

The *dative* of the *interrogative* is **Wem?** for *persons,* and like the English forms *whom* and *to whom* it is used for *persons only.*

(a) **The dative as the indirect object**

In general, the dative expresses the idea of action or gesture toward a person, an institution, an animal, or, in some cases, a reaction to an idea. The most frequent use of the *dative* is to indicate *the indirect object.*

Verb + dat. object and acc. object	*Verb + indir. object and dir. object*
Er gibt **dem Professor** das Buch.	He gives *the professor* the book. He gives the book *to the professor.*
Er zeigt **dem Mann** das Haus.	He shows *the man* the house. He shows the house *to the man.*
Er schickt **dem Mädchen** den Brief.	He sends *the girl* the letter. He sends the letter *to the girl.*

The *dative object* is in most cases a *person.* The *accusative object* is usually a *thing* or a *concept.*

German, however, *never uses* alternative forms such as *He shows the house **to the man*** or *He gives the book **to his friend**,* even when these forms are the only possibility to express the indirect object in English. The *dative itself* implies the relationship expressed in English by the preposition *to.*

Er erklärt **dem Studenten** ein Problem.	He explains a problem *to the student.*
Er beschreibt **dem Mann** das Ereignis.	He describes the event *to the man.*
Er wiederholt **dem Professor** den Satz.	He repeats the sentence *to the professor.*

There is only one exception: **Sagen + dative** is used with *indirect quotes,* **sagen zu + dative** is used with *direct quotes.*

Er **sagt ihm,** daß er bald kommt.	He tells him that he will come soon.
Er **sagt zu ihm:** „Ich komme bald".	He says to him: "I will come soon."

The *dative* is also used with *verbs of deprivation:*

Er nimmt **dem** Freund das Buch.	He takes the book *from* the friend.
Er stiehlt **dem** Mann den Wagen.	He steals the car *from* the man.

Here again, the dative *cannot* be replaced by prepositional expressions like *from the friend* or *from the man.*

(b) **The dative as sole object**

The *dative case* is used for the *sole complement* after *certain verbs,* and with *certain adjectives, perfect participles,* and *nouns.*

The *dative* as a *sole object* after *certain verbs:*

Wir **danken den Ärzten.**	We thank the doctors.
Wir **helfen den** Frauen.	We help the women.
Wir **schaden den** Leuten.	We do harm to the people.
Wir **nützen den** Leuten.	We are useful to the people.
Wir **folgen den** Prinzipien.	We follow the principles.
Wir **glauben den** Professoren.	We believe the professors.
Wir **widersprechen den** Professoren.	We contradict the professors.
Wir **vertrauen den** Jungens.	We trust the boys.
Wir **mißtrauen den** Jungens.	We distrust the boys.
Wir **begegnen den** Leuten.	We meet the people.
Wir **gehorchen den** Eltern.	We obey the parents.
Wir **antworten den** Kindern.	We answer the children.
Was **entgegnet** er **den** Leuten?	What is his reply to the people?
Was **erwidert** er **den** Freunden?	What is his reply to the friends?
Die Bücher **gehören der** Bibliothek.	The books belong to the library.
Die Romane **gefallen dem** Leser.	The novels please the reader.
	The reader likes the novels.
Die Ergebnisse **genügen dem** Studenten.	The results are sufficient for the student.
Die Gedanken **scheinen dem** Autor neu (zu sein).	The ideas seem new to the author.
Die Äpfel **schmecken dem** Mädchen.	The apples taste good to the girl.
Es **gelingt dem** Mann.	The man succeeds.
Es **geht mir gut.**	I am fine.

Adjectives and *perfect participles* with *dative complements:*

Das ist **dem** Jungen gleich.	That does not matter to the boy.
Das ist **dem** Jungen egal.	The boy does not care (one way or the other).
Das ist **dem** Jungen recht.	That is all right with the boy.
Das ist **dem** Studenten zu **leicht.**	That is too easy for the student.
Das ist **dem** Studenten zu **schwer.**	That is too difficult for the student.
Das ist **dem** Leser **bekannt.**	That is familiar to the reader.
Das ist **dem** Leser **fremd.**	That is strange to the reader.
Das ist **dem** Mann **wichtig.**	That is important to the man.
Das ist **dem** Präsidenten **möglich.**	That is possible for the president.
Das ist **dem** Schriftsteller **nützlich.**	That is useful to the writer.
Das ist **dem** Studenten **willkommen.**	That is welcome to the student.
Das ist **dem** Studenten **angenehm.**	That is pleasant for the student.
Er ist **dem** Jungen **böse.**	He is angry with the boy.
Er ist **dem** Mann **dankbar.**	He is grateful to the man.
Es ist **mir kalt.**	I am cold.

Es ist **mir warm.**   I am warm.
Es tut **mir leid.**   I am sorry.

Dative relationships to *nouns:*

Das ist **dem** Stud**enten ein Problem.**   That is a problem for the student.
Das ist **den** Leut**en ein Rätsel.**   That is a puzzle to the people. *Or:* That
                                               puzzles the people.

Drill 6   *Contrastive Drill*   *Give the German equivalent.*

He gives the book to the professor.   He shows the house to the man.
Er gibt **dem** Professor das Buch.   He sends the letter to the girl.
                                               He takes the book from the professor.
He takes the book from the professor.   He repeats the sentence to the professor.
Er nimmt **dem** Professor das Buch.   He describes the event to the man.
                                               He steals the car from the man.
He explains the problem to the student.
He steals the car from the man.

Drill 7   *Contrastive Drill*   *Give the German equivalent.*

We help the women.   We trust the boys.
Wir helfen **den** Frau**en.**   We distrust the boys.
                                               We believe the professors.
We answer the children.   We contradict the professors.
Wir antworten **den** Kindern.   We follow the principles.
                                               We meet the people.
We thank the doctors.   We obey the parents.
We do harm to the people.
We are useful to the people.

Drill 8   *Combination Drill*   *Give the German equivalent.*

We know the women.   We distrust the boys.   We obey the parents.
We help the women.   We see the people.   We see the parents.
We ask the doctors.   We are useful to the people.   We ask the professors.
We thank the doctors.   We know the professors.   We believe the professors.
We understand the principles. We contradict the professors. We meet the people.
We follow the principles.   We answer the children.   We see the people.
We know the boys.   We ask the children.

Drill 9   *Contrastive Drill*   *Give the German equivalent.*

The books belong to the library.   The novels please the reader.
Die Bücher gehören **der** Bibliothek.   Die Romane gefallen **dem** Leser.

The man succeeds.
Es gelingt **dem** Mann.

I am fine.
Es geht **mir** gut.

The man succeeds.

I am fine.
The apples taste good to the girl.
The novels please the reader.
The results are sufficient for the student.
The books belong to the library.
The idea seems new to the author.

Drill 10   *Contrastive Drill*   *Give the German equivalent.*

He is thankful to the man.
Er ist **dem** Mann dankbar.

He is angry with the boy.
Er ist **dem** Jungen böse.

I am cold.
Es ist **mir** kalt.

I am sorry.
Es tut **mir** leid.

I am warm.
I am cold.
I am sorry.
He is angry with the boy.
He is grateful to the man.

Drill 11   *Contrastive Drill*   *Give the German equivalent.*

That does not matter to the boy.
Das ist **dem** Jungen gleich.

That is all right with the boy.
Das ist **dem** Jungen recht.

That is possible for the president.
Das ist **dem** Präsidenten möglich.

That puzzles the man.
Das ist **dem** Mann ein Rätsel.

That is a problem for the student.
Das ist **dem** Studenten ein Problem.

That is welcome to the student.
That is all right with the boy.
That is important to the man.
That puzzles the man.
That is useful to the writer.
That is strange to the reader.
That is familiar to the reader.
That is too difficult for the student.
That is pleasant for the student.
That is too easy for the student.
That is a problem for the student.
That does not matter to the boy.
The boy does not care.

4.   The genitive case

	Masculine I	*Masculine II*	*Neuter*	*Feminine*
Sing. gen.	**des** Satzes	**des** Menschen	**des** Wortes	**der** Frau
	eines Satzes	**eines** Menschen	**eines** Wortes	**einer** Frau
Plur. gen.	**der** Sätze	**der** Menschen	**der** Wörter	**der** Frauen

For all masculine I nouns and all neuter nouns the genitive singular ending is **–s** for words with *two* or *more syllables* and **–es** for *monosyllabic* words:

die Analyse **des** Roman**s**	the analysis of the novel
die Zerstörung **des** Wohnviertel**s**	the destruction of the residential district
das Ende **des** Krieg**es**	the end of the war, the war's end
die Erzählung **des** Kind**es**	the child's story

When these monosyllabic words form the last part of a compound, they usually end only in **–s**:

das Ende **des** Weltkrieg**s**	the end of the world war

The *genitive* of the *interrogative pronoun:*

Wessen Buch ist das? Herrn Meiers Buch.	Whose book is that? Mr. Meier's book.
In **wessen** Wagen kommt er? In Herrn Meiers Wagen.	In whose car is he coming? In Mr. Meier's car.

Like the English interrogative pronoun *whose,* **wessen** is used for *persons* only.

(a) ***The subjective and the objective genitive***

The German genitive is not merely the same as the English possessive or subjective genitive:

Das ist Herrn Meier**s** Haus.	That is Mr. Meier's house.

There is also an objective genitive:

Das ist die Analyse **des** Romans.	That is the analysis of the novel.

Both the subjective and the objective genitive appear normally *after* the noun to which they refer:

die Erzählung **des Kindes**	the child's story
die Analyse **des Romans**	the analysis of the novel

Although the English subjective genitive may and usually does precede the noun, this construction is seldom possible in German:

das Haus **des Mannes**	the man's house
das Stück **des Autors**	the author's play

The genitive may *precede* the noun to which it refers with *proper names:*

Deutschlands Zukunft	Germany's future
Kafkas Parabeln	Kafka's parables

The prepositional form with **von** is an alternative that appears sometimes in colloquial speech:

die Hauptstadt **von** Deutschland	the capital of Germany
das Ende **vom** Krieg	the end of the war

However, this form *must* be used in the *plural* when there is *no article* and the *genitive form would not be recognizable:*

Singular	*Plural*
die Erzählung **eines** Autors	die Erzählung **von** Autoren
die Zerstörung **einer** Stadt	die Zerstörung **von** Städt**en**

But:

die Erzählungen **eines** guten Autors	die Erzählungen gut**er** Autoren
die Zerstörung **einer** alten Stadt	die Zerstörung alt**er** Städte

Note that in these examples the genitive plural form is recognizable in the adjective endings.

(b) Adjective with genitive complements

Er ist **dieser** Leistung **fähig.**	He is capable of this achievement.
Er ist **eines** Preises **würdig.**	He is worthy of a prize.

(c) The use of the genitive to denote indefinite time

Eines Abends kam er.	One evening he came.

These forms appear also as adverbs:

morgen**s** (in the morning), abend**s** (at night), nacht**s** (during the night)

Drill 12   *Contrastive Drill   Give the German equivalent. Follow the examples:*

Kafka's parable
Kafka**s** Parabel

the war's end
das Ende **des** Krieg**es**

the destruction of the residential district
die Zerstörung **des** Wohnviertel**s**

Mr. Meier's book

the author's play
the analysis of the play
Germany's future
the child's story
the topic of the story
the literature of the time
Brecht's work
the man's house
the situation of the writer

B. The Compound Noun

Compound nouns take the gender and declension forms of their last element and usually have the main stress on their first element.

There are three ways of combining the two (or more) elements, although there is no rule governing the formation:

1. *Direct combination:* die Welt, der Krieg   **der Weltkrieg**
2. *An* **–s** *binds two elements:* die Wirtschaft, das Wunder   **das Wirtschaftswunder**
3. *The first element appears in its plural form:* die Frau, –en, die Zeitschrift   **die Frauenzeitschrift**

Compounds are also formed by combining:

1. *An adjective and a noun:* rot, der Wein   **der Rotwein**
2. *A verb and a noun:* erzählen, die Form   **die Erzählform**
3. *A pronoun and a noun:* selbst, die Sucht   **die Selbstsucht** (egoism)
4. *A prefix and a noun:* vor, das Bild   **das Vorbild** (model, standard)

▶ **Remember that in German the *compounds* are always spelled as *one word!***

C. The Gender of Nouns

In German there are no hard and fast rules for the gender of all the nouns. *Therefore always learn the nouns with the article!* Only in the following cases does the meaning, the ending, or the suffix of a noun show its gender.

1. Masculine

Most nouns with the endings **–ig, –ich, –ing, –(is)mus, –en:**

der König (king), **der** Teppich (rug), **der** Flüchtling (refugee), **der** Pessimismus (pessimism), **der** Garten (garden)

Names of the *days, months, seasons,* and *directions:*

der Sonntag, **der** Januar, **der** Sommer, **der** Westen, **der** Osten, **der** Norden, **der** Süden

But: **die** Woche (week), **das** Jahr

2. Neuter

Most nouns with the endings **–tum –(i)um, –ett, –ment,** and the diminutive suffixes **–chen** and **–lein:**

das Eigentum (possessions), **das** Gymnasium (public preparatory school), **das** Lazarett (military hospital), **das** Experiment, **das** Mädchen, **das** Fräulein, **das** Häslein (little rabbit)

Exceptions: **der** Reichtum (wealth), **der** Irrtum (error)

Names of *cities, countries,* and *continents:*

das alte **Augsburg, das** schöne **Italien, das** westliche **Europa**

Exceptions: see Use of the Article, page 21.

All words which are *not ordinarily used as nouns:*

das Rauchen (smoking), **das Gute** und **das Böse** (good and evil), **das Blau, das ABC, das Für und Wider** (pro and con)

3. **Feminine**

Nouns with the endings or suffixes **–ei, –ie, –in, –ion, –tät, –heit, –keit, –ung, –schaft:**

die Gerberei (tannery), **die** Industrie, **die** Lehrerin (female teacher), **die** Generation, **die** Universität, **die** Vergangenheit (past), **die** Wirklichkeit (reality), **die** Erzählung (story), **die** Gesellschaft (society)

Most *disyllabic nouns* with the *ending* **–e:**

die Schule, **die** Kirche (church), **die** Wärme (warmth), **die** Taube (dove)

But: **das** Ende

Drill 13 *Add the correct definite article and give one English meaning of the noun. Follow the example.*

Einführung	moderne Deutschland	ABC
die Einführung introduction	Generation	Taube
Garten	König	Gymnasium
Lehrerin	Experiment	Größe
Fräulein	Pessimismus	Sommer
Mädchen	Vergangenheit	Wagen
Schule	alte München	Würde
Januar	Westen	Teppich
Winter	Ordnung	Erzählung
Kälte	Optimismus	Kirche
Sinnlosigkeit	Wirklichkeit	Osten
Flüchtling	Gesellschaft	Für und Wider
Lazarett	Schönheit	Woche
Rauchen	Wärme	Jahr
Eigentum	Industrie	

III. THE USE OF THE ARTICLE

The following nouns *have an article* in German.

The *names* of *streets, mountains, lakes,* and *rivers:*

die Zugspitze, **der** Bodensee (Lake Constance), **der** Rhein, **die** Donau (Danube River), **die** Wilhelmstraße

Note the following usage: Er wohnt **in der** Wilhelmstraße. *But:* Er wohnt Wilhelmstraße 5.

The *names* of *some countries:*
die Schweiz (Switzerland), **die** Sowjetunion, **die** U.S.A. or **die** Vereinigten Staaten, **die** Niederlande (plural) (Netherlands), **das** Rheinland, **die** Pfalz (county in Germany), **das** Elsaß (Alsace)

All names of *countries ending in* **–ei:**
die Türkei, **die** Tschechoslowakei

All proper nouns (names of persons, cities, countries) when *preceded* by a *qualifying adjective:*

der Alte Fritz ("Old Frederick," Frederick II of Prussia), **das moderne Berlin, das geteilte Deutschland** (divided Germany)

Most abstract nouns:

Die Zeit vergeht schnell.	Time passes quickly.
So ist **das Leben.**	That's life.

The following prepositional expressions:

bei **der** Arbeit	at work	in **der** Tat	in fact
auf **den** ersten Blick	at first sight	**im** Zweifel	in doubt
mit **dem** Zug	by train		

The following nouns *have no article* in German:

Nouns which indicate a *person's profession, religion,* or *nationality* after the verbs **werden, sein, bleiben:**

Er wird Professor.	Er ist Arzt (doctor).	Er bleibt Katholik.

The indefinite article is used if these nouns are preceded by an adjective or followed by a relative clause.

Er ist **ein guter** Arzt.	Er ist **ein Arzt, den** wir kennen.

Drill 14 *Contrastive Drill*   *Give the German equivalent.*

Switzerland	Time passes quickly.	He is coming by train.
divided Germany	in fact	At first sight
modern Berlin	Zugspitze	That's life.
U.S.A.	Danube River	in doubt
Old Frederick	Wilhelm Street	
He is at work.	Lake Constance	

IV. SYLLABIFICATION AT THE END OF A LINE

The German syllabification usually follows phonetic rather than grammatical principles:

Grammatical elements		*Syllabification*
Stem	*Ending*	
geb	en	ge-ben
wiss	en	wis-sen
Kirch	e	Kir-che
Ordn	ung	Ord-nung
Lehr	er in	Leh-re-rin

A single consonant between vowels is placed on the following line:

Glaub	e	Glau-be
hab	en	ha-ben

sch, ch, and **ph** are considered as one consonant:

Tasch	e (pocket)	Ta-sche
Büch	er	Bü-cher
Philosoph	en	Phi-lo-so-phen

The second of two or the last of more consonants are placed on the following line.

folg	en	fol-gen
Wass	er	Was-ser
Ordn	ung	Ord-nung

ck between vowels becomes **k-k:**

Back	e (cheek)	Bak-ke

ng and **sp** between vowels are considered as two consonants:

Hung	er	Hun-ger
Fing	er	Fin-ger
Wesp	e (wasp)	Wes-pe

st is not separable and is placed on the following line if it stands between vowels:

Kist	e (crate)	Ki-ste
geist	ig	gei-stig

Drill 15   *Split the following words.*

der Norden, der Westen, die Kinder, das Fenster, die Erzählung, der Charakter, die Vorbilder, die Menschen, der Präsident, der Schriftsteller, die Professoren, die Wörter, die Studenten, die Ringe, die Wespe, die Philosophen, die Straße, die Tasche, die Kurzgeschichte, machen, wissen, sagen, antworten, geistig, die Kiste, folgendermaßen, die Lehrerin, die Weltliteratur, des Jahrhundert, das Stilexperiment, die Kirche, die Zerstörung

THE PREPOSITIONS

I. **PREPOSITIONS GOVERNING THE ACCUSATIVE:** durch, für, um, ohne, gegen, bis, entlang

Note that in colloquial German one often finds the following *contractions:* **durchs** for **durch das, fürs** for **für das,** and **ums** for **um das.** Both forms are acceptable.

durch

Er geht **durchs** (durch das) Zimmer.	He is walking *through* the room.
Wir sehen das **durch** die Jahrhunderte.	We see that *through* the centuries.

(For **durch** in passive sentences, see Chap. 6.)

für

Er arbeitet **für** seine Familie.	He works *for* his family.

um

Er fährt **um** die Stadt.	He is driving *around* the city.
Er kommt **um** 12 Uhr, **um** Mitternacht.	He comes *at* 12 o'clock, *at* midnight.

ohne

Er kommt **ohne** sein Buch.	He is coming *without* his book.
Er kommt **ohne** Buch.	He is coming *without* a book.

After **ohne** the article is very often not used.

gegen

Sie sind **gegen** den totalen Staat.	They are *against* the totalitarian state.
Er schaut **gegen** die Sonne.	He is looking *toward* the sun.
Er kam **gegen** fünf Uhr.	He came *toward* (*around*) five o'clock.

In literary style **wider** is sometimes used in the sense of *against.*

Er tut es **wider** meinen Willen.	He does it *against* my will.

bis

Er fährt **bis ans** (an das) Haus.	He is driving *up to* the house.
Er geht **bis zur** Universität.	He is going *as far* as the university.

Bis is generally used with another preposition, and this preposition determines the case. **Bis** alone is usually followed by an expression of time or place.

Er bleibt **bis** August.	He is staying *till* August.
Das muß **bis** morgen fertig sein.	That must be done *by* tomorrow.
Er fährt nur **bis** Berlin.	He is driving only *as far as* Berlin.

entlang

Die ganze Straße **entlang** sieht man neue
   Häuser.

One sees new houses *along* the entire street.

But: Sehen Sie die Häuser **entlang** der
   Straße?

Do you see the houses *along* the street?

Entlang governs the *accusative* if it *follows the noun*. It governs the *genitive* if it *precedes the noun*.

Drill 16 *Contrastive Drill* .*Give the German equivalent.*

They are against the totalitarian state.
We see that through the centuries.
He works for his family.
He is walking through the room.
One sees new houses along the entire street.
He is going as far as the university.
He is driving up to the house.
He is only driving as far as Berlin.

He is driving around the city.
He comes at 12 o'clock.
He is coming without his book.
He is coming without a book.
He is staying till the first of August.
He is looking towards the sun.
That must be done by tomorrow.

II. **PREPOSITIONS GOVERNING THE DATIVE:** aus, von, nach, zu, bei, mit, seit, außer, gegenüber

Note that in colloquial German one often finds the following *contractions:* **vom** for **von dem,**
zum for **zu dem, zur** for **zu der,** and **beim** for **bei dem.**

aus

Er kommt **aus** dem Haus.
Er ist **aus** Deutschland.
Dieser Roman ist **aus** dem 20. Jahrhundert.

Der Stuhl ist **aus** Holz.

He is coming *out* of the house.
He is *from* Germany.
This novel is *from* the 20th century. *Or:*
This is a 20th century novel.
The chair is *of* wood.

von

Er kommt **vom** Bahnhof.
Er arbeitet **von** April bis Mai.
die Bevölkerung **von** München
eine Parabel **von** Kafka

He is coming *from* the station.
He works *from* April until May.
the population *of* Munich
a parable *by* Kafka

For **von** + **noun** instead of the genitive, see The Genitive Case, page 18.
For **von** in a passive sentence, see Chapter 6.

nach

Wir fliegen **nach** Deutschland.
Wir fahren **nach** Frankfurt.

We are flying *to* Germany.
We are driving *to* Frankfurt.

Wir fahren **nach** Süden, **nach** Norden.	We are driving south, north.
Er fährt **nach** Hause.	He is driving home.
die Situation **nach** dem Kriege	the situation *after* the war
nach Einstein	*according to* Einstein

To designate direction, **nach** is used for *to* with *geographical names* and with *north, east, south,* and *west:* **nach Europa, nach Deutschland, nach Berlin, nach Norden, nach Osten, nach Süden, nach Westen**

But:

Er geht **nach Hause.**	He is going *home.*

zu

Er fährt **zur** Universität.	He is driving *to* the university.
Er geht **zum** Arzt.	He is going *to* the doctor.
Er geht **zu** Fuß.	He goes *on* foot.

To designate *direction,* **zu** is used with *persons* and with *places* when a geographical name is *not* mentioned.

But:

Er ist **zu Hause.**	He is *at home.*

bei

Er wohnt **bei** seinen Eltern.	He lives *with* his parents.
Er wohnt **beim** Bahnhof.	He lives *near* the station.
Er ist **bei** der Arbeit.	He is *at* work.

mit

Ich komme **mit** dem Wagen.	I am coming *by* car.
Ich komme **mit** meinen Freunden.	I am coming *with* my friends.
Er spricht **mit** leiser (lauter) Stimme.	He speaks *in* a soft (loud) voice.

seit

Er ist **seit** dem 1. Mai hier.	He has been here *since* May 1st.
Er ist **seit** drei Wochen hier.	He has been here *for* three weeks.

Seit is used with the present tense in up-to-now situations.

außer

Außer ihm kommt niemand.	*Besides* him nobody is coming.
Er ist **außer** Gefahr.	He is *out of* danger.
Er ist **außer** sich vor Schrecken.	He is *beside* himself with fear.

gegenüber

Er wohnt der Post **gegenüber.**   He lives *opposite* the post office.
Er wohnt **gegenüber** der Post.

Gegenüber may *precede or follow* the noun which it governs.

Drill 17   *The Use of* **zu** *and* **nach**   *Form sentences with given cues, using* **nach** *or* **zu**, *as shown in the following examples.*

Patterns	*Cues*
Wir fahren **zum Bahnhof.**	Deutschland
Wir fahren **nach Deutschland.**	die Freunde
Wir fahren **zu den Freunden.**	München
Wir fahren **nach München.**	Herr Meier
Wir fahren **zu Herrn Meier.**	Europa
_____	die Studenten
_____	die Universität
_____	Berlin
_____	die Schule
_____	der Arzt
_____	Amerika
_____	die Eltern
_____	die Kirche
_____	Hamburg
_____	Herr Schmidt
_____	die Russen
_____	Rußland
_____	die Jungens
_____	der Präsident

Drill 18   *Contrastive Drill*   *Give the German equivalent.*

I am coming by car.
I am coming with my friends.
He lives with his parents.
He is from Germany.
the population of Munich
a parable by Kafka
The chair is of wood.
He is coming out of the house.
He is coming from the station.
He works from April until May.
He is at home.

He is driving home.
He is driving to the university.
We are flying to Germany.
We are driving south.
He is going to the doctor.
We are driving to Frankfurt.
He goes on foot.
the situation after the war
He lives near the station.
He speaks in a soft voice.
He is at work.

Besides him, nobody is coming.

He has been here for three weeks.

He has been here since May 1.

He is beside himself with fear.

He lives opposite the post office.

Drill 19   *Combination Drill   Give the German equivalent.*

He comes at 12 o'clock.

He is coming without his book.

He is coming without a book.

He is coming from the station.

He is coming out of the house.

I am coming by car.

I am coming with my friends.

He lives near the station.

He lives with his parents.

He lives opposite the post office.

He is at home.

He is at work.

He works for his family.

He is driving to the university.

He is driving to Frankfurt.

He is driving to his friends.

He is driving home.

He is flying to Germany.

He is driving as far as the university.

He is only driving as far as Berlin.

He goes on foot.

He is driving north.

He is walking along the street.

He is walking through the room.

He is driving around the city.

He is driving up to the house.

He has been here for three weeks.

He is from Germany.

He has been here since May 1st.

He works from April until May.

a parable by Kafka

That must be done by tomorrow.

the population of Munich

The chair is of wood.

He is looking toward the sun.

the situation after the war

The novel is from the 20th century.

He is beside himself with fear.

We see that through the centuries.

They are against the totalitarian state.

III.   TWO-WAY PREPOSITIONS – PREPOSITIONS GOVERNING THE ACCUSATIVE AND THE DATIVE:
an, auf, hinter, neben, in, über, unter, vor, zwischen

The following *contractions* are preferred:

ans for **an das, am** for **an dem, ins** for **in das, im** for **in dem**

The *accusative* is used when the prepositional phrase describes *motion toward* a *destination* or *in a specific* direction, i.e., when the question **Wohin?** (Where to) is answered.

Wohin fährt er? Er fährt **in die** Stadt.

Where is he driving (*to*)? He is driving *into* the city.

The *dative* is used when the prepositional phrase indicates *location* or *movement within a place,* i.e., when the question **Wo?** (Where?) is answered:

Wo ist er? Er ist **in der** Stadt.

Wo fährt er **herum?** Er fährt **in der** Stadt **herum.**

Where is he? He is *in* the city.

Where is he driving *around?* He is driving *around in* the city.

Accusative

Wohin geht er?

Er geht **ans** Fenster.
He goes *to* the window.

Er geht **auf den** Berg.
He goes *up* the mountain.

Er geht **hinter das** Haus.
He goes *behind the house* (from somewhere else).

Er geht **neben** den Wagen.
He goes *to* the car and stands *beside* it.

Er geht **über die** Brücke.
He goes *over* the bridge.

Er geht **unter die** Brücke.
He comes *to* the bridge and then goes *under* it.

Er geht **unter die** Leute.
He *mingles with* the people.

Er geht **vor das** Haus.
He goes *in front of* the house (from somewhere else).

Er geht **zwischen die** Mauern.
He goes *between* the walls (from somewhere else).

Er geht **ins** Haus.
He goes *into* the house.

Dative

Wo ist er?

Jetzt ist er **am** Fenster.
Now he is *at* the window.

Jetzt ist er **auf dem** Berg.
Now he is *on* the mountain.

Jetzt ist er **hinter dem** Haus.
Now he is *behind* the house.

Jetzt ist er **neben dem** Wagen.
Now he is *beside* the car.

Jetzt ist er **über dem** Fluß.
Now he is *over (above)* the river.

Jetzt ist er **unter der** Brücke.
Now he is *under* the bridge.

Jetzt ist er **unter den** Leuten.
Now he is *among* the people.

Jetzt ist er **vor dem** Haus.
Now he is *in front of* the house.

Jetzt ist er **zwischen den** Mauern.
Now he is *between* the walls.

Jetzt ist er **im** Haus.
Now he is *in* the house.

Drill 20   *Follow the example.*

Er geht **ans** Fenster.
Jetzt ist er **am** Fenster.

Er geht unter die Brücke.
Er geht neben den Wagen.
Er geht zwischen die Mauern.
Er geht vor das Haus.

Er geht unter die Leute.
Er geht hinter das Haus.
Er geht ans Fenster.
Er geht auf den Berg.
Er geht ins Haus.

Drill 21   *Follow the example.*

Er ist **am** Fenster.
Er ist **ans** Fenster gegangen.

Er ist auf dem Berg.
Er ist zwischen den Mauern.
Er ist hinter dem Haus.

Er ist unter der Brücke.
Er ist vor dem Haus.
Er ist neben dem Wagen.
Er ist unter den Leuten.

Er ist am Fenster.   Er ist im Haus.

When the prepositions **an, in, vor,** and **zwischen** appear in *time expressions* referring to a *point in time,* they take the *dative:*

am Sonntag, **am** Mittag, **am** 3. September	*on* Sunday, *at* noon, *on* September 3rd
im Januar, **im** Herbst, **in** die**ser** Woche	*in* January, *in* the fall, *this* week
vor einem Jahr, **vor dem** 6. Juli	*a* year ago, *before* July 6th
zwischen dem 1. und 3. Mai	*between* May 1st and 3rd

IV. **PREPOSITIONS GOVERNING THE GENITIVE:** während, wegen, statt, trotz, außerhalb, innerhalb, oberhalb, unterhalb

während

Während des Winters waren sie hier.   They were here *during* the winter.

wegen

Wegen des Wetters kommen sie nicht.   *Because of* the weather they are not coming.

statt or anstatt

Statt meines Bruders kam meine Schwester.   My sister came *instead of* my brother.

trotz

Trotz des Regens kamen alle.   They all came *in spite of* the rain.

außerhalb, innerhalb, oberhalb, unterhalb

außerhalb der Stadt	*outside* the city
innerhalb der Stadt	*inside* the city
oberhalb der Brücke	*above* the bridge (*further up* the river)
unterhalb der Brücke	*below* the bridge (*further down* the river)

Drill **22**   *Combination Drill   Give the German equivalent.*

Prepositional time expressions take the dative and prepositional phrases take the genitive:

It happened during the winter.
Es geschah **während des** Winters.

It happened between May 1st and 3rd.
It happened outside the city.
It happened on Sunday.
It happened above the bridge.
It happened in the fall.
It happened because of the weather.
It happened inside the city.
It happened a year ago.
It happened below the bridge.

It happened before July 6th.
It happened this week.
It happened in spite of the rain.
It happened on September 3rd.
It happened in January.
It happened during the week.
It happened at noon.
It happened between May 1st and 3rd.
It happened in spite of the rain.
My sister came instead of my brother.

THE INDEFINITE ARTICLE AND THE POSSESSIVE ADJECTIVES

The *possessive adjectives* have the *same endings* as the *indefinite articles:*

		Masculine	Singular Neuter	Feminine	Plural
Indefinite article	Nom.	ein	ein	eine	keine*
	Acc.	einen	ein	eine	keine
	Dat.	einem	einem	einer	keinen
	Gen.	eines	eines	einer	keiner
ich	Nom.	mein	mein	meine	meine
	Acc.	meinen	mein	meine	meine
	Dat.	meinem	meinem	meiner	meinen
	Gen.	meines	meines	meiner	meiner
du	Nom.	dein	dein	deine	deine
	Acc.	deinen	dein	deine	deine
	Dat.	deinem	deinem	deiner	deinen
	Gen.	deines	deines	deiner	deiner
er, es, man	Nom.	sein	sein	seine	seine
	Acc.	seinen	sein	seine	seine
	Dat.	seinem	seinem	seiner	seinen
	Gen.	seines	seines	seiner	seiner
sie (she)	Nom.	ihr	ihr	ihre	ihre
	Acc.	ihren	ihr	ihre	ihre
	Dat.	ihrem	ihrem	ihrer	ihren
	Gen.	ihres	ihres	ihrer	ihrer
wir	Nom.	unser	unser	unsere	unsere
	Acc.	unseren	unser	unsere	unsere
	Dat.	unserem	unserem	unserer	unseren
	Gen.	unseres	unseres	unserer	unserer
ihr	Nom.	euer	euer	eure	eure
	Acc.	euren	euer	eure	eure
	Dat.	eurem	eurem	eurer	euren
	Gen.	eures	eures	eurer	eurer
sie (they)	Nom.	ihr	ihr	ihre	ihre
	Acc.	ihren	ihr	ihre	ihre
	Dat.	ihrem	ihrem	ihrer	ihren
	Gen.	ihres	ihres	ihrer	ihrer

	Nom.	Ihr	Ihr	Ihre	Ihre
Sie	*Acc.*	Ihren	Ihr	Ihre	Ihre
(you)	*Dat.*	Ihrem	Ihrem	Ihrer	Ihren
	Gen.	Ihres	Ihres	Ihrer	Ihrer

* The indefinite articles **ein, ein, eine** have no plural (**ein Mann**, plural: **Männer**). We have used the negative **keine** to show the plural forms.

Drill 23 *Substitute the given cues. Follow the examples.*

Pattern

Er geht durch **seinen** Garten.
Sie geht durch **ihren** Garten.
Ich gehe durch **meinen** Garten.
Die Leute gehen durch **ihren** Garten.
Wir gehen durch **unseren** Garten.
Wir gehen **in unser Haus.**

_____
_____
_____
_____
_____
_____
_____
_____
_____
_____
_____
_____
_____
_____

Cues

sie geht durch
ich gehe durch
die Leute gehen durch
wir gehen durch
in unser Haus
du gehst in
er geht in
sie geht in
ich gehe in
ich arbeite für
für meine Familie
ihr arbeitet für
wir arbeiten für
er arbeitet für
sie arbeitet für
sie kommt ohne
ohne ihre Bücher
er kommt ohne
ich komme ohne
wir kommen ohne
die Leute kommen ohne

Drill 24 *Substitute the given cues. Follow the examples.*

Pattern

Er kommt mit **seinem** Freund.
Sie kommt mit **ihrem** Freund.
Wir kommen mit **unserem** Freund.
Ich komme mit **meinem** Freund.
Ihr kommt mit **eurem** Freund.
Ihr sprecht **von** eurem Freund.
Ihr sprecht **von eurer Situation.**

Cues

sie kommt mit
wir kommen mit
ich komme mit
ihr kommt mit
ihr sprecht von
von eurer Situation
ich spreche von

_____	er spricht von
_____	sie spricht von
_____	die Leute sprechen von
_____	wir sprechen von
_____	von unseren Eltern
_____	wir wohnen bei
_____	du wohnst bei
_____	ich wohne bei
_____	er wohnt bei
_____	sie wohnt bei
_____	die Jungens wohnen bei
_____	ihr wohnt bei

Drill 25   *Substitute the cues. Follow the example.*

Pattern	*Cues*
Er kommt wegen **seines** Kurses.	**ich** komme wegen
Ich komme wegen **meines** Kurses.	**wir** kommen wegen
_____	du kommst wegen
_____	die Studenten kommen wegen
_____	wegen ihrer Freizeit
_____	die Studenten arbeiten während
_____	er arbeitet während
_____	sie arbeitet während
_____	du arbeitest während
_____	wir arbeiten während
_____	ihr arbeitet während
_____	ich arbeite während
_____	während meiner Ferien
_____	ich studiere während
_____	wir studieren während
_____	er studiert während
_____	sie studiert während
_____	die Studenten studieren während
_____	du studierst während
_____	ihr studiert während

Drill 26   ***Combination Drill***   *Substitute the cues.*

Pattern	*Cues*
Er kommt mit **seinem** Freund.	**wir** kommen mit
_____	sie kommt mit
_____	sie kommt wegen

_____	ich komme wegen
_____	ich komme ohne
_____	wir kommen ohne
_____	ohne unsere Familie
_____	ich komme ohne
_____	ich komme wegen
_____	du kommst wegen
_____	du kommst mit
_____	er kommt mit
_____	er kommt wegen
_____	wegen seines Buches
_____	ich komme wegen
_____	ich komme ohne
_____	sie kommt ohne
_____	sie kommt mit
_____	wir kommen mit
_____	wir kommen wegen
_____	die Studenten kommen wegen
_____	wegen ihrer Eltern
_____	ich komme wegen
_____	ich komme ohne
_____	wir kommen ohne
_____	wir kommen mit
_____	er kommt mit

THE PRONOUNS

I. THE PERSONAL PRONOUNS

		Singular			*Plural*
	Nom.	ich			wir
	Acc.	mich			uns
	Dat.	mir			uns
	Gen.	(meiner)			(unser)
Familiar	*Nom.*	du			ihr
address	*Acc.*	dich			euch
	Dat.	dir			euch
	Gen.	(deiner)			(euer)
Formal	*Nom.*	Sie			Sie
address	*Acc.*	Sie			Sie
	Dat.	Ihnen			Ihnen
	Gen.	(Ihrer)			(Ihrer)
		Masc.	*Neut.*	*Fem.*	
	Nom.	er	es	sie	sie
	Acc.	ihn	es	sie	sie
	Dat.	ihm	ihm	ihr	ihnen
	Gen.	(seiner)	(seiner)	(ihrer)	(ihrer)

A. The Use of the Personal Pronouns

1. Ich

Unlike English, **ich** is not capitalized except when used as a noun: **das Ich,** the ego.

2. The familiar **address** du, ihr **(you), and the formal address** Sie (you)

Du is used only in *intimate* and *familiar address,* between family and close friends (who are then **Duzfreunde**). Children, animals, and the Deity (*English:* thou) are also addressed with **du. Du** is also used frequently among fellow workers, team members, and soldiers. **Ihr** is the plural of **du.**

Sie is used for all other persons, and is the *most common form of address.* **Sie** is always *capitalized* and is used for both *singular* and *plural.*

3. Er, es, sie

Ist **der** Gedanke neu? Ja, **er** ist neu.	Is the idea new? Yes, *it* is.
Ist **das** Kind hier? Ja, **es** ist hier.	Is the child here? Yes, *he* (*she*) is.
Ist **die** Geschichte interessant? Ja, **sie** ist interessant.	Is the story interesting? Yes, *it* is.
Verstehen Sie **den** Satz? Ja, ich verstehe **ihn**.	Do you understand the sentence? Yes, I understand *it*.
Kennen Sie **das** Kind? Ja, ich kenne **es**.	Do you know the child? Yes, I know *him* (*her*).
Lesen Sie **die** Zeitschrift? Ja, ich lese **sie**.	Do you read the periodical? Yes, I read *it*.

Unlike English, German uses **er, es, sie – ihn, es, sie – ihm, ihm, ihr** for *persons* and for *things* and *concepts*.

The *personal pronouns* in German *agree solely* with the *gender* of the *noun* in the singular.

B. The Position of the Personal Pronouns

Er gibt dem Studenten das Buch.	{ He gives the student the book. { He gives the book to the student.
Er gibt **ihm** das Buch.	{ He gives *him* the book. { He gives the book *to him*.
Er gibt **es** dem Studenten.	He gives it to the student.
Er gibt **es ihm**.	He gives it *to him*.

One personal pronoun and *one* noun as objects:

Er gibt dem	Studenten	das Buch.
Er gibt	**ihm**	das Buch.
Er gibt	**es**	dem Studenten.

The pronoun object precedes the noun object.

Two personal pronouns as objects:

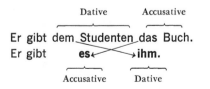

The accusative pronoun object *precedes* the dative pronoun object.

Drill 27 *One pronoun in the nominative. One pronoun in the accusative. Respond to the questions using the correct pronouns. Follow the examples.*

Lesen **Sie das** Drama?
Ja, **ich** lese **es.**

Lesen **Sie die** Novelle auch?
Ja, **ich** lese **sie** auch.

Verstehen Sie das Problem?
Verstehen Sie den Dialog auch?

Kennen Sie das Epos?
Kennen Sie die Erzählung auch?

Verstehen Sie das Wort?
Verstehen Sie den Satz auch?

Lesen Sie das Märchen?
Lesen Sie die Kurzgeschichte auch.

Kennen Sie das Program?
Kennen Sie den Inhalt auch?

Lesen Sie das Buch?
Lesen Sie die Zeitschrift auch?

Kennen Sie das Kind?
Kennen Sie die Mutter auch?

Sehen Sie das Haus?
Sehen Sie die Universität auch?

Kennen Sie die Familie?
Kennen Sie das Kind auch?

Drill 28 *One pronoun in the nominative. One pronoun in the dative. Respond to the questions using the correct pronouns. Follow the examples.*

Gefällt **Ihnen die** Idee?
Ja, **sie** gefällt **mir.**

Gefällt **dem** Schriftsteller **die** Idee auch?
Ja, **sie** gefällt **ihm** auch.

Gefällt den Jungens der Kurs?
Gefällt der Studentin der Kurs auch?

Gefällt dem Kind das Program?
Gefällt der Mutter das Program auch?

Gefällt den Leuten die Zeitung?
Gefällt Ihnen die Zeitung auch?

Gefällt dem Professor das Werk?
Gefällt den Studenten das Werk auch?

Gefällt Ihnen die Kritik?
Gefällt der Studentin die Kritik auch?

Gefällt den Leuten der Rhythmus?
Gefällt Ihnen der Rhythmus auch?

Gefällt dem Professor der Gedanke?
Gefällt den Jungens der Gedanke auch?

Drill 29 *Combination Drill   Respond in the same manner.*

Verstehen Sie das Problem?
Verstehen Sie den Dialog auch?
Gefällt Ihnen die Idee?
Gefällt dem Schriftsteller die Idee auch?
Lesen Sie das Drama?
Lesen Sie die Novelle auch?

Gefällt den Jungens der Kurs?
Gefällt der Studentin der Kurs auch?
Verstehen Sie das Wort?
Verstehen Sie den Satz auch?
Gefällt dem Kind das Programm?
Gefällt der Mutter das Programm auch?

Gefällt Ihnen die Kritik?
Gefällt dem Professor die Kritik auch?
Lesen Sie das Buch?
Lesen Sie die Zeitschrift auch?

Gefällt den Leuten die Zeitung?
Gefällt Ihnen die Zeitung auch?
Kennen Sie die Familie?
Kennen Sie das Kind auch?

Drill 30 *One pronoun in the nominative. One pronoun in the dative. One pronoun in the accusative. Respond to the questions using the correct pronouns. Follow the examples.*

Erklärt **der** Professor **der** Studentin **das** Problem?
Ja, **er** erklärt **es ihr.**

Erklärt **der** Professor **Ihnen das** Problem auch?
Ja, **er** erklärt **es mir** auch.

Schickt der Autor seinem Freund die Kritik?
Schickt der Autor Ihnen die Kritik auch?

Bringen Sie den Leuten die Zeitschrift?
Bringen Sie dem Professor die Zeitschrift auch?

Gibt der Student seiner Schwester das Buch?
Gibt der Student seinem Freund das Buch auch?

Schickt der Student Ihnen den Roman?
Schickt der Student seiner Freundin den Roman auch?

Zeigt der Vater seinen Freunden das Haus?
Zeigt der Vater Ihnen das Haus auch?

Erzählt die Großmutter dem Kind das Märchen?
Erzählt die Großmutter Ihnen das Märchen auch?

Erzählt der Junge seinen Freunden die Geschichte?
Erzählt der Junge seiner Schwester die Geschichte auch?

Drill 31 *Combination Drill   Respond in the same manner.*

Kennen Sie den Roman?
Gefällt Ihnen der Roman?
Schicken Sie Ihrer Freundin den Roman?
Lesen Sie die Zeitschrift?
Gefällt dem Professor die Zeitschrift?
Bringen Sie den Leuten die Zeitschrift?
Kennen Sie die Erzählung?
Gefällt Ihnen die Idee?

Erklärt der Professor Ihnen das Problem?
Verstehen Sie den Dialog?
Gefällt Ihnen der Dialog?
Erklärt der Professor Ihnen den Dialog?
Lesen Sie die Kritik?
Gefällt dem Schriftsteller die Kritik?
Schickt der Schriftsteller Ihnen die Kritik?

C.   Special Use of the Personal Pronoun es and of the Demonstrative Pronouns

Das and **dies** with the auxiliary verb **sein: es (das, dies) ist; es (das, dies) sind:**

Das ist der bekannte Schriftsteller.	*That is* the well-known writer.
Das sind die bekannten Schriftsteller.	*Those are* the well-known writers.

Dies ist das neue Drama.   *This is* the new drama.
Dies sind die neuen Dramen.   *These are* the new dramas.

Es ist der Student, der kommt.   { *It is* the student who is coming.
{ The student is the one who is coming.

Es sind die Studenten, die kommen.   { *It is* the students who are coming.
{ The students are the ones who are coming.

D.   Pronouns das and dies with the Auxiliary Verb sein

Es like **das** and **dies** is used at the beginning of a sentence, in front of **sein,** *which is followed by the subject.* In this case *it is the subject,* not the preceding singular form **es, das,** or **dies,** *which determines the verb form.*

The German equivalent for English *there is* and *there are* is usually **es ist** and **es sind:**

Es sind jetzt 30 Studenten im Kurs.   There are 30 students in the course now.

Remember that **es gibt** is only used if one speaks of *general existence* or *general condition:*

Es gibt viele Studenten in den USA.   There are many students in the USA.

E.   The Abbreviation of es

Es following a verb or pronoun is often abbreviated in colloquial German. In modern literature the following spelling is also to be found:

Wie geht's?   How are you?
Bist du's? Seid ihr's? Sind Sie's?   Is it you?

Was gibts?   What's the matter?
Darauf kommts an!   That's the point!
Gibs ihm!   Give it to him!

Drill 32   *Das ist, das sind, dies ist, dies sind   Render the sentences in the plural. Follow the examples.*

Das ist das neue Wohnviertel.   Dies ist die alte Stadt.
Das sind die neuen Wohnviertel.   Das ist die traditionelle Form.
Dies ist der entscheidende Einfluß.
Dies ist das große Vorbild.   Das ist der heutige Mensch.
Dies sind die großen Vorbilder.   Dies ist die ausgewählte Erzählung.

Das ist der typische Vertreter.

Drill 33 *Es ist, es sind* *Form sentences substituting the given cues. Follow the examples.*

Pattern	*Cues*
Es ist das Ideal.	die Ideale und Vorbilder
Es sind die Ideale und Vorbilder.	der Schriftsteller
Es ist der Schriftsteller.	die Frauen und Kinder
_____	die Universität
_____	die Kirchen und Schulen
_____	das Thema
_____	die Themen und Probleme
_____	das Theater
_____	die Theater und Universitäten

F.   The Genitive Forms of the Personal Pronouns meiner, deiner, seiner

The genitive forms **meiner, deiner, seiner,** etc., are rarely to be found in colloquial German. Therefore they appear in the scheme on page 34 in parentheses. They may be found compounded with the prepositions **wegen** and **um . . . willen.**

Sie kommt nur **seinetwegen.**	She only comes *on his account.*
Meinetwegen kann er gehen.	*As far as I am concerned* he may go.
Er tut es um **ihretwillen.**	He does it *for her sake.*
Er tut es um **unsretwillen.**	He does it *for our sake.*

Note that in these forms the **t** replaces the **r.**

Nevertheless the genitive forms **meiner, deiner, seiner,** etc., still appear in *literary style* after *certain verbs, adjectives,* and *numerals:*

Herr, **gedenke meiner!**	Lord, be mindful of me!
Er wurde **seiner gewahr.**	He perceived him.
Es waren **ihrer drei.**	There were three of them.

II.   THE da- AND wo-COMPOUNDS

Only prepositions governing the accusative and/or dative can form **da-** and **wo-**compounds. However **ohne, außer, seit** *never do.*

A.   Da-Compounds: da(r)—

Hat er **von dieser Person** gesprochen? Ja, er hat **von ihr** gesprochen.	Did he talk about this person? Yes, he talked *about him (her).*
Hat er **von dieser Sache** gesprochen? Ja, er hat **davon** gesprochen.	Did he talk about this matter? Yes, he talked *about it.*
Hat er **von Freiheit** gesprochen? Ja, er hat **davon** gesprochen.	Did he talk about freedom? Yes, he talked *about it.*

Preposition + personal pronoun is used for persons:

von ihm, mit ihr, für sie, etc.

Da(r) + preposition is used for *objects, facts,* and usually for *concepts* (also for *whole sentences*):

darauf, darin, dafür, etc.

B.   Wo-Compounds: wo(r)—

Er hat **von dieser Person** gesprochen. **Von wem** hat er gesprochen?	He talked *about this person. About whom* did he talk?
Er hat **von dieser Sache** gesprochen. **Wovon** hat er gesprochen?	He talked *about this matter. About what* did he talk?
Er hat **von Freiheit** gesprochen. **Wovon** hat er gesprochen?	He talked *about freedom. About what* did he talk?

Preposition + interrogative pronoun is used for *persons:*

von wem, mit wem, für wen, etc.

Wo(r) + preposition is used for *objects, facts,* and usually for *concepts* (also for *whole sentences*):

wovon, worin, worüber, etc.

When the preposition begins with a vowel (**an, auf, über,** etc.), and **r** is inserted between the two components:

da-r-an, wo-r-auf, da-r-über, wo-r-über, etc.
But: da-mit, wo-von, da-für, wo-zu, etc.

C.   Study the Following Verbs with Prepositions before Going through the Drills

1.   Verbs with prepositions + accusative

Sie **arbeiten für die** Familie.	They *work for* the family.
Sie **denken an die** Zukunft.	They *think of (about)* the future.
Sie **warten auf den** Brief.	They *wait for* the letter.
Sie **schreiben über den** Roman.	They *write about* the novel.
Sie **sprechen über die** Situation.	They *talk about* (discuss) the situation in detail.
Sie **bitten um** Kritik	They *ask for* criticism.
Sie **reagieren auf die** Leute.	They *react to* the people.
Sie **glauben an die** Zukunft.	They *believe in* the future.

2. Verbs with prepositions + dative

Sie **sprechen von dem** Autor.	They *talk about* (mention) the author.
Sie **fragen nach den** Büchern.	They *ask about* the books.
Sie **rechnen mit den** Leuten.	They *count on* the people.
Die Geschichten **handeln vom** Krieg.	The stories *deal with* the war.
Die Werke **gehören zur** Weltliteratur.	The works *are part of* world literature.

Note the *different meanings* of **gehören:**

(a) Gehören zu + *dative*

Die Werke **gehören zur** Weltliteratur.   The works *are part of* world literature.

(b) Gehören + *dative*

Das Buch **gehört dem** Studenten.   The book *belongs to* the student. (The student *owns* the book.)

Drill 34 *Contrastive Drill   Verbs with Prepositions + Accusative   Give the German equivalent.*

They work for the family.
Sie **arbeiten für die** Familie.

They ask for criticism.
They write about the novel.
They react to the people.

They talk about (discuss) the situation.
They wait for the letter.
They think about the future.
They believe in the future.
They work for the family.

Drill 35 *Contrastive Drill   Verbs with Prepositions + Dative   Give the German equivalent.*

They talk about (mention) the author.
Sie **sprechen von dem** Autor.

They count on the people.
They ask about the books.

The works are part of world literature.
The stories deal with the war.
They talk about (mention) the author.

Drill 36 *Combination Drill   Give the German equivalent.*

They ask for criticism.
They ask about the books.
They talk about (mention) the author.
They talk about (discuss) the situation.
They think of the future.
The works are part of world literature.
They work for the family.

They wait for the letter.
The stories deal with the war.
They write about the novel.
They react to the people.
They count on the people.
They believe in the future.

Drill 37   *Answer the questions as shown in the examples.*

Spricht er **von dieser Person?**
Ja, er spricht **von ihr.**

Spricht er **von dieser Sache?**
Ja, er spricht **davon.**

Denken Sie **an Ihre Eltern?**
Ja, ich denke **an sie.**

Denken Sie **an Ihre Zukunft?**
Ja, ich denke **daran.**

Warten Sie auf Ihren Freund?
Warten Sie auf den Brief?

Reagiert er auf die Leute?
Reagiert er auf Kritik?
Schreiben Sie über Franz Kafka?
Schreiben Sie über dieses Problem?
Sprechen Sie über den Schriftsteller?
Sprechen Sie über sein Buch?
Arbeiten Sie für Ihre Familie?
Fragt er nach dem Thema?
Glauben Sie an dieses Prinzip?
Bitten Sie um Kritik?
Rechnen Sie mit diesen Leuten?

Drill 38   *Question the given statements as shown in the examples.*

Ich spreche **über den Dichter.**
Über wen sprechen Sie?

Ich spreche **über dieses Thema.**
Worüber sprechen Sie?

Ich rechne **mit diesen Leuten.**
Mit wem rechnen Sie?

Ich rechne **mit Kritik.**
Womit rechnen Sie?

Ich denke an meine Eltern.

Ich denke an meine Zukunft.
Ich schreibe über Wolfgang Borchert.
Ich schreibe über politische Probleme.
Ich warte auf meinen Freund.
Ich warte auf den Brief.
Er reagiert auf diese Personen.
Er reagiert auf diese Situation.
Er spricht vom Wirtschaftswunder.
Ich bitte um Kritik.
Ich rechne mit diesem Herrn.

Drill 39   *Combination Drill*   *Respond to the two statements as shown in the following examples.*

| | Er schreibt **vom Krieg.** |
| *Student:* | **Wovon** schreibt er? |

| | **Vom Krieg.** |
| *Student:* | Aha, **davon.** |

| | Er wartet **auf seinen Freund.** |
| *Student:* | **Auf wen** wartet er? |

| | **Auf seinen Freund.** |
| *Student:* | Aha, **auf ihn.** |

Er spricht über Franz Kafka.
Über Franz Kafka.

Er schreibt vom Krieg und von der Heimkehr.
Vom Krieg und von der Heimkehr.

Er reagiert auf die Frage.
Auf die Frage.

Er rechnet mit den Leuten.
Mit den Leuten.

Er schreibt über politische Probleme.
Über politische Probleme.

Er spricht von dieser Person.
Von dieser Person.

Er bittet um Antwort.
Um Antwort.

Er glaubt an diese Idee.
An diese Idee.

Er schreibt über Wolfgang Borchert.
Über Wolfgang Borchert.

Er denkt an seine Zukunft.
An seine Zukunft.

III. THE REFLEXIVE PRONOUNS

Compare the *personal pronouns* and the *reflexive pronouns*.

Singular

	Personal pronouns	Reflexive pronouns
Acc.	Er kennt **mich.** / He knows me.	**Ich** kenne **mich.** / I know myself.
Dat.	Er schadet **mir.** / He does harm to me.	**Ich** schade **mir.** / I do harm to myself.
Acc.	Er kennt **dich.** / He knows you.	**Du** kennst **dich.** / You know yourself.
Dat.	Er schadet **dir.** / He does harm to you.	**Du** schadest **dir.** / You do harm to yourself.
Acc.	Er kennt **Sie.** / He knows you.	**Sie** kennen **sich.** / You know yourself.
Dat.	Er schadet **Ihnen.** / He does harm to you.	**Sie** schaden **sich.** / You do harm to yourself.
Acc.	Er kennt **ihn.** / He knows him.	**Er** kennt **sich.** / He knows himself.
Dat.	Er schadet **ihm.** / He does harm to him.	**Er** schadet **sich.** / He does harm to himself.
Acc.	Er kennt **es** (das Kind). / He knows him (her).	**Es** (das Kind) kennt **sich.** / The child knows himself.
Dat.	Er schadet **ihm** (dem Kind). / He does harm to him (her).	**Es** (das Kind) schadet **sich.** / The child does harm to himself.
Acc.	Er kennt **sie.** / He knows her.	**Sie** kennt **sich.** / She knows herself.
Dat.	Er schadet **ihr.** / He does harm to her.	**Sie** schadet **sich.** / She does harm to herself.

	Personal pronouns	*Reflexive pronouns*
		Plural
Acc.	Er kennt **uns.** He knows us.	**Wir** kennen **uns.** We know ourselves.
Dat.	Er schadet **uns.** He does harm to us.	**Wir** schaden **uns.** We do harm to ourselves.
Acc.	Er kennt **euch.** He knows you.	**Ihr** kennt **euch.** You know yourselves.
Dat.	Er schadet **euch.** He does harm to you.	**Ihr** schadet **euch.** You do harm to yourselves.
Acc.	Er kennt **Sie.** He knows you.	**Sie** kennen **sich.** You know yourselves.
Dat.	Er schadet **Ihnen.** He does harm to you.	**Sie** schaden **sich.** You do harm to yourselves.
Acc.	Er kennt **sie.** He knows them.	**Sie** kennen **sich.** They know themselves.
Dat.	Er schadet **ihnen.** He does harm to them.	**Sie** schaden **sich.** They do harm to themselves.

Note that the reflexive pronoun of the formal **Sie** is not capitalized: Kennen **Sie sich?**

The reflexive pronoun can be used in the following ways.

1. The direct object:

Nonreflexive

Er kennt **ihn.**
He knows him.

Reflexive

Er kennt **sich.**
He knows himself.

2. The indirect object:

Er kauft **ihm** einen Wagen.
He buys him a car.

Er kauft **sich** einen Wagen.
He buys himself a car.

3. The sole dative object:

Er schadet **ihm.**
He does harm to him.

Er schadet **sich.**
He does harm to himself.

4. The object of a preposition:

Er spricht nur **von ihm.**
He talks only about him.

Er spricht nur **von sich.**
He talks only about himself.

A. Verbs with Reflexive Direct Objects

1. Verbs that are both nonreflexive and reflexive

Some verbs may be used either nonreflexively or reflexively. Compare the following usages:

Nonreflexive		*Reflexive*	
waschen	Er wäscht den Wagen. He is washing the car.	**sich** waschen	Er wäscht **sich.** He is washing.
beugen	Er beugt seinen Kopf über den Tisch. He bends his head over the table.	**sich** beugen	Er beugt **sich** über den Tisch. He bends over the table.
ändern	Er ändert sein Verhalten. He changes his behavior.	**sich** ändern	Er ändert **sich** nie. He never changes.
fürchten	Er fürchtet das Examen. He is afraid of the exam.	**sich** fürchten	Er fürchtet **sich.** He is afraid.
setzen	Er setzt das Kind auf den Stuhl. He puts the child on the chair.	**sich** setzen	Er setzt **sich** auf den Stuhl. He sits down on the chair.
wundern	Das wundert ihn sehr. That surprises him very much.	**sich** wundern	Er wundert **sich** sehr. He is very surprised.
öffnen	Er öffnet die Tür. He opens the door.	**sich** öffnen	Die Tür öffnet **sich.** The door opens.
bewegen	Er bewegt den Vorhang. He moves the curtain.	**sich** bewegen	Der Vorhang bewegt **sich.** The curtain moves.
treffen	Sie treffen ihn oft. They meet him often.	**sich** treffen	Sie treffen **sich** oft. They meet often.
fragen	Er fragt den Studenten. He asks the student.	**sich** fragen	Er fragt **sich,** ob das stimmt. He wonders if that is cor- rect.
vorstellen	Er stellt ihn vor. He introduces him.	**sich** vorstellen	Er stellt **sich** vor. He introduces himself.

Drill 40 *Nonreflexive or Reflexive* *Give the German equivalents.*

He changes his behavior.
He never changes.
He asks the student.
He wonders if that is correct.
That surprises him very much.

He is very surprised.
He is washing the car.
He is washing.
He puts the child on the chair.
He sits down on the chair.

He bends his head over the table.
He bends over the table.
He moves the curtain.
The curtain moves.
He opens the door.
The door opens.
He is afraid of the exam.
He is afraid.
They meet him often.
They meet often.
He introduces him.
He introduces himself.

That surprises him very much.
He wonders if that is correct.
He sits down on the chair.
He changes his behavior.
The curtain moves.
He never changes.
He opens the door.
He is washing.
He bends over the table.
He introduces him.
He is afraid.
He is very surprised.

2. Verbs that are only reflexive

sich befinden	Sie befinden **sich** dort. They are there.
sich verhalten	Sie verhalten **sich** richtig. They behave correctly.
sich entschließen	Sie entschließen **sich** sofort. They decide immediately.
sich ereignen	Es ereignet **sich.** It is happening.

Drill 41   *Give the German equivalents.*

They decide immediately.
They behave correctly.
It is happening.
They are there.

He never changes.
The curtain moves.
He wonders if that is correct.
He bends over the table.

He decides immediately.
He behaves correctly.

B. Verbs with Reflexive Indirect Objects

sich etwas (oder jemand) merken	Ich merke **mir** das. I will keep that in mind.
sich etwas (oder jemand) ansehen	Ich sehe **mir** das Mädchen an. I will have a (close) look at the girl.
sich etwas vorstellen	Ich kann **mir** das gut vorstellen. I can well imagine that.
sich Sorgen machen	Ich mache **mir** Sorgen. I am worrying.

Note the reflexive usage when referring to parts of the body or articles of clothing. The definite article replaces the possessive adjectives before nouns designating parts of the body or articles of clothing. The *relative pronoun* functions as the *indirect object*. Compare the following German sentences with their English equivalents.

Ich wasche **mir die** Hände.	I am washing *my* hands.
Du kämmst **dir das** Haar.	You are combing *your* hair.
Er zieht **sich den** Mantel an.	He is putting on *his* coat.
Ich setze **mir den** Hut auf.	I am putting on *my* hat.

Drill 42   *Give the German equivalents.*

I can well imagine that.	I decide immediately.	I will keep that in mind.
I will have a look at the girl.	I behave correctly.	It is happening.
I will keep that in mind.	The curtain moves.	I am here.
I am worrying.	I can well imagine that.	I wonder if that is correct.

C. Reflexive Verbs with Prepositions

1. Reflexive verbs with prepositions governing the accusative

Sie **freuen sich auf die** Ferien (*plur.*).	They *look forward to* vacation.
Sie **freuen sich über das** Geschenk.	They *are happy about* the present.
Sie **beziehen sich auf den** Inhalt.	They *refer to* the contents.
Sie **erinnern sich an das** Wort.	They *remember the* word.
Sie **konzentrieren sich auf das** Problem.	They *concentrate on* the problem.
Sie **kümmern sich** nicht **um ihre** Zukunft.	They are not *concerned about* their future.
Sie **machen sich** (*dat.*) **um den** Jungen Sorgen.	They are *worried about* the boy.
Ich **mache mir um den** Jungen Sorgen.	I am *worried about* the boy.
Sie **interessieren sich für** Literatur.	They are *interested in* literature.
Sie **beschweren sich über die** Arbeit.	They *complain about* the work.

2. Reflexive verbs with prepositions governing the dative

Sie **irren sich in dieser** Sache.	They are mistaken *about* this matter.
Sie **richten sich nach den** Regeln.	They conform *to* the rules.
Sie **beschäftigen sich mit dem** Roman.	They are busy (busy themselves) *with* the novel.

Note the following prepositional phrases:

Die Erzählung **handelt vom** Krieg.	The story deals *with* the war.
Es handelt sich in dieser Erzählung um den Krieg.	The story deals *with* the war.

Drill 43   *Contrastive Drill   Give the German equivalent.*

They look forward to returning home.
They are happy about the present.
They refer to the theme.
They remember the ruins.
They concentrate on the problem.
They complain about the criticism.

They are interested in this epoch.
They are worried about the boy.
They are mistaken about the interpretation.
They conform to society.
They are not concerned about their future.
They are busy with the novel.

Drill 44   *Contrastive Drill   Give the German equivalent.*

They look forward to returning home.
I am happy about the present.
He refers to the theme.
We remember the ruins.
She concentrates on the problem.
I complain about the criticism.

We are interested in this epoch.
He is worried about the boy.
She is mistaken about the interpretation.
We conform to society.
He is not concerned about his future.
I am busy with the novel.

Drill 45   *Answer the questions as shown in the examples.*

Freuen **Sie sich** auf die Ferien?
Ja, **ich** freue **mich** darauf.

Und der Student?
Er freut **sich** auch darauf.

Interessiere **ich mich** für Literatur?
Ja, **Sie** interessieren **sich** dafür.

Und die Studenten?
Sie interessieren **sich** auch dafür.

Beschweren die Studenten sich über die Arbeit?
Und wir?

Freuen Sie sich über das Geschenk?
Und der Professor?

Beziehe ich mich auf den Inhalt?
Und die Studenten?

Erinnern sich die Leute an die Trümmer?
Und wir?

Beschäftige ich mich mit dem Roman?
Und der Student?

Konzentrieren sich die Studenten auf das Problem? Und wir?

Machen sich die Eltern um den Jungen Sorgen?
Und der Mann?

Irre ich mich in dieser Sache?
Und die Studenten?

Richten sich die Leute nach den Regeln?
Und wir?

Drill 46   *Combination Drill   Give the German equivalent.*

They think of (about) the misery.
We remember the ruins.
They write about the destruction.
They react to the catastrophe.
He talks about the dignity of man.

They ask for criticism.
They are worried about the boy.
The story deals with the war.
They count on the resistance movement.
He looks forward to returning home.

He believes in the future.

They are not concerned about their future.

We are busy with the novel.

They wait for the program.

He works for the industry.

She conforms to society.

We are happy about the present.

I refer to the theme.

He complains about the criticism.

I concentrate on this problem.

We are interested in this epoch.

IV. **THE INDEFINITE PRONOUN** einer, eins, eine — keiner, keins, keine, **THE POSSESSIVE PRONOUNS, AND THE INDEFINITE PRONOUN** man

		Singular		*Plural*
	Masc.	*Neut.*	*Fem.*	
Nom.	einer	eins	eine	welche
	keiner	keins	keine	keine
	meiner	meins	meine	meine
Acc.	einen	eins	eine	welche
	keinen	keins	keine	keine
	meinen	meins	meine	meine
Dat.	einem	einem	einer	—
	keinem	keinem	keiner	keinen
	meinem	meinem	meiner	meinen
Gen.	—	—	—	—

A. **Examples of Singular Usage**

Hier ist **ein** Brief.

Da ist auch **einer.**

Here is a letter.

There is one too.

Hier ist **ein** Programm.

Da ist auch **eins.**

Here is a program.

There is one too.

Hier ist **eine** Zeitung.

Da ist auch **eine.**

Here is a newspaper.

There is one too.

Das ist **kein** Kurs.

Dies ist auch **keiner.**

That is not a course.

(This is not a course either).

Das ist **kein** Problem.

Dies ist auch **keins.**

That is not a problem.

(This is not a problem either).

Das ist **keine** Kurzgeschichte.

Dies ist auch **keine.**

That is not a short story.

(This is not a short story either).

Das ist **mein** Wagen.	That is my car.
Dies ist auch **meiner.**	This is mine too.
Das ist **mein** Haus.	That is my house.
Dies ist auch **meins.**	This is mine too.
Das ist **meine** Zeitung.	That is my newspaper.
Dies ist auch **meine.**	This is mine too.

B. Examples of Plural Usage

Hier sind Briefe, Programme, Zeitungen.	Here are letters, programs, newspapers.
Da sind auch **welche.**	There are some too.
Das sind **keine** Kurse, **keine** Probleme, **keine** Kurzgeschichten.	Those are no courses, no problems, no short stories.
Dies sind auch **keine.**	(These are no courses, no problems, no short stories either.)
Das sind **meine** Wagen, **meine** Häuser, **meine** Zeitungen.	Those are my cars, my houses, my newspapers.
Dies sind auch **meine.**	These are mine too.

Note the difference between the use of the indefinite and the personal pronoun:

Ich lese **dieses Drama.**	Ich lese **es** auch.
Ich lese **ein Drama.**	Ich lese auch **eins.**

The following pronouns take the endings of the direct article:

Pronouns	Direct article
einer	
keiner	der
mein**er**	
eine	
keine	die
meine	
eins	
keins	das
meins	
welche	
keine	die
meine	

Note the difference between German and English in the following expression:

Er ist ein Freund **von mir.**   He is a friend *of* mine.

The German **von** is followed by a *personal pronoun,* whereas the English *of* is followed by a *possessive pronoun.*

C.   The Indefinite Pronoun man

When *declining* **man, einen** is used for the *accusative* and **einem** for the *dative.* As with the indefinite pronouns **einer, keiner,** there is *no genitive* form.

Nom.   **Man** kommt gern hierher.   One likes to come here.
Acc.   Das freut **einen.**   That pleases one (you, people).
Dat.   Er dankt **einem** nie.   He never thanks you (anyone).

Drill 47   *Follow the examples.*

Das ist ein Roman. Dies ist auch einer.
Das sind Romane. Dies sind auch welche.
Das ist kein Problem. Dies ist auch keins.
Das sind keine Probleme. Dies sind auch keine.
Das ist unsere Zeitung. Dies ist auch unsre.
Das sind unsre Zeitungen. Dies sind auch unsre.

Das ist ein Program. Dies ist auch . . .
Das sind Programme. Dies sind auch . . .
Das ist kein Kurs. Dies ist auch . . .
Das sind keine Kurse. Dies sind auch . . .
Das ist ihre Zeitung. Dies ist auch . . .
Das sind ihre Zeitungen. Dies sind auch . . .
Das ist sein Wagen. Dies ist auch . . .
Das sind Wohnviertel. Dies sind auch . . .
Das sind keine Soldaten. Dies sind auch . . .
Das ist unsre Zeitschrift. Dies ist auch . . .
Das sind keine Kurzgeschichten. Dies sind auch . . .
Das sind Romane. Dies sind auch . . .
Das ist ein Roman. Dies ist auch . . .

THE ADJECTIVE, PARTICIPLE, AND ADVERB

I. THE ATTRIBUTIVE ADJECTIVE

In German there are *three declensions* for the adjective preceding a noun:

1. The *adjective declension I* after **der**-words: **der** gut**e** Stil.
2. The *adjective declension II* after **ein**-words: **ein** gut**er** Stil.
3. The *adjective declension III* without limiting **der**- or **ein**-words: gut**er** Stil.

A.   The Adjective Declension I (after der-Words) and the Adjective Declension II (after ein-Words)

	Masculine		*Neuter*		*Feminine*	
Sing. Nom.	der	alte Mann	das	kleine Kind	die	junge Frau
	ein	alter Mann	ein	kleines Kind	eine	junge Frau
Acc.	den	alten Mann	das	kleine Kind	die	junge Frau
	einen	alten Mann	ein	kleines Kind	eine	junge Frau
Dat.	dem / einem	alten Mann	dem / einem	kleinen Kind	der / einer	jungen Frau
Gen.	des / eines	alten Mannes	des / eines	kleinen Kindes	der / einer	jungen Frau
Plur. Nom.	die / keine	alten Männer	die / keine	kleinen Kinder	die / keine	jungen Frauen
Acc.	die / keine	alten Männer	die / keine	kleinen Kinder	die / keine	jungen Frauen
Dat.	den / keinen	alten Männern	den / keinen	kleinen Kindern	den / keinen	jungen Frauen
Gen.	der / keiner	alten Männer	der / keiner	kleinen Kinder	der / keiner	jungen Frauen

Memorize the expressions below:

Masculine	*Neuter*	*Feminine*
der alte Mann	das kleine Kind	die junge Frau
ein alter Mann	ein kleines Kind	eine junge Frau

Every other ending of an adjective preceded by a **der**- or **ein**-word is **–en.**

Pay careful attention to the following irregular forms:

dunk**el**	der dunk**le** Wald	the dark forest
teu**er**	der teu**re** Wagen	the expensive car
ho**ch**	der ho**he** Berg	the high mountain

links	die link**e** Hand	the left hand
rechts	die recht**e** Hand	the right hand
ander**s**	der ander**e** Weg	the other way

1.   The adjective declension I after other der-words

dies**er**	dies**er** typische Zug	this typical feature
jen**er**	jen**es** neue Phänomen	that new phenomenon
jed**er**	jed**e** junge Generation	every (each) young generation
welch**er**	welch**er** totale Staat	which (what) totalitarian state
solch**er**	solch**e** großen Probleme	such big problems
manch**er**	manch**es** gute Jahr	many a good year

(For **welch, solch, manch** *without endings,* see page 58.)

derselbe	**der**selbe moderne Mensch	the same modern man
	dasselbe alte Ideal	the same old ideal
	dieselbe beliebte Erzählung	the same popular story

derselbe is treated as *two elements:* **der + selbe,** which is inflected as an adjective following a **der**-word:

| Ich lese **den**selben neuen Roman. | I am reading the same new novel. |
| Das sind **die**selben alten Themen. | These are the same old topics. |

Adjectives after **alle** take the plural ending **–en:**

| all**e** | all**e** deutsch**en** Schriftsteller | all German writers |

2.   The adjective declension II after other ein-words

kein	kein gut**er** Stil	not a good style
	kein bekannt**es** Gebiet	not a well-known area
	kein**e** echte Überzeugung	not a genuine conviction

All possessive pronouns:

mein	mein alt**er** Freund	my old friend
dein	dein groß**es** Ideal	your great ideal
sein	sein**e** ironische Kritik	his ironic criticism
ihr	ihr deutsch**er** Kurs	her German course
unser	unser öffentlich**es** Leben	our public life
euer	eur**e** politische Idee	your political idea
Ihr	Ihr neuer Anfang	your new beginning
ihr	ih**re** persönlichen Probleme	their personal problems

Note that **–er** of **unser** and **euer** is *not an ending:*

Das ist **ein** neue**s** Buch.   Das ist **kein** neue**s** Buch.
Das ist **unser** neue**s** Buch.   Das ist **euer** neue**s** Buch.

Drill 48   *Follow the examples.*

Das ist der Anfang, der neu ist.
Das ist **der** neu**e** Anfang.

Dies ist auch ein Anfang, der neu ist.
Dies ist auch **ein** neu**er** Anfang.

Das ist das Thema, das beliebt ist.
Das ist **das** beliebt**e** Thema.

Dies ist auch ein Thema, das beliebt ist.
Dies ist auch **ein** beliebt**es** Thema.

Das ist die Kritik, die ironisch ist.
Das ist **die** ironisch**e** Kritik.

Dies ist auch eine Kritik, die ironisch ist.
Dies ist auch **eine** ironisch**e** Kritik.

Das ist der Mensch, der modern ist.
Dies ist auch ein Mensch, der modern ist.

Das ist das Beispiel, das gut ist.
Dies ist auch ein Beispiel, das gut ist.

Das ist die Kurzgeschichte, die interessant ist.
Dies ist auch eine Kurzgeschichte, die interessant ist.

Das ist das Gebiet, das bekannt ist.
Dies ist auch ein Gebiet, das bekannt ist.

Das ist der Stil, der merkwürdig ist.
Dies ist auch ein Stil, der merkwürdig ist.

Das ist das Vorbild, das alt ist.
Dies ist auch ein Vorbild, das alt ist.

Das ist der Zug, der typisch ist.
Dies ist auch ein Zug, der typisch ist.

Das ist das Problem, das persönlich ist.
Dies ist auch ein Problem, das persönlich ist.

Das ist der Krieg, der sinnlos ist.
Dies ist auch ein Krieg, der sinnlos ist.

Das ist das Stilexperiment, das fragwürdig ist.
Dies ist auch ein Stilexperiment, das fragwürdig ist.

Das ist der Einfluß, der entscheidend ist.
Dies ist auch ein Einfluß, der entscheidend ist.

Drill 49   *Follow the examples.*

Das ist der Inhalt, der merkwürdig ist.
Das ist **der** merkwürdig**e** Inhalt.

Wir besprechen den Inhalt, der merkwürdig ist.
Wir besprechen **den** merkwürdig**en** Inhalt.

Das ist der Inhalt, der merkwürdig ist.
Das ist **ein** merkwürdig**er** Inhalt.

Wir besprechen einen Inhalt, der merkwürdig ist.
Wir besprechen **einen** merkwürdig**en** Inhalt.

Das ist jener Einfluß, der stark ist.

Wir empfinden jenen Einfluß, der stark ist.

Das ist kein Bereich, der neu ist.
Wir schreiben über keinen Bereich, der neu ist.

Das ist dieser Schriftsteller, der modern ist.
Wir charakterisieren diesen Schriftsteller, der modern ist.

Das ist mein Stil, der traditionell ist.
Wir sprechen über meinen Stil, der traditionell ist.

Drill 50   *Follow the examples.*

Das ist das Thema, das politisch ist.
Das ist **das** politische Thema.

Er schreibt über das Thema, das politisch ist.
Er schreibt über **das** politische Thema.

Das ist sein Beispiel, das ausgewählt ist.
Das ist **sein** ausgewähltes Beispiel.

Er bittet um unser Beispiel, das ausgewählt ist.
Er bittet um **unser** ausgewähltes Beispiel.

Das ist diese Tradition, die alt ist.
Das ist **diese** alte Tradition.

Er glaubt an jede Tradition, die alt ist.
Er glaubt an **jede** alte Tradition.

Das ist ihre Idee, die neu ist.
Das ist **ihre** neue Idee.

Er bezieht sich auf unsre Idee, die neu ist.
Er bezieht sich auf **unsre** neue Idee.

Das ist das Ereignis, das entscheidend ist.
Er reagiert auf das Ereignis, das entscheidend ist.

Das ist keine Bezeichnung, die typisch ist.
Er liest keine Bezeichnung, die typisch ist.

Das ist unser Problem, das persönlich ist.
Er charakterisiert unser Problem, das persönlich ist.

Das ist meine Geschichte, die interessant ist.
Er spricht über meine Geschichte, die interessant ist.

Drill 51   *Follow the examples.*

Er spricht von der Erzählform, die beliebt ist.
Er spricht von **der** beliebten Erzählform.

Er spricht von den Erzählformen, die beliebt sind.
Er spricht von **den** beliebten Erzählformen.

Er kommt wegen des Stilexperiments, das fragwürdig ist.
Er kommt wegen **des** fragwürdigen Stilexperiments.

Er kommt wegen der Stilexperimente, die fragwürdig sind.
Er kommt wegen **der** fragwürdigen Stilexperimente.

Wir beschäftigen uns mit diesem Roman, der merkwürdig ist.
Wir beschäftigen uns mit diesen Romanen, die merkwürdig sind.

Er kommt wegen seines Problems, das interessant ist.
Er kommt wegen seiner Probleme, die interessant sind.

Die Leute kennen ihren Einfluß, der stark ist.
Die Leute kennen ihre Einflüsse, die stark sind.

Sie spricht von ihrem Thema, das interessant ist.
Sie spricht von ihren Themen, die interessant sind.

Ihr kommt wegen eures Problems, das persönlich ist.
Ihr kommt wegen eurer Probleme, die persönlich sind.

Sie reagieren auf seine Kritik, die ironisch ist.
Sie reagieren auf seine Kritiken, die ironisch sind.

Wir kommen wegen unseres Themas, das bekannt ist.
Wir kommen wegen unserer Themen, die bekannt sind.

Wir beschäftigen uns mit unserer Einführung, die kurz ist.
Wir beschäftigen uns mit unseren Einführungen, die kurz sind.

Drill 52 *Combination Drill* *Respond in the same manner.*

Das ist der Inhalt, der merkwürdig ist.
Das ist ein Mensch, der modern ist.
Das ist das Thema, das beliebt ist.
Das ist ein Ereignis, das entscheidend ist.
Das ist die Tradition, die alt ist.
Das ist eine Geschichte, die neu ist.
Wir besprechen diesen Inhalt, der interessant ist.
Wir besprechen keinen Stil, der traditionell ist.
Wir lesen jene Bezeichnung, die typisch ist.
Wir lesen seine Kurzgeschichte, die bekannt ist.
Wir lesen diese Kurzgeschichten, die merkwürdig sind.
Wir besprechen die Stile, die neu sind.
Wir sprechen von einem Stil, der modern ist.
Wir sprechen von den Problemen, die interessant sind.
Wir kommen wegen der Probleme, die persönlich sind.
Wir kommen wegen des Ereignisses, das entscheidend ist.
Das ist unser Problem, das persönlich ist.
Das ist ihr Anfang, der neu ist.
Wir beschäftigen uns mit einem Inhalt, der merkwürdig ist.
Wir beschäftigen uns mit unserer Einführung, die kurz ist.
Er kommt wegen seiner Kritik, die ironisch ist.
Sie kommen wegen ihrer Probleme, die persönlich sind.
Sie richten sich nach seiner Kritik, die gut ist.
Das ist ein Einfluß, der entscheidend ist.
Das ist unser Einfluß, der entscheidend ist.
Das ist kein Thema, das alt ist.

Drill 53 *Combination Drill* *Give the German equivalent.*

every old friend	your (Ihr) new beginning	which dark forest?
our old friend	the same old ideal	this expensive car
what well-known area?	our old ideal	many a high mountain
not a well-known area	each young generation	my right hand
many a new beginning	our young generation	no other way

| all other ways | the same old topics | all genuine convictions |
| the same new novel | such decisive influences | |

B.   The Adjective Declension III (without Limiting der- or ein-Words)

The *adjectives* take the *endings* of the *definite article* **der, das, die,** except in the masculine and neuter genitive singular.

		Masculine	*Neuter*	*Feminine*
Sing. Nom.		roter Wein	kaltes Wasser	frische Milch
		der Wein	das Wasser	die Milch
Acc.		roten Wein	kaltes Wasser	frische Milch
		den Wein	das Wasser	die Milch
Dat.		rotem Wein	kaltem Wasser	frischer Milch
		dem Wein	dem Wasser	der Milch
Gen.		roten Weines	kalten Wassers	frischer Milch
		des Weines	des Wassers	der Milch
Plur. Nom.		rote Weine		
		die Weine		
Acc.		rote Weine		
		die Weine		
Dat.		roten Weinen		
		den Weinen		
Gen.		roter Weine		
		der Weine		

If there are two or more adjectives preceding a noun, they all have the same endings:

| Das ist gut**er**, alt**er**, rot**er** Wein. | That is good, old, red wine. |
| Das sind gut**e**, alt**e**, deutsch**e** Traditionen. | Those are good, old German traditions. |

1.   The adjective declension III after not limiting words

Andere, einige, mehrere, viele, wenige are *treated as adjectives* and any following adjective takes the same ending.

ander**e**	ander**e** traditionell**e** Formen	other traditional forms
einig**e**	einig**e** ausgewählt**e** Erzählungen	some selected stories
mehrer**e**	mehrer**e** literarisch**e** Stile	several literary styles
viel**e**	viel**e** episch**e** Formen	many epic forms
wenig**e**	wenig**e** gut**e** Gründe	few good reasons

Mehr, viel, ein wenig, etwas, ein paar, ein Paar, *all cardinal numbers (except* **ein–**)**, welch, solch, manch** in their *uninflected form* are also *not limiting words* and any following adjective takes *declension III endings.* **Solch** and **manch** in their *uninflected form* have an *archaic ring.*

mehr	mehr beliebt**e** Romane	more popular novels
viel	viel gut**e** Kritik	much good criticism
ein wenig	ein wenig rot**er** Wein	a little red wine
etwas	etwas frisch**es** Brot	some fresh bread
ein paar	ein paar weiß**e** Kaninchen	some white rabbits
ein Paar	ein Paar weiß**e** Kaninchen	a pair of white rabbits
zwei	zwei entscheidend**e** Einflüsse	two decisive influences
welch	welch gut**er** Stil	what a good style
solch	solch hoh**er** Stil	such a high style
manch	manch schön**er** Tag	many a beautiful day

Drill 54 *Cue Drill* *Follow the examples.*

Patterns	*Cues*
Hier ist rot**er** Wein.	kalt
Hier ist kalt**er** Wein.	wir trinken
_____	weiß
_____	wir sprechen von
_____	rot
_____	das ist der Geschmack (*gen.*)
_____	weiß
_____	hier ist
_____	kalt
_____	kaltes Wasser
_____	wir trinken
_____	wir sprechen von
_____	frisch
_____	das ist der Geschmack
_____	kalt
_____	hier ist
_____	kalte Milch
_____	wir trinken
_____	frisch
_____	wir sprechen von
_____	gut
_____	das ist der Geschmack
_____	kalt

Drill 55 *Put the singular forms into the plural. Follow the examples.*

Das ist **eine** ausgewählte Erzählung.
Das sind ausgewählte Erzählungen.

Wir sprechen von einem interessanten, gesellschaftlichen Problem.
Das sind Themen eines modernen, deutschen Autors.
Wir besprechen ein altes, historisches Problem.
Das sind Erzählungen eines bekannten, deutschen Schriftstellers.
Das ist ein politisches Phänomen.
Wir sprechen über die Probleme eines modernen Menschen.
Wir beschäftigen uns mit einer alten, traditionellen Form.
Wir interessieren uns für ein neues, gesellschaftliches Verhältnis.
Wir sprechen von einem bekannten und beliebten Thema.

Drill 56 *Give the German equivalent.*

more popular novels	such a beautiful day!	a pair of white rabbits
several popular novels	such beautiful days!	some white rabbits
few good reasons	much good criticism	the decisive influences
a little white wine	many epic forms	other big influences
what a good style!	some fresh bread	several good, old German traditions
what good style?	some selected stories	many interesting literary styles

After **etwas, nichts, viel,** and **wenig** the adjective takes declension III and is capitalized if not followed by a noun.

etwas **Neues**	something new	viel **Gutes**	much good
nichts **Neues**	nothing new	wenig **Gutes**	little good

But note:

etwas **anderes**	something else
etwas ganz **anderes**	something quite different

Drill 57 *Contrastive Drill*   *Give the German equivalent.*

something new	much good	something beautiful
something old	something quite different	nothing interesting
nothing good	something else	
nothing bad	little good	

Drill 58 *Combination Drill*   *Give the German equivalent.*

something old	some white rabbits	something quite different
some red wine	something else	much good criticism

much good
many new topics
many a beautiful day
nothing bad
not a bad style

no other way
warm water
a little cold water
little good
few good reasons

many popular novels
all interesting novels
more personal friends
several old friends
all good friends

II. THE PREDICATE ADJECTIVE AND THE ADVERB

As in English, *predicate adjectives* are *not inflected.*

Das Thema ist neu.	The theme is new.
Die Themen sind neu.	The themes are new.
Das Essen wird kalt.	The meal is getting cold.
Wir finden den Roman interessant.	We find the novel interesting.

Contrary to English, *adjectives as adverbs do not have a special form or ending.*

Dieser Autor schreibt gut.	This author writes *well.*
Er schreibt interessant.	He writes interesting*ly.*

III. ADJECTIVES, ABVERBS, AND THEIR OPPOSITES

Drill 59   *Give the English meanings.*

alt	————	jung	————
alt	————	neu	————
arm	————	reich	————
billig	————	teuer	————
breit	————	schmal	————
bunt	————	einfarbig	————
dick	————	dünn	————
einfach	————	kompliziert	————
erfolgreich	————	erfolglos	————
ernst	————	heiter	————
falsch	————	richtig	————
falsch	————	wahr	————
farbig	————	farblos	————
fern	————	nah	————
fleißig	————	faul	————
fremd	————	bekannt	————
froh (event, person)	————	traurig	————
fröhlich (person)	————	traurig	————
früh	————	spät	————
gesund	————	krank	————
groß	————	klein	————

gut	——————	schlecht	——————
gut	——————	böse	——————
hart	——————	weich	——————
häßlich	——————	schön	——————
heiß	——————	(eis)kalt	——————
hell	——————	dunkel	——————
hoch	——————	tief	——————
hoch	——————	niedrig	——————
hungrig	——————	satt	——————
interessant	——————	langweilig	——————
lang	——————	kurz	——————
laut	——————	leise	——————
mächtig	——————	machtlos	——————
mutig	——————	feige	——————
naß	——————	trocken	——————
offen or auf	——————	geschlossen or zu	——————
		abgeschlossen or	
offen or auf	——————	verschlossen	——————
rasch	——————	langsam	——————
schnell	——————	langsam	——————
sauer	——————	süß	——————
schwach	——————	stark	——————
schwer	——————	leicht	——————
schwierig	——————	leicht	——————
selten	——————	häufig	——————
stumpf	——————	scharf	——————
stumpf	——————	spitz	——————
tot	——————	lebend	——————
warm	——————	kalt	——————
weiß	——————	schwarz	——————
voll	——————	leer	——————
zahm	——————	wild	——————

IV. WELCHER – WAS FÜR EIN?

A. Welcher? Welches? Welche?—**Which? What?**

Welcher Roman ist das? **Der** neue Roman.   Which novel is that? The new novel.
Welches Buch ist das? **Das** neue Buch.   Which book is that? The new book.
Welche Erzählung ist das? **Die** neue Erzählung.   Which story is that? The new story.
Welche Ideen sind das? **Die** neuen Ideen.   Which ideas are these? The new ideas.

The *interrogative* **welch–** is a **der**-word. It is used when the questioner anticipates an answer that will call for the *definite article* **der, das, die** plus an *attributive adjective*.

Welcher Stil ist das? **Der** moderne Stil. **Welcher** ist das? **Der** moderne.	Which one is that? The modern one.
Welches Prinzip ist das? **Das** alte Prinzip. **Welches** ist das? **Das** alte.	Which one is that? The old one.
Welche Situation ist das? **Die** typische Situation. **Welche** ist das? **Die** typische.	Which one is that? The typical one.
Welche Formen sind das? **Die** modernen Formen. **Welche** sind das? **Die** modernen.	Which ones are these? The modern ones.

Welch– may also occur *without* a noun. The inflection and the endings remain the same.

B.   Was für ein? – Was für ein? – Was für eine?——**What Kind of? What Sort of?**

The interrogative **was für ein–** is an **ein**-word. It is used when the questioner anticipates an answer that will call for the *indefinite article* **ein, ein, eine** plus an *attributive adjective:*

Was für ein Autor ist er? **Ein** bekannter Autor.	What kind of author is he? A well-known author.
Was für ein Drama ist das? **Ein** bekanntes Drama.	What kind of drama is that? A well-known drama.
Was für eine Geschichte ist das? **Eine** bekannte Geschichte.	What kind of story is that? A well-known story.
Was für Autoren sind sie? Bekannte Autoren.	What kind of authors are they? Well-known authors.

Since there is no plural form of **ein, ein, eine,** *all plural forms* of the interrogative expression **was für ein–** are simply **was für:**

Was für Autoren sind sie?	What kind of authors are they?
Mit was für Büchern arbeiten Sie?	With what kind of books do you work?

Note that **für** in **was für ein–** *does not have the function of a preposition* but is only treated as a *part of the interrogative expression:*

Was für ein Autor ist er?	What kind of author is he?
Mit was für einem Buch arbeiten Sie?	With what kind of book do you work?

Was für ein– may also occur without a noun. The endings in the singular are then the same as those of the indefinite pronoun **einer, eins, eine. Welche** in the plural form **was für welche** *does not* have the meaning of *which.* It is only treated as *a part of the interrogative expression.*

Was für einen Roman lesen Sie?	**Einen** interessanten Roman.

Was für einen?	**Einen** interessanten.
What kind?	An interesting one.

Was für Erzählungen lesen Sie?	Interessante Erzählungen.
Was für welche?	Interessante.
What kind?	Interesting ones.

Drill 60 *Welcher? – Welches? – Welche?* *Follow the examples.*

Das ist **der** äußere Wiederaufbau.
Welcher Wiederaufbau ist das?

Er schreibt **über den** äußeren Wiederaufbau.
Über welchen Wiederaufbau schreibt er?

Das sind **die** neuen Perspektiven.
Welche Perspektiven sind das?

Er spricht **von den** neuen Perspektiven.
Von welchen Perspektiven spricht er?

Er beschreibt die damalige Wirklichkeit.

Er schreibt über die damalige Wirklichkeit.

Er beschäftigt sich mit der abendländischen Bildungswelt.

Er interessiert sich für die europäische Epik.

Er erinnert sich an das deutsche Wirtschaftswunder.

Er bezieht sich auf die großen Werke.

Er beschreibt den Trojanischen Krieg.

Er schreibt über den Trojanischen Krieg.

Drill 61 *Was für ein? – Was für eine?* *Follow the examples.*

Das ist **ein** merkwürdiges Ereignis.
Was für ein Ereignis ist das?

Er spricht **von einem** merkwürdigen Ereignis.
Von was für einem Ereignis spricht er?

Das sind neue Perspektiven.
Was für Perspektiven sind das?

Er spricht **von** neuen Perspektiven.
Von was für Perspektiven spricht er?

Er charakterisiert einen totalen Staat.

Er denkt an einen totalen Staat.

Er studiert einzelne Probleme.

Er beschäftigt sich mit einzelnen Problemen.

Er kennt ein anderes Gebiet.

Er spricht über einen deutschen Autor.

Er spricht über deutsche Autoren.

V. THE COMPARISON OF ADJECTIVES, PERFECT PARTICIPLES, AND ADVERBS

A. The Adjective and Perfect Participle Preceding the Noun

1. Klein, beliebt, interessant

Adjectives and perfect participles preceding a noun form the *comparative degree* by *adding* **–er** and the *superlative degree* by *adding* **–(e)st** to the stem. These forms are inflected like the simple positive forms.

Positive	Comparative	Superlative
der kleine Raum	der kleinere Raum	der kleinste Raum
the small room	the smaller room	the smallest room
das beliebte Thema	das beliebtere Thema	das beliebteste Thema
the popular theme	the more popular theme	the most popular theme
die interessante Epoche	die interessantere Epoche	die interessanteste Epoche
the interesting epoch	the more interesting epoch	the most interesting epoch

–est is used with the *superlative form* when the *positive form ends in –d, –t,* or in an **s**-sound (**–s, –ß, –z**), except with present participles: der entscheidendste Einfluß.

2. Alt, groß, kurz

Most monosyllabic adjectives with stem vowels **a, o, u** are *umlauted* in the comparative and superlative degree.

Positive	Comparative	Superlative
der alte Stil	der ältere Stil	der älteste Stil
the old style	the older style	the oldest style
das große Beispiel	das größere Beispiel	das größte Beispiel
the great example	the greater example	the greatest example
die kurze Erzählung	die kürzere Erzählung	die kürzeste Erzählung
the short story	the shorter story	the shortest story

3. The forms of the adjectives dunkel, teuer, hoch

Positive	Comparative	Superlative
die dunkle Nacht	die dunklere Nacht	die dunkelste Nacht
the dark night	the darker night	the darkest night
das teure Buch	das teurere Buch	das teuerste Buch
the expensive book	the more expensive book	the most expensive book
das hohe Haus	das höhere Haus	das höchste Haus
the high house	the higher house	the highest house

4. Adjectives having irregular forms: gut, viel, wenig

Note that **viel** and **wenig** can occur *either* in their *uninflected* form or in their *inflected forms* in the positive plural. In the *comparative* they *only* occur in their *uninflected form.*

Positive	*Comparative*	*Superlative*
der **gute** Stil	der **bessere** Stil	der **beste** Stil
the good style	the better style	the best style
viel(e) Gründe	**mehr** Gründe	die **meisten** Gründe
many reasons	more reasons	most reasons
wenig(e) Formen	**weniger** Formen	die **wenigsten** Formen
few forms	fewer forms	the fewest forms

B. The Adverb and the Predicate Adjective

1. The comparison of adverbs

Adverbs form the *comparative degree* by *adding* **–er,** and the *superlative degree* by **am . . . –sten.**

Wir fahren schnell.	We drive fast.
Er fährt schnell**er.**	He drives faster.
Sie fährt **am** schnell**sten.**	She drives fastest.

2. The comparison of predicate adjectives

Predicate adjectives form their *comparative* and *superlative degree* like *adverbs* if *dissimilar things* are being compared.

Die Erzählung ist interessant.	The story is interesting.
Die Parabel ist interessant**er.**	The parable is more interesting.
Der Roman ist **am** interessant**esten.**	The novel is most interesting.

If *similar things* or if *persons* are being compared *the superlative degree* may take the inflected form: **der, das, die interessanteste.**

Diese Erzählung ist interessant.	This story is interesting.
Die andere Erzählung ist interessant**er.**	The other story is more interesting.
Und diese Erzählung ist **die** interessant**este.**	An this story is the most interesting.

3. Irregular forms

The same irregularities found in the comparison of adjectives apply here. Note also the following irregularities:

(a) Bald, oft, gern, sehr, nah

Er kam **bald.**	He came soon.
Sie kam **früher (eher).**	She came sooner.
Wir kamen **am frühesten (am ehesten).**	We came soonest.

Sie kommt **oft.**	She comes often.
Wir kommen **öfter.**	We come more often.
Er kommt **am häufigsten.**	He comes most often.
Mathematik studiert er **gern.**	He likes (to study) mathematics.
Geschichte studiert er **lieber.**	He prefers to study history.
Literatur studiert er **am liebsten.**	He likes literature best (of all).
Hans interessiert sich **sehr** dafür.	Hans is very interested in it.
Jürgen interessiert sich **mehr** dafür.	Jürgen is more interested in it.
Elisabeth interessiert sich **am meisten** dafür.	Elizabeth is most interested in it.
Das Ergebnis kommt der Lösung **nah(e).**	The result is close to the solution.
Jenes Ergebnis kommt der Lösung **näher.**	That result is closer to the solution.
Dies Ergebnis kommt der Lösung **am nächsten.**	This result is closest to the solution.

C. Common Adjective Formulas Using Positive and Comparative Forms

1. So . . . wie **and** als

So . . . wie is used for *equivalents,* **als** is used for *comparisons.*

Equivalent: Er ist **so** groß **wie** sie.	He is *as* tall *as* she.
Comparison: Er ist **größer als** sie.	He is *taller than* she.

2. Immer + **comparative**

In German **immer** + *comparative* is used where *two comparatives* are used in *English.*

Er lief **immer schneller.**	He ran faster and faster.
Es wurde **immer kälter.**	It got colder and colder.

D. Special Usages of Comparative and Superlative Forms

1. Comparative form

ein **älterer** Herr	an elderly gentleman
eine **längere** Reise	a fairly long journey
die **neuere** Geschichte	modern history

2. Superlative form

Sie ist **äußerst intelligent.**	She is *exceedingly intelligent.*
Er ist **höchst langweilig.**	He is *most boring.*
Er arbeitet **möglichst schnell.**	He works *as fast as possible.*
erstens	first, in the first place

letztens	finally, last of all
meistens	mostly
wenigstens	at least
höchstens	at most
frühestens	at the earliest
spätestens	at the latest

Drill 62   *Comparison of Adjectives   Follow the examples.*

Er kennt **eine interessante** Geschichte.
Aber ich kenne **eine interessantere** Geschichte.

Er kennt wenig Bücher.
Aber **ich** kenne **weniger** Bücher.

Er spricht von einem großen Werk.
Er schreibt einen guten Stil.
Er interessiert sich für merkwürdige Bücher.

Er schreibt über ein bekanntes Gebiet.
Er bezieht sich auf ein altes Vorbild.
Er gibt eine kurze Einführung.
Er hat viele Gründe.
Er liest humoristische Erzählungen.
Er bekommt ein teures Buch.
Er hat einen dunklen Mantel.
Er hat ein hohes Haus.

Drill 63   *Superlative of Adjectives   Follow the example.*

Das ist **eine alte** Tradition.
Aber dies ist **die älteste** Tradition.

Das ist ein beliebtes Thema.
Das ist ein teures Buch.
Das ist ein entscheidender Einfluß.
Das ist eine kurze Erzählung.

Das ist ein typischer Zug.
Das ist ein kompliziertes Problem.
Das ist ein gutes Beispiel.
Das ist ein dunkler Raum.
Das ist eine interessante Epoche.
Das ist ein hohes Haus.

Drill 64   *Comparison of Predicate Adjectives and Adverbs   Follow the examples.*

Maria ist **jung**. Aber **Elisabeth?**
Elisabeth ist **jünger als** Maria.

Hans spricht **oft** vom Krieg. Aber **Jürgen?**
Jürgen spricht **öfter** vom Krieg **als Hans.**

Die Erzählung ist humoristisch. Aber der Roman?
Hans kam bald nach Hause. Aber Jürgen?
Deutsch studiert er gern. Aber Geschichte?

Elisabeth ist groß. Aber Jürgen?
Die Anekdote ist interessant. Aber die Parabel?
Der Mann ist ironisch. Aber die Frau?
Sie liest viel. Aber er?
Sie arbeitet wenig. Aber er?
Hans interessiert sich sehr dafür. Aber Jürgen?
Das Ergebnis kommt der Lösung nah. Aber jenes Ergebnis?

Drill 65   *Superlative of Adverbs   Follow the examples.*

Wir arbeiten **viel**. Aber **er?**
Er arbeitet **am meisten.**

Wir sprechen **gern** davon. Aber **er?**

Er spricht **am liebsten** davon.

Wir kennen das Drama gut. Aber er?
Wir interessieren uns wenig dafür. Aber er?

Wir beziehen uns oft darauf. Aber er?
Wir erzählen interessant. Aber er?
Wir benehmen uns gut. Aber er?
Wir sprechen wenig. Aber er?
Wir erinnern uns gern daran. Aber er?
Wir schreiben viel darüber. Aber er?

Wir erzählen oft davon. Aber er?
Wir beschäftigen uns viel damit. Aber er?
Wir interessieren uns sehr dafür. Aber er?
Unser Ergebnis kommt der Lösung nah. Aber
sein Ergebnis?

VI. THE PRESENT PARTICIPLE AND THE PERFECT PARTICIPLE

*Present participle (infinitive + **d**)*		*Perfect participle*	
lesen**d**	rea*ding*	gelehr**t**	learn*ed*
geben**d**	gi*ving*	gegeben	gi*ven*

Present participles and perfect participles can be used like adjectives. (For the perfect participle as a predicate adjective see page 60.)

ein Zimmer mit fließend**em** Wasser   a room with running water
ein gelehr**ter** Professor   a learned professor

VII. ADJECTIVES, PRESENT PARTICIPLES, AND PERFECT PARTICIPLES AS NOUNS

Adjectives, a few present participles, and some perfect participles can be used as *nouns*. But they still *follow the adjective declensions!*

Hier kommt **ein fremder** Mann.
Hier kommt **ein Fremder.**

Here comes a strange (unknown) man.
Here comes a stranger.

Wir sprechen **von erwachsenen** Menschen.
Wir sprechen **von Erwachsenen.**

We are speaking of adults (adult persons).
We are speaking of adults.

Dort kommt **der alte** Mann.
Dort kommt **der Alte.**

There comes the old man.
There comes the old man.

Das sind reisend**e** Leute.
Das sind **Reisende.**

These are traveling people.
These are travelers.

Das ist **ein gelehrter** Professor.
Das ist **ein Gelehrter.**

This is a learned professor.
This is a learned man, a scholar.

Er ist deutsch**er** Staatsbürger.
Er ist **Deutscher.**

He is a German citizen.
He is a German.

Sie ist deutsch**e** Staatsbürgerin.
Sie ist **Deutsche.**

She is a German citizen.
She is a German.

Pay special attention to the *difference* between *adjectives as nouns* and the *nouns* of the *masculine declension II:*

Masc. II	Hier kommt **der** Russe	Hier kommt **ein** Russe.
Adj.	Hier kommt **der** Deutsche.	Hier kommt **ein** Deutscher.
Masc. II	Hier kommen **die** Russen.	Hier kommen zwei Russen.
Adj.	Hier kommen **die** Deutschen.	Hier kommen zwei Deutsche.

Drill 66   *Adjectives and Participles as Nouns*   *Follow the examples.*

Hier kommen **zwei** Reisend**e**.
Hier kommen **ein** Reisend**er** und **eine** Reisende.

Dort sehe ich **zwei** Bekannte (acquaintance, friend).
Dort sehe ich **einen** Bekannten und **eine** Bekannt**e**.

Hier kommen zwei Alte.

Dort sehe ich zwei Alte.
Hier kommen zwei Fremde.
Dort sehe ich zwei Fremde.
Hier kommen zwei Deutsche.
Dort sehe ich zwei Deutsche.
Hier kommen zwei Bekannte.
Dort sehe ich zwei Bekannte.

Drill 67   *Adjectives and Participles as Nouns, Masc. II Nouns, and Regular Nouns*   *Follow the examples.*

Hier kommen **zwei** Deutsch**e**.
Hier kommen **ein** Deutscher und **eine** Deutsche.

Dort sehe ich **zwei** Russen.
Dort sehe ich **einen** Russen und **eine** Russ**in**.

Hier kommen zwei Bekannte.
Dort sehe ich zwei Fremde.
Hier kommen zwei Amerikaner.

Dort sehe ich zwei Studenten.
Hier kommen zwei Reisende.
Dort sehe ich zwei Alte.
Hier kommen zwei Deutsche.
Dort sehe ich zwei Tschechen.
Hier kommen zwei Russen.
Dort sehe ich zwei Fremde.

VIII. ADJECTIVES AND PERFECT PARTICIPLES WITH PREPOSITIONS

Adjectives and perfect participles may occur *in front* of or *after the* prepositional phrase. The following usage is preferred:

Er ist mit den Leuten bekannt.	He is acquainted with the people.
Er ist zu dieser Entscheidung fähig.	He is capable of this decision.
Er ist von seinen Ideen überzeugt.	He is convinced of his ideas.
Er ist mit der Arbeit zufrieden.	He is satisfied with the work.
Er ist mit seiner Arbeit fertig.	He is finished with his work.
Sie ist fertig zur Abreise.	She is ready to depart.
Sie ist frei von Vorurteilen.	She is free of prejudices.
Sie ist freundlich zu den Leuten.	She is friendly to the people.
Sie ist stolz auf ihre Leistung.	She is proud of her achievement.
Deutschland ist reich (arm) an Kohle (*dative*).	Germany is rich (poor) in coal.

die **Einleitung, –en** introduction; **besprechen, a, o** to discuss; **der Kurs, –e** course; **aus·wählen** to select, choose; **die Erzählung, –en** narration, story; **der Autor, –en** author; **das Jahrhundert, –e** century; **der Verfasser, –** author; **die Einführung, –en** introduction; **bekannt machen mit** (+ *dat.*) to acquaint with

die **Geschichte, –n** story; **zeigen** to show; **der Inhalt, –e** content(s); **typisch** typical; **der Zug, ⸚e** *here:* feature; **der Zweite Weltkrieg** World War II; **die Parabel, –n** parable; **der Stil, –e** style; **ein Beispiel für** (+ *acc.*) an example of; **gehören zu** (+ *dat.*) *here:* to be part of

politisch political; **nationalsozialistisch** national socialist, Nazi

die **Diktatur, –en** dictatorship; **der Einschnitt, –e** cut, gap; **tief** deep; **der Dichter, –** poet; **der Schriftsteller, –** writer; **verlassen, ie, a** to leave; **total** total, totalitarian; **der Staat, –en** state; **das Exil, –e** exile; **bleiben, ie, ie** to stay, remain; **die meisten** most (people); **die Idee, –n** idea; **sich an·passen** (+ *dat.*) to conform to; **einige** several; **die ‚innere Emigration'** 'inner emigration'; **der Widerstand** *here:* resistance movement; **teil·nehmen, a, o an** (+ *dat.*) to participate in; **führen** to lead; **enden** to end; **der Zusammenbruch, ⸚e** collapse

zurück·blicken to look back; **sich vergegenwärtigen** to visualize

physisch physical; **die Not** *here:* distress, misery; **geistig** intellectual, mental, spiritual; **trennen** to separate; **die Zerstörung, –en** destruction; **die Stadt, ⸚e** city, town; **das Wohnviertel, –** residential district; **die Industrie, –** industry; **die Kirche, –n** church; **die Universität, –en** university; **die Ordnung, –en** order; **die Weltanschauung, –en** philosophy of life; **zwölf Jahre lang** for twelve years; **öffentlich** public

LITERATURE

EINLEITUNG

Wir lesen und besprechen in diesem Kurs zwölf ausgewählte Erzählungen deutscher Autoren des 20. Jahrhunderts. Der Verfasser dieses Buches möchte Ihnen zuerst eine kurze Einführung in die Erzählungen geben und Sie mit den Autoren bekannt machen.

Die ersten vier Geschichten von Wolfgang Borchert, Heinrich Böll und Herbert Malecha zeigen in Form und Inhalt einige typische Züge der deutschen Literatur nach dem Zweiten Weltkrieg. Die letzten acht Geschichten, Bertolt Brechts Erzählungen und Franz Kafkas Parabeln, sind Beispiele für den Stil und die Themen zweier deutscher Schriftsteller, deren Werke zur Weltliteratur gehören.

Die zwölf Jahre der Hitlerdiktatur waren ein tiefer Einschnitt in der politischen Geschichte, aber auch in der Geschichte der Literatur Deutschlands. Viele Dichter und Schriftsteller verließen den totalen Staat Hitlers und gingen ins Exil. Viele aber blieben in Deutschland. Von ihnen paßten sich die meisten der Diktatur an oder folgten aus Überzeugung den nationalsozialistischen Ideen und Prinzipien. Einige aber gingen in die ‚innere Emigration‘ oder nahmen am Widerstand gegen die Diktatur teil. Der totale Staat Hitlers führte zum totalen Krieg. Der totale Krieg endete im totalen Zusammenbruch.

Man kann, wenn man auf die Jahre nach 1945 zurückblickt, die physische Not nicht von der geistigen trennen. Da war die Zerstörung der Städte, der Wohnviertel, der Industrien, der Kirchen, der Schulen, der Universitäten, der Theater . . . , aber da war auch der totale Zusammenbruch der politischen ‚Ordnung‘ und der Weltanschauung, die zwölf Jahre lang die Basis des öffentlichen Lebens gewesen war. Man muß sich das

8. Mai 1945 unconditional surrender of Nazi Germany; **Wolfgang Weyrauch** Modern German writer; **einmal** *here:* at first

folgendermaßen in the following way, as follows, thus; **charakterisieren** to characterize; **sich befinden, a, u** to be; **aus·schicken** to send out; **die Taube, –n** dove; **die Zeitung, –en** newspaper; **das Programm, –e** program; **die Zeitschrift, –en** periodical; **der Grund, ⁀e** ground, reason, cause, foundation; **suchen** to look for, seek; **fast** almost; **verenden** to perish (miserably) (*used for animals*); **an·fangen, i, a** to begin; **der Vertreter, –** representative; **die Katastrophe, –n** catastrophe

Sie kamen aus dem Krieg. They came from the war.; **die Trümmer** (*plur.*) ruins; **in gleichem Maße** to the same extent; **verletzen** to injure, hurt; **sich nahe fühlen** (+ *dat.*) to feel close to; **sich identifizieren** to identify oneself; **an·gehören** (+ *dat.*) to belong to; **zu einem großen Teil** for the most part; **merk- und denkwürdig** strange and noteworthy; **heim·kehren** to return home; **die Heimkehr** returning home; **der Heimkehrer, –** homecomer; **kaum (noch) jemand** hardly anybody; **glauben an** (+ *acc.*) to believe in

Wir schrieben also... So we wrote...; **das Schlagwort, ⁀er** catchword, cliché, slogan; **an·hängen** *here:* to attach, label

etwas vor·finden, a, u to find something awaiting; **ergeben, a, e** to result in

die gesamte abendländische Bildungswelt the entire educated western world; **unverdächtig** above suspicion; **verdächtig** suspicious; **der Stammvater** father; **der Trojanische Krieg** Trojan War; **Troja** Troy; **Odysseus** Ulysses

die Epik epic poetry; **erzählen** to tell, narrate; **die Bezeichnung, –en** designation, label; **sich schämen** (+ *gen.*) to be ashamed of

auf·bauen to build up; **wiederauf·bauen** to rebuild; **die damalige Wirklichkeit** the reality of that time;

das Gebiet, –e area; **das Ideal, –e** ideal; **das Vorbild, –er** example, standard; **gelten, a, o** to be valid, of value; **überhaupt** at all; **der Begriff, –e** concept;

ganz vergegenwärtigen, wenn man die Literatur dieser Zeit verstehen will.

Die geistige Situation des Schriftstellers nach dem 8. Mai 1945 hat Wolfgang Weyrauch folgendermaßen charakterisiert: „1945 und 1946 befanden wir uns alle in der Situation des Noah . . . Wir schickten unsere Tauben aus (die ersten Zeitungen, Radioprogramme, Zeitschriften, Bücher). Die sollten Grund suchen, einmal den Grund, warum wir fast verendet waren, und dann den Grund, auf dem wir wieder anfangen konnten". Wolfgang Borchert und Heinrich Böll sind zwei typische Vertreter der deutschen Schriftstellergeneration, die nach der Katastrophe den neuen Anfang suchte.

Heinrich Böll sagte dazu: „Die Menschen, von denen wir schrieben, lebten in Trümmern, sie kamen aus dem Krieg, Männer und Frauen in gleichem Maße verletzt, auch Kinder. Und wir als Schreibende fühlten uns ihnen so nahe, daß wir uns mit ihnen identifizierten, vor allem natürlich mit der Generation, der wir angehörten und die sich zu einem großen Teil in einer merk- und denkwürdigen Situation befand: sie kehrte heim. Es war die Heimkehr aus einem Krieg, an dessen Ende kaum noch jemand geglaubt hatte.

Wir schrieben also vom Krieg, von der Heimkehr und dem, was wir im Krieg gesehen hatten und bei der Heimkehr vorfanden: von Trümmern; das ergab drei Schlagwörter, die der jungen Literatur angehängt wurden: Kriegs-, Heimkehrer- und Trümmer-literatur . . .

Der Name Homer ist der gesamten abendländischen Bildungswelt unverdächtig: Homer ist der Stammvater europäischer Epik, aber Homer erzählt vom Trojanischen Krieg, von der Zerstörung Trojas und von der Heimkehr des Odysseus — Kriegs-, Trümmer- und Heimkehrerliteratur —, wir haben keinen Grund, uns dieser Bezeichnung zu schämen."

Auf allen Gebieten des öffentlichen Lebens begann man wieder, baute man wieder auf. Aber wo sollte man im geistigen Gebiet, wo in der Literatur beginnen? Welche Ideale, welche Vorbilder galten noch? Ja, galten Ideale und Vorbilder überhaupt noch? In der damaligen Wirklichkeit der physischen und geistigen Zer-

ohnmächtig *here:* helpless; **das Ungenügen** dissatisfaction; **Was ausgedrückt werden wollte . . .** What wanted to be expressed . . . ; **das bloße Überlebenwollen und Überlebenkönnen** the mere wish and ability to survive

die **Größe** *here:* greatness; **die Menschenwürde** man's dignity; **die Schönheit** beauty; **fragwürdig** questionable; **damals** at that time; **empfinden, a, u** to feel, experience; **zunächst** at first; **aus · drücken** to express; **die Unmenschlichkeit** inhumanity; **die Sinnlosigkeit** senselessness; **die Kälte** cold; **das Elend** misery; **früh** early

„Die ungezählte Geliebte" "The Uncounted Sweetheart"; **der äußere Wiederaufbau** external rebuilding, reconstruction

materiell material; **sich ändern** to change; **bald** soon; **die Währungsreform** (*1948*) currency reform; **das Wirtschaftswunder** economic miracle; **humoristisch** humorous; **der Humor** humor; **ironisch** ironic; **die Ironie** irony; **die Kritik, –en** criticism; **begleiten** to accompany

„Die Probe" "The Test"; **veröffentlichen** to publish; **angelsächsisch** Anglo-Saxon; **die Erzählform, –en** narrative form; **das Stilexperiment, –e** experiment in style

die Frage nach the question of; **Stil und Form** style and form; **der Vordergrund** foreground; **der Hintergrund** background; **vor allem** above all; **der Bereich, –e** area, sphere; **beliebt** popular, favorite; **traditionell** traditional; **episch** epic; **der Roman, –e** novel; **die Novelle, –n** novella; **die Anekdote, –n** anecdote; **das Märchen, –** fairy-tale

Die Literatur fragt nach den Verhältnissen Literature inquires into the relationships; **der moderne Mensch überhaupt** modern man altogether

das Werk, –e work; **nicht nur . . . , sondern auch** not only . . . but also; **stark** strong; **entscheidend** decisive; **entscheiden, ie, ie** to decide; **der Einfluß auf** (+ *acc.*) influence on; **wider · spiegeln** to reflect; **der Spiegel, –** mirror; **einzeln** single, individual; **gesellschaftlich** social; **historisch** historical; **psychologisch** psychological; **das Phänomen, –e** phenomenon; **die Epoche, –n** epoch, period; **fragen nach** (+ *dat.*) *here:* to inquire into; **die Grundbedingung, –en** basic condition; **das Verhältnis, –se** relationship; **der heutige Mensch** man of our time; **die Analyse, –n** analysis; **die Gesellschaft** society; **die Deutung, –en** interpretation; **die Existenz** existence

störung waren Begriffe wie Größe, Vaterland, Menschenwürde und Schönheit fragwürdig geworden. „Jeder, der damals schrieb, empfand zunächst ein ohnmächtiges Ungenügen, weil kein Wort ausdrückte, was ausgedrückt werden wollte". Der Krieg in seiner Unmenschlichkeit und Sinnlosigkeit und das bloße Überlebenwollen und Überlebenkönnen in und nach dem Kriege, in den Trümmern der Städte, in Hunger, Kälte und Elend: Das sind die Themen Wolfgang Borcherts und der frühen Erzählungen Heinrich Bölls.

Aber die materielle Situation änderte sich sehr schnell. Schon bald nach der Währungsreform (1948) sprach man vom „Wirtschaftswunder". Eine Perspektive in Heinrich Bölls Erzählung *Die ungezählte Geliebte* ist die humoristische und ironische Kritik dieses äußeren Wiederaufbaus, den kein innerer Wiederaufbau begleitete.

Herbert Malechas *Die Probe*, veröffentlicht 1955, zehn Jahre nach Kriegsende, hat in Thema und Inhalt nichts mehr mit der „Trümmerliteratur" zu tun. Jetzt steht die Frage nach Stil und Form im Vordergrund. Die short story, die Kurzgeschichte, die vor allem im angelsächsischen Bereich schon eine Tradition hatte, war seit 1945 auch in der deutschen Literatur eine beliebte Erzählform geworden. Die traditionellen epischen Formen der deutschen Literatur waren: der Roman, die Erzählung, die Novelle, die Anekdote, die Parabel und das Märchen. Herbert Malechas *Die Probe* ist ein Stilexperiment in der neuen Form der Kurzgeschichte.

In einen ganz anderen Bereich führen uns die Werke Bertolt Brechts und Franz Kafkas. Sie gehören nicht nur zur Weltliteratur, sie hatten und haben auch einen starken und entscheidenden Einfluß auf die Weltliteratur. Diese aber spiegelt im 20. Jahrhundert nicht nur einzelne historische, politische, gesellschaftliche oder psychologische Phänomene und Probleme eines Landes oder einer Epoche wider, sondern fragt nach den Grundbedingungen und Verhältnissen des heutigen Menschen. Brecht gibt in seinem Werk eine Analyse des Verhältnisses von Mensch und Gesellschaft, gestern und heute, Kafkas Romane und Parabeln sind Deutungen der Existenz des modernen Menschen überhaupt.

I. GENERAL INSTRUCTIONS

The ultimate goal of the study of literature in a language course is classroom discussion of works of literature and a probing into style and values. The device traditionally used to proceed toward this goal is a set of direct questions appended to the literary text. The fault of such direct questions lies in the fact that they offer no assistance in formulating your answer and leave you with the necessity of memorizing completely the exact wording of the text. This is not merely tedious; it encourages the use of purely literary turns of phrase in what is meant to be a conversational situation. One solution to this dilemma would be to abandon questions altogether and to try to replace them with other devices. The author of this book has instead introduced new patterns of question and response, so-called *question-naires.*

The questionnaires are divided into three groups: the *A-questions,* which deal with matters of fact and with incidents of the plot of the stories; the *B-questions,* which are concerned with structural features of the stories, with scenes, settings, situations, characters, and relationships; and the *C-questions,* which lead toward free composition and discussion.

In devising the patterns of question and response the author has employed two devices that you will not find familiar.

First, *the questions are formulated and are to be answered in the present-time system* (present tense and perfect tense). This is not an artificial device. Almost all stories are, of course, written in the so-called *narrative past*—the past-time system (imperfect tense and pluperfect tense); but in German as in English we instinctively shift to the present-time system in recounting the events of a story or in discussing the contents of a story detail by detail. (This device will not be applied to the questionnaire of the **Einleitung** since the **Einleitung** is expository prose and not literary style.)

Second, each question is followed by a full set of English keywords, a kind of "dehydrated sentence," that will serve as a nucleus for your response. The keywords will help you to recall the story without tedious memorization and will allow you to concentrate your attention upon *formulating your response by supplying grammatical structure.* Since the keywords are given in English, you will, at the same time, *be developing your active German vocabulary.*

These patterns will only occasionally be altered by special instructions that will call for a variance in the use of tenses or syntactical forms you have been practicing in the parallel grammar chapter.

The responses to the *A-questions* should be prepared orally; those to the *B-questions* first in writing, then orally; and the responses to the *C-questions* will provide opportunity to use the "special expressions" presented after the text of each story as well as to incorporate your accumulated repertory of vocabulary and grammatical patterns.

A. General Instructions for the A- and B-Questions

1. Respond in German *with complete sentences.*

2. Begin your responses to the *A-questions* with the words in **boldface** in the German question. ***Boldface italics*** indicate the initial element of the response, **boldface** the other elements, if any. Reproduce the German equivalents of the English keywords and add articles, pronouns, and prepositions where necessary.

3. Formulate your response in the present-time system (present tense or perfect tense) unless there are special instructions.

4. The symbol // indicates the beginning or end of a sentence. The symbol / is used to set apart the separate keywords or phrases.

a. Example for the A-questions:
Was tun **die Mädchen heute?** // to practice / capital letters //

Heute üben die Mädchen die großen Buchstaben.

b. Example for the B-questions:
Wie sind Jürgens Reaktionen in diesem Teil der Geschichte? // to answer / courageously // to hold / hands / tightly / stick //

Er antwortet mutig. Er hält die Hände fest um den Stock.

5. The symbols /(a)/, /(b)/, etc., are used to indicate separate dependent clauses.

a. Example for the A-questions:
Was **sagt der Mann?** /(a)/ that / he / to leave / now //; /(b)/ that / he / to come back / soon //

Der Mann sagt, daß er jetzt weggeht.
Der Mann sagt, daß er bald zurückkommt.

b. Example for the B-questions:
// boy / to ask / man /(a)/ whether / to leave /;(b)/ when / to come back //

Der Junge fragte den Mann, ob er weggeht.
Der Junge fragt den Mann, wann er zurückkommt.

II. QUESTIONNAIRE

A. Exercises for the A-Questions

Study the following expressions:

1. Wir **machen** Sie **mit** den Autoren **bekannt.**   We *acquaint* you *with* the authors.
2. Dies ist **ein Beispiel für** den Stil des Schriftstellers.   This is *an example of* the author's style.
3. Die meisten **paßten sich** der Diktatur **an.**   Most people *conformed to* the dictatorship.

4. Sie folgten den Prinzipien **aus Überzeugung.**	They followed the principles *out of conviction.*
5. Einige **nahmen am** Widerstand **teil.**	Some *took part in* the resistance movement.
6. Sie **befanden sich** in der Situation des Noah.	They *were* in Noah's situation.
7. Sie **schrieben vom** Krieg.	They *wrote about* the war.
8. Sie **kamen aus** dem Krieg.	They *came from* the war.
9. Sie **fühlten sich** diesen Menschen **nahe.**	They *felt close* to these people.
10. Kaum noch jemand **hatte an** das Ende des Krieges **geglaubt.**	Hardly anyone had *believed in* the end of the war.
11. **bɛi der** Heimkehr	*on returning home*
12. Sie **schämen sich** dieser Bezeichnung nicht.	They *are not ashamed of* this designation.
13. Die Situation **änderte sich** schnell.	The situation *changed* quickly.
14. Man **sprach vom** Wirtschaftswunder.	People *talked about* the economic miracle.
15. **die Frage nach** Stil und Form	*the question of* style and form

Drill 1 *Prepositional and Reflexive Expressions* *Give the German equivalents.*

They acquaint us with the authors.
They write about the destruction.
This is an example of the author's style.
They follow the principles out of conviction.
Most people conform to the dictatorship.
Some take part in the resistance movement.
They come from the war.
They are in Noah's situation.

They believe in the future.
They write about the misery.
They feel close to these people.
They are not ashamed of this designation.
on returning home
People talk about the economic miracle.
The situation changes quickly.
the question of style and form

Drill 2 *Combination Drill* *Give the German equivalents.*

This novel is from the twentieth century.
We see through the centuries.
This is an example of the author's style.
the question of style and form
He works for his family.
They are against the totalitarian state.
They acquaint us with the authors.
He lives with his parents.
a parable by Kafka
The letter comes by mail.
They write about the misery.
the population of Munich
He is coming from the station.

They come from the war.
He is from Germany.
He is at home.
He is going home.
the situation after the war
We fly to Germany.
He is going to the university.
They feel close to these people.
He is going to his friends.
Most people conform to the dictatorship.
on returning home
during the winter
He speaks in a soft voice.

They believe in the future.
He is coming out of the house.

They follow the principles out of conviction.
They take part in the resistance movement.

B. A-Questions

Remember: Answer in present or perfect tense if not otherwise indicated.

1. Was machen *wir* in diesem Kurs? // to read / and / to discuss / twelve selected stories //

2. Was für **Erzählungen lesen wir?** // German authors / 20th century //

3. Warum **möchte** Ihnen *der Verfasser dieses Buches* eine Einführung geben? // (to) acquaint with / authors //

4. Warum lesen wir *Geschichten von Borchert, Böll und Malecha?* // to show / form and contents / typical features / German literature / after / World War II //

5. Was können wir von *den Werken Brechts und Kafkas* sagen? // to be part of / world literature //

6. Was **waren** *die Jahre der Hitlerdiktatur?* // deep cut / in / political history / but / also / history / literature / Germany //

7. Was taten *viele Schriftsteller?* // to leave / totalitarian state / and / to go / exile //

8. Was aber taten *andere?* // to stay / Germany //

9. Wie verhielten sich *die meisten Schriftsteller* unter der Diktatur? // to conform to / dictatorship // to follow / Nazi ideas and principles / out of conviction //

10. Was aber taten *einige?* // to go / "inner emigration" / or / to take part in / resistance movement //

11. Wohin **führte** *der totale Staat Hitlers?* // total war //

12. Wie **endeten** *der totale Staat und der totale Krieg?* // total collapse //

13. Warum konnte man in den Jahren nach 1945 die physische Not nicht von der geistigen trennen? // there / to be / destruction / cities / residential districts / industries / churches / schools / universities / theaters // there / to be / also / total collapse / political order / philosophy of life //

14. Wie war die geistige Situation des Schriftstellers *nach dem 8. Mai 1945?* // all (people) / to be / Noah's / situation //

15. Was taten *die Schriftsteller?* // to send out / newspapers / radio programs / periodicals / and / books //

16. Welchen **Grund sollten** *sie suchen?* // why / Germans / to have almost perished //

17. Welchen **Grund** aber **sollten** *sie auch suchen?* // on which / Germans / to be able / to begin / again //

18. Wer **sind** *Wolfgang Borchert und Heinrich Böll?* // typical representatives / their generation //

19. Was **suchten** *sie?* // new begin / after / catastrophe //

20. Was sagte Heinrich Böll über *die Menschen,* von denen er schrieb? // to live / ruins // to come from / war //

21. Was fühlten *die Schriftsteller?* // to feel close to / these people (Menschen) //

22. Und was taten *sie?* // to identify oneself with //

23. Was sagte Böll über *die Generation,* der er angehörte? // to be / in / strange and noteworthy situation // to return home //

24. **Woran** hatte *kaum noch jemand* geglaubt? // end / war //

25. **Wovon** schrieben *die Schriftsteller?* // war / returning home / and / ruins //

26. Welche drei **Schlagwörter ergab das?** // – – – //

27. Homer ist der Stammvater der europäischen Epik. **Wovon erzählt er?** // Trojan War / destruction of Troy / Ulysses' returning home //

28. Wozu *haben* **die Schriftsteller** also **keinen Grund?** // to be ashamed of / this designation //

29. Auf allen Gebieten des öffentlichen Lebens begann man wieder. Aber welche **Fragen stellte man?** // where / should / one / begin / intellectual area / literature // what ideals / what standards / still / to be valid //

30. Welche *Begriffe* **waren fragwürdig geworden?** // greatness / fatherland / man's dignity / and / beauty //

31. Was **sind** *die Themen Borcherts und Bölls?* // war / inhumanity / senselessness / ruins of the cities / hunger / cold / and / misery //

32. Was aber geschah (happened) **sehr schnell?** // material situation / to change //

33. **Wovon sprach man** *bald?* // after / currency reform / 1948 / economic miracle //

34. Wie war die literarische Situation 1955, zehn Jahre nach Kriegsende? // authors / to have nothing to do anymore with / literature of ruins //

35. Was **steht** *jetzt* **im Vordergrund?** // question of style and form //

36. Welche Erzählform **war sehr beliebt geworden?** // short story //

37. Welches *waren* **die traditionellen epischen Formen der deutschen Literatur?** // novel / novella / narration / anecdote / parable / and / fairytale //

38. Was können wir zunächst über *die Werke Brechts und Kafkas* sagen? // to lead into / quite different area //

39. Was **hatten und haben** *sie?* // strong and decisive influence on / world literature //

40. Wie könnte man zwei typische Züge *der Weltliteratur des 20. Jahrhunderts* charakterisieren? // to reflect / historical, political, social, or psychological problems / epoch // to inquire into / basic conditions / and / relationships / modern man //

C. B-Questions

1. Was machen wir in diesem Kurs, und was möchte der Verfasser dieses Buches? // to read / to discuss / twelve selected stories / German authors / twentieth century // to acquaint with / authors //

2. Warum lesen wir Geschichten von Borchert, Böll, Malecha, Brecht und Kafka? // Borchert's, Böll's, and Malecha's stories / to show / form and contents / typical features / German literature / after / World War II / Brecht's and Kafka's works / to be part of / world literature //

3. Was war die Hitlerdiktatur für die Literatur und die Schriftsteller, und wie endete sie? // deep cut / in / political history / and / in / history / literature / Germany // many writers / to leave / totalitarian state / and / to go / exile // others / to stay Germany // most of them / to conform to / dictatorship / or / to follow / Nazi ideas and principles / out of conviction // some / to go / inner emigration / or / to take part in / resistance movement // totalitarian state / to lead / total war // total war / to lead / total collapse //

4. Was muß man sich vergegenwärtigen, wenn man die Literatur nach dem 8. Mai 1945 verstehen will? // there / to be / destruction / cities / residential districts / industries / churches / schools / universities / theaters // there / to be / also / total collapse / political order / philosophy of life // after May 8, 1945 / all / to be / Noah's situation // writers / to send out / newspapers / radio programs / periodicals / books // they / should / look for / grounds // grounds / why / to have almost perished // grounds / on which / to be able / to begin / again //

5. Wer sind Wolfgang Borchert und Heinrich Böll? Was sagte Heinrich Böll über die Menschen, von denen er schrieb, über seine Generation und über die junge Literatur? // Borchert / Böll / to be / typical representatives / their generation // to seek / new beginning / after / catastrophe // people / to live / ruins // to come / war // writers / to feel close to // to identify oneself with // generation / to be / strange and noteworthy situation // to return home // hardly anybody / to have believed in / end / war // writers / to write about / war / returning home / ruins // that / to result in / three catchwords / — — — // Homer / to tell about / Trojan War / destruction of Troy / Ulysses' returning home // writers / to have no reason / to be ashamed of / designation //

6. Was waren die Fragen und Themen der Trümmerliteratur? // where / should / one / begin / intellectual area / literature // what ideals / what standards / still / to be valid // concepts / like / greatness / fatherland / man's dignity / beauty / to have become questionable // Borchert's and Böll's themes / to be / war / inhumanity / senselessness / ruins of the cities / hunger / cold / misery //

7. Was geschah bald nach 1948, und wie war die literarische Situation 1955, zehn Jahre nach

Kriegsende? // material situation / to change / quickly // soon / after / currency reform 1948 / one / to speak about / economic miracle // 1955 / authors / to have nothing to do anymore with / literature of ruins // now / question of style and form / to stand / foreground // short story / to have become / very popular // traditional epic forms / German literature / to be / novel / novella / narration / anecdote / parable / fairy-tale //

8. Was können wir über die Werke Brechts und Kafkas sagen? // to have / strong / and decisive influence on / world literature // to reflect / historical, political, social, or psychological problems / epoch // to inquire into / basic conditions / and / relationships / modern man //

D. Word Study

Follow the examples. Give one or two English meanings of the verb, form the German noun by adding –**ung** to the verb stem, and then give one or two English meanings of the noun.

1. besprech-en, a, o	to discuss	die Besprechung	discussion
2. sich anpass-en	to conform, adapt	die Anpassung	adaptation
3. führ-en	_____	_____	_____
4. trenn-en	_____	_____	_____
5. charakterisier-en	_____	_____	_____
6. vertret-en, a, e	_____	_____	_____
7. verletz-en	_____	_____	_____
8. schreib-en, ie, ie	_____	_____	_____
9. gelt-en, a, o	_____	_____	_____
10. empfind-en, a, u	_____	_____	_____
11. sich änder-n	_____	_____	_____
12. begleit-en	_____	_____	_____
13. veröffentlich-en	_____	_____	_____
14. sich entscheid-en, ie, ie	_____	_____	_____
15. spiegel-n	_____	_____	_____

Follow the examples. Give one or two English meanings for the noun, form the German verb by adding –**en** to the noun stem, and then give one or two English meanings of the verb.

16. die Erzähl-ung	story, narration	erzählen	to narrate, tell
17. die (Welt)anschau-ung	philosophy of life	anschauen	to look at, consider
18. die Überzeug-ung	_____	_____	_____
19. die Einführ-ung	_____	_____	_____
20. die Zerstör-ung	_____	_____	_____
21. die Ordn-ung	_____	_____	_____
22. die Deut-ung	_____	_____	_____
23. die Beding-ung	_____	_____	_____
24. die Bezeichn-ung	_____	_____	_____

Follow the examples. Give one or two English meanings of the noun, try to find the German verb to which the noun is related, and then give one or two English meanings of the verb.

25. der Zug, ⸚e	feature, train	ziehen, o, o	to draw, pull, haul
26. die Geschichte, –n	story, history	geschehen, a, e	to happen
27. die Auswahl –			
28. der Einschnitt, –e			
29. der Widerstand, ⸚e			
30. der Zusammenbruch, ⸚e			
31. der Blick, –e			
32. der Grund, ⸚e			
33. der Anfang, ⸚e			
34. der (das) Teil, –e			
35. die Heimkehr			
36. die Schrift, –en			
37. der Ergebnis, –se			
38. das Gebiet, –e			
39. der Begriff, –e			
40. der Ausdruck, ⸚e			
41. das Wunder, –			
42. die Kritik, –en			
43. der Aufbau			
44. die Form, –en			

CHAPTER

GRAMMATICAL REVIEW

THE VERB

I. REGULAR AND IRREGULAR VERBS

All regular and irregular verbs form the *perfect and pluperfect tenses* with the auxiliary verbs **haben** or **sein** and the *perfect participle* of the *main verb*. The perfect participle is the last element in a simple sentence. *All regular and irregular verbs* form the *future tense* with the auxiliary verb **werden** and the *infinitive* of the *main verb*. The infinitive is the last element in a simple sentence.

	1. *Weak or regular verbs*		**2.** *Strong or irregular verbs*	
	a	*b*	*a*	*b*
Present	ich frag **e**	ich arbeit **e**	ich bleib **e**	ich geb **e**
	du frag **st**	du arbeit **e st**	du bleib **st**	du gib **st**
	er frag **t**	er arbeit **e t**	er bleib **t**	er gib **t**
	wir frag **en**	wir arbeit **en**	wir bleib **en**	wir geb **en**
	ihr frag **t**	ihr arbeit **e t**	ihr bleib **t**	ihr geb **t**
	sie frag **en**	sie arbeit **en**	sie bleib **en**	sie geb **en**
Imperfect	ich frag **t e**	ich arbeit **e t e**	ich blieb	ich gab
	du frag **t e st**	du arbeit **e t e st**	du blieb **st**	du gab **st**
	er frag **t e**	er arbeit **e t e**	er blieb	er gab
	wir frag **t en**	wir arbeit **e t en**	wir blieb **en**	wir gab **en**
	ihr frag **t e t**	ihr arbeit **e t e t**	ihr blieb **t**	ihr gab **t**
	sie frag **t en**	sie arbeit **e t en**	sie blieb **en**	sie gab **en**
Perfect	ich habe ... **ge** frag **t**	ich habe ... **ge** arbeit **e t**	ich bin ... **ge** blieb **en**	ich habe ... **ge** geb **en**
	du hast ... **ge** frag **t**	du hast ... **ge** arbeit **e t**	du bist ... **ge** blieb **en**	du hast ... **ge** geb **en**
	etc.	etc.	etc.	etc.
Pluperfect	ich hatte ... **ge** frag **t**	ich hatte ... **ge** arbeit **e t**	ich war ... **ge** blieb **en**	ich hatte ... **ge** geb **en**
	du hattest ... **ge** frag **t**	du hattest ... **ge** arbeit **e t**	du warst ... **ge** blieb **en**	du hattest ... **ge** geb **en**
	etc.	etc.	etc.	etc.
Future	ich werde ... frag **en**	ich werde ... arbeit **en**	ich werde ... bleib **en**	ich werde ... geb **en**
	du wirst ... frag **en**	du wirst ... arbeit **en**	du wirst ... bleib **en**	du wirst ... geb **en**
	etc.	etc.	etc.	etc.

A. Regular Verbs

1. Group 1a: present, imperfect, and perfect participle

Regular verbs of group 1a form *the present tense* by adding the personal endings to the verb stem, the *imperfect tense* by adding the infix –t– before the personal endings, and the *perfect participle* by using the prefix **ge–** before the verb stem and adding the ending –t to it. For the perfect and pluperfect tenses with **haben** and **sein,** see page 95.

	Pronoun	Stem	Personal ending	
Present	sie	**frag**	en	

	Pronoun	Stem	Infix	Personal ending
Imperfect	sie	**frag**	t	en

	Prefix	Stem	Ending	
Perfect participle	**ge**	**frag**	t	

Verbs with the ending **–ieren,** which are always regular, form the *perfect participle without* the prefix **ge–.**

Infinitive	*Perfect participle*
kriti**sieren**	kritisier **t**
charakteri**sieren**	charakterisier **t**
stud**ieren**	studier **t**

2. Group 1b: present, imperfect, and perfect participle

If the verb stem ends in **–t** (arbeit en, to work), in **–d** (red en, to speak), in **–chn** (rechn en, to figure out), in **–gn** (begegn en, to meet), or in **–ffn** (öffn en, to open), in the *present tense* an **–e–** is inserted between the stem and the endings **–st** and **–t,** in the *imperfect tense* between the stem and the **–t–** infix, and also between the **–t–** infix and the endings **–st** and **–t.** In the *perfect participle* an **–e–** is also inserted between the stem and the **–t** ending.

Present	du arbeit e st	du red e st	du rechn e st	du öffn e st
	er arbeit e t	er red e t	er rechn e t	er öffn e t
	ihr arbeit e t	ihr red e t	ihr rechn e t	ihr öffn e t
Imperfect	du arbeit e te st	du red e te st	du rechn e te st	du öffn e te st
	ihr arbeit e te t	ihr red e te t	ihr rechn e te t	ihr öffn e te t
Perfect participle	ge arbeit e t	ge red e t	ge rechn e t	ge öffn e t

Irregular verbs also follow the same pattern in the **du, er,** and **ihr** forms of the *present tense, except* when they have an *umlauted stem vowel.*

finden: Er find e t das.
raten: Er rät ihm gut. He advises him well.

B. Irregular Verbs

1. Group 2a: present, imperfect, and perfect participle

Irregular verbs undergo a *change of the stem vowel* to form the *imperfect tense* and the *perfect participle.*

Present	wir bleib en
Imperfect	wir blieb en
Perfect participle	ge blieb en

Some irregular verbs have the *same stem vowel* in the *infinitive* and in the *perfect participle.*

Infinitive	*Imperfect*	*Perfect participle*
sehen	sah	gesehen
lesen	las	gelesen
tragen	trug	getragen
schlafen	schlief	geschlafen
kommen	kam	gekommen

Some irregular verbs have the *same stem vowel* in the *imperfect tense* and in the *perfect participle.*

Infinitive	*Imperfect*	*Perfect participle*
schreiben	schrieb	geschrieben
schießen	schoß	geschossen
stehen	stand	gestanden

Some irregular verbs have a *progressive change of the stem vowel.*

Infinitive	*Imperfect*	*Perfect participle*
finden	fand	gefunden
rinnen (to run, flow)	rann	geronnen
sitzen	saß	gesessen
sprechen	sprach	gesprochen
gelten	galt	gegolten
gehen	ging	gegangen

2. Group 2b: present tense and familiar command

Some irregular verbs also have an *additional change of the stem vowel* in the **du** and **er** forms of the *present tense*.

Present	ich gebe	ich nehme	ich trage	ich laufe
	du gibst	**du** nimmst	**du** trägst	**du** läufst
	er gibt	**er** nimmt	**er** trägt	**er** läuft

Pay special attention to the following forms of the familiar command:

Infinitive	**Du**-*form*	*Familiar command*
nehmen	du nimmst	Nimm das Buch!
helfen	du hilfst	Hilf ihm!
essen	du ißt	Iß das Brot!
sehen	du siehst	Sieh(e) da!
geben	du gibst	Gib mir das!

Note that there are *also other irregularities* in addition to the vowel change! Refer always to the list of irregular verbs in the appendix.

C. Verbs That Follow Neither the Regular nor the Irregular Verb Patterns

These verbs have a *change of the stem vowel* but *regular endings in* the *imperfect tense* and in the *perfect participle*. Those verbs are:

Present	sie bringen (bring)	sie brennen (burn)	sie kennen (know)
Imperfect	sie brachten	sie brannten	sie kannten
Perfect	sie haben . . . gebracht	sie haben . . . gebrannt	sie haben . . . gekannt
Present	sie nennen (name)	sie rennen (run)	sie senden (send)
Imperfect	sie nannten	sie rannten	sie sandten
Perfect	sie haben . . . genannt	sie sind . . . gerannt	sie haben . . . gesandt
Present	sie denken (think)	sie wissen (know)	sie wenden (turn)
Imperfect	sie dachten	sie wußten	sie wandten (wendeten)
Perfect	sie haben . . . gedacht	sie haben . . . gewußt	sie haben . . . gewandt (gewendet)

Pay special attention to the **ich, du,** and **er** forms of the *present tense* of **wissen**: ich weiß, du weißt, er weiß.

Drill 1   *Put the sentences (a) into the imperfect (b) into the perfect. Follow the examples.*

Wir **lesen** moderne Kurzgeschichten.
Wir **lasen** moderne Kurzgeschichten.

Wir **lesen** moderne Kurzgeschichten.
Wir **haben** moderne Kurzgeschichten **gelesen**.

Der Verfasser gibt uns eine Einführung.
Die Schriftsteller stehen vor einer schwierigen
　　Entscheidung.
Die alten Vorbilder gelten nicht mehr.

Wir nehmen dieses Beispiel.
Man findet das Ereignis interessant.
Die Lehrerin spricht mit leiser Stimme.
Die Mädchen schreiben die großen Buch-
　　staben.
Alle sitzen vor der großen Tafel.
Er trägt einen roten Schal.
Wir sehen das Schild an der Tür.
Die Scharfschützen schießen sofort.

Drill 2   *Put the sentences (a) into the imperfect (b) into the perfect. Follow the examples.*

Der Mann **weiß** das nicht.
Der Mann **wußte** das nicht.

Der Mann **weiß** das nicht.
Der Mann **hat** das nicht **gewußt**.

Die Stadt brennt drei Tage lang.
Die Leute denken an den Krieg.

Er kennt seine Leute gut.
Der Junge weiß das nicht.
Er wendet sich zu ihm.
Man nennt das ein Wirtschaftswunder.
Der Junge bringt ihm Zigaretten.
Er sendet das Paket an die Ostfront.

Drill 3   *Combination Drill*   *Put the sentences (a) into the imperfect (b) into the perfect.*

Der Junge weiß das nicht.
Er kennt seine Leute gut.
Wir lesen moderne Kurzgeschichten.
Die Leute denken an den Krieg.
Wir nehmen dieses Beispiel.
Der Verfasser gibt uns eine Einführung.
Er wendet sich zu ihm.
Alle sitzen vor der großen Tafel.

Der Junge bringt ihm Zigaretten.
Man findet das Ereignis interessant.
Die Scharfschützen schießen sofort.
Die Stadt brennt drei Tage lang.
Die Mädchen schreiben die großen Buch-
　　staben.
Die Lehrerin spricht mit leiser Stimme.

II. SEPARABLE AND INSEPARABLE VERBS

A. Separable Verbs

A verb with a *stressed prefix is separable*. The separable prefix appears at the end of the main clause.

Ich denke, daß wir das Buch **auswählen**. Ja, wir **wählen** es **aus**.
Ich denke, daß wir heute **anfangen**. Ja, wir **fangen** heute **an**.

In the perfect participles and in the infinitives with **zu, ge–** and **zu** are placed between the prefixes and verb stems.

ge–	*zu*
ausgewählt	auszuwählen
angefangen	anzufangen
widergespiegelt	widerzuspiegeln

B. Inseparable Verbs

Verbs with an *unstressed prefix* are *inseparable*. The prefixes **ge–, be–, er–, ver–, zer–, ent–, emp–, hinter–,** and **miß–** are *unstressed* and *not separable*. Note that **miß–** is stressed, but not separable if it is followed by another inseparable prefix: Er **mißver**steht mich.

Ich denke, daß ihm die Erzählungen **gefallen.** Ja, sie **gefallen** ihm.	I think that he likes the stories.
Ich denke, daß wir das **begreifen.** Ja, wir **begreifen** das.	I think that we understand it.
Ich denke, daß wir ihm alles **erzählen.** Ja, wir **erzählen** ihm alles.	I think that we will tell him everything.
Ich denke, daß wir das Problem **verstehen.** Ja, wir **verstehen** es.	I think that we understand the problem.
Ich hoffe, daß wir hier nichts **zerstören.** Nein, wir **zerstören** hier nichts.	I hope that we won't destroy anything here.
Ich denke, daß wir das jetzt **entscheiden.** Ja, wir **entscheiden** das jetzt.	I think that we decide it now.
Ich denke, daß wir das alle **empfinden.** Ja, wir **empfinden** das alle.	I think that we all feel it.
Ich hoffe, daß sie eine Nachricht **hinterlassen.** Ja, sie **hinterlassen** eine Nachricht.	I hope that they will leave (behind) a message.
Ich vermute, daß sie ihm **mißtrauen.** Ja, sie **mißtrauen** ihm.	I guess that they distrust him.

The prefixes **unter–, durch–,** and **um–** are *inseparable* if they are *unstressed!* They are *separable* if they are *stressed.*

Ich hoffe, daß Sie sich gut **unterhalten.** Ja, ich **unterhalte** mich gut.	I hope that you are having a good time.
Ich finde, daß sie sich gut **unterhalten.** Ja, sie **unterhalten** sich gut.	I find that they are having a good conversation (that they converse well with each other).
Ich finde, daß sie uns gut **unterhalten.** Ja, sie **unterhalten** uns gut.	I find that they entertain us well.

Ich glaube, daß wir ihn **überzeugen**. Ja, wir **überzeugen** ihn.

I believe that we shall convince him.

Ich denke, daß sie alles **durchsuchen**. Ja, sie **durchsuchen** alles.

I think that they are searching everything.

Ich denke, daß er diesen Ausdruck **umschreibt**. Ja, er **umschreibt** ihn.

I think that he will paraphrase this expression.

Verbs with *unstressed prefixes* form the perfect participle *without* **ge–**:

gefallen	entschieden	überzeugt
begriffen	empfunden	durchsucht
erzählt	hinterlassen	umschrieben
verstanden	mißtraut	
zerstört	unterhalten	

Drill 4 *Separable Verbs, Present Tense* *Follow the example.*

Ich denke, daß er das Buch **auswählt**.
Ja, er **wählt** das Buch **aus**.

Ich glaube, daß er heute anfängt.
Ich hoffe, daß er gut aufpaßt.
Ich denke, daß er den Schal abnimmt.
Ich glaube, daß er am Kurs teilnimmt.
Ich hoffe, daß er das durchhält.

Ich finde, daß sie gut aussieht.
Ich denke, daß wir die Bücher zumachen.
Ich finde, daß er sich gut ausdrückt.
Ich finde, daß das Buch die Probleme widerspiegelt.
Ich glaube, daß der die Zigarette ansteckt.
Ich denke, daß er sich der Diktatur anpaßt.

Drill 5 *Inseparable Verbs, Present Tense* *Follow the example.*

Ich hoffe, daß er eine Nachricht **hinterläßt**.
Ja, er **hinterläßt** eine Nachricht.

Ich denke, daß wir das begreifen.
Ich glaube, daß wir ihn überzeugen.
Ich denke, daß wir das entscheiden.
Ich finde, daß er uns gut unterhält.
Ich glaube, daß wir alles verstehen.

Ich denke, daß er alles durchsucht.
Ich glaube, daß er alles zerstört.
Ich denke, daß er diesen Ausdruck umschreibt.
Ich denke, daß wir alles erzählen.
Ich glaube, daß er uns mißtraut.
Ich glaube, daß wir das alle empfinden.
Ich denke, daß ihm die Erzählung gefällt.

Drill 6 *Combination Drill* *Respond in the same manner.*

Ich denke, daß er das Buch auswählt.
Ich hoffe, daß er eine Nachricht hinterläßt.
Ich hoffe, daß er das durchhält.
Ich finde, daß er uns gut unterhält.
Ich glaube, daß wir ihn überzeugen.
Ich denke, daß wir die Bücher zumachen.

Ich finde, daß er sich gut ausdrückt.
Ich glaube, daß er alles zerstört.
Ich denke, daß wir das entscheiden.
Ich hoffe, daß er gut aufpaßt.
Ich glaube, daß er heute anfängt.
Ich denke, daß er alles durchsucht.

Ich hoffe, daß er das durchhält.
Ich denke, daß er diesen Ausdruck umschreibt.
Ich finde, daß das Buch die Probleme wider-
spiegelt.

Ich denke, daß er die Zigarette ansteckt.
Ich denke, daß er sich der Diktatur anpaßt.
Ich glaube, daß er uns mißtraut.
Ich glaube, daß wir das alle empfinden.

Drill 7   *Separable Verbs, Perfect Tense*   *Put the sentences into the perfect tense. Follow the example.*

Er **wählt** den Roman **aus.**
Er **hat** den Roman **ausgewählt.**

Die Mädchen schreiben die Sätze ab.
Die Studenten fangen heute an.
Die Leute bauen die Städte wieder auf.
Er nimmt den Schal ab.
Er macht das Buch zu.
Er steckt eine Zigarette an.

Er wirft die Zigarette weg.
Er hält das durch.
Er findet zu Hause nichts mehr vor.
Die Geschichte spiegelt die psychologischen
Probleme wider.
Er führt uns in die Erzählung ein.
Er drückt sich kompliziert aus.

Drill 8   *Inseparable Verbs and Verbs with the Ending* –ieren, *Perfect Tense*   *Put the sentences into the perfect tense. Follow the examples.*

Er **überzeugt** alle Leute.
Er **hat** alle Leute **überzeugt.**

Er **charakterisiert** den modernen Menschen.
Er **hat** den modernen Menschen **charakterisiert.**

Er versteht das Thema.
Er unterhält uns gut.

Er kritisiert den schlechten Stil.
Er entscheidet das sofort.
Er umschreibt den schwierigen Ausdruck.
Er studiert Geschichte.
Er begreift das schnell.
Er identifiziert sich mit seiner Generation.

Drill 9   *Combination Drill*   *Put the sentences into the perfect tense.*

Die Studenten fangen heute an.
Er wirft die Zigarette weg.
Er begreift das schnell.
Er entscheidet das sofort.
Die Geschichte spiegelt die psychologischen
Probleme wider.
Er charakterisiert den modernen Menschen.
Er führt uns in die Erzählung ein.
Er umschreibt den schwierigen Ausdruck.

Er findet zu Hause nichts mehr vor.
Er macht das Buch zu.
Er überzeugt alle Leute.
Er hält das durch.
Er unterhält uns gut.
Er identifiziert sich mit seiner Generation.
Er findet zu Hause nichts mehr vor.
Er kritisiert den schlechten Stil.

III. THE PERFECT AND PLUPERFECT TENSES WITH haben AND sein

	haben	*sein*
Perfect	sie **haben** gefragt	sie **sind** gekommen
	sie **haben** gesprochen	sie **sind** gegangen
Pluperfect	sie **hatten** gefragt	sie **waren** gekommen
	sie **hatten** gesprochen	sie **waren** gegangen

Most German verbs take **haben** as their auxiliary in forming the perfect and pluperfect tenses. Only the following verbs require **sein!**

1. Verbs *without an accusative object:* which express (a) a *change of place* or (b) a *change of condition.*

   (a) sie sind gekommen
       wir waren gegangen

   (b) sie sind gestorben   (they died)
       sie waren gewachsen (they had grown)

2. Also the following verbs:

   sein
   werden
   bleiben

   sie **sind gewesen**
   sie **sind geworden**
   sie **sind geblieben**

3. The following *impersonal expressions* also form the *perfect* and *pluperfect tenses* with **sein:**

   Es geschieht nichts.
   Nothing happens.

   Es **ist** nichts **geschehen.**

   Das kommt oft vor.
   That occurs often.

   Das **ist** oft **vorgekommen.**

   Es gelingt ihm immer.
   He always succeeds.

   Es **ist** ihm immer **gelungen.**

   Es mißlingt ihm manchmal.
   He sometimes fails.

   Es **ist** ihm manchmal **mißlungen.**

   Es geht mir gut.
   I am fine.

   Es **ist** mir gut **gegangen.**

Drill 10   *The Perfect Tense with* sein   *Follow the example.*

   Er **kommt** zur zweiten Kompanie.
   Er **ist** zur zweiten Kompanie **gekommen.**

   Es geschieht in dieser Woche nichts.
   Sie geht in die Zauberflöte.

Er kehrt in diesem Jahr heim.
Er bleibt zu Hause.
Das kommt oft vor.
Die Schwester steht langsam auf.
Es gelingt ihm immer.

Er wird Hauptmann und Kompaniechef.
Es geht mir gut.
Er ist mehr für das Leichte.
Es mißlingt ihm manchmal.
Die Kinder wachsen schnell.

Drill 11   *Combination Drill   The Perfect Tense with* **sein** *or* **haben**   *Put the sentences into the perfect tense.*

Er erzieht die Leute gut.
Er kommt zur zweiten Kompanie.
Er wird Hauptmann und Kompaniechef.
Er entscheidet das sofort.
Er verläßt die Stadt.
Die Schwester steht langsam auf.
Es geschieht in dieser Woche.
Er ist mehr für das Leichte.

Er nimmt den Schal ab.
Er bleibt zu Hause.
Das kommt oft vor.
Sie geht in die Zauberflöte.
Die Schwester hält das durch.
Er kehrt in diesem Jahr heim.
Es gelingt ihm immer.

IV. THE USE OF VERB TENSES IN COLLOQUIAL SPEECH

Generally it can be said that usually *two tenses* are used in *conversational German:* the *present tense* and the *perfect tense.*

A. The Use of the Present and Perfect Tenses

The *present tense* is the common conversational form for *general statements,* for the *present time,* and for the *future time.*

An *expression of time* (morgen, nächste Woche, etc.) is usually used *to distinguish* between the *present* and the *future.*

Er schreibt einen Bericht.

He *writes* a report.
He *is writing* a report.
He *does write* a report.

Er schreibt morgen einen Bericht.

He *will write* a report tomorrow.
He *is going to write* a report tomorrow.

There is *also* the form **werden** + *infinitive* for *future time.* (Er **wird** einen Bericht **schreiben.**) This form, the so-called *future tense,* is preferred when *no expression of time* is used, and when it is *not clear from the context* that the sentence has a *future meaning.*

The *perfect tense* is the *conversational form for the past.*

Er hat einen Bericht **geschrieben.**

He *wrote* a report.
He *has written* a report.

But one often uses the *imperfect forms* for the *past* with *auxiliary* and *modal verbs.*

Er **war** Student.   Er **sollte** gehen.   Er **mußte** nach Hause.
Er **hatte** Zeit.   Er **konnte** Deutsch.   Er **mochte** nichts essen.
Er **wollte** kommen.   Er **durfte** bleiben.

The *perfect tense* is *also used* when something is *to be ended by a specific time in the future:*

Er **hat** den Bericht **bis morgen geschrieben.**   He *will have written* the report *by tomorrow.*

Er **hat** seine Arbeit **bis morgen beendet.**   He *will have finished* his work *by tomorrow.*

B. The Use of the Imperfect and Pluperfect Tenses

The *imperfect tense* is the *narrative past.* It is used in *stories* and *reports* when the *contents are related and have no direct connection with the present.*

Es **war** einmal . . .   Once upon a time there *was* . . .

The *pluperfect tense* is used to describe events or situations which *precede events* or *situations that occurred in the past.*

Er **kam** nach Hause. Er **war** in Deutschland **gewesen.**

THE GERMAN SENTENCE

I. THE SPLIT PREDICATE

The most *characteristic feature of German syntax* is the *framework* built by the *split predicate,* i.e., by *the split verbal complex* of a sentence. The difference between the predicate in English and the split predicate of a German sentence is easily shown by this example:

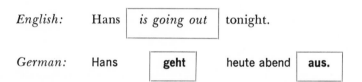

English: Hans | *is going out* | tonight.

German: Hans   **geht**   heute abend   **aus.**

We call the field *between* the two parts of the split predicate the **Satzfeld.** Whatever appears *in front of it* is called the **Vorfeld,** and what appears *after* it is called the **Nachfeld.**

Vorfeld ——— | *First part of predicate (P1)* | —— Satzfeld —— | *Second part of predicate (P2)* | ——Nachfeld——

Hans   **geht**   heute abend   **aus,**   wie immer.

Not all German sentences use the entire pattern. The following patterns are possible:

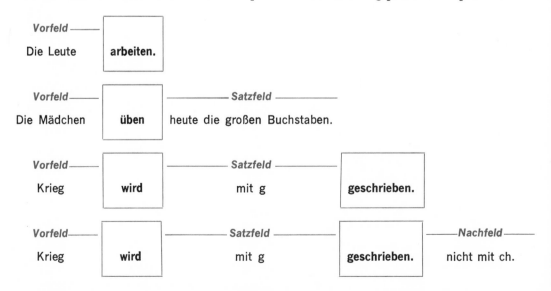

Vorfeld ———
Die Leute   **arbeiten.**

Vorfeld———   ———— Satzfeld ————
Die Mädchen   **üben**   heute die großen Buchstaben.

Vorfeld———   ——— Satzfeld ———
Krieg   **wird**   mit g   **geschrieben.**

Vorfeld———   ——— Satzfeld ———   ———Nachfeld———
Krieg   **wird**   mit g   **geschrieben.**   nicht mit ch.

A. The Six Possible Split Predicates

Split predicates may consist of the following elements:

		P1			*P2*
1. Verb + separable prefix:	Alle	**fangen**	heute		**an.**
2. Auxiliary verb + perfect participle:	Er	**hat**	einen Brief		**geschrieben.**
3. Auxiliary verb + infinitive without **zu**:	Wir	**werden**	vielleicht		**kommen.**
4. Modal verb + infinitive without **zu**:	Sie	**wollen**	jetzt		**arbeiten.**
5. Other verbs + infinitive without **zu**:	Sie	**sieht**	die Kinder		**kommen.**
6. Other verbs + infinitive with **zu**:	Ich	**brauche**	heute nicht		**zu kommen.**

(For 3, 4, 5, and 6, see also Chapter 5.)

B. Expressions Treated Like Split Predicates

We can say that every predicate expresses a *verbal idea*. The verbal idea, for instance, in the sentence **Wir gehen jetzt** is simply that of *going* or *walking*. If we compare the following three sentences

	P1		*P2*
Wir	**gehen**	jetzt.	
Wir	**gehen**	jetzt	**aus.**
Wir	**gehen**	jetzt	**nach Hause.**

it can easily be seen that the *separable prefix* **aus** and the *verbal complement* **nach Hause** change the simple verbal idea of *going* or *walking* in a similar way. The *verbal complement* **nach Hause** has the *same function* as the *prefix* **aus,** namely, to give the sentence **Wir gehen jetzt** a *different meaning*. Therefore, **nach Hause** is treated like **aus,** i.e., like a separable prefix.

The following verbs + verbal complements are treated like split predicates:

1. Verb + directive

(that is, a prepositional phrase which answers the question **Wohin?**)

		P1			*P2*
nach Deutschland fahren	Wir	**fahren**	dieses Jahr		**nach Deutschland.**

2. Sein or werden + predicate adjective

korrekt sein	Er	**war**	immer	**korrekt.**
reich werden	Er	**wurde**	schnell	**reich.**

3. Sein or werden + predicate noun

Student sein	Er	**ist**	seit einem Jahr	**Student.**
Professor werden	Er	**wird**	nächstes Jahr	**Professor.**

4. Other expressions in which the verbal complement is part of the verbal idea

Zeit haben	Wir	**haben**	heute nachmittag	**Zeit.**
Kaffee trinken	Sie	**trinken**	um zehn Uhr	**Kaffee.**
Deutsch sprechen	Er	**spricht**	sehr gut	**Deutsch.**
zu Hause sein	Wir	**sind**	heute abend	**zu Hause.**

When a sentence consists of a split predicate *and* a verbal complement, it is the *verbal complement* that *precedes a prefix, perfect participle,* or *infinitive.*

	P1		*P2*	
			a	*b*
Er	**kam**	um drei Uhr	**zu Hause**	**an.**
Er	**ist**	immer sehr	**korrekt**	**gewesen.**
Er	**muß**	jetzt	**nach Hause**	**gehen.**

Drill 12   *Give the German equivalent. Use the present tense.*

We are at home today.
He is getting rich fast.
We are going to Germany this year.
He is a student now.
We have time today.
They drink coffee at nine o'clock.

We are going home now.
He will become a professor this year.
They are going to the university at eight o'clock.
He speaks German very well.

II. THE VORFELD

A. Elements of the Satzfeld in the Vorfeld

It is only the *first part of the predicate* (P1) that has a *fixed position.* Aside from this, *any one of the elements of the Satzfeld can replace the subject in the Vorfeld, except the pronoun object* **es.** The *subject* then *becomes the first element after P1.*

Vorfeld	P1	Satzfeld	P2
Die Mädchen	haben	heute in der Schule die großen Buchstaben	geübt.
Heute	haben	die Mädchen in der Schule die großen Buchstaben	geübt.
In der Schule	haben	die Mädchen heute die großen Buchstaben	geübt.
Die großen Buchstaben	haben	die Mädchen heute in der Schule	geübt.

The coordinating conjunctions **denn, aber, sondern, und, oder** *do not affect the word order.*

	Vorfeld ———	P1 ———	Satzfeld ———————	P2
	Er	hat	seiner Frau einen Brief	geschrieben.
Denn	er	hat	seiner Frau einen Brief	geschrieben.
Aber	seiner Frau	hat	er einen Brief	geschrieben.
.., sondern	einen Brief	hat	er seiner Frau	geschrieben.
.., und	seiner Frau	hat	er einen Brief	geschrieben.
.., oder	er	hat	seiner Frau einen Brief	geschrieben.

Drill 13 *Begin each sentence with one of the words or expressions in parentheses. Place the subject after P1 when moving it into the Satzfeld.*

Die Mädchen üben (am Dienstag) (in der Schule) (die großen Buchstaben).

Sie schreibt (den Satz) (am Abend) (zehnmal) ab.

Er nimmt (den roten Schal) (auf dem Wege zur zweiten Kompanie) ab.

Die Leute sind (nachts) (mit den Zigaretten) vorsichtig.

Sie haben (dem Hauptmann) (ein Paar Handschuhe) an die Front geschickt.

Die Jungens haben (dieses Jahr) (einen schlechten Winter) (draußen).

B. The Second Part of the Predicate or the Verbal Complement of the Vorfeld

If the Vorfeld is occupied by a word or phrase other than the subject of the sentence, this word or phrase usually refers to something already mentioned.

Die Woche hat **einen Dienstag.** Das Jahr ein halbes Hundert. Der Krieg hat viele **Dienstage. An diesem Dienstag** übten sie in der Schule die großen Buchstaben.

If this reference to a word or phrase already mentioned is *emphasized,* then even the *second part of the predicate (P2)* or the *verbal complement* may appear in the *Vorfeld. Only separable prefixes cannot occupy the Vorfeld.*

When the second part of the predicate or the verbal complement is placed in the Vorfeld, a clause with **aber** usually follows to denote the special emphasis on P2. The word order in both clauses then follows the same pattern.

Vorfeld ———	P1 ———	Satzfeld —————— P2
Er	hat	uns einen Brief **geschrieben.**
Geschrieben	hat	er uns einen Brief, aber **angekommen** ist dieser Brief noch nicht.
Sie	werden	vielleicht **kommen.**
Kommen	werden	sie vielleicht, aber **bleiben** werden sie nicht lange.
Er	braucht	nicht **zu kommen.**
Zu kommen	braucht	er nicht, aber **telefonieren** könnte er doch.
Wir	fahren	selten **nach Berlin.**
Nach Berlin	fahren	wir selten, aber **nach München** fahren wir jedes Wochenende.

Er	war	immer **korrekt.**
Korrekt	war	er immer, aber **freundlich** war er selten.
Er	hat	immer **Zeit.**
Zeit	hat	er immer, aber **Geld** hat er nie.
Er	spricht	sehr gut **Deutsch.**
Deutsch	spricht	er sehr gut, aber **Französisch** spricht er noch besser.

Drill 14   *Put the second part of the predicate or the verbal complement into the Vorfeld. Follow the example.*

Sie werden vielleicht **kommen,** aber sie werden nicht lange **bleiben.**
Kommen werden sie vielleicht, aber bleiben werden sie nicht lange.

Er hat eine Zigarette angesteckt, aber er hat sie nicht geraucht.
Sie hat das Buch gekannt, aber sie hat es nicht ganz gelesen.
Er fühlt sich nicht gut, aber er ist auch nicht krank.
Er ist immer korrekt, aber er ist selten freundlich.
Er fährt oft nach Hamburg, aber er kommt selten nach Berlin.
Er spricht gut Deutsch, aber er spricht schlecht Russisch.
Sie hat den Brief geschrieben, aber sie hat ihn nicht abgeschickt.
Er trinkt gern Kaffee, aber er trinkt lieber Bier.
Sie ist selten zu Hause, aber sie ist oft im Kino.
Er hat immer Zeit, aber er hat nie Geld.

C.   The Impersonal es in the Vorfeld

We have already learned that one may say:

	Vorfeld	P1	Satzfeld	P2
	Es	sind	jetzt 30 Studenten	im Kurs.
instead of	30 Studenten	sind	jetzt	im Kurs.
or	Jetzt	sind	30 Studenten	im Kurs.
or	Im Kurs	sind	jetzt 30 Studenten	

We call this **es,** which is *neither the subject* of the sentence *nor an object,* the impersonal **es.** It is *nothing but a filler* which has *no meaning* of itself. Besides expressions like **es ist . . .** or **es sind . . .** (there is . . . , there are . . .), this impersonal **es** *can occupy any Vorfeld* if, for *specific stylistic reasons,* the speaker or writer wishes the subject to follow the verb.

Vorfeld	P1	Satzfeld
Viele Leute	kommen	heute.
Heute	kommen	viele Leute.
es	kommen	heute viele Leute.

But this impersonal **es** *cannot occupy a Vorfeld* if the *subject of the sentence* is a *pronoun* itself.

Vorfeld	P1	Satzfeld
Sie	kommen	heute.
Heute	kommen	sie.

In the following sentence it is the *subject* of the sentence (30 Studenten) and *not the impersonal* **es** *which determines the verb form.*

Es sind jetzt 30 Studenten im Kurs.

This impersonal **es** disappears as soon as the *subject* of the sentence or *another element* is put into the *Vorfeld*.

Vorfeld	P1	Satzfeld	P2
Es	sind	jetzt 30 Studenten	im Kurs.
30 Studenten	sind	jetzt	im Kurs.
Es	sind	viele Briefe von der Front	gekommen.
Viele Briefe	sind	von der Front	gekommen.
Von der Front	sind	viele Briefe	gekommen.

D. Sentences without a Vorfeld

Certain kinds of sentences *lack a Vorfeld,* and the *inflected verb form* (P1) appears in *front position.*

1. Questions without interrogative pronouns:

P1	Satzfeld	P2
Sind	das	die Studenten?
Gehen	Sie jetzt	weg?

2. Command forms:

P1	Satzfeld	P2	
Schreib(e)	den Satz zehnmal	ab!	
Paßt	bitte gut	auf!	
Seien	Sie bitte	vorsichtig!	
Gehen	wir jetzt	nach Hause!	(Let's go home!)

3. Unreal wishes:

P1	Satzfeld	P2
Kämen	unsere Freunde doch	nach Hause!

(For item 3 see Chapter 6.)

III. THE SATZFELD

A. The Position of the Subject

1. If a *pronoun subject like* **er, sie, wir,** etc., is placed within the Satzfeld, it *follows P1 immediately:*

   Vorfeld ———— P1 ———————— Satzfeld ——————

   An diesem Tag   **übten**   **sie** die großen Buchstaben.

2. If a *noun subject* is placed within the Satzfeld, it follows P1 *immediately:*

   Vorfeld ———— P1 ——————————— Satzfeld ——————

   An diesem Tag   **übten**   **die Mädchen** die großen Buchstaben.
   Jetzt   **antwortet**   **der Junge** ihm.

   But a *noun subject* within the Satzfeld *may also be preceded by a pronoun object* if the noun subject is emphasized.

   Vorfeld ————————— P1 ———————————— Satzfeld ——————————

   Jetzt   **antwortet**   ihm der **Junge.**
   In einem anderen Bereich   **führen**   uns **die Werke** Brechts und Kafkas.
   Was   **zeigen**   Ihnen **der Anfang** und **der Schluß** der Erzählung?

The sentence Was **zeigen** der Anfang und der Schluß der Erzählung **Ihnen?** would mean: What do the beginning and the end of the story show *especially to you?*

B. The Positions of Indirect and Direct Objects

1. *Dative noun objects* precede *accusative noun objects:*

   Vorfeld — P1 ———————— Satzfeld ——————

   Er   gibt   **dem Studenten das Buch.**

2. *Accusative pronoun objects* precede *dative pronoun objects:*

   Vorfeld — P1 ———— Satzfeld ——

   Er   gibt   **es ihm.**

3. *Pronoun objects* precede *noun objects:*

   Vorfeld — P1 ————————— Satzfeld ——

   Er   gibt   **ihm das Buch.**
   Er   gibt   **es dem Studenten.**

(See also p. 35.)

But the following word order is also possible, if the *accusative object* has a *definite article* and the *dative object* has an *indefinite article* or a *possessive adjective,* and is *emphasized.*

Vorfeld ——	P1 ——————————	Satzfeld ———————
Er·	gibt	**das** Buch **einem** Studenten.
Er	schreibt	**den** Brief **seiner** Frau.

C. The Positions of Adverbs and Prepositional Phrases

Adverbs and prepositional phrases placed within the Satzfeld usually follow the sequence *time–manner–place* (**Wann? – Wie? – Wo? Woher?**).

Vorfeld —	P1 ———————————————	Satzfeld	——————————	P2
		Time: wann?	*Manner: wie?* *Place: wo? woher?*	
Er	ist	**an diesem Tag**	**ganz krumm** **durch den Saal**	gegangen.

Drill 15   *Complete the sentences using the elements in parentheses in the correct order.*

Wir gehen (zu Fuß) (durch die Stadt) (heute).
Er kommt (von München) (morgen) (mit dem Wagen).
Er arbeitet (fleißig) (in der Bibliothek) (den ganzen Tag).
Der Arzt kam (aus dem Lazarett) (langsam) (an diesem Tag).
Die Nebelkrähen saßen (auf dem Schulhof) (hungrig) (am Morgen).
Viele blieben (in Deutschland) (aus Überzeugung) (während der 12 Jahre).

IV. THE NACHFELD

The *Nachfeld* may be used for a *phrase* that *contrasts with the first statement,* or for an *afterthought.*

Vorfeld ——	P1 ——	Satzfeld ——	P2 ——————	Nachfeld
Er	ist	nicht heute	gekommen,	**sondern gestern.**
Sie	kann	gut	Deutsch sprechen,	**wie alle hier.**

In many cases the phrase of the Nachfeld can also be placed *within* the Satzfeld.

Vorfeld —	P1 ———————	Satzfeld ———————	P2
Er	ist	nicht heute, **sondern gestern**	gekommen.

As we shall see in Chapter 3, the Nachfeld may also be a subordinate clause.

V. THE NEGATION WITH nicht AND kein–

A. The Use of nicht

With **nicht** one may either negate the predicate (and thereby the entire sentence) or various parts of the sentence.

1. The position of nicht

In sentences in which the *predicate* (and thereby the *entire assertion*) is *negated,* **nicht** is placed at the *end of the Satzfeld.*

Sentences *without objects:*

Vorfeld	P1	Satzfeld		P2
Er	kommt	—	—	**nicht** —.
Er	fängt	—	—	**nicht** an.
Er	ist	—	—	**nicht** angekommen.
Er	kann	—	—	**nicht** kommen.

Sentences *with objects:*

Vorfeld	P1	Satzfeld		P2
Er	liest	**die Erzählung**		**nicht** —.
Er	liest	**sie**		**nicht** —.
Er	fängt	**das Werk**		**nicht** an.
Er	erklärt	**ihm das Problem**		**nicht** —.
Er	hat	**es ihm**		**nicht** erklärt.
Er	kann	**es dem Studenten**		**nicht** erklären.
Er	kann	**den Leuten**		**nicht** helfen.

Sentences with expressions stating a specific time like **gestern, heute, morgen, jetzt, diese Woche, in diesem Monat, nächstes Jahr,** etc. :

Vorfeld	P1	Satzfeld		P2
Er	kommt	—	**heute**	**nicht** —.
Er	fängt	—	**jetzt**	**nicht** an.
Er	hat	—	**gestern**	**nicht** angefangen.
Er	will	es	**heute**	**nicht** erklären.
Er	erklärt	es	**jetzt**	**nicht** —.
Er	hat	es	**diese Woche**	**nicht** gelesen.
Er	kann	es	**in diesem Monat**	**nicht** lesen.

Sentences *with prepositional phrases:*

Vorfeld	P1	Satzfeld		P2
Er	fährt	—	—	**nicht** **nach Berlin.**
Er	ist	—	—	**nicht** **zu Hause gewesen.**
Er	denkt	—	—	**nicht** **an die Zukunft.**

Sentences with *adverbs, predicate adjectives,* and *predicate nouns* with definite articles:

Vorfeld —	P1	—	Satzfeld —		P2
Er	fährt	–	–	nicht schnell	–.
Er	ist	–	–	nicht	typisch.
Er	ist	–	–	nicht	der bekannte Schriftsteller.

▶ *Rule of thumb:* **Nicht** is placed *after objects and expressions* stating a specific time and *before prepositional phrases and adverbs* (except *expressions* stating a specific time).

With **nicht** one may negate *various parts* of the sentence *for emphasis.* A clause with **sondern** usually follows. **Nicht** *precedes the emphasized part.*

Er liest **den Roman nicht. (Er liest die Novelle.)**
Er liest **nicht den Roman, sondern die Novelle.**

Er geht **nicht** auf die Universität. (**Sie** geht auf die Universität.)
Nicht er geht auf die Universität, **sondern sie.**

Er geht **heute nicht** ins Theater. (Er geht morgen.)
Er geht **nicht heute** ins Theater, **sondern morgen.**

Nicht usually *precedes* **jeder, jedes, jede,** and **alle.**

Ich kenne **nicht jeden** Menschen.
Ich kenne **nicht jeden.**

Ich kenne **nicht alle** Menschen.
Ich kenne **nicht alle.**

But:

Ich kenne **jenen** Menschen **nicht.**

Ich kenne **diesen** Menschen **nicht.**

B.   The Use of nicht and kein–

The question whether to use **nicht** or **kein–** for negation is acute only in *sentences with objects* or *predicate nouns.*

1.   The use of nicht

Sentences with objects or predicate nouns are negated with **nicht** if the *nouns* have *a definite article* (**der, das, die,** etc.), *a demonstrative adjective* (**dies–, jen–**), or *a possessive adjective* (**mein–, dein–,** etc.).

Kennen Sie **den** Roman?
Kennen Sie **dieses** Buch?
Kennen Sie **jenes** Theater dort?
Kennen Sie **meine** Familie?

Nein, ich kenne **den** Roman **nicht.**
Nein, ich kenne **dieses** Buch **nicht.**
Nein, ich kenne **jenes** Theater dort **nicht.**
Nein, ich kenne **Ihre** Familie **nicht.**

2. The use of kein—

Sentences with objects or predicate nouns are negated with **kein–** (no, not a, not any) if the objects have an *indefinite article* **(ein ein, eine)** or *no article*.

Ist das **eine** Parabel?	Nein, das ist **keine** Parabel.
Haben Sie **ein** Beispiel?	Nein, ich habe **kein** Beispiel.
Sind dies Novellen?	Nein, dies sind **keine** Novellen.
Haben Sie Beispiele?	Nein, ich habe **keine** Beispiele.
Haben Sie Hunger?	Nein, ich habe **keinen** Hunger.
Trinken Sie Kaffee?	Nein, ich trinke **keinen** Kaffee.
Haben Sie Zeit?	Nein, ich habe **keine** Zeit.

Either **nicht** or **kein–** negate *predicate nouns* which have no article, and which indicate *a person's profession, religion, or nationality.*

Sind Sie Arzt?	Nein, ich bin **kein Arzt.**
	Nein, ich bin **nicht Arzt.**

German **nicht ein–** corresponds to English *not one* or *not a single:*

Ich kenne hier auch **nicht einen** Menschen.	I do *not* know even *one* person around here.
Ich habe hier **nicht einen** Freund.	I do *not* have a *single* friend around here.

Drill 16   *The Position of* **nicht**   *Follow the examples.*

Lesen wir **diese Erzählung?**
Nein, wir lesen **diese Erzählung nicht.**

Kommt er **heute?**
Nein, er kommt **heute nicht.**

Erklärt er **ihm das Problem?**
Nein, er erklärt **ihm das Problem nicht.**

Hat er gestern angefangen?

Hat er ihm das Problem gestern erklärt?
Hat sie den Satz abgeschrieben?
Hat er den Roman diese Woche gelesen?
Bespricht er die interessante Kurzgeschichte heute?
Hat er das moderne Drama kritisiert?
Hat er diesen Monat angefangen?

Drill 17   *The Position of* **nicht**   *Follow the examples.*

Arbeitet er **in der Bibliothek?**
Nein, er arbeitet **nicht in der Bibliothek.**

Hat er **gut** angefangen?
Nein, er hat **nicht gut** angefangen.

Ist das der neue Student?
Nein, das ist **nicht der neue Student.**

Fährt er nach Berlin?

Ist er zu Hause gewesen?
Ist das typisch?
Fährt er schnell?
Ist das der bekannte Schriftsteller?
Sind das die Ärzte gewesen?
Ist er in die Universität gegangen?
Drückt er sich gut aus?
Ist das der moderne Autor?

Drill 18   *Combination Drill*

Kennen Sie die Universität?
Studiert er auf der Universität?
Kennen Sie die Bibliothek?
Arbeitet er in der Bibliothek?
Kommt er diese Woche?
Kommt er nach Hause?
Ist das der moderne Autor?
Kennen Sie den modernen Autor?
Fährt er nach Berlin?

Kennen Sie diese Stadt?
Ist das typisch?
Ist das der bekannte Schriftsteller?
Kennen Sie den bekannten Schriftsteller?
Bespricht er heute die interessante Kurzge-
schichte?
Hat er gut angefangen?
Hat er heute angefangen?

Drill 19   *The Use of* **kein–**   *Follow the examples.*

Ist das **eine** Parabel?
Nein, das ist **keine** Parabel.

Sind das Parabeln?
Nein, das sind **keine** Parabeln.

Haben Sie Hunger?
Nein, ich habe **keinen** Hunger.

Haben Sie Zeit?
Nein, ich habe **keine** Zeit.
Ist das ein Drama?
Sind das Dramen?
Trinken Sie Kaffee?
Gibt es hier eine Universität?
Haben Sie Beispiele?

Ist das Unsinn?
Ist das Literatur?
Lesen Sie Zeitungen?
Haben Sie Zigaretten?
Schreiben Sie Briefe?

Drill 20   *Combination Drill   The Use of* **nicht** *and* **kein–**

Gehen Sie in die Universität?
Kennen Sie die Universität?
Gibt es hier eine Universität?
Ist er Student?
Sind das die neuen Studenten?
Sind das Studenten?
Lesen Sie Zeitungen?

Ist das der moderne Autor?
Arbeiten Sie in der Bibliothek?
Haben Sie Beispiele?
Kennen Sie diese Beispiele?
Drückt er sich gut aus?
Ist er zu Hause gewesen?
Fängt er diese Woche an?

Hat er den Roman gelesen?
Haben Sie Zeit?
Sind das Parabeln?
Kennen Sie diese Parabeln?
Kennen Sie eine Parabel?
Ist das Unsinn?

das schmale Werk *here:* the small body of works

der Feindeinsatz, ⸚e combat; **Kalinin** Russian city, 100 miles NW of Moscow; **denunzieren** to denounce; **das Kriegsgericht, –e** court-martial; **die Todesstrafe beantragen** to demand the death penalty; **die Zelle, –n** cell; **in einer Einzelzelle sitzen, a, e** to be in solitary confinement; **begnadigen** to pardon; **eine immer schwerer werdende Krankheit** an illness that became progressively worse

in **Gefangenschaft geraten, ie, a** to be taken prisoner; **aus·brechen, a, o** to break out, escape; **700 Kilometer** 437.5 miles; **Draußen vor der Tür** *The Man Outside;* **ausgebombt** bombed out; **die Hamburger Kammerspiele** *name of a theater in Hamburg;* **das Spital, ⸚er** hospital

sich entwickeln to develop; **reifen** to mature; **besitzen, a, e** to possess; **die Front, –en** front (-line); **das Gefängnis, –se** prison; **das Krankenhaus, ⸚er** hospital

Er wurde 1921 geboren He was born *in* 1921; **die Schlacht, –en** battle; **die Äußerung, –en** remark; **der Witz, –e** joke; **zeigen** to show; **leidenschaftlich** passionate; **die Leidenschaft, –en** passion; **der Gegner, –** opponent; **gegen** against; **beim ersten Male** the first time; **der Einundzwanzigjährige** (*adj.*) the 21-year old; **warten auf** (+ *acc.*) to wait for; **das Urteil, –e** *here:* verdict, sentence; **der Fall, ⸚e** case; **der Zufall, ⸚e** coincidence

als Folge as a result; **die Krankheit, –en** sickness; **die Gesundheit** health; **kurz** short(ly); **unheilbar** incurable; **sich auf den Weg machen nach** (+ *dat.*) to set out for; **zu Fuß** on foot; **fieberhaft** feverish; **das Hörspiel, –e** radio play; **das Bewußtsein** consciousness; **in dem Bewußtsein** *here:* with the knowledge; **wissen, u, u** to know; **da** *here:* since, because; **schicken** to send; **zu spät** too late; **die Uraufführung** opening night, premiere; **die Aufführung, –en** performance; **sterben, a, o** to die

LITERATURE

Wolfgang Borchert

Biographie   Wolfgang Borcherts großes Talent hatte wenig Zeit, sich zu entwickeln und zu reifen. Er schrieb das schmale Werk, das wir von ihm besitzen, in wenigen Jahren, — an der Front, in Gefängnissen und in Krankenhäusern.

Borchert wurde 1921 in Hamburg geboren. Er war 18 Jahre alt, als der Krieg ausbrach, und 20 bei seinem ersten „Feindeinsatz" in der russischen Winterschlacht vor Kalinin. Die Briefe an seine Eltern und Freunde und seine ironischen Äußerungen und politischen Witze gegen das Nazi-Regime zeigten ihn als leidenschaftlichen Gegner der Diktatur und des Krieges. Aber man öffnete seine Briefe und man denunzierte ihn. Dreimal stand er vor einem Kriegsgericht, das beim ersten Male gegen den Einundzwanzigjährigen die Todesstrafe beantragte. Hundert Tage saß er in einer Einzelzelle und wartete auf sein Urteil. Er wurde begnadigt. „Aber Begnadigung", sagt Heinrich Böll, „war in solchen Fällen nur einer jener Zufälle", die auch zur Diktatur gehören.

Krieg, Gefängnis und — als Folge — eine immer schwerer werdende Krankheit hatten seine Gesundheit zerstört. Kurz vor dem Ende des Krieges kam er noch an die Westfront, wo er in französische Gefangenschaft geriet. Er brach aus, und machte sich — bereits unheilbar krank — zu Fuß auf den 700-Kilometer langen Weg nach Hamburg, nach Hause. Hier begann er wieder zu schreiben, leidenschaftlich und fieberhaft: Gedichte, Kurzgeschichten und das Hörspiel (Drama) *Draußen vor der Tür*. Er schrieb in dem Bewußtsein, daß seine Krankheit ihm nur noch kurze Zeit ließ. Da dem Todkranken im ausgebombten Hamburg niemand helfen konnte, schickten Freunde ihn in die Schweiz. Aber es war zu spät. Am 20. November, einen Tag vor der Uraufführung von *Draußen vor der Tür* in den Hamburger Kammerspielen, starb Wolfgang Borchert, 26 Jahre alt, im Clara-Spital in Basel.

die **Woche**, –n week; **ein halbes Hundert** half a hundred; **der Krieg**, –e war

der Buchstabe, –n (*Masc. II*) letter; **die kleinen Buchstaben** small letters, lower case; **der Rand**, ̈er *here:* rim

üben to practice; **die großen Buchstaben** capital letters; **die Brille**, –n glasses; **das Glas**, ̈er *here:* lens; **dick** thick; **das Auge**, –n eye; **ganz leise** very quiet, *here:* very gentle; **aus·sehen**, a, e to look

die Tafel, –n blackboard

der Becher, – mug, cup, goblet

der Trinkbecher, – drinking mug; **das Blech**, –e tin, sheet metal; **schießen**, o, o to shoot; **der Schuß**, ̈e shot; **bis Paris** as far as Paris; **der Soldat**, –en (*Masc. II*) soldier

Sie kam mit der Zungenspitze bis an die Nase She touched her nose with the tip of her tongue; **jemand an·stoßen**, ie, o to give someone a push; **Sie machte einen Haken hinter den Namen** She put a check beside the name; **zu morgen** for tomorrow; **die Abschrift**, –en copy; **schön sauber** nice and neat

die Zunge, –n tongue; **die Nase**, –n nose; **schon** already; **die Grube**, –n pit, grave (*idiom.*); **graben**, u, a to dig; **das Grab**, ̈er grave; **ab·schreiben**, ie, ie to copy; **die mit ihrer Brille** her with her glasses; **der Schulhof**, ̈e school yard; **fressen**, a, e to eat (*animals*), to devour; **die Nebelkrähe**, –n hooded crow; **die Krähe**, –n crow; **weg·werfen**, a, o to throw away; **das Brot**, –e bread

der Befehl, –e order

der Bataillonskommandeur, –e batallion commander; **befehlen**, a, o to order

der Schal, –s shawl, scarf; **ab·nehmen**, a, o to take off, remove

in der Zweiten (Kompanie) in the second company

sowas = so etwas that sort of thing

AN DIESEM DIENSTAG

Die Woche hat einen Dienstag.
Das Jahr ein halbes Hundert.
Der Krieg hat viele Dienstage.

An diesem Dienstag
übten sie in der Schule die großen Buchstaben. Die Lehrerin
hatte eine Brille mit dicken Gläsern. Die hatten keinen Rand.
Sie waren so dick, daß die Augen ganz leise aussahen.

Zweiundvierzig Mädchen saßen vor der schwarzen Tafel und
schrieben mit großen Buchstaben:

DER ALTE FRITZ[1] HATTE EINEN TRINKBECHER AUS BLECH! DIE DICKE
BERTA[2] SCHOSS BIS PARIS! IM KRIEGE SIND ALLE VÄTER SOLDAT.

Ulla kam mit der Zungenspitze bis an die Nase. Da stieß die
Lehrerin sie an. Du hast Krieg mit ch geschrieben, Ulla.[3] Krieg
wird mit g geschrieben. G wie Grube. Wie oft habe ich das
schon gesagt. Die Lehrerin nahm ein Buch und machte einen
Haken hinter Ullas Namen. Zu morgen schreibst du den Satz
zehnmal ab, schön sauber, verstehst du? Ja, sagte Ulla und
dachte: Die mit ihrer Brille. Auf dem Schulhof fraßen die
Nebelkrähen das weggeworfene Brot.

An diesem Dienstag
wurde Leutnant Ehlers zum Bataillonskommandeur befohlen.

Sie müssen den roten Schal abnehmen, Herr Ehlers.

Herr Major?

Doch, Ehlers. In der Zweiten ist sowas nicht beliebt.

---

[1] **Der alte Fritz**   Frederick II (Friedrich II., or Friedrich der Zweite), also known in German history as Frederick the Great, King of Prussia (1740–1786), founder of Prussian political greatness and military power, called by the people „Der Alte Fritz."

[2] **Die Dicke Berta**   Cannon in World War I from the Krupp steel works, named after Mrs. Bertha Krupp.

[3] **Ulla hat Krieg mit ch geschrieben**   Many people in Middle and Northern Germany pronounce the g in end position (Krieg, Hamburg, etc.) as ch (Kriech, Hamburch, etc.).

Da kommen Sie nicht mit durch (*slang*) = **Damit kommen Sie nicht durch** You won't get away with it; **Mit dem Schal läßt die Kompanie Sie glatt stehen** With that shawl the company will cut you dead

gewöhnt sein an (+ *acc.*) to be accustomed to; **das Korrekte** (*adj.*) exactness; **der Hauptmann, –leute** captain; **tragen, u, a** to wear

die Wunde, –n wound

verwundet wounded, hurt

flau slack; **Na ja, Ehlers** Well, Ehlers

nee (*slang*) = **nein** no; **sich krank melden** to go on sick call; **sich fühlen** to feel; **sonst** *here:* formerly, at any other time; **korrekt** exact; **Sehen Sie zu** See to it; **fertig werden mit** (+ *dat.*) to be able to handle; **erziehen, o, o** to educate; *here:* to train

türlich = **natürlich** naturally

anständig decent; **der Scharfschütze, –n** (*Masc. II*) sharpshooter, sniper; **der Zeigefinger, –** index finger; *here:* trigger finger; **jucken** to itch; **das Glühwürmchen, –** glowworm; **herum·schwirren** to whirl around

auf·passen to watch out, *here:* to see to it; **vorsichtig** careful; **die Zigarette, –n** cigarette; **vorige Woche** last week; **der Kopfschuß, ⁔e** shot in the head

der Führer, – leader; **führen** to lead

eine Zigarette an·stecken to light a cigarette; **der Kompanieführer, –** company commander; **laut** loud

Da schoß es A shot rang out

mal wieder was (*slang*) = **einmal wieder etwas** something once again; **rauchen** to smoke; **knabbern** to nibble on, chew; **der Handschuh, –e** glove; **Sie haben einen verdammt schlechten Winter draußen** They have a damn bad winter out there

Ich komme in die zweite Kompanie?

Ja, und die lieben sowas nicht. Da kommen sie nicht mit durch. Die Zweite ist an das Korrekte gewöhnt. Mit dem roten Schal läßt die Kompanie Sie glatt stehen. Hauptmann Hesse trug sowas nicht.

Ist Hesse verwundet?

Nee, er hat sich krank gemeldet. Fühlte sich nicht gut, sagte er. Seit er Hauptmann ist, ist er ein bißchen flau geworden, der Hesse. Versteh ich nicht. War sonst immer so korrekt. Na ja, Ehlers, sehen Sie zu, daß Sie mit der Kompanie fertig werden. Hesse hat die Leute gut erzogen. Und den Schal nehmen Sie ab, klar?

Türlich, Herr Major.

Und passen Sie auf, daß die Leute mit den Zigaretten vorsichtig sind. Da muß ja jedem anständigen Scharfschützen der Zeigefinger jucken, wenn er diese Glühwürmchen herumschwirren sieht. Vorige Woche hatten wir fünf Kopfschüsse. Also passen Sie ein bißchen auf, ja?

Jawohl, Herr Major.

Auf dem Wege zur zweiten Kompanie nahm Leutnant Ehlers den roten Schal ab. Er steckte eine Zigarette an. Kompanieführer Ehlers, sagte er laut.

Da schoß es.

An diesem Dienstag
sagte Herr Hansen zu Fräulein Severin:

Wir müssen dem Hesse auch mal wieder was schicken, Severinchen. Was zu rauchen, was zu knabbern. Ein bißchen Literatur. Ein Paar Handschuhe oder sowas. Die Jungens haben einen verdammt schlechten Winter draußen. Ich kenne das. Vielen Dank.

vielleicht perhaps

der **Sinn** sense, meaning; **ruhig** calm, quiet; *here:* better (*idiom.*); **oder so** or something like that

der **Unsinn** nonsense; **freundlich** friendly, pleasant; **Er war doch mehr für das Leichte** He was really always more for the light stuff; **Er lacht doch gern, das wissen Sie doch** He does like to laugh, you know that; **Was kann dieser Hesse lachen** How that Hesse can laugh

tragen, u, a *here:* to carry; **die Bahre, –n** stretcher, bier; **die Entlausungsanstalt, –en** delousing station; **das Schild, –er** sign

der **General, ⸚e** general; der **Grenadier, –e** grenadier, infantryman; **das Haar, –e** hair

das **Spinnenbein, –e** spider's leg; der **Knöchel, –** knuckle; **gerötet** reddened; das **Fleckfieber** spotted fever, typhus; der **Verdacht** suspicion; die **Seuche, –n** epidemic; das **Lazarett, –e** military hospital

scheren, o, o to shear, shave; der **Sanitäter, –** medical orderly; **dünn** thin; **ab·reiben, ie, ie** to rub down; **riechen, o, o nach** (+ *dat.*) to smell like; **die Apotheke, –n** pharmacy; **fühlen nach** (+ *dat.*) to feel for; **41,6°** centigrade 106.9° Fahrenheit; der **Puls, –e** pulse; **ohne Besinnung** unconscious; der **Fleckfieberverdacht** suspicion of typhus; **zu·machen** to close; **das Seuchenlazarett, –e** isolation hospital

hoch·nehmen, a, o to lift; **Sein Kopf pendelte aus den Decken heraus und immer hin und her** His head dangled from out of the covers and swung to and fro; **Und dabei hatte er immer gelacht** And yet it was he who had always laughed; der **Schnupfen** cold

die **Treppe, –n** stairs; die **Stufe, –n** step; **Es steht drauf** It says; der **Träger, –** carrier, bearer

der **Nachbar, –** (*Masc. I* or *II*) neighbor (*male*); **Die Tür ging zu** The door closed; **wedeln** to wag, *here:* to wave; die **Kälte** cold (ness)

klingeln to ring the bell; die **Nachbarin, –nen** neighbor (*female*); **Die Tür ging auf** The door opened; der **Chef, –s** boss, *here:* commander

Hölderlin[4] vielleicht, Herr Hansen?

Unsinn, Severinchen, Unsinn. Nein, ruhig ein bißchen freund-
licher. Wilhelm Busch[5] oder so, Hesse war doch mehr für das
Leichte. Lacht doch gern, das wissen Sie doch. Mein Gott,
Severinchen, was kann dieser Hesse lachen!

Ja, das kann er, sagte Fräulein Severin.

An diesem Dienstag
. trugen sie Hauptmann Hesse auf einer Bahre in die Entlausungsanstalt. An der Tür war ein Schild:

> OB GENERAL, OB GRENADIER:
> DIE HAARE BLEIBEN HIER.

Er wurde geschoren. Der Sanitäter hatte lange, dünne Finger.
Wie Spinnenbeine. An den Knöcheln waren sie etwas gerötet.
Sie rieben ihn mit etwas ab, das roch nach Apotheke. Dann
fühlten die Spinnenbeine nach seinem Puls und schrieben in
ein dickes Buch: Temperatur 41,6. Puls 116. Ohne Besinnung.
Fleckfieberverdacht. Der Sanitäter machte das dicke Buch zu.
Seuchenlazarett Smolensk stand da drauf. Und darunter:
Vierzehnhundert Betten.

Die Träger nahmen die Bahre hoch. Auf der Treppe pendelte
sein Kopf aus den Decken heraus und immer hin und her bei
jeder Stufe. Und kurzgeschoren. Und dabei hatte er immer über
die Russen gelacht.[6] Der eine Träger hatte Schnupfen.

An diesem Dienstag
klingelte Frau Hesse bei ihrer Nachbarin. Als die Tür aufging,
wedelte sie mit dem Brief. Er ist Hauptmann geworden. Hauptmann und Kompaniechef, schreibt er. Und sie haben über 40

---

[4] **Friedrich Hölderlin** Famous German classical-romantic poet (1770–1843). Borchert probably was thinking of Hölderlin's poem „Der Tod fürs Vaterland" which was included in most anthologies edited for German soldiers.

[5] **Wilhelm Busch** Great German humorist. Poet and cartoonist (1832–1908).

[6] Every man who joins the Russian army gets his head shaved for hygienic reasons. Since the German soldiers were allowed to have a "normal" haircut—except when entering a military hospital—they used to laugh about the shaved heads of the Russians.

40 Grad Kälte = −40° centigrade, 40° below zero;
9 Tage hat der Brief gedauert The letter took 9
days; oben drauf *here:* at the top of the page

hoch·halten, ie, a to hold up; Sie sah nicht hin She
did not look at it

arm poor; die Jungs = die Jungens (*plur.*) (*Masc. II*)
boys

der Oberfeldarzt, ⸚e high-ranking military doctor;
der Chefarzt, ⸚e superintendent of the hospital

scheußlich disgusting

dabei = beim Reden while talking; Sie sahen sich
nicht an They did not look at each other

spielen to play; die Zauberflöte *The Magic Flute* by
W. A. Mozart; Sie hatte sich die Lippen rot gemacht
She had put on lipstick

der Unterarzt, ⸚e low ranking military doctor; Als
trüge er = Als ob er trüge As though he carried

die Schwester, −n *here:* nurse; schreiben, ie, ie an
(+ *acc.*) to write to; durch·halten, ie, a to endure;
Ohne Gott hält man das gar nicht durch Without
God one cannot endure it; auf·stehen, a, a to stand
up, to rise; krumm crooked, *here:* bent; der Saal, ⸚e
large room, *here:* word

Als ob er sich schämte As though he were ashamed

poltern to thump; bumsen to bump

der Tote, −n (*adj.*) dead man; hin·legen to lay down;
die Erde ground, earth

Grad Kälte. Neun Tage hat der Brief gedauert. An Frau Hauptmann Hesse hat er oben drauf geschrieben.

Sie hielt den Brief hoch. Aber die Nachbarin sah nicht hin.

40 Grad Kälte, sagte sie, die armen Jungs. 40 Grad Kälte.

An diesem Dienstag.
fragte der Oberfeldarzt den Chefarzt des Seuchenlazaretts Smolensk[7]:
Wieviel sind es jeden Tag?

Ein halbes Dutzend.

Scheußlich, sagte der Oberfeldarzt.

Ja, scheußlich, sagte der Chefarzt.

Dabei sahen sie sich nicht an.

An diesem Dienstag
spielten sie die Zauberflöte. Frau Hesse hatte sich die Lippen rot gemacht.

An diesem Dienstag
schrieb Schwester Elisabeth an ihre Eltern: Ohne Gott hält man das gar nicht durch. Aber als der Unterarzt kam, stand sie auf. Er ging so krumm, als trüge er ganz Rußland durch den Saal.

Soll ich ihm noch was geben? fragte die Schwester.

Nein, sagte der Unterarzt. Er sagte das so leise, als ob er sich schämte.

Dann trugen sie Hauptmann Hesse hinaus. Draußen polterte es. Die bumsen immer so. Warum können sie die Toten nicht langsam hinlegen. Jedesmal lassen sie sie so auf die Erde bumsen. Das sagte einer.

[7] **Smolensk**   Old Russian city on the river Dnjepr.

schneidig snappy, dashing

tagelang for days; **Nächte durch** throughout the nights; **davon·stolpern** to stumble away; **leer** empty

abends in the evening; **malen** to paint, draw, *here:* write slowly; **das Schreibheft, –e** exercise book, notebook

Und sein Nachbar sang ganz leise:

> Zicke zacke juppheidi
> Schneidig ist die Infantrie.

Der Unterarzt ging von Bett zu Bett. Jeden Tag. Tag und Nacht. Tagelang. Nächte durch. Krumm ging er. Er trug ganz Rußland durch den Saal. Draußen stolperten zwei Krankenträger mit einer leeren Bahre davon. Nummer 4, sagte der eine. Er hatte Schnupfen.

An diesem Dienstag
saß Ulla abends und malte in ihr Schreibheft mit großen Buchstaben:

> IM KRIEG SIND ALLE VÄTER SOLDAT.
> IM KRIEG SIND ALLE VÄTER SOLDAT.

Zehnmal schrieb sie das. Mit großen Buchstaben. Und Krieg mit G. Wie Grube.

I. QUESTIONNAIRE

A. Exercises for the A-Questions

1. Study the following expressions

1. **an diesem** Dienstag, **am** Abend, **um** 9 Uhr, **um** Mitternacht, **im** Herbst, **im** Mai, **in der** Woche, **in der** Nacht — this Tuesday, in the evening, at 9 o'clock, at midnight, in the fall, in May, during the week, during the night
2. Die Zweite **ist an das** Korrekte **gewöhnt.** — The second company is accustomed to exactness.
3. Er **fühlte sich** nicht gut. — He did not feel well.
4. Er **wird mit der** Kompanie **fertig.** — He can handle the company.
5. Sie **fühlten nach dem** Puls. — They felt for the pulse.
6. Das **roch nach** Apotheke. — That smelled like a pharmacy (like a hospital).
7. **Auf dem** Schild **steht** . . . Es **steht drauf** . . . — The sign says . . . . It says . . . .
8. Sie hatte sich die Lippen rot gemacht. — She had put on lipstick.
9. **beim** Reden — while speaking

10. Der Autor **teilt** seine Erzählung **in** zehn **Abschnitte.**	The author divides his story into ten sections.
11. Der dritte Abschnitt **spielt an der** Ostfront, **in** Rußland.	The third section is set on the Eastern front, in Russia.
12. Die Abschnitte **führen** uns **in die** Schule, **nach** Smolensk, **an die** Ostfront, **in die** Heimatstadt Hauptmann Hesses.	The sections take us into the school, to Smolensk, to the Eastern front, to Captain Hesse's home town.
13. **Auf welche** Schauplätze führt uns die Erzählung?	To what settings does the story take us?
14. Was **erfahren wir über** Leutnant Ehlers?	What do we learn about Lieutenant Ehlers?
15. **in diesem** Augenblick	at this moment
16. Was **findet an** diesem Dienstag **statt?**	What takes place on this Tuesday?

2. The use of an, in, um **with time expressions**

An is used with (a) parts of the day, (b) specific days, and (c) holidays:

(a) **am** Morgen, **am** Mittag, **am** Abend
(b) **am** Montag, **am** Dienstag, **am** achten Mai or **am** 8. Mai
(c) **an** Weihnachten, **an** Ostern

In is used with (a) weeks, (b) months, (c) seasons, (d) years, (e) centuries, and (f) **die Nacht:**

(a) **in dieser** Woche
(b) **im** April, **im** Juni
(c) **im** Frühling, **im** Sommer, **im** Herbst, **im** Winter
(d) **im** Jahre 1948
(e) **im** zwanzigsten Jahrhundert or **im** 20. Jahrhundert
(f) **in der** Nacht

Um is used with (a) specific clock times, and (b) **die Mitternacht:**

(a) **um** zwölf Uhr, **um** drei Uhr
(b) **um** Mitternacht (at midnight)

Drill 1   *The Use of* an, in, um *with Time Expressions*   *Use the cues following the examples.*

Patterns	Cues
am Dienstag	der Mittwoch
am Mittwoch	die Woche
in der Woche	der Morgen
_____	die Nacht
_____	der Mittag
_____	12 Uhr

————————	die Mitternacht
————————	der Abend
————————	das Jahr 1948
————————	Weihnachten
————————	der Winter
————————	der Montag
————————	das 20. Jahrhundert.
————————	8 Uhr
————————	die Nacht
————————	der Sommer
————————	der 8. Mai
————————	der Sonntag
————————	3 Uhr
————————	die Woche

3. Das deutsche Alphabet

Lesen und lernen Sie:

a b c d e f g h i j k l m n o p q r s t u v w x y z

Note that **ch** is spelled: **c-h,** and **sch** is spelled: **s-c-h.**

Drill 2 *Buchstabieren Sie (spell):*

W o l f g a n g   B o r c h e r t.   D e r   K r i e g.   D e r   A l t e   F r i t z.   D i e   Z u n g e n s p i t z e. H a u p t m a n n   H e s s e.   S e u c h e n l a z a r e t t   S m o l e n s k.   S c h w e s t e r   E l i s a b e t h.

Buchstabieren Sie Ihren Namen (your name).

Drill 3 *Diktatübung* *Schreiben Sie:*

/d/i/e/ /R/e/i/h/e/n/f/o/l/g/e/, /d/e/r/ /W/i/d/e/r/s/t/a/n/d/, /d/a/s/ /S/t/i/l/m/i/t/- /t/e/l/, /d/i/e/ /W/e/l/t/a/n/s/c/h/a/u/u/n/g/, /d/e/r/ /K/r/i/e/g/.

4. The use of kennen und wissen (to know)

Kennen is used in the sense of *to be acquainted with, to be familiar with* (*a*) a person, (*b*) a fact, (*c*) an idea:

Er kennt Hauptmann Hesse.　　　　Er kennt den russischen Winter.
Er kennt den totalen Krieg.　　　　Er kennt die Idee.

Wissen is used in the sense of *to have a knowledge of a fact:*

Er kommt heute.　　　　Ich weiß es. *Or:* Ich weiß.

In most cases **wissen** is *followed* by a *dependent clause:*

Ich weiß, daß er heute kommt.   Ich weiß, wohin er geht.

Drill 4   *The Use of* **kennen** *and* **wissen**   *Fill in either* **Er kennt** *or* **Er weiß.** *Follow the examples.*

_____ Hauptmann Hesse.

Er kennt Hauptmann Hesse.

_____, daß Hauptmann Hesse krank ist.

Er weiß, daß Hauptmann Hesse krank ist.

_____ die Lehrerin.
_____, daß die Lehrerin eine Brille hat.
_____ die Situation nach dem Krieg.
_____, daß die Situation sich schnell ändert.
_____ den Krieg.
_____, daß Krieg mit g geschrieben wird.
_____ die Kurzgeschichte.
_____, daß die Kurzgeschichte sehr beliebt ist.
_____ die Trümmerliteratur.
_____ den russischen Winter.
_____, daß der totale Krieg im totalen Zusammenbruch endete.
_____ den totalen Krieg.
_____ die Nazi Ideen.

5. Replacement of the personal pronouns er, es, sie **by the demonstrative pronouns** der, das, die

Die Lehrerin hatte eine Brille mit dicken Gläsern.
Die Gläser hatten keinen Rand.
Sie hatten keinen Rand.
Die hatten keinen Rand.

Der Bataillonskommandeur sagte: ,,Sie kommen in die zweite Kompanie!''
''**Die Leute** lieben sowas nicht''.
,,**Sie** lieben sowas nicht''.
,,**Die** lieben sowas nicht''.

Ulla dachte: **Diese Lehrerin** mit ihrer Brille!
          Die mit ihrer Brille!

In *informal German,* the personal pronouns **er, es, sie** are sometimes replaced by the demonstrative pronouns **der, das, die** in the nominative, accusative, and dative.

Kommt Ihr Freund heute?	Kennen Sie den russischen Winter?	Glauben Sie diesen Leuten?
Ja, **er** kommt heute.	Ja, ich kenne **ihn.**	Ja, ich glaube **ihnen.**
Ja, **der** kommt heute.	Ja, **den** kenne ich.	Ja, **denen** glaube ich.

The demonstrative pronouns **der, das, die** normally *precede* the *inflected verb form.* They *must precede* it if they are *stressed.*

The nominative, accusative, and dative forms are identical with those of the definitive articles, except the dative plural **(denen).**

6. Demonstrative pronouns and da-compounds

Demonstrative pronouns *may be used* after *prepositions,* even if they *refer to things, facts,* or *concepts,* and if these *things, facts,* or *concepts* are *strongly stressed.*

Interessieren Sie sich **für das Thema?**	Nein, ich interessiere mich nicht **dafür.**
Interessieren Sie sich für **dieses Thema?**	Nein, **dafür** interessiere ich mich nicht.
	Nein, **für das** interessiere ich mich nicht.

Drill 5 *Answer the questions using (a) a personal pronoun (b) a demonstrative pronoun. Follow the example.*

Verstehen Sie den Satz?	Glauben Sie den Leuten?
Ja, ich verstehe **ihn.**	Glauben Sie diesen Leuten auch?
Verstehen Sie diesen Satz auch?	Haben Sie den Jungens geantwortet?
Ja, **den** verstehe ich auch.	Haben Sie diesen Jungens auch geantwortet?
	Haben Sie den Satz abgeschrieben?
Kennen Sie das Lazarett?	Haben Sie diesen Satz auch abgeschrieben?
Kennen Sie dieses Lazarett auch?	

B. A-Questions

Answer with complete sentences. *Remember:* Use the present or perfect tense if not otherwise indicated. (Since Borchert wrote this story in very colloquial German, direct quotes from the text are unavoidable in your answers.)

1. Wolfgang Borchert hat seine Erzählung in zehn Abschnitte geteilt. **Mit** welcher **Feststellung** (statement) **beginnt er?** // week / to have / one Tuesday // year / half a hundred // war / to have / many Tuesdays //

2. Der zweite Abschnitt spielt in der Schule.

   Was tun *die Mädchen?* // to practice / capital letters //
   Was *hat die Lehrerin?* // glasses / with / thick lenses //
   Wo sind *die zweiundvierzig Mädchen?* // to sit / in front of / blackboard //
   Was **schreiben** *die Mädchen* mit großen Buchstaben? // der Alte Fritz / to have (*imperf.*) / drinking mug / tin // die Dicke Berta / to shoot (*imperf.*) / Paris // war / all fathers / to be / soldiers //
   Warum stößt die Lehrerin *Ulla* an? // to have written / war / ch // war / to be written / g / like / ditch //

Was **sagt** *sie* **zu Ulla?** // for tomorrow / to copy / sentence / ten times //
Was **denkt** *Ulla?* // her and her glasses //
Wie schließt Borchert den zweiten Abschnitt? // school yard / hooded crows / to devour /
thrown away bread //

3. Der dritte Abschnitt spielt an der Ostfront, in Rußland. Leutnant Ehlers ist zum Bataillonskommandeur befohlen.

Was **sagt** *der Bataillonskommandeur* **zu Leutnant Ehlers?** // to have to take off / red
scarf //
Warum sagt er das? // in second company / that sort of thing / to be / not popular //
Welche **Frage stellt** *Leutnant Ehlers* da? // to come / second company //
Was **antwortet** *der Bataillonskommandeur?* // yes / they / not / to love / that sort of
thing //
Was erfahren wir über *die zweite Kompanie?* // to be accustomed to / exactness //
Was sagt der Bataillonskommandeur über *Hauptmann Hesse?* // not / to have worn / that
sort of thing //
Was **fragt** *Leutnant Ehlers?* // Hesse / to be wounded //
Und was **antwortet** *der Bataillonskommandeur?* // to have gone on sick call // not / to
have felt well //
Warum versteht der Bataillonskommandeur nicht, daß *Hauptmann Hesse* „ein bißchen flau"
geworden ist? // always / to be (*imperf.*) / so exact //
Was **sagt** *er* **zu Ehlers?** // to see to it / that / to be able / to handle / company //
Worauf **soll** *Leutnant Ehlers* **aufpassen?** // that / people / to be careful / cigarettes //
Warum sollen die Leute aufpassen? // last week / they / to have (*imperf.*) / five shots in
the head //
Was tut **Leutnant Ehlers** *auf dem Wege zur zweiten Kompanie?* // to take off / red scarf //
to light / cigarette // to say / company commander Ehlers //
Was geschieht *in diesem Augenblick?* // shot / to ring out //

4. Der vierte Abschnitt führt uns in die Heimatstadt Hauptmann Hesses.

Was **sagt** *Herr Hansen,* der wohl ein Freund Hauptmann Hesses ist, **zu seiner Sekretärin,**
Fräulein Severin? // to have to send / something / to Hesse // something to smoke, to
nibble // literature / a pair of gloves //
Was **sagt** *er* über den russischen Winter? // boys / to have / damn bad winter / out
there // to know / that //
Was **fragt** *Fräulein Severin?* // Hölderlin / perhaps //
Und was **antwortet** *Herr Hansen?* // nonsense / a little more friendly //
Warum will Herr Hansen *Hauptmann Hesse* kein Werk von Hölderlin schicken? // to be
(*imperf.*) more for light stuff // to like to laugh // he / to say / how that Hesse can
laugh //

5. Der fünfte Abschnitt spielt im Seuchenlazarett Smolensk.

Was erfahren wir über **Hauptmann Hesse?** // they / to carry / stretcher / delousing station //

Was **steht** *auf dem Schild* an der Tür? // general / grenadier / hair / to remain / here //
Womit reibt *der Sanitäter* Hauptmann Hesse ab? // something / to smell like a pharmacy (hospital) //
Was tut **der Sanitäter** *dann?* // to feel for / pulse // to write / thick book / temperature 41,6 / pulse 116 / unconscious / suspicion of typhus // to close / thick book //
Was **steht** *auf dem Buch?* // isolation hospital Smolensk / 1400 beds //
Die Träger nehmen die Bahre hoch. Was sagt Borchert dann über Hauptmann Hesse? // his head / to be shorn short //

6. Im sechsten Abschnitt lernen wir Frau Hesse kennen. Sie hat einen Brief von der Front bekommen.

Was **erzählt** *sie* der Nachbarin? // he / to have become / captain and company commander // they / to have / over 40 degrees below //
Was sagt sie über den *Brief?* // to have taken / nine days //
Wie ist die Briefadresse? // he / to have written on it / to Mrs. ... //
Was **antwortet** *die Nachbarin?* // 40 degrees below / the poor boys //

7. Der siebte Abschnitt führt uns wieder an die Ostfront.

Was **fragt** *der Oberfeldarzt* den Chefarzt? // how many / to be / every day //
Was **antwortet** *der Chefarzt?* // half a dozen //
Wie reagieren sie *beide?* // to say / disgusting //
Was tun **sie** *beim Reden* nicht? // to look at each other //

8. Der achte Abschnitt zeigt uns noch einmal Frau Hesse.

Was findet *an diesem Dienstag* statt // they / to play / The Magic Flute //
Was hat *Frau Hesse* gemacht? // to have put on // lipstick //

9. Der neunte Abschnitt spielt wieder im Seuchenlazarett Smolensk.

Was **schreibt** *Schwester Elisabeth* an ihre Eltern? // without God / not / to endure / it //
Der Unterarzt kommt. Was **fragt ihn** *Schwester Elisabeth?* // to give / some more //
Der Unterarzt antwortet: Nein. Wie **sagt er das?** // as though / to be ashamed //
Die Sanitäter tragen Hauptmann Hesse hinaus. Draußen poltert es. Was **fragt** *einer im Saal?* // why / they / not / to be able / to lay down / dead persons / slowly //
Was **singt** *sein Nachbar* leise? // ... / snappy / to be / infantry //
Was erfahren wir über den *Unterarzt?* // to go / from bed to bed // every day // day and night // for days // throughout the nights //
Wie **geht er?** // bent // to carry / all of Russia / room //
Was geschieht *draußen?* // two carriers / to stumble away / empty stretcher //
Was **sagt** *der eine?* // number 4 //

10. Der zehnte und letzte Abschnitt bringt uns zurück zu Ulla.

Was **malt** *sie am Abend* mit großen Buchstaben in ihr Schreibheft? // war / all fathers / to be / soldiers //
Wie **schreibt** *sie das?* // ten times / capital letters / war / g / like / ditch //

C. Exercises for the B-Questions

Drill 6   *Give the German equivalents.*

The second company is accustomed to exactness.

They behave correctly.

They wonder if that is correct.

She feels close to the soldiers.

They feel for the pulse.

He does not feel well.

on returning home

while speaking

This is an example of the author's style.

The story deals with the war.

They believe in the future.

He is able to handle the company.

She has put on lipstick.

What do we learn about Lieutenant Ehlers?

That smells like a hospital (pharmacy).

The sign says . . . .

The third section is set on the Eastern front

The situation changes quickly.

The section takes us to Captain Hesse's home town.

The author divides his story into ten sections.

They refer to the contents.

To what setting does the story take us?

They are mistaken about this matter.

She reacts to the letter.

She worries about the poor boys.

What takes place on this Tuesday?

D. B-Questions

Study the following vocabulary:

das Kunstwerk, –e	work of art
lösen	to solve
versuchen	to try
das Stilmittel, –	technique
wählen	to choose
der Kontrast, –e	contrast
der Gegensatz, ⁀e	contrast
Das steht zu seiner Meinung im Gegensatz.	That is in contrast to or contrary to his opinion.
das Gegenteil, –e	contrary, opposite
Das Gegenteil ist richtig.	The opposite is correct.
im Gegenteil	on the contrary
der Widerspruch, ⁀e	contradiction
eine Rolle spielen	to play a part, to be of significance
wesentlich	essential
die Stimmung, –en	atmosphere
die Reihenfolge	sequence

Answer in the present or perfect tense.

1. Die Stilmittel

Wie beginnt der Autor die Erzählung und wie jeden Abschnitt?
Was, glauben Sie, will er damit sagen?
Auf welche Schauplätze führt uns die Erzählung?
Wie ist die Reihenfolge dieser Schauplätze?
Warum, glauben Sie, wählt der Autor diese Reihenfolge? (Answer with the expressions *contrast, contrary to, opposite,* and *contradiction*).

2. Der Inhalt

Unsere nächste Perspektive auf die Erzählung ist: die Menschen und der Krieg.

Was ist der Krieg für die Personen der Erzählung? (*a*) für die Lehrerin; (*b*) für Ulla; (*c*) für den Bataillonskommandeur; (*d*) für Leutnant Ehlers und Hauptmann Hesse; (*e*) für Herrn Hansen und Fräulein Severin; (*f*) für den Sanitäter und die Krankenträger; (*g*) für Frau Hesse; (*h*) für die Nachbarin; (*i*) für den Oberfeldarzt und den Chefarzt; (*k*) für Schwester Elisabeth; (*l*) für den Unterarzt; (*m*) für zwei Soldaten im Lazarett.

E. C-Questions (Essay)

1. Der Bataillonskommandeur sagt im dritten Abschnitt: „Die Zweite ist an das Korrekte (*exactness*) gewöhnt". Der Gegensatz von **exakt** und **unexakt** spielt in der Geschichte eine wesentliche Rolle. Beschreiben Sie einige Personen unter dem Aspekt des Exakten und des Unexakten. Wie sehen die exakten Menschen den Krieg, und wie sehen ihn die unexakten?

2. Wie sieht der Autor selbst den Krieg?
   Wie ist die ganze Stimmung der Erzählung?
   Unsere erste Frage war: Wie beginnt der Autor die Erzählung?
   Die letzte Frage ist: Wie schließt er seine Erzählung?
   Was zeigen uns der Anfang und der Schluß, sowie die ganze Atmosphäre der Geschichte von der Weltanschauung des Autors?

Drill 7 *Follow the example: Give one or two English meanings of the noun and the expression of time, form the adjective by using the endings* **–ig, –isch, –(a)tisch, –istisch, –lich;** *then give the meaning of the complete expression.*

–ig

der Geist, spirit, intellect   **die geistige Situation,**   the intellectual situation

die Würd(e)	_____	der	_____	Alte _____
die Vorsicht	_____	der	_____	Bataillonskommandeur _____
der Verdacht	_____	der	_____	Mann _____

der Vordergrund	die	Kritik
der Hintergrund	die	Geschichte
die Gegenwart	die	Katastrophe
heut(e)	der	Mensch
gest(e)r(n)	das	Ereignis
morg(en)	der	Tag

–isch

der Typ	der	Zug
die Stadt	die	Industrie
die Anekdot(e)	der	Stil
die Iron(ie)	die	Kritik
die Histor(ie)	die	Situation
die Psycholog(ie)	das	Phänomen
die Krit(ik)	die	Analyse
die Ep(ik)	das	Werk

–(a)tisch

das Drama	die	Form
das Schema	der	Aufbau
das Problem	die	Deutung
das Programm	die	Zeitschrift

–istisch

der Charakter	das	Stilmittel
der Humor	die	Erzählung
der Stil	das	Prinzip
das Ideal	die	Weltanschauung

–lich

der Geist	der	Herr
die Schrift	der	Ausdruck
der Staat	die	Ordnung
das Vorbild	der	Arzt
die Gesellschaft	die	Situation
der Grund	die	Arbeit
der Ausdruck	die	Bedingung
die Geschicht(e)	die	Situation
die Kirch(e)	das	Gebiet
der Tag	die	Zeitung
der Monat	das	Programm
das Jahr	der	Rhythmus

CHAPTER

GRAMMATICAL REVIEW

THE SUBORDINATE CLAUSE: PART I

I. THE FRAMEWORK OF THE SUBORDINATE CLAUSE

In contrast to English, there is a clear distinction between the word order of the main clause (see Chapter 2, page 98) and that of the subordinate clause. The *subordinate clause* has *its own framework,* consisting of the following:

1. A *connecting word* in the *first position* which can be either a *subordinating conjunction,* an *interrogative conjunction,* or a *relative pronoun.*

2. The *complete predicate* (all parts of the verb or verbal expression together) in the *final position.* The *inflected verb form* is placed at the *very end.*

	Connecting word		*Predicate*
Er merkt,	**daß**	jemand ganz leise	**gekommen ist.**
Er fragt,	**ob**	der Junge auf Geld	**aufpaßt.**
Er sagt nicht,	**was**	er	**im Korb hat.**
Er weiß,	**wieviel**	drei mal neun	**sind.**
Das ist der Mann,	**der**	siebenundzwanzig Kaninchen	**hat.**

Subordinate clauses are attached to main clauses ("sentences") as syntactical units. The *subordinate clause* may be either the *Nachfeld* or the *Vorfeld* of the *main clause.*

1. The *subordinate clause* as the *Nachfeld* of the main clause:

Vorfeld	P1	Satzfeld	P2	Nachfeld
Der Mann	hat	den Jungen	gefragt,	**wie** alt er	ist.
Er	hat	den Jungen	gefragt,	**ob** er denn gar nicht	nach Hause geht.
Der Junge	hat	gleich	gewußt,	**daß** drei mal drei neun	ist.

2. The *subordinate clause* as the Vorfeld of the main clause:

Vorfeld	P1	Satzfeld	P2
Daß der Junge sehr müde **ist,**	sieht	der Mann sofort.	—
Wieviel drei mal drei **sind,**	weiß	der Junge gleich.	—

All subordinate clauses are marked off by commas!

Der Junge merkt, daß jemand gekommen ist.
Daß der Junge müde ist, merkt der Mann sofort.

Notice that when the subordinate clause takes the Vorfeld of the main clause the *inflected verbs of both clauses meet at the comma:*

——————— *Vorfeld* ——————— *P1* ——— *Satzfeld* ——

Daß   der Junge sehr müde **ist, sieht** der Mann sofort.

II.   SUBORDINATING CONJUNCTIONS: daß

The subordination of one main clause to another is achieved by linkage with **daß.**

Drill 1   Daß-*Clauses with Inseparable Verbs*   *Follow the example.*

Jemand **kommt** durch die Trümmer.
Er sieht, daß jemand durch die Trümmer **kommt.**

Jemand steht vor ihm.
Der Mann hat ein Messer in der Hand.
Der Mann hat einen Korb in der Hand.
Der Mann nimmt den Korb.

Der Mann hat etwas Erde an den Fingerspitzen.
Der Mann stößt mit dem Fuß an den Korb.
Der Mann ist etwas verwundert.
Der Mann bückt sich zu seinem Korb.
Der Mann ist ganz unruhig.

Drill 2   Daß-*Clauses with Separable Verbs*   *Follow the example.*

Der Mann denkt: Der Junge **paßt** auf Geld **auf.**
Der Mann denkt, **daß** der Junge auf Geld **aufpaßt.**

Der Junge sieht: Der Mann setzt den Korb ab.
Der Junge sieht: Der Mann klappt das Messer zu.
Der Mann sieht: Der Junge hebt einen Stein hoch.
Der Junge sieht: Der Mann geht weg.

Der Mann merkt: der Junge faßt seinen Stock fest an.
Der Junge sieht: Der Mann richtet sich auf.
Der Junge sieht: Der Mann dreht sich um.
Der Junge sieht: Der Mann kommt einen Schritt zurück.
Der Mann merkt: Der Junge sieht auf einmal müde aus.

Drill 3   *Combining Two* daß-*Clauses*   *Follow the examples.*

Der Junge merkt: Jemand **ist gekommen.**
Der Junge merkt, **daß** jemand **gekommen ist.**

Der Junge merkt: Jemand **steht** vor ihm.
Der Junge merkt, **daß** jemand vor ihm **steht.**

Der Junge merkt: Jemand **ist gekommen** und **steht** vor ihm.
Der Junge merkt, **daß** jemand **gekommen ist** und vor ihm **steht.**

Der Junge sieht: Der Mann setzt den Korb ab.
Der Junge sieht: Der Mann wischt das Messer hin und her.

Der Junge sieht: Der Mann setzt den Korb ab und wischt das Messer hin und her.
Der Junge sieht: Der Mann stößt mit dem Fuß an den Korb.
Der Junge sieht: Der Mann klappt das Messer zu.
Der Junge sieht: Der Mann stößt mit dem Fuß an den Korb und klappt das Messer zu.
Der Junge sieht: Der Mann nimmt den Korb hoch.
Der Junge sieht: Der Mann richtet sich auf.
Der Junge sieht: Der Mann nimmt den Korb hoch und richtet sich auf.

Note carefully the basic contrasts between German and English. The *English constructions* can be *expressed in German only* by means of a *subordinate clause introduced by* **daß.**

Sie **wollen, daß** er kommt.	They want him to come.
Sie **möchten, daß** er geht.	They would like him to go.
Sie **erwarten, daß** er bleibt.	They expect him to stay.

Drill 4   *Give the German equivalents.*

The man would like the boy to answer.
The man wants him to say everything.
The man expects the boy to react.
The man would like him to wait for him.
The man wants the boy to go home at night.
The man expects him to answer.

The man would like the boy to choose a rabbit.
The boy wants the man to believe him.
The boy would like the man to come back.
The boy expects the man to understand him.

The indirect statement is likewise produced by linkage with **daß.** Pay special attention to the *change* of the *personal* and reflexive *pronouns* in the *indirect forms* of the *statements.* It is the same in English! Remember that **sagen + zu** (to say to) is used with *direct quotes* but that **sagen + dative** (to tell) is used with *indirect quotes.* Words for emphasis such as **doch, ja,** etc., are usually *omitted* in the *indirect forms* of statements, commands, and questions.

Der Junge sagt: „**Ich kann mir denken**, was in dem Korb ist".
Der Junge sagt, **daß er sich denken kann,** was in dem Korb ist.

Die Jungens sagen: „**Wir müssen doch aufpassen**".
Die Jungens sagen, **daß sie aufpassen müssen.**

Der Mann **sagt zu** dem Jungen: „**Du bist** ja ein fixer Kerl".
Der Mann **sagt** dem Jungen, **daß er** ein fixer Kerl **ist.**

Der Mann **sagt zu** den Jungens: „**Ihr seid** ja fixe Kerle".
Der Mann **sagt** den Jungens, **daß sie** fixe Kerle **sind.**

Der Junge **sagt zu** dem Mann: „ **Sie können mir glauben**".
Der Junge **sagt** dem Mann, **daß er ihm glauben kann.**

Der Junge **sagt zu** den Leuten: „**Sie können mir glauben**".
Der Junge **sagt** den Leuten, **daß sie ihm glauben können.**

Drill 5 *Follow the example.*

Der Junge **sagt zu** dem Mann: „**Ich** schlafe nicht".
Der Junge **sagt** dem Mann, **daß er** nicht schläft.

Der Junge sagt zu dem Mann: „Ich muß aufpassen".
Der Junge sagt zu dem Mann: „Ich kann das nicht sagen".
Der Junge sagt zu dem Mann: „Ich passe nicht auf Geld auf".
Der Junge sagt zu dem Mann: „Ich kann mir denken, was in dem Korb ist".
Der Junge sagt zu dem Mann: „Ich habe gleich gewußt, wieviel dreimal neun sind".
Der Mann sagt zu dem Jungen: „Du bist ein fixer Kerl".
Der Mann sagt zu dem Jungen: „Du mußt noch warten".
Der Mann sagt zu dem Jungen: „Du mußt etwas essen".
Der Mann sagt zu dem Jungen: „Du kannst die Kaninchen sehen, wenn du willst".
Der Mann sagt zu dem Jungen: „Du mußt wissen, wie man einen Kaninchenstall baut".

The indirect command is likewise produced by linkage with **daß,** and requires the *use of the modal verb* **sollen** *in the subordinate clause.*

Der Mann sagt zu dem Jungen: „Geh nach Hause!"
Der Mann sagt dem Jungen, **daß er** nach Hause gehen **soll.**

Die Lehrerin sagt zu den Mädchen: „Schreibt mit großen Buchstaben!"
Die Lehrerin sagt den Mädchen, **daß sie** mit großen Buchstaben schreiben **sollen.**

Note carefully the basic contrast between German and English:

Der Mann sagt dem Jungen, **daß er** nach Hause gehen **soll.**

The man tells the boy to go home.

Die Lehrerin sagt Ulla, **daß sie** den Satz zehnmal abschreiben **soll.**

The teacher tells Ulla to copy the sentence ten times.

Drill 6 *Give the German equivalents.*

The man tells the boy to go home.
The man tells the boy to answer.
The man tells the boy to wait for him.
The man tells the boy to believe him.

The man tells the boy to decide.
The man tells the boy to trust him.
The man tells the boy to follow him.

III. SUBORDINATE CLAUSES WITH INTERROGATIVE CONJUNCTIONS

Direct questions are converted to indirect questions by using the original interrogative as an interrogative conjunction.

Er fragt den Jungen: „**Wie** alt **bist du?**"
Er fragt den Jungen, **wie** alt **er ist.**

Indirect questions are always subordinate clauses.

Drill 7 *Express the direct questions indirectly.*

Er fragt den Jungen: ,,Wie alt bist du?''
Er fragt den Jungen: ,,Wofür hast du den großen Stock?''
Er fragt den Jungen: ,,Worauf paßt du auf?''
Er fragt den Jungen: ,,Wieviel sind drei mal neun?''
Er fragt den Jungen: ,,Wer hat das gesagt?''
Er fragt den Jungen: ,,Was für ein Kaninchen willst du?''

Direct questions without an interrogative are *converted to indirect questions* by linkage with **ob.**

Er fragt den Jungen: ,,**Schläfst du** hier?''
Er fragt den Jungen, **ob er** hier **schläft.**

Drill 8 *Express the direct questions indirectly.*

Er fragt den Jungen: ,,Schläfst du hier?''
Er fragt den Jungen: ,,Hast du dafür den großen Stock?''
Er fragt den Jungen: ,,Paßt du auf Geld auf?''
Er fragt den Jungen: ,,Willst du die Kaninchen sehen?''
Er fragt den Jungen: ,,Mußt du nachts auch aufpassen?''
Er fragt den Jungen: ,,Rauchst du?''
Er fragt den Jungen: ,,Hast du eine Pfeife?''
Er fragt den Jungen: ,,Gehst du nicht nach Hause, wenn es dunkel wird?''
Er fragt den Jungen: ,,Hat der Lehrer nicht gesagt, daß die Ratten nachts schlafen?''

Note a basic contrast between German and English. The *English constructions* can be *expressed in German only* by means of an *indirect question* introduced by an *interrogative conjunction.* The modal verb **sollen** is required in the *subordinate clause.*

Sie **sagen** ihm, **was er machen soll.**	They tell him what to do.
Sie **sagen** ihm, **wohin er gehen soll.**	They tell him where to go.
Sie **sagen** ihm, **wie er es machen soll.**	They tell him how to do it.
Er **weiß, was er sagen soll.**	He knows what to say.
Er **weiß** nicht, **wie er sich verhalten soll.**	He does not know how to behave.

Drill 9 *Give the German equivalents.*

He does not know what to do.	They tell him how to do it.
They tell him what to do.	He does not know what to say.
He does not know where to go.	They tell him what to say.
They tell him where to go.	He does not know how to behave.
He does not know how to do it.	They tell him how to behave.

Drill 10   *Combination Drill   Indirect Statements and Questions* *Express the direct statements and questions indirectly.*

Der Mann fragt den Jungen: ,,Schläfst du?''

Der Junge sagt: ,,Ich schlafe nicht''.

Er sagt: ,,Ich muß aufpassen''.

Der Mann fragt den Jungen: ,,Hast du dafür den großen Stock?''

Er fragt den Jungen: ,,Worauf paßt du auf?''

Der Junge sagt: ,,Ich kann das nicht sagen''.

Der Mann fragt den Jungen: ,,Paßt du auf Geld auf?''

Der Junge antwortet: ,,Ich passe auf etwas anderes auf''.

Der Mann sagt: ,,Ich sage dir auch nicht, was ich im Korb habe''.

Der Junge sagt: ,,Ich kann mir denken, was in dem Korb ist''.

Der Mann sagt: ,,Du bist ein fixer Kerl''.

Er fragt den Jungen: ,,Wie alt bist du?''

Er fragt: ,,Wieviel sind drei mal neun?''

Der Junge sagt: ,,Ich habe gleich gewußt, wieviel drei mal neun sind''.

Der Mann sagt: ,,Du kannst die Kaninchen sehen, wenn du willst''.

Der Mann fragt: ,,Gehst du nicht nach Hause, wenn es dunkel wird?''

Der Mann fragt: ,,Hat der Lehrer nicht gesagt, daß die Ratten nachts schlafen?''

Der Mann sagt: ,,Du mußt wissen, wie man einen Kaninchenstall baut''.

Drill 11   *Combination Drill   Daß-Clauses, Indirect Commands, and Indirect Questions* *Give the German equivalents.*

The man would like the boy to answer.

The man tells the boy to answer.

The boy does not know what to answer.

The man wants the boy to go home.

The man tells the boy to go home.

The man tells the boy where to go.

The boy does not know where to go.

The man expects the boy to trust him.

The man tells the boy to trust him.

The man tells the boy what to do.

The boy does not know what to do.

IV.   SUBORDINATE CLAUSES REQUIRING AN ANTICIPATING da-COMPOUND

Da-*compounds* (page 39) are often used to *subsume a complete statement.*

Der Junge bleibt hier. Der Mann besteht **darauf.**

Der Mann hat recht. Der Junge zweifelt **daran.**

Er bekommt ein Kaninchen. Er freut sich **darauf.**

The *initial statement* can be *converted into a subordinate clause* by linkage with **daß.** The **da**-*compound* then anticipates the *content* of the *subordinate clause.*

Der Mann besteht **darauf, daß** der Junge hier bleibt.

Der Junge zweifelt **daran, daß** der Mann recht hat.

Er freut sich **darauf, daß** er ein Kaninchen bekommt.

Note carefully these basic contrasts between German and English:

Der Mann besteht **darauf, daß** der Junge hier   The man insists on the boy's staying here.
    bleibt.

Der Junge wartet **darauf, daß** der Mann zurückkommt.	The boy is waiting for the man to return.
Der Junge zweifelt **daran, daß** der Mann recht hat.	The boy doubts that the man is right.
Er freut sich **darauf, daß** er ein Kaninchen bekommt.	He is looking forward to getting a rabbit.
Der Mann hat **davon** gesprochen, **daß** er siebenundzwanzig Kaninchen hat.	The man spoke about the fact that he has twenty-seven rabbits.

Drill 12   *Answer the questions following the example.*

Der Junge sitzt in der Schuttwüste. Der Mann wundert sich **darüber.**
Worüber wundert sich der Mann? . . . **darüber, daß** der Junge in der Schuttwüste sitzt.

Er hat siebenundzwanzig Kaninchen. Der Mann spricht davon.
Wovon spricht der Mann? . . .

Der Junge antwortet ihm. Der Mann freut sich darüber.
Worüber freut sich der Mann? . . .

Der Junge möchte ein Kaninchen. Der Mann ist überzeugt davon.
Wovon ist der Mann überzeugt? . . .

Der Junge wartet auf ihn. Der Mann besteht darauf.
Worauf besteht der Mann? . . .

Der Junge glaubt dem Mann. Es geht darum.
Worum geht es? . . .

Jemand kommt. Der Junge wundert sich darüber.
Worüber wundert sich der Junge? . . .

Der Mann hat recht. Der Junge zweifelt daran.
Woran zweifelt der Junge? . . .

Der Mann kommt zurück. Der Junge verläßt sich darauf.
Worauf verläßt sich der Junge? . . .

Er bekommt ein weißes Kaninchen. Der Junge freut sich darauf.
Worauf freut sich der Junge? . . .

Der Mann holt ihn ab. Der Junge wartet darauf.
Worauf wartet der Junge? . . .

Er hat Kistenbretter zu Hause. Der Junge spricht davon.
Wovon spricht der Junge? . . .

Drill 13   *Now repeat Drill 12, answering the questions with complete sentences, following the example.*

Der Junge sizt in der Schuttwüste. Der Mann wundert sich **darüber.**
Worüber wundert sich der Mann?
Der Mann wundert sich **darüber, daß** der Junge in der Schuttwüste sitzt.

gähnen to yawn, gape; flimmern to glimmer, flicker; steilgereckt *here:* steeply rising

Nachts schlafen die Ratten doch But rats sleep at night; **hohl** hollow, *here:* empty, without glass; **vereinsamt** *here:* deserted; **einsam** lonely; **die Mauer, –n** wall; **das Staubgewölk(e)** (*sing.*) clouds of dust; **die Schornsteinreste** (*plur.*) the remains of chimneys; **der Schutt** rubble, debris; **die Wüste, –n** desert, wilderness; **dösen** to doze

ein bißchen a little; **blinzeln** to blink, *here:* to peek; **mit einmal = auf einmal** all at once; **leise** *here:* quiet; **das Geblinzel** blink, *here:* peek; **die Hose, –n** trousers, pants; **an den Hosenbeinen hoch** up the trouser legs

Er hatte die Augen zu His eyes were closed; **auf einmal** all at once; **noch dunkler** even darker; **merken** to notice; **ärmlich** *here:* shabby; **behost** "trousered"; **ziemlich** rather; **krumme Beine** bowlegs; **riskieren** to risk; **erkennen, a, a** to recognize; **das Messer, –** knife; **der Korb, ⸚e** basket; **die Erde** *here:* soil; **die Fingerspitze, –n** fingertip

Du schläfst hier wohl I assume you sleep here; **Er sah auf das Haargestrüpp herunter** He looked down at the mop of hair; **von oben** from above

auf·passen *here:* to watch out, stand guard; **nicken** to nod; **der Stock, ⸚e** stick

der Mut courage

mutig courageous, brave; **fest·halten, ie, a** to hold tightly

auf·passen auf (+ *acc.*) *here:* to stand guard over, watch out for

der Hosenboden, ⸚ seat of the pants

das Geld, –er money; **ab·setzen** to set down, put down; **wischen** to wipe; **hin und her** back and forth

verachten to despise, scorn; **die Verachtung** contempt, scorn

überhaupt nicht not at all; **verächtlich** scornful; **ganz etwas anderes** something quite different

LITERATURE

NACHTS SCHLAFEN DIE RATTEN DOCH
Wolfgang Borchert

Das hohle Fenster in der vereinsamten Mauer gähnte blaurot voll früher Abendsonne. Staubgewölke flimmerte zwischen den steilgereckten Schornsteinresten. Die Schuttwüste döste.

Er hatte die Augen zu. Mit einmal wurde es noch dunkler. Er merkte, daß jemand gekommen war und nun vor ihm stand, dunkel, leise. Jetzt haben sie mich! dachte er. Aber als er ein bißchen blinzelte, sah er nur zwei ärmlich behoste Beine. Die standen ziemlich krumm vor ihm, daß er zwischen ihnen hindurchsehen konnte. Er riskierte ein kleines Geblinzel an den Hosenbeinen hoch und erkannte einen älteren Mann. Der hatte ein Messer und einen Korb in der Hand. Und etwas Erde an den Fingerspitzen.

Du schläfst hier wohl, was? fragte der Mann und sah von oben auf das Haargestrüpp herunter. Jürgen blinzelte zwischen den Beinen des Mannes hindurch in die Sonne und sagte: Nein, ich schlafe nicht. Ich muß hier aufpassen. Der Mann nickte: So, dafür hast du wohl den großen Stock da?

Ja, antwortete Jürgen mutig und hielt den Stock fest.

Worauf paßt du denn auf?

Das kann ich nicht sagen. Er hielt die Hände fest um den Stock.

Wohl auf Geld, was? Der Mann setzte den Korb ab und wischte das Messer an seinem Hosenboden hin und her.

Nein, auf Geld überhaupt nicht, sagte Jürgen verächtlich. Auf ganz etwas anderes.

Was anderes eben Just something else

Na, denn nicht Well, don't then; **der Stoß, ⁻e** push, kick

stoßen, ie, o to push, kick; **der Fuß, ⁻e** foot; **zu·klappen** to close, snap shut

schätzen to esteem, value; **etwas gering·schätzen** to treat something with contempt; **füttern** to feed

Ich kann es mir denken I can imagine; **meinen** *here:* to say; **geringschätzig** contemptuous, disparaging; **das Kaninchenfutter** rabbit feed

Donnerwetter, ja! Good Heavens! You're right!; **Bist ja ein fixer Kerl** You really are a smart fellow

verwundert surprised, astonished

Oha, denk mal an, neun also Aha, think of that, so you're nine; **wie?** *here:* don't you? Eh?

drei mal neun three times nine

um Zeit zu gewinnen to gain time

klar clear, sure; **leicht** easy; **hindurch·sehen, a, e durch** (+ *acc.*) to look through; **noch mal = noch einmal** again; **gleich** at once, immediately

(das) stimmt (that's) right, correct; **genau soviel** exactly that many; **das Kaninchen, –** rabbit

Er machte einen runden Mund He gaped

noch ganz jung still very young

die Sicherheit certainty, safety; **sicher** certain

unsicher uncertain

immerzu = immer always

das Geflüster whispering

Seit Sonnabend schon Ever since Saturday; **flüstern** to whisper

das Brot, –e bread, loaf of bread

hoch·heben, o, o to lift up; **ein halbes Brot** half a loaf of bread; **die Blechschachtel, –n** tin box

Na, was denn?

Ich kann es nicht sagen. Was anderes eben.

Na, denn nicht. Dann sage ich dir natürlich auch nicht, was ich hier im Korb habe. Der Mann stieß mit dem Fuß an den Korb und klappte das Messer zu.

Pah, ich kann mir denken, was in dem Korb ist, meinte Jürgen geringschätzig, Kaninchenfutter.

Donnerwetter, ja! sagte der Mann verwundert, bist ja ein fixer Kerl. Wie alt bist du denn?

Neun.

Oha, denk mal an, neun also. Dann weißt du ja auch, wieviel drei mal neun sind, wie?

Klar, sagte Jürgen und um Zeit zu gewinnen, sagte er noch: Das ist ja ganz leicht. Und er sah durch die Beine des Mannes hindurch. Drei mal neun, nicht? fragte er noch mal, siebenundzwanzig. Das wußte ich gleich.

Stimmt, sagte der Mann, genau soviel Kaninchen habe ich.

Jürgen machte einen runden Mund: Siebenundzwanzig?

Du kannst sie sehen. Viele sind noch ganz jung. Willst du?

Ich kann doch nicht. Ich muß doch aufpassen, sagte Jürgen unsicher.

Immerzu, fragte der Mann, nachts auch?

Nachts auch. Immerzu. Immer. Jürgen sah an den krummen Beinen hoch. Seit Sonnabend schon, flüsterte er.

Aber gehst du denn gar nicht nach Hause? Du mußt doch essen.

Jürgen hob einen Stein hoch. Da lag ein halbes Brot. Und eine Blechschachtel.

rauchen to smoke; **die Pfeife, –n** pipe

drehen to turn; **Ich drehe = Ich drehe meine Zigaretten** I roll my own cigarettes; **die Zaghaftigkeit** shyness, timidity

an·fassen to take hold of, grasp; **zaghaft** shy, timid

Die hättest du ruhig mal ansehen können You'd have been welcome to look at them; **Vielleicht hättest du dir eines ausgesucht** Perhaps you would have chosen one for yourself

schade too bad; **sich bücken** to bend down; **vor allem** above all; **das Junge, –n** (adj.) the young one; **Aber du kannst hier ja nicht weg** But you can't get away from here

traurig sad

verraten, ie, a to betray, reveal, give something away; **der Verrat** betrayal, treason

sich auf·richten to straighten up; **sich um·drehen** to turn around; **der Schritt, –e** step

Da leben sie doch von = Davon leben sie doch That's what they live on

essen, a, e to eat; **essen von** (+ dat.) here: to feed on

zusammen·sacken to collapse

liegen, a, e to lie; **nämlich** namely, here: you see; **zeigen auf** (+acc.) to point at; **kriegen** to get, receive; **die Bombe, –n** bomb; **Das Licht war weg** The light was gone; **der Keller, –** cellar; **rufen, ie, u** to call; **erst vier** only four (years old)

plötzlich suddenly

müde tired

Du rauchst? fragte der Mann, hast du denn eine Pfeife?

Jürgen faßte seinen Stock fest an und sagte zaghaft: Ich drehe. Pfeife mag ich nicht.

Schade, der Mann bückte sich zu seinem Korb, die Kaninchen hättest du ruhig mal ansehen können. Vor allem die Jungen. Vielleicht hättest du dir eines ausgesucht. Aber du kannst hier ja nicht weg.

Nein, sagte Jürgen traurig, nein, nein.

Der Mann nahm den Korb und richtete sich auf. Na ja, wenn du hierbleiben mußt – schade. Und er drehte sich um. Wenn du mich nicht verrätst, sagte Jürgen da schnell, es ist wegen den Ratten. Die krummen Beine kamen einen Schritt zurück: Wegen den Ratten?

Ja, die essen doch von Toten. Von Menschen. Da leben sie doch von.

Wer sagt das?

Unser Lehrer.

Und du paßt nun auf die Ratten auf? fragte der Mann.

Auf die doch nicht! Und dann sagte er ganz leise: Mein Bruder, der liegt nämlich da unten. Da. Jürgen zeigte mit dem Stock auf die zusammengesackten Mauern. Unser Haus kriegte eine Bombe. Mit einmal war das Licht weg im Keller. Und er auch. Wir haben noch gerufen. Er war viel kleiner als ich. Erst vier. Er muß hier ja noch sein. Er ist doch viel kleiner als ich.

Der Mann sah von oben auf das Haargestrüpp. Aber dann sagte er plötzlich: Ja, hat euer Lehrer euch denn nicht gesagt, daß die Ratten nachts schlafen?

Nein, flüsterte Jürgen und sah mit einmal ganz müde aus, das hat er nicht gesagt.

Das ist aber ein Lehrer That's some teacher; **ruhig** *here:* safely, without worrying

nicht mal = **nicht einmal** not even

die Kuhle, –n = **die Grube** pit, hole; **lauter** *here:* lots of; **unruhig** restless; **ab·holen** to pick up; **mit·bringen, a, a** to bring along

grau grey; **leise** *here:* softly; **sehen, a, e auf** (+ *acc.*) to look at

steigen, ie, ie to climb; **Euer Lehrer soll einpacken** Your teacher ought to pack up

auf·stehen, a, a to stand up

so ein = **solch ein** such a

versuchen to try; **schon im Weggehen** already leaving, already walking away; **solange** *here:* a while; **warten** to wait; **der Kaninchenstall, ⁻e** rabbit cage, hutch; **bauen,** to build

bestimmt definite, certain; **das Brett, –er** board; **die Kiste, –n** crate

auf·regen to excite; **da drin** = **darin**

Er lief auf die Sonne zu He ran toward the sun; **hindurch·scheinen, ie, ie durch** (+ *acc.*) to shine through; **schwenken** to swing; **aufgeregt** excited

Na, sagte der Mann, das ist aber ein Lehrer, wenn er das nicht mal weiß. Nachts schlafen die Ratten doch. Nachts kannst du ruhig nach Hause gehen. Nachts schlafen sie immer. Wenn es dunkel wird, schon.

Jürgen machte mit seinem Stock kleine Kuhlen in den Schutt. Lauter kleine Betten sind das, dachte er, alles kleine Betten. Da sagte der Mann (und seine krummen Beine waren ganz unruhig dabei): Weißt du was? Jetzt füttere ich schnell meine Kaninchen und wenn es dunkel wird, hole ich dich ab. Vielleicht kann ich eins mitbringen. Ein kleines oder, was meinst du?

Jürgen machte kleine Kuhlen in den Schutt. Lauter kleine Kaninchen. Weiße, graue, weißgraue. Ich weiß nicht, sagte er leise und sah auf die krummen Beine, wenn sie wirklich nachts schlafen.

Der Mann stieg über die Mauerreste weg auf die Straße. Natürlich, sagte er von da, euer Lehrer soll einpacken, wenn er das nicht mal weiß.

Da stand Jürgen auf und fragte: Wenn ich eins kriegen kann? Ein weißes vielleicht?

Ich will mal versuchen, rief der Mann schon im Weggehen, aber du mußt hier solange warten. Ich gehe dann mit dir nach Hause, weißt du? Ich muß deinem Vater doch sagen, wie so ein Kaninchenstall gebaut wird. Denn das müßt ihr ja wissen.

Ja, rief Jürgen, ich warte. Ich muß ja noch aufpassen, bis es dunkel wird. Ich warte bestimmt. Und er rief: Wir haben auch noch Bretter zu Hause. Kistenbretter, rief er.

Aber das hörte der Mann schon nicht mehr. Er lief mit seinen krummen Beinen auf die Sonne zu. Die war schon rot vom Abend und Jürgen konnte sehen, wie sie durch die Beine hindurchschien, so krumm waren sie. Und der Korb schwenkte aufgeregt hin und her. Kaninchenfutter war da drin. Grünes Kaninchenfutter, das war etwas grau vom Schutt.

I. QUESTIONNAIRE

A. Exercises for the A-Questions

1. The use of the modifying words doch, ja, wohl, denn, ruhig

Borchert uses many modifying words characteristic of colloquial speech. One reacts more subjectively to something which has been said by using **doch, ja, wohl, denn,** and **ruhig:**

(a) In statements

With **doch** you can express an opinion more emphatically.

Er war doch mehr für das Leichte.	He really was more for light stuff.
Er lacht doch gern.	He really likes to laugh.
Das wissen Sie doch!	You do know that!
Du mußt doch essen!	You do have to eat!

With **doch** you can show that you are of the opposite opinion.

Nachts schlafen die Ratten doch!	But rats sleep at night!
Ich kann doch nicht!	But I can't!
Ich muß doch aufpassen!	But I have to watch out!

With **ja** you can express surprise.

Du bist ja ein fixer Kerl.	You are a smart lad.

With **ja** you can also confirm a well-known fact.

Denn das müßt ihr ja wissen.	For you have to know that.
Ich muß ja noch aufpassen.	I still have to watch out!

With **ruhig,** used as a sentence adverb, you show that you have no objections or want to give assurance.

Du kannst die Kaninchen ruhig ansehen.	You are welcome to look at the rabbits.
Nachts kannst du ruhig nach Hause gehen.	You can go home at night without worrying.

(b) In questions

With **wohl** you show that a positive answer is expected.

Du schläfst hier wohl?	I take it you sleep here?
Dafür hast du wohl den Stock da?	I take it that is why you have that stick?
Du paßt wohl auf Geld auf?	I suppose you are standing guard over money?

With **denn** you show an immediate interest.

Worauf paßt du denn auf?   What *are* you watching out for?
Wie alt bist du denn?   How old *are* you?

(c) In exclamations

With **ja** you can express your surprise.

Donnerwetter, ja!   Good Heavens!

With **denn** you show your resoluteness.

Na, denn nicht!   Don't then!
Nun gut denn!   All right then!

2. **Study the following expressions**

1. Er **paßt** nicht **auf die** Ratten **auf.**   He does not watch out for the rats.
2. Er **paßt** nicht **auf** Geld **auf.**   He does not stand guard over money.
3. Er kann **es sich denken.**   He can imagine.
4. Er **bückt sich** zu seinem Korb.   He bends down to his basket.
5. Er **richtet sich auf.**   He straightens up.
6. Er **dreht sich um.**   He turns around.
7. Er **zeigt** mit dem Stock **auf die** Mauern.   He points with his stick at the walls.
8. Sein kleiner Bruder war **erst** vier Jahre alt.   His little brother was only four years old.
9. Er weiß das **nicht einmal.**   He does not even know that.
10. Er weiß das **sogar.**   He even knows that.
11. Er **sieht auf die** krummen Beine.   He looks at the bandy-legs.
12. Was sagt er **noch?**   What else does he say?
13. Er **wechselt das Thema.**   He changes the topic.
14. Er **macht einen Vorschlag.**   He makes a suggestion.
15. Er **stellt eine Frage.**   He asks a question.
16. Er sagt eine **Notlüge.**   He tells a white lie.
17. Welcher Zusammenhang **besteht zwischen den** beiden Erzählungen?   What connection exists between the two stories?
18. Er **zweifelt an dieser** Aussage.   He doubts this statement.
19. Er **besteht auf dieser** Bedingung.   He insists on this condition.
20. Er **hat Mitleid mit dem** Jungen.   He pities the boy.
21. **Es geht um die** Zukunft des Jungen.   The boy's future is at stake.
22. Er **verläßt sich auf seinen** Freund.   He relies on his friend.

Drill 1   Ich kann es mir denken *(I can imagine)*   *Follow the example.*

> **Ich** kann es **mir** denken.   **Er**
> **Er** kann es **sich** denken.   **Wir**

> Wir _____
> Die Frau _____
> Du _____
> Das Kind _____
> Ihr _____
> Die Leute _____

Drill 2   *The Use of* sogar *(even) and of* nicht einmal *(not even)*   **Sogar** *and* **nicht einmal** *take the same position as the negation* **nicht**. *Refer* **sogar** *to the word in bold print. Follow the examples.*

> **Er** weiß das.   **Sogar er** weiß das.
> Er **weiß** das.   Er **weiß** das **sogar**.
> Er weiß **das**.   Er weiß **sogar das**.

> Er **kennt** ihn.   _____
> **Er** kennt ihn.   _____
> Er kennt **ihn**.   _____

> **Er** versteht das.   _____
> Er **versteht** das.   _____
> Er versteht **das**.   _____

> Er **antwortet** ihm.   _____
> Er fragt **ihn**.   _____
> **Er** sieht ihn.   _____

Now practice this drill again, this time using **nicht einmal.** Do it in the same way.

B. A-Questions

Answer with complete sentences. Change the direct quotes to indirect quotes, if not otherwise indicated. Drop the modifying words **doch, ja, wohl, denn,** and **ruhig** when quoting indirectly.

1. Wolfgang Borchert beginnt seine Erzählung mit einer Beschreibung.

   Woraus besteht *der Schauplatz der Erzählung?* // hollow window / deserted wall / clouds of dust / remains of chimneys //
   Wie ist die Atmosphäre des Schauplatzes? // wilderness of rubble / to doze //

2. Nach der Beschreibung des Schauplatzes lernen wir die Personen der Erzählung kennen.

   Wie sitzt *Jürgen* in den Trümmern? // eyes / closed //
   Was bemerkt er *auf einmal?* // to become / even darker //
   Was **merkt er?** // that / somebody / to have come / and / to stand in front of //

Was **denkt er?** // that / they / to have / now //
Er blinzelt ein bißchen. Was **sieht er?** // two / shabbily trousered legs //
Was **kann er?** // to look through / between / them //
Wen **erkennt er?** // older man //
Wie sieht *der Mann* aus? // to have / knife / and / basket / hand / and / soil / finger-tips //

3. Der Mann beginnt ein Gespräch.

Was **fragt er Jürgen?** // whether / he / to sleep / there //
Was **erwidert Jürgen?** // that / he / not / to sleep //
Was **sagt er?** // that / he / to have to watch out //
Der Mann nickt. Was **fragt er dann?** // whether / Jürgen / to have / big stick / for that //
Wie reagiert *Jürgen?* // to answer / courageously / yes // to hold / stick / tightly //
Der Mann fragt weiter. Was **will er wissen?** // what / Jürgen / to stand guard over //
Was **entgegnet Jürgen?** // that / he / not / to be able / to say / that //
Wie verhält *er* sich dabei? // to hold / hands / stick //
Was **glaubt der Mann?** // that / Jürgen / to stand guard over money //
Was tut *er?* // to set down / basket //
Was **sagt Jürgen verächtlich?** / (a) / that / he / not at all / to stand guard over / money / (b) / that / he / to watch out for / something quite different //
Was **kann Jürgen aber nicht?** // to say it //

4. Der Mann wechselt das Thema.

Was **sagt er Jürgen auch nicht?** // what / he / to have / basket //
Was tut *der Mann* dann? // to kick / foot / basket / and / to clap shut / knife //
Was **meint Jürgen** da **geringschätzig?** // that / he / can / imagine / what / to be / basket // rabbit food //
Der Mann ist verwundert. Was **fragt er Jürgen?** // how old / he / to be //
Wie **alt ist Jürgen?** // nine years //
Was **fragt der Mann** Jürgen? // whether / he / to know / how much / to be / three times nine //
Jürgen sagt: Klar. Was **erwidert er?** // that / that / to be / quite easy //
Was **hat er gleich gewußt?** // that / three times nine / to be / twenty-seven //
Der Mann sagt: Stimmt. Was **erzählt er Jürgen jetzt?** // that / he / to have / exactly that many rabbits //
Wie reagiert *Jürgen* darauf? // to gape //

5. Der Mann macht einen Vorschlag.

Was **schlägt der Mann vor?** // that / Jürgen / can / see / them //
Was **sagt er** über die Kaninchen? // that / many / to be / still very young //
Was **fragt er Jürgen?** // whether / he / to want / to see / them //
Was **erwidert Jürgen?** / (a) / that / he / not / to be able / (b) / that / he / to have to watch out //
Was **erfährt der Mann jetzt?** // that / Jürgen / to watch out / always / even / at night //
Was **flüstert Jürgen?** // that / he / to watch out / ever / since / Saturday //

Welche **Frage stellt *der Mann*** da? // whether / he / not at all / to go home //
Was **meint *er* noch?** // that / Jürgen / to have to eat //
Wie reagiert *Jürgen* darauf? // to lift up / stone //
Was befindet sich ***unter dem Stein?*** // to lie / half a loaf of bread / and / tin box //
Was **fragt *der Mann*** Jürgen? / (*a*) / whether / he / to smoke / (*b*) / whether / he / to have / pipe //
Wie **antwortet *Jürgen?*** // shy // to grasp / stick / tightly //
Was **entgegnet *er?*** // that / he / to roll / cigarettes //

6. Die Erzählung erreicht ihren Wendepunkt. Jürgen erzählt seine Geschichte.

Der Mann sagt: Schade. Welchen zweiten **Vorschlag macht *er?*** // that / Jürgen / to choose / one / for himself //
Wie **antwortet *Jürgen?*** // sad / no //
Was macht *der Mann* da? // to take / basket / and / to turn around //
Was **sagt Jürgen *da schnell?*** // "it is because of the rats" // (*direct quote*)
Was **sagt *Jürgen*** über die Ratten? // that / rats / to feed on / dead bodies / people //
Wer **sagt das?** // teacher //
Welche **Frage stellt *der Mann?*** // whether / Jürgen / to watch out for / rats //
Was **erzählt *Jürgen* dem Mann da leise?** // that / brother / to lie / down there //
Was **tut *Jürgen?*** // to point at / walls / stick //
Was **erzählt *er* weiter?** // that / house / to get (*imperf.*) bomb // that / light / to be gone (*imperf.*) / cellar / all at once // and / brother / too //
that / they / still / to have called // that / he / to be (*imperf.*) much smaller / than / Jürgen // that / he / to be (*imperf.*) only four // that / he / must be / still there //

7. Der Mann sagt eine Notlüge und macht einen dritten Vorschlag.

Was **fragt *er* plötzlich?** // whether / teacher / not / to have said / that / rats / to sleep / at night //
Was **erwidert *Jürgen?*** // that / teacher / not / to have said / that //
Wie antwortet *er?* // to whisper / and / to look / all at once / quite tired //
Was **sagt *der Mann* noch einmal?** // that / rats / sleep / at night //
Was **kann *Jürgen* nachts?** // to go home / without worrying //
Was **macht *Jürgen* jetzt mit seinem Stock?** // little holes / rubble //
Was **denkt *er* dabei?** // that / these / to be / lots of little beds //
Wie verhält sich der Mann? // his bowlegs / to be / quite restless //
Was **sagt *er* darauf?** // that / he / quickly / to feed / rabbits //
Was **schlägt *er* Jürgen vor?** // that / he / to pick up / him / when / it / to become / dark //
Was **kann *er* vielleicht?** // (to) bring along / one //
Was **macht *Jürgen* wieder?** // little holes / rubble //
Was **sieht *er* in seiner Phantasie?** // lots of little rabbits // white ones / grey ones / white-grey ones //
Was sagt *er* leise? // if / they / to sleep / really / at night //

Den Mann steigt über die Mauerreste weg auf die Straße. Was **sagt er** jetzt über den Lehrer? // that / teacher / ought / to pack up / if / he / not even / to know / that //

8. Wie endet die Geschichte?

Wie reagiert *Jürgen* jetzt? // to stand up //
Welche **Frage stellt er** jetzt? // if / he / can / get / one //
Der Mann ist schon im Weggehen. Was **ruft er?** // that / Jürgen / to have to wait / a while //
Was **soll Jürgen wissen?** // that / he / then / to go home / with him //
Was **müssen der Vater und Jürgen wissen?** // how / one (man) / to build / such a rabbit cage //
Was **ruft Jürgen zurück?** // that / he / to wait / certainly //
Was **muß er noch?** // (to) stand guard / until / to become dark //
Was **ruft er noch?** // that / they / to have / crate boards / at home //
Wie reagiert *der Mann?* // not / to hear / that / anymore //
Wie geht **er** weg? // to run / towards / sun //
Was **kann Jürgen sehen?** // how / sun / to shine / through / bowlegs //
Was **sieht er noch?** // that / basket / to swing / excited / back and forth //
Wie **ist das Kaninchenfutter im Korb?** // green / a little grey / rubble //

C. Exercises for the B-Questions

Drill 3 *Give the German equivalents.*

He bends down to his basket.
We can imagine.
He straightens up.
He turns around.
He changes the topic.
The boy does not watch out for the rats.
The boy does not stand guard over money.
The man doubts this statement.
His little brother was only four years old.
He points with his stick at the wall.
He looks at the bowlegs.
He even knows that.

He does not even know that.
The man pities the boy.
What else does he say?
The boy's future is at stake.
What connection exists between the two stories?
He asks a question.
He insists on this condition.
He tells a white lie.
He makes a suggestion.
He relies on his friend.

Drill 4 *Combination Drill* *Give the German equivalents.*

He is sitting in front of the wall.
He sits down in front of the wall.
He bends down to his basket.
He straightens up.
The boy thinks of his brother.

I can imagine.
The situation changes.
He changes the topic.
He is looking forward to the rabbits.
He is looking at the bowlegs.

He is surprised about the boy.

He wonders if that is correct.

The teacher is mistaken about this matter.

He is convinced of his idea.

He is only nine years old.

He decides immediately.

He relies on his friend.

He does not live with his parents.

He does not stand guard over money.

He doubts this statement.

He does not watch out for the rats.

He turns around.

He is surprised about the boy.

He worries about the boy.

He is concerned about the boy.

He pities the boy.

He makes a suggestion.

He strives for a solution.

He insists on this condition.

He tells a white lie.

He asks a question.

What connection exists between the two stories?

That puzzles the boy.

That is a problem for the boy.

That is important for the man.

That does not matter to the boy.

The boy's future is at stake.

D. B-Questions

Answer with complete sentences. Quote indirectly if not otherwise indicated. Begin each quote with: **Er sagt, er fragt,** or **er antwortet . . .**

1. **Woraus besteht die Welt Jürgens am Anfang der Erzählung?**

   Wo sitzt Jürgen? // in front of / hollow window / beside / deserted wall / under / clouds of dust / between / remains of chimneys / in / wilderness of rubble //

2. **In diese Welt kommt ein älterer Mann.**

   Wie sieht Jürgen ihn? // eyes closed // all at once / darker // to notice / somebody / to have come / and / to stand in front of // to see / two shabbily trousered legs // to be able / to look through // to recognize / older man // to have / knife / basket / hand / soil / fingertips //
   Wie ist Jürgens Reaktion? // to think / to have him / now //
   Warum reagiert Jürgen so?

3. **Wie verhält sich der alte Mann zunächst, und wie reagiert Jürgen?**

   Was will der Mann wissen? / (a) / Jürgen / to sleep / there / (b) / for what / to have / big stick / (c) / what / Jürgen / to stand guard over / (d) / whether / to stand guard over / money //
   Wie antwortet Jürgen dem Mann zunächst? / (a) / not / to sleep / (b) / not / to stand guard over money / (c) / to watch out for / something / quite different / (d) / not to be able / to say it //
   Wie sind Jürgens Reaktionen in diesem Teil der Geschichte? // to answer / courageously // to hold / hands / tightly / stick // to speak / scornfully //
   Warum, glauben Sie, reagiert Jürgen in dieser Weise?

4. Wie erfährt der Mann, warum Jürgen in der Schuttwüste sitzt und worauf er aufpaßt? // to change / topic //

Welche Fragen stellt er? // to ask / Jürgen / (a) / how old / (b) / how much / three times nine // to say / to have / exactly that many rabbits // to make / first suggestion // to say / (a) / Jürgen / can / see / them / (b) / many / still very young //
Welche Fragen stellt er dann? // to ask / Jürgen / (a) / to want / to see / (b) / always / to stand guard / also / at night / (c) / not at all to go home / (d) / to smoke / (e) / to have / pipe //
Wie sind Jürgens Reaktionen jetzt? // at first / to answer / contemptuously // he / to imagine / what / to be / basket // rabbit food // then / to say / (a) / to be nine years old / (b) / to have known immediately / how much / three times nine // then / he / to learn about / rabbits / and / to purse up his lips // now / to whisper / to have to watch out / always / at night too // ever / since Saturday // to lift up / stone / and / to show / man / half a loaf / tin box // to grasp / stick / tightly // to say shyly / to roll / cigarettes //
Warum reagiert Jürgen plötzlich anders?

5. Wie erreicht die Erzählung ihren Wendepunkt? // man / to make / second suggestion // to tell / Jürgen / to choose / one // Jürgen / to answer sad // no // man / to take / basket / and / to turn around // then / Jürgen / to say / quickly / because of / rats (*direct quote*) // man / to ask / Jürgen / to watch out for / rats //
Warum sagt Jürgen auf einmal, warum er in der Schuttwüste sitzt?

6. Erzählen Sie Jürgens Geschichte! Beginnen Sie alle Sätze mit: **Jürgen sagt, ...** / (a) / brother / to lie / down there / (b) / house / to get (*imperf.*) / bomb / (c) / light / to be gone (*imperf.*) / cellar / brother / too / (d) / to have called / (e) / he / to be / much smaller / (f) / to be / only four / (g) / must be / still there / (h) / teacher / to have said / rats / to feed on / dead bodies //

7. Was macht der Mann nach Jürgens Erzählung? Und wie verhält sich Jürgen jetzt? // to tell / white lie // to ask / teacher / not / to have said / rats / to sleep / at night // to tell / Jürgen / to go home / without worrying / at night // to say / to feed / rabbits / quickly // then / to make / third suggestion // to say / to bring along / one // Jürgen / to whisper // to look / quite tired // to make little holes / stick / rubble // to think / lots of little beds // to think / lots of little rabbits // to say / softly / if / to sleep / really / at night (*direct quote*) //
Wie verstehen Sie Jürgens Verhalten?

8. Wie sieht die Welt Jürgens am Schluß der Geschichte aus? // Jürgen / to stand up // to ask / question / if I can get one (*direct quote*) // to know / man / to go home / with him // to have to know / how / one / to build // to call / (a) / to wait / certainly / (b) / to have to watch out / until / to become dark / (c) / to have / crate boards // to see / (a) / how / man / to run / sun / (b) / how / sun / to shine / through / (c) / how /

basket / to swing / excited // to know / green grass / to be / basket // a little grey / rubble //

Was hat Jürgens Verhalten geändert?

E. C-Questions (Essay)

1. Wie ist die „äußere" und wie die „innere" Welt Jürgens vor und nach dem Wendepunkt der Erzählung?

2. Wie hilft der alte Mann Jürgen?

3. Warum könnte man sagen, daß der letzte Satz der Erzählung symbolisch für die Geschichte ist?

4. Wie ist die Atmosphäre in der ersten Geschichte und wie in der zweiten?
    Vergleichen Sie das Ende der ersten Geschichte mit dem Schluß der zweiten.
    Was können Sie jetzt über die Weltanschauung des Autors sagen?

Wolfang Borchert hat ein kleines Gedicht geschrieben:

der Leuchtturm, ⸚e lighthouse

der Dorsch, –e cod (fish)
der Stint, –e smelt

die Not distress

Ich möchte Leuchtturm sein
in Nacht und Wind —
für Dorsch und Stint,
für jedes Boot —
und bin doch selbst
ein Schiff in Not!

Welchen Zusammenhang können Sie zwischen diesem Gedicht und den beiden Erzählungen sehen?

CHAPTER

CHAPTER 9

GRAMMATICAL REVIEW

4

THE SUBORDINATE CLAUSE: PART II

I. THE TEMPORAL CONJUNCTIONS wenn AND als

A. Wenn (Whenever)

If the *event* or *action* of the subordinate clause *occurs* or *occurred repeatedly,* **wenn** is used with the future tense, present tense, and all past tenses. In this case, **wenn** basically means *whenever.*

Wenn (immer wenn) er ihnen das Ergebnis mitteilt, strahlen ihre Gesichter.
Wenn (immer wenn) er ihnen das Ergebnis mitteilte, strahlten ihre Gesichter.
Wenn (immer wenn) er ihnen das Ergebnis mitteilte, haben ihre Gesichter gestrahlt.

B. Wenn (When) or als (When)

If the *event* or *action* of the subordinate clause *occurs or occurred once,* **wenn** is used with the future tense and present tense, **als** is used with all past tenses.

Wenn (als) er das Ergebnis dieses Tages sieht, klopft er ihm auf die Schulter.
Als er das Ergebnis dieses Tages sah, klopfte er ihm auf die Schulter.
Als er das Ergebnis dieses Tages sah, hat er ihm auf die Schulter geklopft.

However, **als** may *also* be used in *narrating past events* in the *present tense,* as we generally do in the A-Questions of the questionnaires.

	Past	*Present*	*Future*
Whenever	wenn	wenn	wenn
When	als	wenn, als	wenn

1. The use of the past tenses in wenn- and als-clauses

The *imperfect* is preferred in **wenn-** and **als-**clauses, when the main clause uses the perfect tense, and the *events* or *actions* of *both* clauses occurred *at the same time.*

Als man ihn **kontrollierte, hat** er höllisch **aufgepaßt.**

159

The *pluperfect* is used, when the *event* or *action* of the subordinate clause occurred *before* the event or action of the main clause.

Als sie **weggegangen war, hat** er wieder **angefangen** zu zählen.

C.   **Distinguish between** wenn **and** wann

Wenn meaning *at the time when* introduces *time clauses*. **Wann** meaning *at what time* introduces *direct and indirect questions.*

1.   **Direct question**

Er fragt: ,,**Wann** kommt der Junge nach Hause?"

2.   **Indirect question**

Wir wissen nicht, **wann** der Junge nach Hause kommt.

3.   **Time clause**

Er kommt nach Hause, **wenn** es dunkel wird.

The subordinate clause introduced by **wenn** or **als** may be either the Vorfeld or the Nachfeld of the main clause.

Vorfeld	P2	Satzfeld	P2	Nachfeld
Wenn es dunkel wird,	holt	der Mann den Jungen	ab.	
Der Mann	holt	den Jungen	ab,	**wenn es dunkel wird.**
Als es dunkel wurde,	holte	der Mann den Jungen	ab.	
Der Mann	holte	den Jungen	ab,	**als es dunkel wurde.**

II.   **THE CONDITIONAL** wenn **(IF)**

Wenn introduces *conditional* as well as *temporal clauses.*

Compare the use of the temporal **wenn** (whenever, when) with the conditional **wenn** (if):

Es macht nicht viel, **wenn** er sich um einen in der Stunde verzählt.
Er paßt höllisch auf, **wenn** er zählt.

It does not matter much *if* he miscounts one an hour.
He is terribly careful *when* (*whenever*) he counts.

III. THE MEANINGS OF als

Der Kumpel hat ihm geholfen, **als** es um seine Existenz ging.

The buddy helped him *when* it was a question of his existence.

Als Oberstatistiker verzählt er sich nicht.

As a head statistician he does not miscount.

Er war **schneller als** die andern.

He was *faster than* the others.

Nichts als Zahlen.

Nothing but numbers.

IV. THE MEANINGS OF da

Wer ist **da?**

Who is *there?*

Da bin ich!

Here I am.

Da hat er höllisch aufgepaßt.

Then he was terribly careful.

Da er nichts zu rauchen hat, ist er wütend.

Since he has nothing to smoke, he is furious.

Drill 1   Wenn-*Clauses*   *The event occurs often. Follow the example.*

Er teilt ihnen das Ergebnis mit. Dann strahlen ihre Gesichter.
Wann strahlen ihre Gesichter?
. . ., **wenn** er ihnen das Ergebnis mitteilt.

Er empfindet Mitleid. Dann schenkt er ihnen ein paar Ziffern.
Wann schenkt er ihnen ein paar Ziffern?

Er hat nichts zu rauchen. Dann gibt er nur den Durchschnitt an.
Wann gibt er nur den Durchschnitt an?

Er ist wütend. Dann gibt er unter dem Durchschnitt an.
Wann gibt er unter dem Durchschnitt an?

Er ist froh. Dann ist er großzügig.
Wann ist er großzügig?

Die Zahl ist fünfstellig. Dann sind sie zufrieden.
Wann sind sie zufrieden?

Drill 2   *Now repeat Drill 1 and answer the questions with complete sentences. Follow the example.*

Er teilt ihnen das Ergebnis mit. Dann strahlen ihre Gesichter.
Wann strahlen ihre Gesichter?
Ihre Gesichter strahlen, **wenn** er ihnen das Ergebnis mitteilt.

Drill 3   Wenn-*Clauses*   *The event occurred often. Follow the example.*

Er empfand Mitleid. Dann hat er ihnen ein paar Ziffern geschenkt.
Wann hat er ihnen ein paar Ziffern geschenkt?
Wenn er Mitleid empfand, hat er ihnen ein paar Ziffern geschenkt.

Seine kleine Geliebte kam über die Brücke. Dann ist sein Herz stehen geblieben.
Wann ist sein Herz stehen geblieben?

Sie kam abends zurück. Dann hat sein Herz wieder ausgesetzt.
Wann hat sein Herz wieder ausgesetzt?

Sie ging auf der andern Seite vorbei. Dann hat er aufgehört zu zählen.
Wann hat er aufgehört zu zählen?

Sie war nicht mehr zu sehen. Dann hat er wieder angefangen zu zählen.
Wann hat er wieder angefangen zu zählen?

Drill 4   Als-*Clauses*   *The event occurred once. Following the example.*

Man kontrollierte ihn. Da (*then*) hat er höllisch aufgepaßt.
Wann hat er höllisch aufgepaßt?
Als man ihn kontrollierte, hat er höllisch aufgepaßt.

Es ging um seine Existenz. Da hat ihm der Kumpel geholfen.
Wann hat ihm der Kumpel geholfen?

Der Oberstatistiker stellte sich auf die andere Seite. Da hat er gezählt wie verrückt.
Wann hat er gezählt wie verrückt?

Man verglich die Ergebnisse. Da hatte der Oberstatistiker nur eins mehr.
Wann hatte der Oberstatistiker nur eins mehr?

Seine kleine Geliebte war vorbeigekommen. Da hatte er sich um eins verzählt.
Wann hatte er sich um eins verzählt?

Der Oberstatistiker sah das Ergebnis. Da hat er ihm auf die Schulter geklopft.
Wann hat er ihm auf die Schulter geklopft?

Drill 5   *Combination Drill*   Als *or* wenn   *The event occurred either once or often. Answer the questions following the examples.*

Er hatte nichts zu rauchen. Dann gab er (immer) nur den Durchschnitt an.
Wann gab er (immer) nur den Durchschnitt an?
. . . ., **wenn** er nichts zu rauchen hatte.

Es ging um seine Existenz. Da hat ihm der Kumpel geholfen.
Wann hat ihm der Kumpel geholfen?
. . . ., **als** es um seine Existenz ging.

Man kontrollierte ihn einmal. Da hat er höllisch aufgepaßt.
Wann hat er höllisch aufgepaßt?

Er war wütend. Dann gab er (immer) unter dem Durchschnitt an.
Wann gab er (immer) unter dem Durchschnitt an?

Der Oberstatistiker stellte sich auf die andere Seite. Da hat er gezählt wie verrückt.
Wann hat er gezählt wie verrückt?

Man verglich die Ergebnisse. Da hatte der Oberstatistiker nur eins mehr.
Wann hatte der Oberstatistiker nur eins mehr?

Seine kleine Geliebte ging auf der anderen Seite vorbei. Dann hat er (immer) aufgehört zu zählen.
Wann hat er (immer) aufgehört zu zählen?

Sie war nicht mehr zu sehen. Dann hat er (immer) wieder angefangen zu zählen.
Wann hat er (immer) wieder angefangen zu zählen?

Seine kleine Geliebte war vorbeigekommen. Da hatte er sich um eins verzählt.
Wann hatte er sich um eins verzählt?

Der Oberstatistiker sah das Ergebnis. Da hat er ihm auf die Schulter geklopft.
Wann hat er ihm auf die Schulter geklopft?

Er teilte den andern das Ergebnis mit. Dann strahlten (immer) ihre Gesichter.
Wann strahlten (immer) ihre Gesichter?

V. THE CONJUNCTIONS weil AND da

The subordinate clause beginning with **weil** (because) is usually the Nachfeld and the subordinate clause beginning with **da** (since) is usually the Vorfeld of the main clause.

Vorfeld —	*P1*	*Satzfeld*	*P2*	— *Nachfeld* —
Die Leute	sind	zufrieden,		**weil täglich viele Tausende über ihre neue Brücke gehen.**

— *Vorfeld* —	*P1*	— *Satzfeld* —
Da er ein unzuverlässiger Mensch ist,	stimmt	die Statistik nicht.

Drill 6   Weil-*Clauses*   *Answer the questions following the example.*

Die Leute sind zufrieden. Denn viele Tausende gehen über ihre neue Brücke.
Warum sind die Leute zufrieden?
Sie sind zufrieden, **weil** viele Tausende über ihre neue Brücke gehen.

Die Statistik stimmt nicht. Denn er ist ein unzuverlässiger Mensch.
Warum stimmt die Statistik nicht?

Er hat höllisch aufgepaßt. Denn es ging um seine Existenz.
Warum hat er höllisch aufgepaßt?

Er hat gezählt wie verrückt. Denn der Oberstatistiker hat sich auf die andere Seite gestellt.
Warum hat er gezählt wie verrückt?

Der Oberstatistiker hat ihm auf die Schulter geklopft. Denn er hat sich nur um eins verzählt.
Warum hat der Oberstatistiker ihm auf die Schulter geklopft?

Pferdewagen ist ein Lenz. Denn zwischen vier und acht dürfen keine Pferdewagen über die Brücke.
Warum ist Pferdewagen ein Lenz?

Drill 7   Da-*Clauses*   *Follow the example.*

Er hat nichts zu rauchen. Darum (*therefore*) ist er wütend.
Da er nichts zu rauchen hat, ist er wütend.

Der Kumpel hat ihn gewarnt. Darum ist er ihm dankbar gewesen.
Er ist zuverlässig und treu. Darum wird er zu den Pferdewagen versetzt.
Zwischen vier und fünf dürfen keine Pferdewagen über die Brücke. Darum kann er spazieren gehen.
Er hat jetzt Zeit. Darum kann er das Mädchen nach Hause bringen.
Er kann jetzt in die Eisdiele gehen. Darum gefällt ihm das Leben.

VI.   THE CONJUNCTIONS obwohl, obgleich, obschon

The subordinate clause introduced by **obwohl, obgleich, obschon** (although) which are of synonymic meaning, is either the Vorfeld or the Nachfeld of the main clause.

Vorfeld	*P1*	*Satzfeld*	*Nachfeld*
Obwohl er nicht zuverlässig ist,	klopfen	sie ihm auf die Schulter.	
Sie	klopfen	ihm auf die Schulter,	**obwohl er nicht zuverlässig ist.**

Drill 8   Obwohl-*Clauses*   *Follow the example.*

Er ist nicht zuverlässig. Trotzdem (nevertheless) klopfen sie ihm auf die Schulter.
Obwohl er nicht zuverlässig ist, klopfen sie ihm auf die Schulter.

Diese Ziffern sind ein sinnloses Nichts. Trotzdem berauschen sie sich daran.
Sie multiplizieren und dividieren. Trotzdem stimmt die Statistik nicht.
Seine kleine Geliebte kommt über die Brücke. Trotzdem muß er zählen.
Es geht um seine Existenz. Trotzdem zählt er seine kleine Geliebte nicht.
Er hat sich verzählt. Trotzdem versetzen sie ihn zu den Pferdewagen.

VII. THE RELATIVE CLAUSE

A.   The Relative Pronoun der, das, die

The most commonly used relative pronoun is **der, das, die.** It has *the same forms* as *the definite article,* except for the genitive case, singular and plural, and the dative plural.

	Masculine	*Neuter*	*Feminine*
Sing. Nom.	. . . , der . . .	. . . , das . . .	. . . , die . . .
Acc.	. . . , den . . .	. . . , das . . .	. . . , die . . .
Dat.	. . . , dem . . .	. . . , dem . . .	. . . , der . . .
Gen.	. . . , **des**sen . . .	. . . , **des**sen . . .	. . . , deren . . .

Plur. Nom.	. . . , die . . .	. . . , die . . .	. . . , die . . .
Acc.	. . . , die . . .	. . . , die . . .	. . . , die . . .
Dat.	. . . , denen . . .	. . . , denen . . .	. . . , denen . . .
Gen.	. . . , deren . . .	. . . , deren . . .	. . . , deren . . .

The relative pronoun agrees in *gender* and *number* with its *antecedent,* that is, with the noun to which it refers. Its *case* is determined by its *use* in its *own clause.*

Er liest einen Roman, **der** ihm sehr gefällt.
Sie kennt den Schriftsteller, **der** diese Novellen geschrieben hat.
Das ist das Thema, **das** wir besprochen haben.
Dort kommt das Mädchen, **das** er kennt.
Er grüßt die Frau, **der** er begegnet.
Er charakterisiert die Generation, **der** er angehört.
Wir sprechen über den Autor, **dessen** Kurzgeschichte wir lesen.
Die Erzählung, **deren** Stil wir besprechen, ist modern.
Das sind die Professoren, **denen** wir gern widersprechen.
Dies sind die Schriftsteller, **deren** Werke zur Weltliteratur gehören.
Hier ist ein Problem, **über das** wir nachdenken müssen.
Das ist der Mann, **mit dessen** Theorie wir nicht übereinstimmen.
Hier ist der Brief, **von dessen** Inhalt alles abhängt.

▶ *Notice:* The relative pronoun is *never omitted* in German.

Das Buch, **das** er gelesen hat, war interessant.   The book he read was interesting.

Welcher, welches, welche is occasionally used as relative pronoun, especially to avoid repetition.

Er spricht mit dem Schriftsteller, **der der** Vertreter des neuen Stils ist.
Er spricht mit dem Schriftsteller, **welcher der** Vertreter des neuen Stils ist.

Drill 9   *Begin all sentences with:* **Wir sprechen von dem Mann, . . .** *Follow the examples.*

Er zählt die Leute.
Wir sprechen von dem Mann, **der** die Leute zählt.

Über ihn beschwert sich niemand.
Wir sprechen von dem Mann, **über den** sich niemand beschwert.

Ihn hat der Oberstatistiker kontrolliert.

Auf ihn verlassen sich alle.
Ihm vertrauen alle.
In ihm irrt sich der Oberstatistiker.
Er ist unzuverlässig.
Ihm ist die Statistik gleich.
Er interessiert sich für das Mädchen.
Ihm ist niemand böse.
Er hat mit den Verantwortlichen Mitleid.

Drill 10   *Begin all sentences with:* **Kir kennen den Mann, . . .** *Follow the examples.*

Seine Ergebnisse stimmen nicht.
Wir kennen den Mann, **dessen** Ergebnisse nicht stimmen.

An seinen Ergebnissen zweifelt niemand.
Wir kennen den Mann, **an dessen** Ergebnissen niemand zweifelt.

Seine Großzügigkeit ist bekannt.

Auf seine Zahlen freut sich jeder.
Sein Mund geht wie ein Uhrwerk.
Auf seine Ergebnisse reagieren alle.
Seine kleine Geliebte kommt täglich über die Brücke.
Sein Herz bleibt dann stehen.
Um seine Existenz geht es.
An seine Zuverlässigkeit glaubt jeder.

Drill 11   *Combination Drill*   *Begin all sentences with:* **Wir interessieren uns für den Mann, . . .**

Er ist unzuverlässig.
An seiner Zuverlässigkeit zweifelt niemand.
Ihm vertrauen alle.
Auf seine Ergebnisse reagieren alle.
Seine Großzügigkeit ist bekannt.

In ihm irrt sich der Oberstatistiker.
Sein Mund geht wie ein Uhrwerk.
Ihm ist die Statistik gleich.
Ihn hat der Oberstatistiker kontrolliert.
Um seine Existenz geht es.

Drill 12   *Begin all sentences with:* **Kennen Sie die junge Dame, . . .?** *Follow the examples.*

Sie kommt zweimal am Tage über die Brücke.
Kennen Sie die junge Dame, **die** zweimal am Tage über die Brücke kommt?

Von ihr handelt die Geschichte.
Kennen Sie die junge Dame, **von der** die Geschichte handelt?

Sie arbeitet in einer Eisdiele.

Auf sie wartet er jeden Tag.
Sie zählt er nicht.
An sie denkt er immer.
Ihr folgt er in die Eisdiele.
Von ihr hängt die Statistik ab.
Für sie interessiert er sich.
Sie geht nicht in die Ewigkeit der Statistik ein.

Drill 13   *Begin all sentences with:* **Das ist die junge Dame, . . .** *Follow the examples.*

Ihr Haar gefällt ihm.
Das ist die junge Dame, **deren** Haar ihm gefällt.

Um ihr Glück geht es auch.
Das ist die junge Dame, **um deren** Glück es auch geht.

Ihre Existenz ist ihm nicht gleich.
Ihren Weg kennt er.
In ihre Eisdiele kommt er.
Ihr Weg führt über die Brücke.
Ihre Existenz wirft alle Berechnungen über den Haufen.

Drill 14   *Combination Drill*   *Begin all sentences with:* **Wir sprechen von der jungen Dame, . . .**

Sie arbeitet in einer Eisdiele.
Auf sie wartet er jeden Tag.
Ihr Weg führt über die Brücke.
Um ihr Glück geht es auch.
Für sie interessiert er sich.
Von ihr hängt die Statistik ab.

Ihre Existenz wirft alle Berechnungen über den Haufen.
Sie geht nicht in die Ewigkeit der Statistik ein.
Ihr folgt er in die Eisdiele.
In ihre Eisdiele kommt er.
An sie denkt er immer.

Drill 15   *Begin each sentence with:* **Wir interessieren uns für die Leute,** . . . *Follow the examples.*

Ihnen sind nur Zahlen wichtig.
Wir interessieren uns für die Leute, **denen** nur
   Zahlen wichtig sind.

Mit ihnen empfindet er Mitleid.
Wir interessieren uns für die Leute, **mit denen**
   er Mitleid empfindet.
Sie berauschen sich an den Zahlen.

Sie haben ihm einen Posten gegeben.
Ihnen schenkt er ein paar Zahlen.
Für sie zählt er die Pferdewagen.
Sie tun ihm leid.
Ihnen macht das Multiplizieren Spaß.
Sie lieben das zweite Futur.

Drill 16   *Begin each sentence with:* **Das sind die Leute,** . . . *Follow the examples.*

Ihr Glück liegt in seiner Hand.
Das sind die Leute, **deren** Glück in seiner Hand liegt.

Auf ihre Statistik kann man sich nicht verlassen.
Das sind die Leute, **auf deren** Statistik man sich nicht verlassen kann.

Ihre Statistik stimmt nicht.
An ihre Tüchtigkeit glaubt jeder.
Ihre Spezialität ist das zweite Futur.
Ihre Berechnungen sind falsch.

Drill 17   *Combination Drill*   *Begin each sentence with:* **Das sind die Leute,** . . .

Ihnen sind nur Zahlen wichtig.
Mit ihnen empfindet er Mitleid.
Ihr Glück liegt in seiner Hand.
Sie tun ihm leid.

Auf ihre Statistik kann man sich nicht verlassen.
Ihnen schenkt er ein paar Zahlen.

B.   The Indefinite Relative Pronouns wer and was

1. **Wer,** in the sense of *whoever, he who,* or *anyone who,* and **was,** in the sense of *whatever, that which, no matter what,* or simply *what,* are used as relative pronouns if there is no antecedent.

   Wer may be used in all four cases. However, the genitive **wessen** occurs only in proverbs and in literary style.

   Wer mir hilft, dem helfe ich auch.
   Wen ich kenne, den grüße ich auch.
   Wem ich vertraue, dem glaube ich auch.
   Wessen Freundschaft man gewinnen will, dessen Vertrauen muß man besitzen.

   Was occurs only in the nominative and accusative cases.

   Was er sagt, das stimmt.   **Was** ich sehe, das glaube ich.

Wer and **was** are usually followed by a demonstrative pronoun in the next clause. After a clause introduced by **wer** the demonstrative pronoun **der** may be omitted if both pronouns are in the nominative.

Wer nicht für mich ist, **der** ist gegen mich.   **Wer** nicht für mich ist, ist gegen mich.

After a clause introduced by **was** the demonstrative pronoun **das** may always be omitted.

Was er gesagt hat, **das** ist nicht wahr.   **Was** er gesagt hat, ist nicht wahr.

Was occurs in the nominative and accusative cases only.

2. **Was** is used instead of the definite relative pronoun **das** or **welches** if *an indefinite neuter form* such as **alles, nichts, manches, vieles,** or **etwas** or *a neuter superlative* is the antecedent.

Das ist **alles, was** ich weiß.   Das ist **das Beste, was** ich gelesen habe.

If the antecedent is a noun, **was** cannot be used.

Das ist **das Beste, was** ich gelesen habe.   Das ist **das beste Buch, das** ich gelesen habe.

3. **Was** may also refer to *an entire concept* or *clause.*

Er hatte nichts zu rauchen, **was** ihn immer sehr wütend machte.
Er schenkte ihnen ein paar Zahlen, **was** sie sehr glücklich machte.

4. **Wo(r)**-compounds may also be used as indefinite relative pronouns if they refer to *an entire concept* or *clause.*

Er schenkte ihnen ein paar Zahlen, **worüber** sie sehr glücklich waren.
But:
Es waren nur **Ziffern** und **Zahlen, über die** sie sich freuten.

Drill 18 *The Indefinite Relative Pronoun* **wer** *Fill in the blanks using the correct indefinite and demonstrative pronouns. Follow the example.*

_____ sucht, _____ findet.
Wer sucht, **der** findet.

_____ nicht für mich ist, _____ ist gegen mich.
_____ ich kenne, _____ grüße ich auch.
_____ ich helfe, _____ hilft mir auch.
_____ Freundschaft man gewinnen will, _____ Vertrauen muß man besitzen.
_____ Buch ich lese, _____ Meinungen interessieren mich.
_____ ich vertraue, _____ glaube ich auch.
_____ Sorgen hat, _____ hat auch Likör.

Drill 19   *The Indefinite Relative Pronoun* **was**   *Fill in the blanks using either the indefinite relative pronoun* **was** *or the definite relative pronoun* **der, die, das.** *Follow the examples.*

Er kennt nichts, _____ ich nicht auch kenne.
Er kennt **nichts, was** ich nicht auch kenne.

Er kennt nicht ein Buch, _____ ich nicht auch kenne.
Er kennt **nicht ein Buch, das** ich nicht auch kenne.

Das ist alles, _____ ich besitze.
Das ist alles Geld, _____ ich besitze.

Er sagt manches, _____ ich nicht sagen würde.
Er sagt manches Wort, _____ ich nicht sagen würde.

Das ist das Beste, _____ ich gelesen habe.
Das ist das beste Buch, _____ ich gelesen habe.

Das ist das Schönste, _____ ich gesehen habe.
Das ist das schönste Bild, _____ ich gesehen habe.

Das ist das Letzte, _____ ich gehört habe.
Das ist die letzte Zahl, _____ ich gehört habe.

Er schreibt vieles, _____ ich nicht schreiben würde.
Er schreibt viele Dinge, _____ ich nicht schreiben würde.

Er konnte den Beitritt zur Hitlerjugend vermeiden He was able to avoid joining the Hitler Youth; **der Arbeitsdienst** premilitary labor service; **der Wehrdienst** military service; **eingezogen werden** to be drafted; **der Infanterist, –en** (*Masc. II*) infantryman; **das Militär** military (life); **die Hungerjahre** lean years; **notdürftig renoviert** scantily renovated

das Hinterhaus, ⸚er back building; **die Mietskaserne, –n** tenement; **der Schreiner, –** joiner; **der Bildhauer, –** sculptor; **die Werkstatt, ⸚en** workshop; **der Besuch** *here:* attendance; **der Lehrling, –e** apprentice; **die Buchhandlung, –en** bookshop; **das Studium der Germanistik** study of German language and literature; **sich vertiefen** *here:* to deepen; **die Überzeugung, –en** conviction; **sinnlos** senseless; **langweilig** boring; **erleben** to experience; **erscheinen, ie, ie** to appear; **ungeheuer** monstrous; **nichts anderes als** nothing but; **der Volkszähler, –** census taker; **das Statistische Amt** Bureau of Statistics

Der Preis der Gruppe 47 *literary award of the Group 47, an avant-garde group of democratic German writers formed in 1947*

der Erfolg, –e success; **erhalten, ie, a** to receive; **einschließlich** including

im Streben nach materiellem Wohlstand in striving for material prosperity

sich richten gegen (+ *acc.*) to be directed against; **die Ursache, –n** cause; **drohen** to threaten

Heinrich Böll

Biographie   Heinrich Böll ist 1917 in Köln, im Hinterhaus einer Mietskaserne, geboren, wo sein Vater eine Schreiner- und Bildhauerwerkstatt hatte. Nach dem Besuch des Gymnasiums (1937) arbeitete Böll, der den Beitritt zur Hitlerjugend vermeiden konnte, als Lehrling in einer Buchhandlung, kam 1938 zum Arbeitsdienst und begann 1939 das Studium der Germanistik an der Universität Köln, als er zum Wehrdienst eingezogen wurde. Sechs Jahre lang, vom Beginn bis zum Ende des Krieges, war er Infanterist an verschiedenen Fronten. ,,In diesen sechs Jahren'', schrieb Böll, ,,vertiefte sich meine Überzeugung, daß es nichts Sinnloseres, nichts Langweiligeres gibt als das Militär. Der Krieg – obwohl ich ihn ,interessant' genug erlebte – erschien mir als nichts anderes als eine ungeheure Maschinerie...'' 1945 kam er ins zerstörte Köln zurück. Dort lebte er in den Hungerjahren nach dem Kriege mit seiner Familie, seiner Frau und drei Söhnen, in zwei kleinen Räumen eines notdürftig renovierten Ruinenhauses. Er arbeitete zunächst in der väterlichen Schreinerei, dann ein Jahr lang als Volkszähler beim Statistischen Amt der Stadt Köln.

Schon 1946 hatte Böll in verschiedenen Zeitschriften Kurzgeschichten veröffentlicht, aber sein literarischer Erfolg begann erst, als er 1951 den ,,Preis der Gruppe 47'' erhielt. Seitdem sind Bölls Erzählungen und Romane Bestseller. Die Übersetzungen seiner Bücher erscheinen in achtzehn Ländern, einschließlich Rußland.

Heinrich Böll ist Katholik und nennt sich selbst einen christlichen Schriftsteller. Seine Kritik richtet sich gegen den Krieg und gegen alle, die im Streben nach materiellem Wohlstand den Krieg und seine Ursachen zu schnell vergessen. Und sie richtet sich gegen alles, was das Leben zu einer sinnlosen Maschinerie zu machen droht.

besitzen, a, e to possess

indem while; häufen to pile up; die Schicht, –e *here:* shift; je höher . . . , um so mehr . . . the higher . . . the more . . .

Die ungezählte Geliebte the uncounted sweetheart; flicken to patch; der Posten, – = die Stellung job, post, position; zählen to count; die Brücke, –n bridge; Es macht ihnen Spaß They have fun; die Tüchtigkeit efficiency, competence; die Zahl, –en number; belegen to authenticate, prove; sich berauschen an (+*dat.*) to intoxicate oneself with; die Ziffer, –n figure; stumm silent, mute; das Uhrwerk clockwork; schenken to give (as a present), bestow upon; das Gesicht, –er face; strahlen to beam, shine; das Ergebnis, –se result; mit·teilen to report, announce; Grund haben to have reason; befriedigt satisfied, content; täglich daily

Ich verstehe es, den Eindruck von Biederkeit zu erwecken I know how to give the impression of honesty

Die Statistik stimmt nicht The statistics are not correct; unzuverlässig unreliable

insgeheim secretly; Mein Herz schlägt auf My heart beats high; verströmen to stream forth, to flow; förmlich *here:* veritably, literally; prozentualisieren to figure percentages

Es macht mir Freude It gives me pleasure; manchmal sometimes; unterschlagen, u, a to embezzle, *here:* steal; das Mitleid pity; empfinden, a, u *here:* to feel; ein paar schenken to give a few extra; das Glück good luck, success, happiness; wütend furious, angry; den Durchschnitt an·geben, a, e to give the average; froh happy; die Großzügigkeit generosity; großzügig generous; die fünfstellige Zahl five-digit number; glücklich happy; reißen, i, i to tear, snatch; auf·leuchten to become bright, light up; klopfen *here:* to pat; ahnen to suspect, sense; aus·rechnen to calculate, figure out; Sie werden gegangen sein They will have gone; das zweite Futur future perfect

Böll besitzt Humor. Nach den beiden Beispielen der Kriegs-
und Trümmerliteratur von Borchert lesen wir nun eine Heimkehrergeschichte. Aber sie ist aus der Perspektive des Humors
geschrieben.

DIE UNGEZÄHLTE GELIEBTE

Die haben mir meine Beine geflickt und haben mir einen
Posten gegeben, wo ich sitzen kann: ich zähle die Leute, die
über die neue Brücke gehen. Es macht ihnen ja Spaß, sich ihre
Tüchtigkeit mit Zahlen zu belegen, sie berauschen sich an
diesem sinnlosen Nichts aus ein paar Ziffern, und den ganzen
Tag, den ganzen Tag, geht mein stummer Mund wie ein
Uhrwerk, indem ich Nummer auf Nummer häufe, um ihnen
abends den Triumph einer Zahl zu schenken. Ihre Gesichter
strahlen, wenn ich ihnen das Ergebnis meiner Schicht mitteile,
je höher die Zahl, um so mehr strahlen sie, und sie haben
Grund, sich befriedigt ins Bett zu legen, denn viele Tausende
gehen täglich über ihre neue Brücke . . .

Aber ihre Statistik stimmt nicht. Es tut mir leid, aber sie stimmt
nicht. Ich bin ein unzuverlässiger Mensch, obwohl ich es verstehe, den Eindruck von Biederkeit zu erwecken.

Insgeheim macht es mir Freude, manchmal einen zu unterschlagen und dann wieder, wenn ich Mitleid empfinde, ihnen
ein paar zu schenken. Ihr Glück liegt in meiner Hand. Wenn ich
wütend bin, wenn ich nichts zu rauchen habe, gebe ich nur den
Durchschnitt an, manchmal unter dem Durchschnitt, und wenn
mein Herz aufschlägt, wenn ich froh bin, lasse ich meine
Großzügigkeit in einer fünfstelligen Zahl verströmen. Sie sind
ja so glücklich: Sie reißen mir jedesmal das Ergebnis förmlich
aus der Hand, und ihre Augen leuchten auf, und sie klopfen
mir auf die Schulter. Sie ahnen ja nichts! Und dann fangen sie
an zu multiplizieren, zu dividieren, zu prozentualisieren, ich
weiß nicht was. Sie rechnen aus, wieviel heute jede Minute
über die Brücke gehen und wieviel in zehn Jahren über die
Brücke gegangen sein werden. Sie lieben das zweite Futur, das

unermüdlich untiring; **aus·setzen** to make a pause; **ein·biegen, o, o** in (+*acc.*) to turn into; **verschwinden, a, u** to disappear; **Ich lasse sie mir nicht nehmen** I won't give them up; **der Gehsteig, –e** sidewalk; **defilieren** to march past (*military expression*)

stehen bleiben, ie, ie to stand still; **Sein Herz setzt aus** His heart skips a beat; **die Allee, –n** avenue; **passieren** *here:* to pass by; **verschweigen, ie, ie** *here:* to leave unmentioned; **die Eisdiele, –n** ice cream parlor; **inzwischen** in the meantime, meanwhile; **Sie ist zu sehen** She is to be seen; **Sie gehen nicht in die Ewigkeit der Statistik ein** They do not enter the eternity of statistics; **der Schatten, –** shadow; **Schattenmänner und Schattenfrauen** phantom men and phantom women; **nichtige Wesen** nonentities; **mitmarschieren** to march along

ahnen *here:* to find out; **erfahren, u, a** to learn; **ungeheuer** appalling, immense; **auf welche Weise** in what way; **Sie wirft alle Berechnungen über den Haufen** She upsets all the calculations; **ahnungslos** unsuspecting, unconscious; **unschuldig** innocent; **zart** delicate; **das Trinkgeld, –er** tip

der Kilometerzähler, – odometer, mileage indicator; **Ich will sie nicht transportieren lassen** I will not have her transported

neulich recently, the other day; **kontrollieren** to check up on; **der Kumpel, –** chum, buddy; **auf·passen** *here:* to be careful; **höllisch** hellishly, mighty, terribly; **verrückt** crazy; **der Oberstatistiker, –** head statistician; **vergleichen, i, i** to compare; **vorbei·kommen, a, o** to pass (by); **hübsch** pretty, nice; **das Nichts** *here:* nonentity; **verwandeln** to transform, to convert; **Mein Herz hat mir geblutet** My heart bled; **nach·sehen, a, e** (+ *dat.*) to look at

zweite Futur ist ihre Spezialität — und doch, es tut mir leid, daß alles nicht stimmt . . .

Wenn meine kleine Geliebte über die Brücke kommt — und sie kommt zweimal am Tage — dann bleibt mein Herz einfach stehen. Das unermüdliche Ticken meines Herzens setzt einfach aus, bis sie in die Allee eingebogen und verschwunden ist. Und alle, die in dieser Zeit passieren, verschweige ich ihnen. Diese zwei Minuten gehören mir, mir ganz allein, und ich lasse sie mir nicht nehmen. Und auch wenn sie abends wieder zurückkommt aus ihrer Eisdiele — ich weiß inzwischen, daß sie in einer Eisdiele arbeitet —, wenn sie auf der anderen Seite des Gehsteiges meinen stummen Mund passiert, der zählen, zählen muß, dann setzt mein Herz wieder aus, und ich fange erst wieder an zu zählen, wenn sie nicht mehr zu sehen ist. Und alle, die das Glück haben, in diesen Minuten vor meinen blinden Augen zu defilieren, gehen nicht in die Ewigkeit der Statistik ein: Schattenmänner und Schattenfrauen, nichtige Wesen, die im zweiten Futur der Statistik nicht mitmarschieren werden . . .

Es ist klar, daß ich sie liebe. Aber sie weiß nichts davon, und ich möchte auch nicht, daß sie es erfährt. Sie soll nicht ahnen, auf welche ungeheure Weise sie alle Berechnungen über den Haufen wirft, und ahnungslos und unschuldig soll sie mit ihren langen braunen Haaren und den zarten Füßen in ihre Eisdiele marschieren, und sie soll viel Trinkgeld bekommen. Ich liebe sie. Es ist ganz klar, daß ich sie liebe.

Neulich haben sie mich kontrolliert. Der Kumpel, der auf der anderen Seite sitzt und die Autos zählen muß, hat mich früh genug gewarnt, und ich habe höllisch aufgepaßt. Ich habe gezählt wie verrückt, ein Kilometerzähler kann nicht besser zählen. Der Oberstatistiker selbst hat sich drüben auf die andere Seite gestellt und hat später sein Ergebnis einer Stunde mit meinem Stundenergebnis verglichen. Ich hatte nur einen weniger als er. Meine kleine Geliebte war vorbeigekommen, und niemals im Leben werde ich dieses hübsche Kind ins zweite Futur transportieren lassen, diese meine kleine Geliebte soll nicht multipliziert und dividiert und in ein prozentuales Nichts verwandelt werden. Mein Herz hat mir geblutet, daß ich zählen mußte, ohne ihr nachsehen zu können, und dem Kumpel drü-

Es ging glatt um meine Existenz It was simply a question of my existence

sowieso anyway; hinzu·zählen to add; gewiß certain; der Verschleiß depreciation, *here:* loss

treu loyal, faithful; sich verzählen to miscount; (Das) macht nicht viel That doesn't matter much; beantragen to propose; der Pferdewagen, – cart, carriage; versetzen to transfer, *here:* to promote

der Lenz, –e = der Frühling spring

Das ist die Masche That's the ticket (*slang*); Das ist ein Lenz That's a snap (*slang*); wie nie zuvor like never before; höchstens at the most; das Gehirn, –e brain

herrlich splendid; spazierengehen, i, a to go for a stroll; Ich könnte sie mir an·schauen I could have a look at her; Er bringt sie ein Stück nach Hause He takes her part of the way home

ben, der die Autos zählen muß, bin ich sehr dankbar gewesen. Es ging ja glatt um meine Existenz.

Der Oberstatistiker hat mir auf die Schulter geklopft und hat gesagt, daß ich gut bin, zuverlässig und treu. „Eins in der Stunde verzählt", hat er gesagt, „macht nicht viel. Wir zählen sowieso einen gewissen prozentualen Verschleiß hinzu. Ich werde beantragen, daß Sie zu den Pferdewagen versetzt werden".

Pferdewagen ist natürlich die Masche. Pferdewagen ist ein Lenz wie nie zuvor. Pferdewagen gibt es höchstens fünfundzwanzig am Tage, und alle halbe Stunde einmal in seinem Gehirn die nächste Nummer fallen zu lassen, das ist ein Lenz!

Pferdewagen wäre herrlich. Zwischen vier und acht dürfen überhaupt keine Pferdewagen über die Brücke, und ich könnte spazierengehen oder in die Eisdiele, könnte sie mir lange anschauen oder sie vielleicht ein Stück nach Hause bringen, meine kleine ungezählte Geliebte . . .

I. QUESTIONNAIRE

A. Exercises for the A-Questions

1. Study the following expressions

1. Es macht ihnen Spaß.
   They have fun.
2. Es macht mir Freude.
   It gives me joy.
3. Sie wirft alle Berechnungen über den Haufen.
   She upsets all calculations.
4. **Es geht** glatt **um** seine Existenz.
   It is simply a question of his existence.
5. Er **verzählt sich um** einen (oder um eins).
   He miscounts by one.
6. Das macht nicht viel.
   That doesn't matter much.
7. Das ist die Masche.
   That's the ticket.
8. Das ist ein Lenz.
   That's a snap.
9. Er **schaut** sie **sich an.** (See also p. 46.)
   He takes a look at her.
10. Die Welt der Verantwortlichen **unterscheidet sich von** der Welt des Erzählers.
    The world of those who are in charge differs from the narrator's world.

11. Die Kritik **richtet sich gegen** die Gesellschaft. | The criticism is directed against society.
12. Alles **hängt von** ihm ab. | Everything depends on him.
13. Das **macht** ihn **zu** einem glücklichen Menschen. | That makes him a happy man.
14. Die Welt der Verantwortlichen **besteht** nur **aus** Zahlen. | The world of those who are in charge consists of numbers only.

2. The use of some reflexive verbs with the prefix ver–

The expression **einen in der Stunde verzählt** is an example of bureaucratic language. The correct German would be:

Er hat sich um einen (or **um eins**) in der Stunde **verzählt.**

The use of the reflexive pronoun and the addition of the prefix **ver–** gives the verb **zählen** the meaning of *to count incorrectly unconsciously* = **aus Versehen falsch zählen.**

The following verbs use the same pattern. Follow the example.

Er zählt aus Versehen falsch.	Er verzählt sich.
Er rechnet aus Versehen falsch.	Er _____
Er sieht aus Versehen (!) falsch.	Er _____
Er hört aus Versehen falsch.	Er _____
Er schreibt aus Versehen falsch.	Er _____
Er spricht aus Versehen falsch.	Er _____
Er fährt aus Versehen in falscher Richtung.	Er _____
Er läuft (*walks*) aus Versehen in falscher Richtung.	Er _____

3. The use of the words Zahl, Ziffer, and Nummer

Zahl and **Ziffer** represent the *mathematical* concepts *digit, figure*. **Nummer** represents the *concrete* concept, the *number* as it appears written, printed, or stamped on a surface.

4. Intransitive and factitive verbs

The verbs **stehen, sitzen,** and **liegen** are *irregular verbs* which describe a *condition*. They cannot take a direct object.

stehen, stand, gestanden	to stand
sitzen, saß, gesessen	to sit
liegen, lag, gelegen	to lie

The verbs **(sich) stellen, (sich) setzen, (sich) legen** are *regular verbs* which describe an *action*. They take a direct object.

stellen, stellte, gestellt	to put, to place
setzen, setzte, gesetzt	to put, to set
legen, legte, gelegt	to put, to lay, to place

sich stellen, er stellte sich, er hat sich gestellt	to go and stand
sich setzen, er setzte sich, er hat sich gesetzt	to sit down
sich legen, er legte sich, er hat sich gelegt	to lie down

The direct object of these reflexive verbs is the reflexive pronoun.

The verbs **(sich) stellen, (sich) setzen, (sich) legen** require the *accusative* if a prepositional phrase is used. They answer the question **wohin?** (Where . . . to?)

Er **stellt** den Tisch **ans** Fenster.
He puts the table at the window.

Er **stellt sich ans** Fenster.
He goes and stands at the window.

Er **setzt** das Kind **auf den** Stuhl.
He puts the child on the chair.

Er **setzt sich auf den** Stuhl.
He sits down on the chair.

Er **legt** die Decke **auf das** Bett.
He puts the blanket on the bed.

Er **legt sich auf das** Bett.
He lies down on the bed.

The verbs **stehen, sitzen, liegen** require the *dative* if a prepositional phrase is used. They answer the question **wo?** (Where?)

Jetzt **steht** der Tisch **am** Fenster.
Now the table is at the window.

Jetzt **steht** er **am** Fenster.
Now he stands at the window.

Jetzt **sitzt** das Kind **auf dem** Stuhl.
Now the child sits on the chair.

Jetzt **sitzt** er **auf dem** Stuhl.
Now he sits on the chair.

Jetzt **liegt** die Decke **auf dem** Bett.
Now the blanket is on the bed.

Jetzt **liegt** er **auf dem** Bett.
Now he lies on the bed.

Drill 1   *Follow the examples.*

Der Mann **stellt** das Auto **auf die** andere Seite.
Jetzt **steht** das Auto **auf der** anderen Seite.

Der Mann **stellt sich** auf **die** andere Seite.
Jetzt **steht** er **auf der** andern Seite.

Er setzt das Kind auf die Bank.

Er setzt sich auf die Bank.
Er legt das Buch auf den Tisch.
Er legt sich auf das Bett.
Er stellt das Auto vor die Tür.
Er stellt sich vor die Tür.

Drill 2   *Follow the examples.*

Das Auto **steht auf der** andern Seite.
Er **hat** das Auto **auf die** andere Seite **gestellt.**

Er **steht auf der** andern Seite.
Er **hat sich auf die** andere Seite **gestellt.**

Das Kind sitzt auf dem Stuhl.

Er sitzt am Tisch.
Die Decke liegt auf dem Bett.
Er liegt auf dem Bett.
Der Tisch steht am Fenster.
Er steht am Fenster.

B. A-Questions

Heinrich Böll erzählt seine Geschichte in der ich-Form. Antworten Sie auf alle Fragen über den Erzähler in der er-Form.

Böll gebraucht das Demonstrativpronomen **die** und das Personalpronomen **sie** für diejenigen, die die Verantwortung (responsibility) tragen, für die Verantwortlichen (= for those who are in charge.)

Der Erzähler, das Ich dieser Geschichte, ist ein Kriegsverletzter (disabled veteran) dem **sie** die Beine geflickt haben, sodaß er wieder arbeiten kann.

1. Was sagt der Erzähler über seine Arbeit?

   Was **hat er bekommen?** // job / where he can sit //
   Was **ist** *seine Aufgabe?* (*task*) // to count (*infinitive*) / people / who / to cross / new bridge //
   Was *macht den Verantwortlichen Spaß?* // to prove to themselves (*infinitive*) / efficiency / with / numbers //
   Woran **berauschen** *sie sich?* // senseless nothingness of a few numbers //
   Was tut der Erzähler *den ganzen Tag?* // his silent lips / to go / like / clockwork //
   Wann **strahlen** *ihre Gesichter?* // (*a*) / when / he / at night / to give / to them / triumph of a number // (*b*) / when / he / to report / to them / result /
   Warum **haben** *sie* **Grund, sich befriedigt ins Bett zu legen?** // because (**weil**) / daily / many thousands / to cross / new bridge //

2. Wie arbeitet der Erzähler?

   Was **sagt er von der Statistik?** // that / it / to be / not correct //
   Was **sagt er von sich selbst?** // (*a*) / that / he / to be sorry // (*b*) / that / he / to be / unreliable person //
   Was **macht ihm** *insgeheim* **Freude?** // sometimes / to steal (*infinitive*) / one //
   Was tut er, *wenn er Mitleid empfindet?* // to give / them / a few extra //
   Was **weiß er?** // that / their happiness / to lie / in / his hand //
   Was tut er, *wenn er nichts zu rauchen hat und wütend ist?* // to report / only / average //
   Was tut er, *wenn er froh ist?* // (*a*) / to be / generous // (*b*) to report / five-digit number //

3. Wie sind die Reaktionen der Verantwortlichen?

  Was geschieht *jedesmal, wenn er das Ergebnis mitteilt?* // (a) / they / to snatch / it / out of his hand // (b) / eyes / to light up // (c) / they / to pat / shoulder //
  Warum **sind sie so glücklich?** // because / they / to suspect / nothing //
  Was **fangen sie** *dann an?* // to multiply // to divide / to figure out percentages //
  Was **rechnen** *sie aus?* // (a) / how many / today / every minute / to cross / bridge // (b) / how many / in ten years / to have crossed (*future perfect*) / bridge //
  Warum **rechnen sie das aus?** // (a) / because / they / to love / future perfect // (b) / because / future perfect / to be / specialty //

4. Warum stimmt die Statistik nicht?

  Wer **kommt zweimal am Tage?** // little sweetheart / bridge //
  Was geschieht, **wenn sie über die Brücke kommt?** // heart / simply / to stand still //
  Was tut **er in dieser Zeit?** // to leave unmentioned / to them / all / who / to pass by //
  Warum? // these two minutes / to belong to //
  Was **weiß er inzwischen?** // that / she / to work / ice cream parlor //
  Wann **setz sein Herz wieder aus?** // when / she / to come back / at night / ice-cream parlor //
  Wann **fängt er erst wieder an zu zählen?** // when / she / no longer / to be seen //
  Was **sagt** *der Erzähler* von allen, die in diesen Minuten vorbeigehen? // (a) / that / they / not / to enter / eternity / statistics // (b) / that / they / to be / phantom men / and / phantom women // (c) / that / they / to be / nonentities / who / not / to march along / future perfect / statistics //
  Was **ist klar?** // that / he / to love / her //
  Was **ist auch klar?** // that / she / to know / nothing / about it //
  Denn was **möchte er nicht?** // that / she / to find it out //
  Was **soll** *sie nicht ahnen?* // in what way / she / to upset / all calculations //
  Was **wünscht er ihr?** // (a) / that / she / to march / unsuspecting / and / innocent / ice-cream parlor // (b) / that / she / to get / a lot of tips //

5. Warum stimmt die Statistik eines Tages beinahe?

  Was ist *neulich* geschehen? // they / to have checked up on //
  Wer **hat ihn früh genug gewarnt?** // buddy / who / to sit / other side / and / to count / cars //
  Wie hat *der Erzähler* reagiert? // (a) / to have been terribly careful // (b) / to have counted / like crazy //
  Was hat *der Oberstatistiker* gemacht? // (a) / to come and stand (*perfect*) / other side // (b) / to have compared / results //
  Wie war das Ergebnis? // he / to have (*imperfect*) / only / one less //
  Warum? // little sweetheart / to have passed by //
  Was **will** *der Erzähler* nicht? // (a) / that / one (man) / to transport / little / sweetheart / future perfect // (b) / that / one / to multiply / and / to divide / her // (c) / that / one / to transform / her / percental nothing //

Warum ist er dem Kumpel dankbar gewesen? // because / it / to have been / question of his existence //

6. **Welche Folgen (consequences) hat die Kontrolle für den Erzähler?**

Was hat der Oberstatistiker getan? // to have patted / shoulder //
Was hat er gesagt? // that / he / to be / reliable / and / loyal //
Was hat er noch gesagt? // one miscounted per hour doesn't matter much (*direct quote*) //
Was wird der Oberstatistiker beantragen? // that / he / to be transferred / horse carts //
Was sagt der Erzähler darüber, daß er Pferdewagen zählen darf? // (*a*) / (to count) horse carts, that's the ticket // (*b*) / that's a snap // (*direct quotes*)
Warum freut er sich darüber? // (*a*) / because / there to be / daily / at the most twenty-five // (*b*) / because / between 4 and 8 / no horse carts at all / to be allowed / (to cross) bridge //
Was könnte er machen? // (*a*) / (to) go for a stroll // (*b*) (to go) ice-cream parlor // (*c*) / to have a look at her // (*d*) / perhaps / to take her home //

C. B-Questions

Answer with complete sentences.

1. **Wie sieht der Erzähler die Verantwortlichen?**

Wie charakterisiert er sie? // to have fun / to prove to oneself / efficiency / to intoxicate oneself / with / nothingness // faces / to shine // (*a*) / when / he / to give / triumph / number // (*b*) / when / he / to report / result // (*c*) / because / many thousands / to cross // when / he / to report / result // (*a*) they / to snatch / it / out of / hand // (*b*) / eyes / to light up // (*c*) / to pat / shoulder // they / to be happy / because / to suspect / nothing // to begin / to multiply / to divide / to figure percentages // to figure out // (*a*) / how many / every minute // (*b*) / how many / in ten years // to figure it out // (*a*) / because / to love / future perfect // (*b*) / because / future perfect / specialty //
Woraus besteht die Welt der Verantwortlichen? – Was für eine Welt ist das?

2. **Wie sieht der Erzähler sich selbst?**

Was sagt er über seine Arbeit // job / where // to count people / who // silent lips / clockwork // but / to be sorry // statistics / not correct //
Was sagt er von sich selbst? // to be sorry // to be / unreliable person // it / to give / him / joy / sometimes / to steal // when / to feel pity / to give / a few extra // to know / that / happiness / to lie / hand // when / to have / nothing to smoke / to report / only / average // when / to be happy // (*a*) / to be / generous // (*b*) / to report / five-digit number //
Was sagt er über seine kleine Geliebte? // when / she / to cross / bridge / and / when / she / to come back / ice-cream parlor / heart / to stand still // two minutes / to belong to // to be clear / that / to love //

Was möchte er nicht? // (a) / that / she / to find it out // (b) / that / she / to know / that / she / to upset / all calculations //

Was sagt er über die Leute, die er den Verantwortlichen verschweigt? // not / to enter / eternity // to be / phantom men / and / phantom women // to be / nonentities / who / not / to march along / future perfect / statistics //

Woraus besteht die Welt des Erzählers?

In welchem Konflikt befindet er sich?

Was für ein Mensch ist er?

3. Wie findet der Konflikt des Erzählers seine Lösung?

Was ist eines Tages geschehen? // to have checked up on // to have been thankful to / buddy / who / to sit / other side // (a) / because / to have warned // (b) / because / to be (*imperf.*) question / existence // when / head statistician / to come and stand (*perfect*) / other side // (a) / he / to have been terribly careful // (b) / to have counted / crazy // when / they / to have compared / results / he / to have had / only one less // he / to have miscounted by / one / because / little sweetheart / to have passed by //

Was will der Erzähler nicht? // (a) / that / one (man) / to transport / her / future perfect // (b) / that / one / to multiply / and / to divide / her // (c) / that / one / to transform / her / percental nothing //

Wie reagiert der Oberstatistiker? // although / he / to have miscounted by / one / he / to have patted / shoulder // to say / that / he / to be / reliable / and / loyal // head statistician / to propose / that / he / to be transferred / horse carts //

Welche Perspektiven öffnen sich dem Erzähler? // there / to be / daily / at the most twenty-five // between 4 and 8 / no horse carts at all / to be allowed / (to cross) bridge // he / could // (a) / go for a stroll // (b) / (go) ice-cream parlor // (c) / have a look at her // (d) / perhaps take her home //

Was glauben Sie, möchte Böll mit dieser humoristischen Lösung sagen?

D. Exercises for the C-Questions

Go through the following expressions before answering the C-questions:

Those who are in charge trust him.
That puzzles him.
They believe in the figures.
They count on him.
That makes him a happy man.
They are satisfied with his work.
They rely on him.
It is a question of his existence.
They identify themselves with the numbers.
They look forward to the results.

Their world consists of numbers only.
That is important to them.
They are mistaken about the man.
These minutes belong to him.
They have fun.
She upsets all the calculations.
It gives him joy.
He miscounts by one.
That doesn't matter much.

E. C-Questions (Essay)

   1. Worin unterscheidet sich die Welt der Verantwortlichen von der Welt des Erzählers?

   2. Gegen welche Züge unserer modernen Gesellschaft richtet sich Bölls humoristische Kritik?

CHAPTER

GRAMMATICAL REVIEW **5**

THE SUBORDINATE CLAUSE: PART III

I. **THE CONJUNCTIONS** nachdem, bevor, während, seit

Distinguish carefully between preposition, conjunctions, and adverbs:

Preposition		*Conjunction*		*Adverb*	
nach	after	**nachdem**	after	**danach**	after that
				nachher	afterwards
vor	before	**bevor, ehe**	before	**vorher**	before that
während	during	**während**	while	**dabei**	at the same time
				währenddessen	meanwhile
seit	since, for	**seit, seitdem**	since	**seitdem**	ever since
				seither	since then

A. Nach, nachdem, danach

Prep.: **Nach** der Arbeit steckt er sich eine Zigarette an.
Conj.: **Nachdem** er gearbeitet hat, steckt er sich eine Zigarette an.
Adv.: Er arbeitet. **Danach** steckt er sich eine Zigarette an.

The *perfect tense* is used *in a subordinate clause* with **nachdem** if *the present tense* is used *in the main clause.*

Nachdem er sich hingesetzt **hat, beginnt** der Musikautomat zu hämmern.

The *pluperfect tense* is used *in a subordinate clause* with **nachdem** if *the imperfect tense* or *the perfect tense* is used *in the main clause.*

Subordinate clauses introduced by **nachdem** may either be the Vorfeld or the Nachfeld of the main clause. But they are usually the Vorfeld.

Nachdem er sich hingesetzt **hatte, begann** der Musikautomat zu hämmern.
Nachdem er sich hingesetzt **hatte, hat** der Musikautomat zu hämmern **begonnen**.

Drill 1   *Change the prepositional expression with* **nach** *into a subordinate clause with* **nachdem,** *following the examples. Pay attention to the tenses!*

Nach dem Schlafen trinkt er Kaffee.
Nachdem er geschlafen **hat,** trinkt er Kaffee.

Nach dem Schlafen hat er Kaffee getrunken.
Nachdem er geschlafen **hatte,** hat er Kaffee getrunken.

Nach dem Kaffeetrinken geht er in die Universität.
Nach dem Kaffeetrinken ist er in die Universität gegangen.

Nach dem Arbeiten steckt er sich eine Zigarette an.
Nach dem Arbeiten hat er sich eine Zigarette angesteckt.

Nach dem Essen liest er die Zeitung.
Nach dem Essen hat er die Zeitung gelesen.

Nach dem Lesen geht er weg.
Nach dem Lesen ist er weggegangen.

Nach dem Telefonieren geht er in die Stadt.
Nach dem Telefonieren ist er in die Stadt gegangen.

Drill 2   *Further Subordinate Clauses with* nachdem   *Follow the example.*

Er macht sich frei. **Danach** starrt der Alte ihm nach.
Nachdem er sich frei gemacht **hat,** starrt der Alte ihm nach.

Er steckt sich eine Zigarette an. Danach fühlt er sich besser.
Eine Wagentür fällt zu. Danach kommen zwei Männer herein.
Der Große beendet seine Runde. Danach steuert er auf ihn zu.
Der Polizist bittet um den Paß. Danach blättert er darin.
Die beiden gehen. Danach verschwindet die Spannung in ihm.
Er verläßt das Lokal. Danach atmet er tief.
Er besteht die Probe. Danach ist ihm wie nach Sekt.
Er zwängt sich durch den Einlaß. Danach hört er ein Gewirr von Stimmen.

Drill 3   *Further Subordinate Clauses with* nachdem   *Follow the example.*

Er setzte sich hin. **Danach** begann der Musikautomat zu hämmern.
Nachdem er sich hingesetzt **hatte,** begann der Musikautomat zu hämmern.

Er ging durch den Einlaß. Danach deutete jemand hinter ihm her.
Jemand drückte ihm einen Riesenblumenstrauß in die Hände. Danach hakten zwei Mädchen ihn
    unter.
Jemand gratulierte Redluff. Danach fragte er ihn nach seinem Namen.
Er sagte seinen richtigen Namen. Danach hörte er ihn aus allen Lautsprechern.
Die Polizisten hörten den Namen Jens Redluff. Danach kamen sie auf ihn zu.

B. Vor, bevor, vorher

> *Prep.:* **Vor dem Lesen** steckt er sich eine Zigarette an.
> *Conj.:* **Bevor** er liest, steckt er sich eine Zigarette an.
> *Adv.:* Er liest. **Vorher** steckt er sich eine Zigarette an.

C. Während, während, dabei (währenddessen)

> The *main clause* and the *subordinate clause* introduced by **bevor** or **während** have the *same tenses.*
>
> **Während des Essens** unterhalten wir uns.
> **Während** wir essen, unterhalten wir uns.
> Wir essen. **Dabei** unterhalten wir uns.

D. Seit – seit, seitdem – seitdem

> The preposition **seit,** the conjunctions **seit, seitdem,** and the adverb **seitdem** refer to a *period of time.*
>
> In contrast to English, German uses the *present tense* when **seit** or **seitdem** refers to a *continuing action* in a so-called *up-to-now situation.*

Prep.: **Seit drei Monaten sucht** er ein Schiff.	He *has been looking* for a ship *for three months.*
Conj.: **Seit (seitdem)** er in der Stadt **ist, sucht** er ein Schiff.	*Since* he *has been* in the city he *has been looking for a ship.*
Adv.: Er **ist** drei Monate in der Stadt. **Seitdem sucht** er ein Schiff.	He *has been* in the city *for* three months. He *has been looking* for a ship *for that long.*

> German uses the *imperfect tense* when the text is written in the *narrative past* and **seit** or **seitdem** refers to a *continuing action* in a so-called *up-to-then situation.*

Prep.: **Seit drei Monaten suchte** er ein Schiff.	He *had been looking* for a ship *for three months.*
Conj.: **Seit (seitdem)** er in der Stadt **war, suchte** er ein Schiff.	*Since* he had been in the city he *had been looking* for a ship.
Adv.: Er **war** drei Monate in der Stadt. **Seitdem suchte** er ein Schiff.	He *had been* in the city *for* three months. He *had been looking* for a ship *for that long.*

> German uses the *perfect tense* in the *subordinate clause* when **seit** or **seitdem** refer to a *one-time past action* in a so-called *up-to-now situation.*

Prep.: **Seit seiner Ankunft sucht** er ein Schiff.	*Since his arrival* he *has been looking* for a ship.

Conj.:	**Seit (seitdem)** er **angekommen ist,** **sucht** er ein Schiff.	*Since* he *arrived* he *has been looking* for a ship.
Adv.:	Er **ist** vor drei Monaten **angekommen.** **Seitdem sucht** er ein Schiff.	He *arrived* three months ago. *Since then* he *has been looking* for a ship.

The *pluperfect* is used in the *subordinate clause* when the text is written in the *narrative past* and **seit** or **seitdem** refers to a *one-time past action* in a so-called *up-to-then situation.*

Seit (seitdem) er **angekommen war, suchte** er ein Schiff.	*Since* he *had arrived* he *had been looking* for a ship.

Subordinate clauses introduced by **bevor, während** or **seit (seitdem)** may either be the **Vorfeld** or the **Nachfeld** of the main clause. Usually they are the **Vorfeld**.

Drill 4 *Während, bevor, seit (seitdem)* *Follow the examples.*

Er denkt an die Polizei. **Dabei fühlt** er Schwäche und Übelkeit.
Während er an die Polizei **denkt, fühlt** er Schwäche und Übelkeit.

Er setzt sich an einen leeren Tisch. **Vorher bestellt** er einen doppelten Konjak.
Bevor er sich an einen leeren Tisch **setzt, bestellt** er einen doppelten Konjak.

Er ist in der Hafenstadt. **Seitdem sucht** er ein Schiff.
Seit er in der Hafenstadt **ist, sucht** er ein Schiff.

Er hat einen falschen Paß. Seitdem will er die Stadt verlassen.
Er geht die hellen Straßen entlang. Dabei sieht er Autos und Reklamelichter.
Er ist wieder unter Menschen. Seitdem hat er Angst.
Er öffnet seinen Kragen. Dabei fröstelt ihn.
Der Polizist kommt auf ihn zu. Vorher geht er zum Nachbartisch.
Er sieht das runde Metall in der Hand. Dabei wird er ganz ruhig.
Der Polizist hebt den Paß in das Licht. Vorher blättert er darin.
Er klammert sich an die Tischkante. Dabei entfärben sich seine Fingernägel.
Er geht in die große Halle. Vorher nimmt ihm jemand die Einlaßkarte ab.

THE INFINITIVE PHRASES

I. THE INFINITIVE WITHOUT zu

The infinitive without **zu** appears after *(a)* the modal verbs **können, mögen, dürfen, müssen, wollen, sollen;** *(b)* the verbs **hören, sehen, helfen, lassen;** *(c)* the verbs **lernen, bleiben, fühlen, spüren, gehen, fahren, reiten, kommen, schicken, (sich) legen.**

A. The Modal Verbs

In contrast to English, *German modal verbs,* which directly govern an infinitive, *are conjugated in all tenses.* The conjugational endings are the same as those of the regular verbs.

können	*mögen*	*dürfen*	*müssen*	*wollen*	*sollen*
		Present tense			
ich kann	ich mag	ich darf	ich muß	ich will	ich soll
du kannst	du magst	du darfst	du mußt	du willst	du sollst
er kann	er mag	er darf	er muß	er will	er soll
wir können	wir mögen	wir dürfen	wir müssen	wir wollen	wir sollen
ihr könnt	ihr mögt	ihr dürft	ihr müßt	ihr wollt	ihr sollt
sie können	sie mögen	sie dürfen	sie müssen	sie wollen	sie sollen
		Imperfect tense			
ich konnte	ich mochte	ich durfte	ich mußte	ich wollte	ich sollte
		etc.			

Modal verbs with a *dependent infinitive* form the *perfect* and *pluperfect tenses* with a *double infinitive.*

Perfect tense	*Pluperfect tense*
Ich habe **lesen können.**	Ich hatte **lesen können.**
Ich habe nicht **weggehen mögen.**	etc.
Ich habe **bleiben dürfen.**	
Ich habe **arbeiten müssen.**	
Ich habe **anfangen wollen.**	
Ich habe **kommen sollen.**	

Only a few modal forms have survived in English. The function of the German modals is performed by verbs or verb phrases that require *to* before the infinitive.

können   to be able to

mögen	to like to
dürfen	to be allowed to
müssen	to have to
wollen	to want to
sollen	to be supposed (expected) to

Können has both present and imperfect tense modal equivalents in English:

| Er **kann** kommen. | He can (is able to) come. |
| Er **konnte** kommen. | He could (was able to) come. |

Dürfen has two different present tense modal equivalents in English:

| Er **darf** bleiben. | He may (is allowed to) stay. |
| Er **darf** nicht bleiben. | He must not (is not allowed to) stay. |

Müssen has only one present tense modal equivalent in English:

| Er **muß** arbeiten. | He must (has to) work. |

Mögen has the English present tense equivalent *may* in subjective statements only (see p. 197).

| Er **mag** sich irren. | He may be mistaken. |

Wollen and **sollen** have no modal equivalents in modern colloquial English.

In contrast to English, German modal verbs may also be used simply as main verbs in expressions in which a dependent infinitive is understood.

Er kann das.	He can (is able to) do that.
Er mag sie nicht.	He does not like her.
Er darf das nicht.	He must not (is not allowed to) do that.
Er muß nach Hause.	He must (has to) go home.
Er will nichts.	He does not want anything.
Er soll in die Schule.	He is supposed (expected) to go to school.

Modal verbs as main verbs form the perfect and pluperfect tenses with the perfect participle:

Perfect tense	*Pluperfect tense*
Ich habe das gekonnt.	Ich hatte das gekonnt.
Ich habe sie nicht gemocht.	etc.
Ich habe das nicht gedurft.	
Ich habe nach Hause gemußt.	
Ich habe nichts gewollt.	
Ich habe es gesollt.	

B.   **The Verbs** hören, sehen, helfen, lassen

The verbs **hören, sehen, helfen, lassen** can also directly govern an infinitive and also form the *perfect* and *pluperfect tenses* with a *double infinitive.*

Er **hört** die Leute.	Er **hört** die Leute **lachen.**
Er **hat** die Leute **gehört.**	Er **hat** die Leute **lachen hören.**
Er **sieht** die Polizisten.	Er **sieht** die Polizisten **kommen.**
Er **hat** die Polizisten **gesehen.**	Er **hat** die Polizisten **kommen sehen.**
Er **hilft** ihm.	Er **hilft** ihm **arbeiten.**
Er **hat** ihm **geholfen.**	Er **hat** ihm **arbeiten helfen.**
Er **läßt** den Paß zu Hause.	Er **läßt** den Paß zu Hause **liegen.**
Er **hat** den Paß zu Hause **gelassen.**	Er **hat** den Paß zu Hause **liegen lassen.**

The *double infinitive* always takes *the last position* both in a main clause and in a subordinate clause. The double infinitive in a subordinate clause appears in literary style only.

Er hat heute viel **arbeiten müssen.**	Er hat die Leute **lachen hören.**
Es stimmt, daß er heute viel hat **arbeiten müssen.**	Es ist sicher, daß er die Leute hat **lachen hören.**
	Er hat die Polizisten **kommen sehen.**
Er hat gestern **kommen sollen.**	Es ist sicher, daß er die Polizisten hat **kommen sehen.**
Es stimmt, daß er gestern hat **kommen sollen.**	

Drill 5   *Perfect Tense of Modal Verbs and of the Verbs* hören, sehen, helfen, lassen *without and with a Dependent Infinitive   Follow the examples.*

Er **kann** das.	Ich **will** das nicht.	Er **darf** das nicht.
Er **hat** das **gekonnt.**	Ich will heute anfangen.	Er darf nicht hierbleiben.
Er **kann** lesen.	Er mag das Mädchen nicht.	Er läßt den Paß zu Hause.
Er **hat** lesen **können.**	Er mag nicht weggehen.	Er läßt den Paß zu Hause liegen.
Wir helfen unserm Freund.	Ich sehe die Polizei.	
Wir helfen unserm Freund arbeiten.	Ich sehe die Polizei kommen.	Wir hören die Leute.
		Wir hören die Leute lachen.

Drill 6   *Perfect Tense of Modal Verbs and the Verbs* hören, sehen, helfen, lassen *with a Dependent Infinitive   Follow the example.*

Er **hörte** die Bremsen quietschen.	Er mußte unauffällig weiterlaufen.
Er **hat** die Bremsen **quietschen hören.**	Er wollte wieder mit dem Leben Kontakt aufnehmen.
Er sah das Auto nicht kommen.	Er ließ sich einen falschen Paß machen.
Er durfte nicht schwach werden.	

Er mußte für den Paß nicht schlecht bezahlen.
Er sah die Autos anfahren.
Er mußte sich sehr anstrengen.
Er hörte jemand lachen.
Er konnte in der Menge nicht eintauchen.
Er hörte den Musikautomaten hämmern.
Er konnte nichts verstehen.

Er sah den Polizisten auf sich zukommen.
Er hörte sich selber sprechen.
Er sah die beiden weggehen.
Er ließ seinen Hut liegen.
Seine Ruhe half ihm die Probe bestehen.
Er konnte jetzt frei atmen.
Er hörte die Leute lachen und schwatzen.

C.   The Verbs lernen, bleiben, fühlen, spüren, gehen, fahren, reiten, kommen, schicken, (sich) legen

The infinitive without *zu* also appears after those verbs as given in the following table. But these verbs form the *perfect* and *pluperfect tenses regularly*, i.e., without the double infinitive.

Present tense	*Perfect tense*
Er **lernt** Deutsch **sprechen.**	Er **hat** Deutsch **sprechen gelernt.**
Er **bleibt** in der Kneipe **sitzen.**	Er **ist** in der Kneipe **sitzen geblieben.**
Er **fühlt** das Unglück **kommen.**	Er **hat** das Unglück **kommen gefühlt.**
Er **spürt** den Sturm **kommen.**	Er **hat** den Sturm **kommen gespürt.**
Er **geht** die Post **abholen.**	Er **ist** die Post **abholen gegangen.**
Er **fährt** heute **spazieren.**	Er **ist** heute **spazieren gefahren.**
Er **reitet** heute spazieren.	Er **ist** heute **spazieren geritten.**
Er **kommt** uns **besuchen.**	Er **ist** uns **besuchen gekommen.**
Er **schickt** ihn **einkaufen.**	Er **hat** ihn **einkaufen geschickt.**
Sie **legt** das Kind **schlafen.**	Sie **hat** das Kind **schlafen gelegt.**
Er **legt** sich **schlafen.**	Er **hat** sich **schlafen gelegt.**

Note the exception with the verb kommen:

Er kommt gelaufen.   He comes running.

Drill 7   *Perfect Tense of the Verbs* lernen, bleiben, fühlen, sich legen, gehen, schicken, fahren *with a Dependent Infinitive   Follow the example.*

Er **lernt** Deutsch **schreiben.**
Er **hat** Deutsch **schreiben gelernt.**

Er bleibt in der Kneipe sitzen.
Er fühlt das Unglück nicht kommen.
Er geht auf der hellen Straße spazieren.
Er legt sich schlafen.

Er lernt Deutsch sprechen.
Er bleibt in der großen Halle stehen.
Er schickt ihn einkaufen.
Er geht den Paß abholen.
Er fährt in der Stadt spazieren.

Drill 8   *Combination Drill of Perfect Forms with Dependent Infinitives*

Er geht den Paß abholen.	Er muß unauffällig weiterlaufen.
Er muß für den Paß bezahlen.	Er lernt Deutsch sprechen.
Er hört den Musikautomaten hämmern.	Er läßt seinen Hut liegen.
Er bleibt in der Kneipe sitzen.	Er hört die Leute lachen und schwatzen.
Er sieht den Polizisten auf sich zukommen.	Er legt sich schlafen.
Er fühlt das Unglück nicht kommen.	Er kann jetzt frei atmen.
Er geht in den hellen Straßen spazieren.	Er bleibt in der großen Halle stehen.

D.   Uses and Meanings of the Modal Verbs and of the Auxiliary Verb werden

1. Modal verbs and the auxiliary verb **werden** can be used *(a)* in *objective statements* in which the speaker or writer refers to facts; *(b)* in *subjective statements* in which the speaker or writer wants to express a conclusion he has drawn, his opinion, conviction, or doubt, i.e., his subjective standpoint.

Compare the following sentences:

(a) Er **kann** alles verstehen.	He can understand everything.
(b) Das **kann** wahr sein.	That may be true.
(a) Er **mag** jetzt nicht weggehen.	He does not want to leave now.
(b) Er **mag** sich irren.	He may be mistaken.
(a) Er **muß** ein Schiff finden.	He must find a ship.
(b) Er **muß** ein Verbrecher sein.	He must be a criminal.
(a) Er **will** kein Verbrecher sein.	He does not want to be a criminal.
(b) Er **will** kein Verbrecher sein.	He claims not to be a criminal.
(a) Er **soll** dem Polizisten seinen Paß zeigen.	He is supposed to show his passport to the policeman.
(b) Er **soll** einen falschen Paß haben.	He is said (supposed) to have a fake passport.
(a) Er **wird** nicht kommen.	He will not come.
(b) Er **wird** heute in München sein.	He probably is in Munich today.

2. The objective and the subjective uses of the modal verbs take the same present tense forms.

(a) Er **kann** kommen.	He can come.
(b) Das **kann** sein.	That may be.

But the *objective* and the *subjective uses* of the modal verbs take *different perfect* and *pluperfect tense forms.*

We have already learned that modal verbs with a dependent infinitive form the *perfect* and *pluperfect tenses* with a *double infinitive.* Usually this is true when the modal verbs are used *objectively.*

Present infinitive	*Double present infinitive*
(*a*) Er muß ein Schiff **finden.**	Er hat ein Schiff **finden müssen.**
He must find a ship.	He had to find a ship.

When a modal verb is used subjectively it is only the infinitive that takes the perfect form.

Present infinitive	*Perfect infinitive*
(*b*) Er muß ein Verbrecher **sein.**	Er muß ein Verbrecher **gewesen sein.**
He must be a criminal.	He must have been a criminal.

Since German modal verbs have imperfect forms, one may make the subjective statement in the narrative past:

(*a*) Er mußte in der Stadt sein.	He had to be in the city.
(*b*) Er mußte in der Stadt gewesen sein, als es passierte.	I was sure that he was in the city when it happened.

But only **können, mögen,** and **müssen** may have imperfect forms when used subjectively in the narrative past. There are no perfect and pluperfect tenses.

1. Objective and subjective uses of the modal verbs and of the auxiliary verb werden

(a) Können

Objective use

die Fähigkeit	*ability*
Er kann alles verstehen.	He can (is able to) understand everything.
die Unfähigkeit	*inability*
Er kann sich nicht mehr konzentrieren.	He cannot (is not able to) concentrate any longer.
die Möglichkeit	*possibility*
Mit dem falschen Paß kann er die Stadt verlassen.	He can leave the city with his fake passport.

die Unmöglichkeit	*impossibility*
Ohne Paß kann er nicht über die Grenze.	Without a passport he cannot cross the border.
die Erlaubnis	*permission*
Kann ich ein Kaninchen haben?	May I have a rabbit?
Können wir ins Kino gehen?	May we go to the movies?

Subjective use

eine ziemlich sichere Vermutung	*a rather certain assumption*
Er kann recht haben.	He may be right.
(Ich denke, daß er recht hat.)	(I think he is right).

(b) Mögen

When **mögen** is used without a dependent infinitive it means *to like;* when used with a dependent infinitive it means *to want to.*

It is the subjunctive forms of **mögen, ich möchte** (I would like to) etc., which are used most frequently. However, the indicative forms, **ich mag** (I like to), etc., are possible too.

Objective use

die Neigung	*inclination, liking, desire*
Er mag das Mädchen.	He likes the girl.
die Abneigung	*aversion, dislike*
Er mag diesen Menschen nicht.	He does not like this person.
Er mag noch nicht weggehen.	He does not want to leave yet.

Subjective use

eine mögliche Annahme	*a possible assumption*
Es mag nur Einbildung sein.	It may be only an illusion.
(Ich halte es für möglich, daß es nur Einbildung ist.)	(I consider it possible that it is only an illusion.)

(c) Dürfen

Objective use

eine Erlaubnis meistens als Belohnung	*a permission usually as a reward*
Alle Kinder dürfen ins Kino; denn alle haben sich gut benommen.	All the children may (are permitted to) go to the movies because they all behaved well.
ein Verbot	*a restriction*
Du darfst das nicht tun!	You must not do that!

eine höfliche Bitte oder Aussage	*a polite request or statement*
Darf ich Ihnen einen Stuhl anbieten?	May I offer you a chair?
Ich darf Ihnen gratulieren!	May I congratulate you!

Dürfen is not used very often since it suggests a kind of master-servant relationship. In colloquial German **können** is preferred.

Können wir jetzt weggehen?	May we leave now?

Subjective use

eine Wahrscheinlichkeit	*a probability*
Sie dürfte zwanzig Jahre alt sein.	She is probably twenty years old.
(Ich nehme an, daß sie zwanzig Jahre alt ist.)	(I assume that she is twenty years old.)

The subjective use of **dürfen** is possible only with the subjunctive form **er dürfte,** etc.

(d) Müssen

Objective use

die Notwendigkeit	*necessity*
Er muß ein Schiff finden.	He must find a ship.
das Fehlen einer Notwendigkeit	*lack of necessity*
Er braucht die Ausstellung nicht zu betreten.	He need not enter the exhibition.
Er muß nicht arbeiten!	He does not have to work!

The usual negation of **müssen** is **nicht brauchen** + infinitive with **zu.** The negation **nicht müssen** + infinitive without **zu** is only used if **müssen** is emphasized strongly.

Er muß nicht arbeiten. Niemand zwingt ihn dazu.	He does not have to work. Nobody forces him to do so.

Subjective use

eine sichere Überzeugung	*a sure conviction*
Er muß viel Geld haben.	He must have a lot of money.
(Ich bin überzeugt, daß er viel Geld hat.)	(I am convinced that he has a lot of money.)

(e) Wollen

Objective use

eine Absicht, ein Plan, der Wille	*an intention, a plan, volition*
Er will die Stadt verlassen.	He wants to leave the city.

ein Wunsch	*a wish*
Er will ein Kaninchen haben.	He wants to have a rabbit.
Er will den Paß sehen.	He wants to see the passport.
eine Behauptung, an der der Sprecher zweifelt	a statement which the speaker doubts
Er will Deutscher sein, aber spricht mit einem amerikanischen Akzent.	He claims to be a German yet speaks with an American accent.
(Er behauptet, Deutscher zu sein.)	(He claims to be a German.)

In the present tense it is the context only which shows whether **wollen** is used objectively or subjectively. The subjective use of **wollen** occurs most frequently with the perfect infinitive.

Er will Professor gewesen sein.	He claims to have been a professor.

(f) Sollen

Objective use

ein Befehl, ein Auftrag, oder ein Wunsch einer dritten Person	*an order, an assignment, or a wish of a third person*
Er soll seinen richtigen Namen nennen.	He is supposed to tell his real name.
Er soll die Briefe zur Post bringen.	He is supposed to bring the letters to the post office.
Sie soll viel Trinkgeld bekommen.	I hope she gets lots of tips.
eine moralische Verpflichtung	*a moral obligation*
Man soll hilfreich sein.	One ought to be helpful.

Subjective use

eine Annahme auf Grund einer Information	*an assumption based on information*
Er soll in Deutschland sein.	He is said to be in Germany.
(Ich habe gehört, oder man sagt, daß er in Deutschland ist.)	(I heard, or people say, that he is in Germany.)

(g) Werden

Objective use

Futur	*future tense*
Ich werde kommen.	I shall come.

Subjective use

die Wahrscheinlichkeit	*probability*
Er wird jetzt zu Hause sein.	He probably is at home now.
(Ich vermute, daß er jetzt zu Hause ist.)	(I suspect that he is at home now.)

Er wird gestern abgefahren sein.   He probably left yesterday.
(Ich vermute, daß er gestern abgegefahren   (I suspect that he left yesterday.)
   ist.)

When **werden** is used subjectively, adverbs such as **wohl, wahrscheinlich, vielleicht,** and **sicher**
are usually included.

Er wird jetzt **wohl** in der Ausstellung sein.   He probably is in the exhibition now.

Drill 9   *The Objective Use of Modal Verbs and of* **werden**   *Give the German equivalent.*

He can leave the city with his fake passport.   He must find a ship.
May I have a rabbit?   You (Sie) must not do that!
He cannot concentrate any longer.   He need not enter the exhibition.
He wants to see the passport.   All the children are permitted to go to the
He is supposed to say his real name.   movies.
He does not like this person.   One ought to be helpful.
He wants to leave the city.   He will not come.
Without a passport he cannot cross the
   border.

Drill 10   *Objective and Subjective Use of Modal Verbs*   *Form the perfect tense and give the English*
equivalent. Follow the examples.

(*a*) Er muß ein Schiff finden.   (*a*) Er will kein Verbrecher sein.
       Er hat ein Schiff finden müssen.   (*b*) Er will kein Verbrecher sein.
       He had to find a ship.
                                                                   (*a*) Er soll dem Polizisten den Paß zeigen.
(*b*) Er muß ein Verbrecher sein.   (*b*) Er soll einen falschen Paß haben.
       Er muß ein Verbrecher gewesen sein.
       He must have been a criminal.   (*a*) Alle Kinder dürfen ins Kino gehen.
                                                                   (*b*) Sie dürfte zwanzig Jahre alt sein.
(*a*) Er kann alles verstehen.
(*b*) Das kann wahr sein.   (*a*) Er muß die Stadt verlassen.
                                                                   (*b*) Er muß viel Geld haben.
(*a*) Er mag jetzt nicht weggehen.
(*b*) Er mag sich irren.

Drill 11   *The Subjective Use of Modal Verbs and of* **werden**   *Express the meaning of the following*
sentences by using a modal verb or the auxiliary verb **werden***. Follow the examples.*

Ich denke, daß er recht hat.   Man sagt, daß er noch in der Stadt ist.
Er kann recht haben.   Ich vermute, daß er jetzt in der Kneipe sitzt.
                                                                   Ich bin überzeugt, daß er viel Geld hat.
Ich denke, daß er recht gehabt hat.   Ich denke, daß er sich geirrt hat.
Er kann recht gehabt haben.

Ich vermute, daß er in der Ausstellung gewesen ist.

Er behauptet, kein Verbrecher gewesen zu sein.

Ich nehme an, daß er zu viel getrunken hat.

Ich bin überzeugt, daß er Angst gehabt hat.

Ich halte es für möglich, daß es nur Einbildung ist.

Er behauptet, Herr Wolters zu sein.

Ich nehme an, daß er vierzig Jahre alt ist.

Ich habe gehört, daß sein Name in den Zeitung gestanden hat.

Ich bin überzeugt, daß das Bild schlecht gewesen ist.

E. The Meanings and Uses of lassen

1. To let (to cause or to permit)

Ich lasse ihn kommen.	I let (or have) him come.
Ich lasse ihn meinen Wagen fahren.	I let him (permit him to) drive my car.

2. To have something done

Er läßt seinen Wagen waschen.	He has his car washed.
Er läßt sich die Haare schneiden.	He has his hair cut.

3. To leave (behind)

Lassen in the sense of *to leave (behind)* is frequently used in combination with **liegen, stehen,** and **hängen.**

Er läßt seinen Hut in der Kneipe.	He leaves his hat in the bar.
Er läßt seinen Hut in der Kneipe liegen.	He leaves his hat in the bar.
Er läßt seinen Wagen auf der Straße.	He leaves his car in the street.
Er läßt seinen Wagen auf der Straße stehen.	He leaves his car in the street.
Er läßt seinen Mantel im Lokal.	He leaves his coat in the restaurant.
Er läßt seinen Mantel im Lokal hängen.	He leaves his coat in the restaurant.

4. Perfect and pluperfect tenses of lassen

Lassen is grammatically treated like a modal verb.

(a) With a *dependent infinitive* it forms the *perfect and pluperfect* tenses with a *double infinitive:*

Er **hat** sich einen falschen Paß **machen lassen.**	He had a fake passport made for himself.

(b) In the sense of *to leave (behind)* without **liegen, stehen, hängen, lassen** forms the *perfect and pluperfect tenses* with a *perfect participle:*

Er **hat** den Hut in der Kneipe **gelassen.**
But:
Er **hat** den Hut in der Kneipe **liegen lassen.**

Drill 12   *Follow the example.*

Wäscht er seinen Wagen selbst?
Nein, er **läßt** seinen Wagen **waschen.**

Schneidet er sich die Haare selbst?
Schreibt er die Briefe selbst?
Rechnet er die Ergebnisse selbst aus?

Macht er sich den falschen Paß selbst?
Holt er das Buch selbst ab?
Macht er die Arbeit selbst?
Zählt er die Pferdewagen selbst?

Drill 13   *Follow the example.*

Hat er den Wagen selbst **geholt?**
Nein, er **hat** den Wagen **holen lassen.**
Hat er den Brief selbst geschrieben?
Hat er die Ergebnisse selbst ausgerechnet?

Hat er sich den Paß selbst gemacht?
Hat er das Buch selbst abgeholt?
Hat er die Autos selbst gezählt?

II.   THE INFINITIVE WITH zu

The use of German infinitive constructions with **zu** is similar to that of English constructions with *to:*

Er hat sich entschlossen, heute nachmittag in die Stadt zu gehen.

He decided to go to town this afternoon.

Er ist bereit, heute nachmittag in die Stadt zu gehen.

He is ready to go to town this afternoon.

But there are differences. German infinitives with **zu** can either be the *second part of the predicate* (P2), or can occur as the Nachfeld.

Vorfeld —— *P1* —————— *Satzfeld* —————— *P2*			
Er	braucht	heute nicht	**zu arbeiten**

Vorfeld —— *P1* —————— *Satzfeld* —————— *P2* —————— *Nachfeld*				
Er	hat sich	heute morgen	entschlossen,	nicht **zu arbeiten.**

A.   The Infinitive with zu as the Second Part of the Predicate (P2)

1.   Nicht brauchen *(need not)*

Vorfeld —— *P1* —————— *Satzfeld* ——————— *P2*

Er   braucht   heute   nicht **zu kommen.**

He *need not come* today.

Vorfeld — *P1* ———— *Satzfeld* ————————— *P2*

Er   hat   heute nicht   **zu kommen brauchen.**

He did not *have to come* today.

Although **brauchen** is not a modal verb, it forms the *perfect and pluperfect tenses* with a *double infinitive.*

2.   Scheinen *(to seem)*

Vorfeld —— *P1* —————— *Satzfeld* ———— *P2*

Er   **scheint**   nicht hier   **zu sein.**

He does not *seem to be* here.

Vorfeld —— *P1* —————— *Satzfeld* ————————— *P2*

Er   **scheint**   nicht hier   **gewesen zu sein.**

He does not *seem to have been* here.

3.   Haben *(to have)*

Whereas English *to have to* is the equivalent of *must,* German **haben zu** is *not* the exact equivalent of **müssen.**

Er **hat** sofort **zu kommen** means that someone is giving him *the strict order* to come immediately.

Vorfeld — *P1* ————————— *Satzfeld* ————————— *P2*

Er   **hat**   seine Arbeit einfach   **fertig zu machen!**

He simply *must finish* his work!

However, **haben** + infinitive with **zu** occurs frequently together with **etwas, nichts, wenig,** and **viel** in the same sense as its English equivalent.

Vorfeld —— *P1* —————————— *Satzfeld* —————————— *P2*

  Wir   **haben**   **viel (wenig, nichts, etwas)**   **zu tun.**

We *have much (little, nothing, something) to do.*

Vorfeld —— *P1* —— *Satzfeld* —————————— *P2*

  Wir   **haben**   heute   **nichts zu tun gehabt.**

We *did not have anything to do* today.

4. **Sein** *(to be)*

Vorfeld —— *P1* —— *Satzfeld* —————— *P2*

  Das   **war**   leicht   **zu machen.**

That *was* easy *to do.*

Vorfeld —— *P1* —— *Satzfeld* —————— *P2*

  Da   **ist**   nichts   **zu machen.**

There *is* nothing *to be done.*

The use of the *passive infinitive* after **sein** does *not* exist in German. That the infinitive with **zu** after **nicht brauchen, scheinen, haben,** and **sein** in the use described above belongs to the predicate is clearly to be seen when the main clause is changed to a subordinate clause.

Er braucht nicht wegzugehen.
Er **scheint** nicht mehr hier **zu sein.**
Er **hat** hier nichts mehr **zu tun.**
Hier **ist** nichts mehr **zu machen.**

Er weiß, **daß** er nicht wegzugehen **braucht.**
Wir hören, **daß** er nicht mehr hier zu sein **scheint.**
Er weiß, **daß** er hier nichts mehr zu tun **hat.**
Es ist klar, **daß** hier nichts mehr zu machen **ist.**

Drill 14   *Change the second clause to a* **daß**-*clause. Follow the example.*

Es ist klar, er **braucht** die Stadt nicht **zu ver-lassen.**
Es ist klar, **daß** er die Stadt nicht zu verlassen **braucht.**

Er weiß, er hat hier nichts mehr zu tun.
Er ist der Meinung, die Probe war leicht zu bestehen.

Er weiß jetzt, er braucht keine Angst mehr zu haben.
Er sagt, er hatte für den Paß viel zu bezahlen.
Wir hören, er scheint noch in der Stadt zu sein.
Es ist klar, er braucht dem Mädchen nicht zu folgen.
Er weiß, er hat noch viel zu tun.

Es ist klar, er braucht die Ausstellung nicht zu betreten.
Wir hören, er scheint nicht mehr in der Kneipe gewesen zu sein.

Es ist klar, er braucht seinen Namen nicht zu sagen.
Es ist klar, er scheint nicht zu wissen, was er sagt.

B. The Infinitive with zu as the Nachfeld

Compare the following sentences:

Vorfeld	P1	Satzfeld		P2
Er	braucht	die Stadt nicht		zu verlassen.
Er	hat	die Stadt nicht		zu verlassen brauchen.

Vorfeld	P1	Satzfeld	P2	Nachfeld
Er	versucht	seit gestern, ...		die Stadt zu verlassen.
Er	hat	seit gestern versucht,		die Stadt zu verlassen.

After verbs other than **nicht brauchen, scheinen, haben,** and **sein** and after some predicate adjectives the infinitive with **zu** occupies the Nachfeld and is therefore separated from the main clause by a comma.

However, when the infinitive with **zu** has no other element (object, prepositional phrase, etc.), the comma is omitted, and after a few verbs the infinitive may even be incorporated into the Satzfeld.

Vorfeld	P1	Satzfeld	P2	Nachfeld
Jetzt	fängt	er	an	zu laufen.
Jetzt	fängt	er zu laufen	an.	
But:				
Jetzt	fängt	er	an,	hin und her zu laufen.

The infinitive with **zu** may also depend on a **da**-compound when the subject of the main clause is the same as the subject of the infinitive construction.

Er besteht darauf, daß **er Herr Wolters** ist.
Er besteht darauf, **Herr Wolters zu sein.**

Drill 15   *Change the second clause to a* **daß***-clause. Follow the examples.*

Es ist klar, er vergißt, vorsichtig zu sein.
Es ist klar, daß er vergißt, vorsichtig zu sein.

Es ist klar, er hat vorsichtig zu sein.
Es ist klar, daß er vorsichtig zu sein hat.

Er fühlt, er hört auf, Angst zu haben.

Er fühlt, er braucht keine Angst mehr zu haben.

Wir hören, er scheint die Probe bestanden zu haben.

Wir hören, er ist sicher, die Probe bestanden zu haben.

Wir sehen, er vergißt, seinen Hut mitzunehmen.

Wir sehen, er scheint seinen Hut zu vergessen.

Wir hören, er ist sicher, das Mädchen zu kennen.

Wir hören, er hat dem Polizisten seinen Paß zu zeigen.

Wir sehen, er ist bereit, dem Polizisten seinen Paß zu zeigen.

C.   Um . . . zu, ohne . . . zu, (an)statt . . . zu

Die Polizisten sind in die Kneipe gekommen, **um** die Ausweise **zu kontrollieren.**

Er sagt dem Mann seinen richtigen Namen, **ohne** es **zu merken.**

Er folgt dem Mädchen in die Ausstellung, **statt** in den Hafen **zu gehen.**

The policemen came into the bar (in order) to check the identification cards.

He tells the man his real name without noticing it.

He follows the girl into the exhibition instead of going to the harbor.

In German you *must* use **um . . . zu** whenever you *may* use *in order . . . to* in English!

Wir sind hier, **um** Deutsch **zu** lernen.

We are here *(in order) to* learn German.

Infinitives with **um . . . zu, ohne . . . zu,** and **(an)statt . . . zu** may either be the Nachfeld or the Vorfeld.

Um den Paß besser sehen **zu können,** hebt ihn der Polizist in das Licht.

Ohne ein Wort **zu sagen,** verlassen beide den Raum.

Statt auf dem Gehweg **zu** bleiben, läuft er auf die Straße.

Um . . . zu, ohne . . . zu, (an)statt . . . zu can only be used if the *subject* of the *infinitive construction* is the *same* as the *subject* of the *main clause*. Otherwise a dependent clause introduced by **damit, ohne daß, (an)statt daß** must replace the infinitive construction.

Er geht in die Bar, **um** einen Konjak **zu** trinken.

Er geht in die Bar, **damit** ihn **niemand** auf der Straße sieht.

Die beiden verlassen den Raum, **ohne** ein Wort zu sagen.

Die beiden verlassen den Raum, **ohne daß jemand** ein Wort sagt.

Drill 16   *Change the second clause to an infinitive construction with* **um . . . zu.** *Follow the example.*

Die beiden betreten das Lokal. Sie wollen die Ausweise kontrollieren.

Die beiden betreten das Lokal, **um** die Ausweise **zu kontrollieren.**

Der Polizist hebt den Paß in das Licht. Er will ihn besser sehen können.

Der Verbrecher verläßt das Hause. Er will ein Schiff finden.

Er muß raus. Er will mit dem Leben wieder Kontakt aufnehmen.

Er geht in das Lokal. Er will einen Konjak trinken.

Der Mann kommt auf ihn zu. Er will ihm gratulieren.

Der Mann spricht mit ihm. Er will seinen Namen erfahren.

Drill 17 *Change the second clause to an infinitive construction with* **ohne . . . zu**. *Follow the example.*

Er läuft auf die Straße. Er paßt nicht auf.

Er läuft auf die Straße, **ohne aufzupassen.**

Die Menschen gehen an ihm vorbei. Sie erkennen ihn nicht.

Die beiden verlassen die Bar. Sie sagen kein Wort.

Er betritt die große Halle. Er merkt nicht, wohin er geht.

Er sagt dem Mann seinen richtigen Namen. Er weiß nicht, was er sagt.

Er setzte sich wieder auf die Schulbank He went back to school; Er verdiente sich sein Studium He earned his tuition; Der Bauarbeiter, – construction worker; der Landarbeiter, – farmhand; der Fabrikarbeiter, – factory worker; das Staatsexamen, – university diploma for high school teachers

teilen *here:* to share; das Schicksal, –e fate; Er machte das Abitur He got his high school diploma; die Germanistik study of German language and literature; die Anglistik study of English language and literature; die Geschichte *here:* history; der Bibliothekar, –e librarian; der Vertreter, – *here:* traveling salesman; Schwäbisch-Hall *city in Württemberg;* der Gastdozent, –en *(MII)* guest lecturer

Der Erzählerwettbewerb, – writers' contest; die Wochenzeitung, –en weekly newspaper; der Spiegel, – mirror; Sie hat zum Thema It has its theme; das Bewußtsein consciousness; das Unterbewußte *(part.)* subconscious; im engsten Rahmen *here:* within the tightest possible framework; ein Thema gestalten to develop a theme

Das Gesicht des Fahrers verzog sich ärgerlich The driver's face became distorted with anger; taumelig staggering; der Gehweg, –e sidewalk

quietschen to screech; die Bremse, –n brake; ärgerlich angry; der Schritt, –e step; Hat es Ihnen was gemacht? Were you hurt?; der Ellbogen, – elbow; an·fassen an (+ *dat.*) to take hold of by

Herbert Malecha

Biographie   Herbert Malecha ist 1927 in Ratibor, in Ober-
schlesien, geboren. Auch er teilte das Schicksal seiner Generation, und wurde mit siebzehn Jahren, noch kurz vor dem Ende
des Krieges, Soldat. 1945 kehre er nicht in seine Heimat, die
nun zu Polen gehört, zurück, sondern ging nach Süddeutschland, wo er sich im Schwäbisch-Haller Gymnasium wieder
auf die Schulbank setzte, um sein Abitur zu machen. 1947
begann er an der Universität Tübingen Germanistik, Anglistik
und Geschichte zu studieren. Er verdiente sich sein Studium
während der Semester als Bibliothekar und als Vertreter, und
in den Ferien als Bau-, Land- und Fabrikarbeiter. 1953 verließ
er die Universität mit dem Staatsexamen. Er lehrt heute am
Gymnasium in Schwäbisch-Hall. 1960 war er Gastdozent am
Middlebury College, Vt.

Seine Kurzgeschichte *Die Probe* gewann 1955 den ersten Preis
im Erzählerwettbewerb der Hamburger Wochenzeitung *Die Zeit*.
Diese Erzählung hat nichts mehr mit der Kriegs-, Trümmer- und
Heimkehrerliteratur zu tun. Sie ist kein Spiegel der Zeit, sondern hat ein psychologisches Problem, den Konflikt zwischen
dem Bewußtsein und dem Unterbewußten, zum Thema. Herbert
Malechas *Die Probe* ist ein Versuch, dieses Thema im engsten
Rahmen, in der konzentrierten Form der Kurzgeschichte, zu
gestalten.

DIE PROBE

Redluff sah, das schrille Quietschen der Bremsen noch in den
Ohren, wie sich das Gesicht des Fahrers ärgerlich verzog. Mit
zwei taumeligen Schritten war er wieder auf dem Gehweg. „Hat
es Ihnen was gemacht?" Er fühlte sich am Ellbogen angefaßt.

beinah *here:* almost; **Schon gut** It's all right

sich frei·machen to free oneself; **merken** to notice; **die Bewegung, –en** movement; **nach·starren** *(+ dat.)* to stare after

die Welle, –n wave; **aufsteigen, ie, ie** to climb up, to arise; **unauffällig** inconspicuous; **Langsam ließ das Klopfen im Halse nach** The pounding in his throat subsided slowly; **ewig** *here:* forever; **das Loch, ⁀er** hole; **sich verkriechen, o, o** to hide away, to hole up; **Seine Hand fuhr über die linke Brustseite seines Jacketts** He ran his hand over the left side of his jacket

die Schwäche, –n weakness; **die Übelkeit, –en** sickness, nausea; **Das hätte ihm gerade gefehlt!** That's all he needed; **angefahren** hit, run over (by a car); **gaffen** to gape; **die Menge** crowd; **weiter·laufen, ie, au** to go on, to keep going; **Ich darf jetzt nicht schwach werden** I must not become weak (I cannot let myself become weak); **Er mußte wieder Kontakt auf·nehmen mit dem Leben** He had to get in contact with life again; **Ein Schiff mußte sich finden lassen = Es mußte möglich sein, ein Schiff zu finden; möglichst** if at all possible; **spüren** to feel, to sense; **der Paß, ⁀sse** passport; **die Innentasche, ‑‑n** inside pocket

Die Autos waren zu einer Kette angefahren The cars had formed a line; **Nur stockend schoben sie sich vorwärts** They proceeded only in spurts; **der Platzregen, –** shower; **ausgesetzt sein** *(+ dat.)* to be exposed to; **schlagen, u, a an** *(+ acc.)* to strike; **der Blick, –e** glance; **haften an** *(+ dat.)* to be fixed upon; **schwarzgerändert** bordered in black; **an·fahren, u, a** to start; **auf·summen** to begin to purr; **vorbei·schrammen** to squeak past; **unwillkürlich** involuntary

die Kette, –n chain; **vorbei·gehen, i, a, an** *(+ dat.)* to go past; **entgegen·kommen, a, o** *(+ dat.)* to come toward; **Er achtete darauf, daß . . .** He saw to it that . . . ; **streifen** to brush against; **fahl** pale; **das wechselnde Reklamelicht, –r** flashing advertisement lights; **sich verfärben** to change colors; **sich an·strengen** to exert oneself; **an·nehmen, a, o** *here:* to adapt to; **mit·schwimmen, a, o** to swim along; **der Strom, ⁀e** stream, current; **die Stimme, –n** voice; **abgerissene Gesprächsfetzen** torn bits of conversation; **bemalt** painted; **die Straßenbahn, –en** streetcar; **flutend** surging; **hundertfach** hundredfold; **der Kragen, –** collar; **das Hals, ⁀** *here:* throat; **schweißig** perspiring, sweaty

ein·tauchen to submerge

Wovor hab' ich denn eigentlich Angst? What am I actually afraid of?; **die Einbildung, –en** imagination; **erkennen, a, a** to recognize; **genau** clear, precise

Mit einer fast brüsken Bewegung machte er sich frei. „Nein, nein, schon gut. Danke", sagte er noch, beinah schon über die Schulter, als er merkte, daß ihm der Alte nachstarrte.

Eine Welle von Schwäche stieg von seinen Knien auf, wurde fast zur Übelkeit. Das hätte ihm gerade gefehlt, angefahren auf der Straße zu liegen, eine gaffende Menge und dann die Polizei. Er durfte jetzt nicht schwach werden, nur weiterlaufen, unauffällig weiterlaufen zwischen den vielen auf der hellen Straße. Langsam ließ das Klopfen im Halse nach. Seit drei Monaten war er zum erstenmal wieder in der Stadt, zum erstenmal wieder unter so viel Menschen. Ewig konnte er in dem Loch sich ja nicht verkriechen, er mußte einmal wieder raus, wieder Kontakt aufnehmen mit dem Leben, überhaupt raus aus allem. Ein Schiff mußte sich finden lassen, möglichst noch, bevor es Winter wurde. Seine Hand fuhr leicht über die linke Brustseite seines Jacketts, er spürte den Paß, der in der Innentasche steckte; gute Arbeit war dieser Paß, er hatte auch nicht schlecht dafür bezahlt.

Die Autos auf der Straße waren zu einer langen Kette aufgefahren. Nur stockend schoben sie sich vorwärts. Menschen gingen an ihm vorbei, kamen ihm entgegen; er achtete darauf, daß sie ihn nicht streiften. Einem Platzregen von Gesichtern war er ausgesetzt, fahle Ovale, die sich mit dem wechselnden Reklamelicht verfärbten. Redluff strengte sich an, den Schritt der vielen anzunehmen, mitzuschwimmen in dem Strom. Stimmen, abgerissene Gesprächsfetzen schlugen an sein Ohr, jemand lachte. Für eine Sekunde haftete sein Blick an dem Gesicht einer Frau, ihr offener, bemalter Mund sah schwarzgerändert aus. Die Autos fuhren jetzt an, ihre Motoren summten auf. Eine Straßenbahn schrammte vorbei. Und wieder Menschen, Menschen, ein Strom flutender Gesichter, Sprechen und hundertfache Schritte. Redluff fuhr unwillkürlich mit der Hand an seinen Kragen. An seinem Hals merkte er, daß seine Finger kalt und schweißig waren.

Wovor hab' ich denn eigentlich Angst, verdammte Einbildung, wer soll mich denn schon erkennen in dieser Menge, sagte er sich. Aber er spürte nur zu genau, daß er in ihr nicht eintauchen konnte, daß er wie ein Kork auf dem Wasser tanzte,

fett fat; *here:* in bold print; **rutschen** to slip; **die Spalte, –n** *here:* newspaper column

abgestoßen repelled; **weitergetrieben** driven on; **Ihn fror** He felt cold; **anders** different; **die Anschlagsäule, –n** advertisement pillar, billboard; **das Fragezeichen, –** question mark; **die Schlagzeilen** headlines; **das Blatt, ∸er = die Zeitung, –en; verschwinden, a, u** to disappear

ab·biegen, o, o to turn off; **das Rinnsal, –e** rivulet, rill; **sich auf·lösen** to break up, to dissolve; **zerfallen, ie, a** *here:* to separate; **brackig** brackish; **der Lufthauch** breath of air; **der Hafen, ∸** harbor

einzeln *here:* single; **die Gestalt, –en** shape; *here:* figure; **die Krawatte, –n** tie; **nach·lassen, ie, a** *here:* to loosen; **Ihn fröstelte** He felt chilly

das Lichtband, ∸er stream of light; **quer** diagonal; **der Dunst, ∸e nach** (+ *dat.*) smell of; **der Qualm** smoke; **aufgetakelt** rigged up; **die Ecke, –n** corner; **die Theke, –n** bar, counter; **auf·schauen** to look up; **flüchtig** fleeting, hasty

das Lokal, –e restaurant; **die Kneipe, –n** bar, joint; **grell** gaudy, garish; **die Gesellschaft** *here:* company; **pathetisch** sentimental; *here:* overexpressive, pretentious; **der Schirm, –e** lamp shade; **der Musikautomat, –en** juke box; **lehnen** to lean; **dick** fat; **der Bursche, –n** fellow; **bloß** bare

der Zug, ∸e *here:* puff, draw; **leicht benommen** slightly dizzy; **gezogen jaulende Gitarretöne** drawn out howling guitar sounds; **spitz** sharp

der Kellner, – waiter; **schön warm** nice and warm; **aus·strecken** to stretch out; **Gut saß es sich hier** It was good to sit here

drehen to turn; **schlagend zufallen, ie, a** to slam shut; **gleich darauf** right after that; **hinüber·schielen** to glance over

stockig stocky; **der Ledermantel, ∸** leather coat; **Er steuerte auf den Nachbartisch zu** He headed for the next table

abgestoßen und weitergetrieben. Ihn fror plötzlich. Nichts wie verdammte Einbildung, sagte er sich wieder. Vor drei Monaten war das ja noch anders, da stand sein Name schwarz auf rotem Papier auf jeder Anschlagsäule zu lesen, Jens Redluff; nur gut, daß das Foto so schlecht war. Der Name stand damals fett in den Schlagzeilen der Blätter, wurde dann klein und kleiner, auch das Fragezeichen dahinter, rutschte in die letzten Spalten und verschwand bald ganz.

Redluff war jetzt in eine Seitenstraße abgebogen, der Menschenstrom wurde dünner, noch ein paar Abbiegungen, und die Rinnsale lösten sich auf, zerfielen in einzelne Gestalten, einzelne Schritte. Hier war es dunkler. Er konnte den Kragen öffnen und die Krawatte nachlassen. Der Wind brachte einen brackigen Lufthauch vom Hafen her. Ihn fröstelte.

Ein breites Lichtband fiel quer vor ihm über die Straße, jemand kam aus dem kleinen Lokal, mit ihm ein Dunst nach Bier, Qualm und Essen. Redluff ging hinein. Die kleine, als Cafe aufgetakelte Kneipe war fast leer, ein paar Soldaten saßen herum, grelle Damen in ihrer Gesellschaft. Auf den kleinen Tischen standen Lämpchen mit pathetisch roten Schirmen. Ein Musikautomat begann aus der Ecke zu hämmern. Hinter der Theke lehnte ein dicker Bursche mit bloßen Armen. Er schaute nur flüchtig auf.

„Konjak, doppelt", sagte Redluff zu dem Kellner. Er merkte, daß er seinen Hut noch in der Hand hielt und legte ihn auf den leeren Stuhl neben sich. Er steckte sich eine Zigarette an, die ersten tiefen Züge machten ihn leicht benommen. Schön warm war es hier, er streckte seine Füße lang aus. Die Musik hatte gewechselt. Über gezogen jaulenden Gitarretönen hörte er halblautes Sprechen, ein spitzes Lachen vom Nachbartisch. Gut saß es sich hier.

Der Dicke hinter der Theke drehte jetzt seinen Kopf nach der Tür. Draußen fiel eine Wagentür schlagend zu. Gleich darauf kamen zwei Männer herein, klein und stockig der eine von ihnen. Er blieb in der Mitte stehen, der andere, im langen Ledermantel, steuerte auf den Nachbartisch zu. Keiner von beiden nahm seinen Hut ab. Redluff versuchte hinüberzuschielen,

Es durchfuhr ihn A shiver ran through his body; **etwas Blinkendes** something shiny; **aus·setzen** *here:* to stop; **wulstig** thick; **kramen** to rummage for; **eigensinnig** stubborn; **scheinen, ie, ie** *here:* to seem; **leicht** slightly; **schwanken** to sway; **Ihm war, als . . .** It seemed to him as if . . . ; **der sich neigende Boden** slanting floor; **samt** together with; **rutschen** slide; **die Runde, –n** round

sich beugen to bend; **kurz** briefly; **eine bunte Karte** *here:* registration card; **die Handtasche, –n** pocketbook; **sich klammern an** (+ *acc.*) to cling to; **die Tischkante, –n** edge of the table; **der Fingernagel, ⸚** fingernail; **sich entfärben** to lose color; **geradewegs** straight

entschuldigen to excuse; **das runde Metall** *here:* badge; **der Stoff, –e** material; **berühren** to touch; **die Falte, –n** fold; *here:* crease; **gerunzelt** wrinkled; **die Stirn, –en** forehead; **zögern** to hesitate; **spröde** harsh; **grinsen** to grin; **der Witz, –e** joke; „**Feuer?**" "A light?" **schieben, o, o** to push; **brennen, a, a** to burn; **das Streichholz, ⸚er** match; **längs** along

der Ausweis, –e identification; **aus·drücken** *here:* to put out; **völlig ruhig** completely calm; **blättern** to leaf through; **heben, o, o** to lift, to hold up; **kontrollieren** to check up on; **der Verbrecher, –** criminal; **jemand(em) ähnlich sehen** to resemble someone

sich zurück·lehnen to lean back; **zerbröckeln** to crumble; **schmelzen, o, o** to melt; **jubeln** to rejoice, to shout for joy; **wieder ein·setzen** to start up again

die Spannung, –en tension; **die Probe bestehen, a, a** to pass the test

es durchfuhr ihn. Er sah, wie der Große sich über den Tisch beugte, kurz etwas Blinkendes in der Hand hielt. Die Musik hatte ausgesetzt. „What's he want?" hörte er den Neger vom Nebentisch sagen. „What's he want?" Er sah seine wulstigen Lippen sich bewegen. Das Mädchen kramte eine bunte Karte aus ihrer Handtasche. „What's he want?" sagte der Neger eigensinnig. Der Mann war schon zum nächsten Tisch gegangen. Redluff klammerte sich mit der einen Hand an die Tischkante. Er sah, wie die Fingernägel sich entfärbten. Der rauchige Raum schien ganz leicht zu schwanken, ganz leicht. Ihm war, als müßte er auf dem sich neigenden Boden jetzt langsam samt Tisch und Stuhl auf die andere Seite rutschen. Der Große hatte seine Runde beendet und ging auf den anderen zu, der immer noch mitten im Raum stand, die Hände in den Manteltaschen. Redluff sah, wie er zu dem Großen etwas sagte. Er konnte es nicht verstehen. Dann kam er geradewegs auf ihn zu.

„Sie entschuldigen", sagte er, „Ihren Ausweis bitte!" Redluff schaute erst gar nicht auf das runde Metall in seiner Hand. Er drückte seine Zigarette aus und war plötzlich völlig ruhig. Er wußte es selbst nicht, was ihn mit einmal so ruhig machte, aber seine Hand, die in die Innentasche seines Jacketts fuhr, fühlte den Stoff nicht, den sie berührte, sie war wie von Holz. Der Mann blätterte langsam in dem Paß, hob ihn besser in das Licht. Redluff sah die Falten auf der gerunzelten Stirn, eins, zwei, drei. Der Mann gab ihm den Paß zurück. „Danke, Herr Wolters", sagte er. Aus seiner unnatürlichen Ruhe heraus hörte Redluff sich selber sprechen. „Das hat man gern, so kontrolliert zu werden wie —", er zögerte etwas, „ein Verbrecher!" Seine Stimme stand spröde im Raum. Er hatte doch gar nicht so laut gesprochen. „Man sieht manchmal jemand ähnlich", sagte der Mann, grinste, als hätte er einen feinen Witz gemacht. „Feuer?" Er fingerte eine halbe Zigarette aus der Manteltasche. Redluff schob seine Hand mit dem brennenden Streichholz längs der Tischkante ihm entgegen. Die beiden gingen.

Redluff lehnte sich in seinen Stuhl zurück. Die Spannung in ihm zerbröckelte, die eisige Ruhe schmolz. Er hätte jubeln können. Das war es, das war die Probe, und er hatte sie bestanden. Triumphierend setzte der Musikautomat wieder ein. „He, Sie vergessen Ihren Hut", sagte der Dicke hinter der Theke.

atmen to breathe; **Seine Schritte schwangen weit aus**
He took long strides

belebt *here:* busy, frequented; **zu·nehmen, a, o** to
increase; **der Laden, ⁻n** shop; **das Kino, –s** movie
house, theater; **der Knäuel** knot; **schwatzen** to chatter; **lächeln** to smile; **enttäuscht** disappointed;
nesteln an (+ *dat.*) to fuss with; **dunkel glänzend**
dark shiny; **blank** shiny; **(sich) ergießen, o, o** to
pour; **aus·rufen, ie, u** to call out; **die Abendausgabe,**
–n evening edition; **beschlagen** *here:* fogged up,
steamed up; **die Spiegelglasscheibe, –n** plateglass
window; **undeutlich** indistinct, blurred; **pulsieren**
to pulsate, hum; **dringen, a, u** to penetrate; **abge-**
dämpft faint, muted; **der Sog** wake; **die Glühlampe,**
–n electric light; **riesig** giant; **das Transparent, –e**
poster, billboard; **die Kasse, –n** ticket window; **der**
Einlaß entrance; **(sich) drängen** to crowd and shove;
dicht hinter ihr close behind her; **wenden, a, a** to
turn; **(sich) zwängen** to squeeze; **suchen** to seek;
die Ordnung, –en order; **das Gedränge** mob, pushing
crowd; **blitzend** gleaming, flashing; **der Anzug, ⁻e**
suit; **gleißend** dazzling; **übergießen, o, o** to flood;
der Fotoblitz, –e flashbulb; **zucken** *here:* to flash;
zu allem on top of it all; **dröhnen** to boom; **vor**
innerer Freudigkeit from sheer joy; **bersten, a, o** to
burst; **wert** *here:* honorable; **Die Stimme schmalzte**
The voice oozed; **unwiderstehlich** irresistible

Am liebsten hätte er gesungen He felt like singing

Es tat ihm wohl It did him good; **der Zeitungsver-**
käufer, – newspaperboy; **das Paar, –e** couple; **Ihm**
war wie nach Sekt He felt as though he should have
champagne (i.e., should celebrate); **Es machte ihm**
keine Mühe mehr It was not an effort for him anymore; **der Platz, ⁻e** square; **fluten** *here:* to pour out;
von vorhin from before; **die Reihe, –n** line; **spüren**
to sense; **der Hauch** whiff; **das Gewirr** *here:* confusion; **der Portier, –s** doorkeeper; **die Art, –en** kind,
sort; **ab·nehmen, a, o** to take (from); **die Einlaßkarte,**
–n ticket; **Er deutete hinter ihm her** He pointed after
him; **das Scheinwerferlicht** spotlight; **der Riesenblu-**
menstrauß, ⁻e giant bouquet; **Sie hakten ihn unter**
They linked arms with him; **geölt** oily; **der Besucher,**
– visitor; **die Ausstellung, –en** exhibition; **betäubt**
stunned

Draußen atmete er tief, seine Schritte schwangen weit aus, am liebsten hätte er gesungen.

Langsam kam er wieder in belebtere Straßen, die Lichter nahmen zu, die Läden, die Leuchtzeichen an den Wänden. Aus einem Kino kam ein Knäuel Menschen, sie lachten und schwatzten, er mitten unter ihnen. Es tat ihm wohl, wenn sie ihn streiften. „Hans", hörte er eine Frauenstimme hinter sich, jemand faßte seinen Arm. „Tut mir leid", sagte er und lächelte in das enttäuschte Gesicht. Verdammt hübsch, sagte er zu sich. Im Weitergehen nestelte er an seiner Krawatte. Dunkelglänzende Wagen sangen über den blanken Asphalt, Kaskaden wechselnden Lichts ergossen sich von den Fassaden, Zeitungsverkäufer riefen die Abendausgaben aus. Hinter einer großen, leicht beschlagenen Spiegelglasscheibe sah er undeutlich tanzende Paare; pulsierend drang die Musik abgedämpft bis auf die Straße. Ihm war wie nach Sekt. Ewig hätte er so gehen können, so wie jetzt. Er gehörte wieder dazu, er hatte den Schritt der vielen, es machte ihm keine Mühe mehr. Im Sog der Menge ging er über den großen Platz auf die große Halle zu mit ihren Ketten von Glühlampen und riesigen Transparenten. Um die Kassen vor dem Einlaß drängten sich Menschen. Von irgendwoher flutete Lautsprechermusik. Stand dort nicht das Mädchen von vorhin? Redluff stellte sich hinter sie in die Reihe. Sie wandte den Kopf, er spürte einen Hauch von Parfüm. Dicht hinter ihr zwängte er sich durch den Einlaß. Immer noch flutete die Musik, er hörte ein Gewirr von Hunderten von Stimmen. Ein paar Polizisten suchten etwas Ordnung in das Gedränge zu bringen. Ein Mann in einer Art von Portiersuniform nahm ihm seine Einlaßkarte ab. „Der, der!" rief er auf einmal und deutete aufgeregt hinter ihm her. Gesichter wandten sich, jemand im schwarzen Anzug kam auf ihn zu, ein blitzendes Ding in der Hand. Gleißendes Scheinwerferlicht übergoß ihn. Jemand drückte ihm einen Riesenblumenstrauß in die Hände. Zwei strahlend lächelnde Mädchen hakten ihn rechts und links unter, Fotoblitze zuckten. Und zu allem dröhnte eine geölte Stimme, die vor innerer Freudigkeit fast zu bersten schien: „Ich darf Ihnen im Namen der Direktion von ganzem Herzen gratulieren, Sie sind der hunderttausendste Besucher der Ausstellung!" Redluff stand wie betäubt. „Und jetzt sagen Sie uns Ihren werten Namen", schmalzte die Stimme unwiderstehlich weiter.

der **Winkel**, – *here:* corner

eben noch until then

der **Kordon** cordon; *here:* barrier; **sich auf·lösen** to dissolve, to break up

„Redluff, Jens Redluff", sagte er, noch ehe er wußte, was er sagte, und schon hatten es die Lautsprecher dröhnend bis in den letzten Winkel der riesigen Halle getragen.

Der Kordon der Polizisten, der eben noch die applaudierende Menge zurückgehalten hatte, löste sich langsam auf. Sie kamen auf ihn zu.

I. QUESTIONNAIRE

A. Exercises for the A-Questions

Study the following expressions:

1. Er **machte sich frei.**	He freed himself.
2. Das hätte ihm gerade gefehlt.	That is all he needed.
3. Er mußte wieder **mit dem** Leben Kontakt **aufnehmen.**	He had to get in contact with life again.
4. Er **achtete** darauf, daß die Menschen ihn nicht streiften.	He saw to it that people did not brush against him.
5. Die Gesichter **verfärbten sich.**	The faces changed colors.
6. Er **strengte sich an.**	He exerted himself.
7. Er hatte **Angst vor der** Polizei.	He was afraid of the police.
8. Gut **saß es sich** hier.	It was good to sit here.
9. Er **klammerte sich an die** Tischkante.	He clung to the edge of the table.
10. Ihm war wie nach Sekt.	He felt as though he had champagne.
11. Die Gesichter **wandten sich** ihm **zu.**	The faces turned toward him.
12. Der Kordon der Polizisten **löste sich auf.**	The barrier of policemen broke up.
13. Er war **stolz auf seinen** falschen Paß.	He was proud of his fake passport.

The following expressions emphasize the completion of an action: **Hin** indicates motion *away from the speaker,* **her** refers to motion *toward the speaker.*

herauskommen **aus**	Er kommt **aus** dem Haus **heraus.**
herumfahren **um**	Er fährt **um** die Stadt **herum.**
herangehen **an**	Er geht **an** das Haus **heran.**
hineinlaufen **in**	Er läuft **in** das Haus **hinein.**
hinauffahren **auf**	Er fährt **auf** den Berg **hinauf.**
hindurchgehen **durch**	Er geht **durch** die Halle **hindurch.**
hinüberfahren **über**	Er fährt **über** den Fluß **hinüber.**

Drill 1   *Form sentences following the examples above.*

hineingehen, die Kneipe   hineinlaufen, die Halle   hinüberschwimmen, der Fluß
herauskommen, das Lokal   herumgehen, die Ecke   hindurchgehen, die Halle
herantreten, der Nachbartisch hinaufgehen, der Berg

In expressions like the following, **her** indicates a *gesture* or *continuous motion in the same direction in which the object of the preposition is moving.*

Er zeigt **hinter ihm her.**	He points after him.
Er fährt **neben ihm her.**	He is driving beside him.
Er läuft **vor ihm her.**	He is running in front of him.
Er geht **hinter ihm her.**	He is following him.

The following expression emphasizes *the direction of a movement.*

Der Polizist geht **auf ihn zu.**	The policeman is heading toward him.
Sie kommen **auf ihn zu.**	They are heading toward him.

Drill 2   *Give the German equivalent.*

We are heading for the house.   They are heading for the little bar.
They are heading for us.   He is heading for the next table.
He is heading for the large hall.   They are heading for me.

B. A-Questions

1. Was erfahren wir zu Beginn der Geschichte?

   Was **hört** *Redluff?* // shrill screeching / brakes //
   Was **sieht** *er?* // the driver's angry face //
   Mit zwei Schritten ist er wieder auf dem Gehweg. Was **fragt** *jemand?* // Were you hurt? *(direct quote)* //
   Was tut *der Alte?* // to take hold of by / elbow //
   Wie reagiert *Redluff?* // to free oneself //
   Was **bemerkt** *er?* // that /old man / to stare after / him //

2. Welche Empfindungen und welche Gedanken hat Redluff auf der Straße?

   Was **fühlt** *er zunächst?* // weakness / and / nausea //
   Was *hätte ihm gerade gefehlt?* // to lie run over / on / street //
   Vor wem hat *er Angst?* // gaping crowd / and / police //
   Was **darf** *er jetzt nicht?* // to become weak //
   Wo **ist** er *seit drei Monaten* **zum ersten Mal wieder?** // in / city / among / people //
   Was **muß** er wieder? // to get in contact with / life //
   Was **hat** *er in der Innentasche?* // passport //
   Was **erfahren** *wir* über den Paß? // that / to be / good work / and / that / to have paid well for it //

3. Redluff läuft die nächtliche Straße entlang. Welche Eindrücke hat er dabei?

   Was alles **sieht er?** // a long line of cars // pale faces and flashing advertisement lights // the face of a woman with open, painted lips // cars and a stream of faces //
   Was alles **hört er?** // voices and torn bits of conversation // somebody laugh // motors and a streetcar // speaking and hundreds of footsteps //

4. Wie verhält er sich?

   Worauf achtet er? // that / people / not / to brush against / him //
   Was macht **er,** um den Schritt der vielen andern Menschen anzunehmen? // to exert oneself //
   Er greift mit der Hand an den Kragen. Was **merkt er?** // that / fingers / to be / cold / and / sweaty //

5. Welche Einbildungen hat er und was fühlt er?

   Was **fragt er sich?** // what / to be afraid of //
   Was **fragt er sich** noch? // who / to recognize / him //
   Was **spürt er genau?** // that / to dance / like /cork / water // that / to be repelled / and / driven on //
   Welches **Gefühl hat er plötzlich?** // that / to feel cold //

6. Was erfahren wir über seine Vergangenheit?

   Wo **hat man seinen Namen** *vor drei Monaten* **gelesen?** // billboards / and / headlines of the newspapers //
   Was aber *ist nur gut für ihn gewesen?* // that / photo / to have been / bad //
   Was ist *später* geschehen? // name / to have disappeared / completely / from (aus) newspapers //

7. Redluff ist in eine dunkle Seitenstraße eingebogen. Wie verhält er sich jetzt?
   Was **sieht er noch?** // single figures //
   Was **hört er noch?** // single footsteps //
   Was **kann er** *jetzt* **tun?** // to open / collar / and / to loosen / tie //
   Aber welches **Gefühl hat er wieder?** // that / to feel chilly //

8. Redluff sieht eine kleine Kneipe und geht hinein. Beschreiben Sie die Kneipe.
   Sind viele Leute in dem Lokal? // bar / to be / almost empty //
   Wer **sitzt dort herum?** // a few soldiers //
   Wer **befindet sich in ihrer Gesellschaft?** // gaudy women //
   Was steht *auf den kleinen Tischen?* // lamps / overexpressively sentimental / red shades //
   Und was **hämmert** *aus der Ecke?* // jukebox //
   Was für ein Mann **steht** *hinter der Theke?* // fat fellow / bare arms //

9. Wie verhält sich Redluff in der Kneipe und was denkt er?
   Was **bestellt er?** // double cognac //
   Wo **hat er seinen Hut?** // in his hand //

Was macht *er* damit? // to put / it / chair //
Was tut *er* dann? // to light / cigarette / and / to stretch out / feet //
Was **denkt er dabei?** // to be / nice and warm / here // to be good / to sit / here //

10. Draußen fällt eine Wagentür zu. Der dicke Bursche dreht seinen Kopf nach der Tür. Wie ändert sich die Situation?

Wer **kommt herein?** // two men //
Wie sieht *der eine* aus? // to be / small / and / stocky //
Was trägt *der andere?* // leather coat //
Wohin geht *der Große?* // to head for / next table //
Was tun beide nicht? // neither one of them / to take off / hat //
Was **sieht Redluff?** // how / big one / to bend / over / table //
Was nimmt *das Mädchen* aus ihrer **Handtasche?** // registration card //
Wie reagiert *Redluff* in diesem Augenblick? // to cling to / edge of table //
Was **sieht er?** // how / fingernails / to lose / color //

11. Was geschieht, nachdem der Große seine Runde beendet hat?

Was **tut er?** // to head for / Redluff //
Was **sagt er?** // excuse // identification //
Wie reagiert *Redluff?* // to put out / cigarette // to be / suddenly / completely calm //
Was macht *der Mann* mit Redluffs Paß // to leaf through / slowly / passport // to hold up to / light //
Mit welchen **Worten gibt er Redluff den Paß zurück?** // thanks / Mr. . . . . //
Was **sagt Redluff da?** // one / to like / that / to be checked up on / like / criminal //
Was **antwortet ihm der Große?** // one / to resemble / sometimes / someone //

12. Die beiden verlassen die Kneipe. Was bedeutet Redluff die Kontrolle?

Was **verschwindet?** // tension / and / calm //
Was **glaubt er?** // that / that / to have been / test // that / to have passed / test //
Er steht auf und geht. Was **sagt der Dicke?** // to forget / hat // *(direct quote)*
Draußen atmet er tief. Was **hätte er jetzt am liebsten** getan? // to sing //

13. Er kommt wieder in belebtere Straßen zurück. Wie verhält er sich jetzt?

Was *tut ihm wohl?* // when / people / to brush / against / him //
Wie reagiert er auf die Frau, die ihn mit einem falschen Namen anredet? // to say / that / to be sorry // to smile / disappointed face //
Was alles **bemerkt er jetzt?** // cars / newspaper boys / and / dancing couples //
Welches Gefühl hat er? // he feels as though he should have champagne *(direct quote)* // to belong / again //
Wohin **geht er?** //large square / large hall //
Was **fragt er sich?** // whether / there / not / to be / girl from before //
Was tut *er?* // to go and stand / behind / her //
Was **spürt er?** // whiff of perfume //

14. Er zwängt sich durch den Einlaß. Wie endet die Geschichte?

Was **hört** *Redluff?* // confusion of voices //
Was tut **ein Mann in einer Art Portiersuniform?** // to take / ticket // to call / and / to point / after / him //
Was **sieht** *Redluff* im Scheinwerferlicht? // that / faces / to turn to / him // that / somebody / black suit / to head for / him // giant bouquet //
Was geschieht noch? // two smiling girls / to link arms with him //
Was **sagt** *eine geölte Stimme?* // may / congratulate // *(direct quote)* // that / to be / 100,000th visitor / exhibition //
Wie reagiert **Redluff?** // to stand / as though / stunned //
Was **möchte** *der Mann wissen?* // his name //
Wie **antwortet** *Redluff?* // with / real name / before / to know / what / to say //
Was ist **sofort** geschehen? // loudspeakers / to have carried / it / last corner / big hall //
Wie reagieren die Polizisten? // barrier / policemen / to break up // to head for him //

C.   Exercises for the B-Questions

Drill 3   *Give the English equivalents.*

He frees himself.
He has to get in contact with life again.
It is a question of his existence.
He exerts himself.
The faces change colors.
He sees to it that people do not brush against him.
He enters the bar.
He sits down at a table.
It is good to sit there.
He lights a cigarette.
The policeman heads for him.
He bends over the table.
He asks for his passport.
He distrusts him.
The criminal is afraid of the test.
His fingernails lose color.

He clings to the edge of the table.
He relies on his fake passport.
He wonders whether they recognize him.
The situation changes.
He changes his behavior.
He is proud of himself.
He feels as though he should have champagne.
But he is mistaken about the test.
He adapts himself to the people on the street.
He reacts to the perfume.
He decides to follow the girl.
He does not care.
The faces turn to him.
The barrier of policemen breaks up.
They head for him.

D.   B-Questions

1. Welche Tatsachen erfahren wir zu Beginn der Erzählung über die Hauptfigur, Jens Redluff, und seine Vergangenheit?
   // for three months / to be / for the first time / again / in / city / among / people //
   // to have to get in contact with / life / again //

// to feel / passport / in / inside pocket //
// to be / good work // to have paid / well / for it //
// three months ago / one / to have read / name / billboards / and / headlines / newspapers //
// to have been good / that / photo / bad //
// later / name / to have disappeared / completely / papers //
Was sagen uns diese Tatsachen über die Hauptfigur der Erzählung und ihren Paß? Versuchen
Sie, mit Modalverben, **werden** und **scheinen** zu antworten.

2. Redluff glaubt, daß die Paßkontrolle in der Kneipe die Probe für ihn gewesen ist, und daß er
diese Probe bestanden hat. Er hat danach keine Angst mehr. Vergleichen Sie seine Eindrücke
und Reaktionen **vor** und **nach** der Probe. Beginnen Sie Ihre Sätze mit den Präpositionen **vor**
und **nach**, mit den Konjunktionen **bevor** und **nachdem**, oder mit den Adverbien **vorher** und
danach. Zum Beispiel:

vor	*nach*
Vor der Probe . . .	**Nach** der Probe . . .
Vor der Paßkontrolle . . .	**Nach** der Paßkontrolle . . .

bevor	*nachdem*
Bevor er die Probe besteht, . . .	**Nachdem** er die Probe bestanden **hat,** . . .
Bevor er die Kneipe betritt, . . .	**Nachdem** er die Kneipe verlassen **hat,** . . .
Bevor die Polizei seinen Paß kontrolliert, . . .	**Nachdem** die Polizei seinen Paß kontrolliert **hat,** . . .

vorher	*danach*
Vorher fühlt er Schwäche und Übelkeit.	**Danach** ist ihm wie nach Sekt.

// before the test / somebody / to take hold of by / elbow / and / to ask / whether /
he / to have been hurt //
// after the test / somebody / to take / arm // Redluff / to hear / a woman's voice /
saying / Hans //
// before / to stand / test / Redluff / to free oneself / brusk movement //
// after / to have passed / test / Redluff / to reply / to be sorry / and / to smile /
disappointed face //
// before / Redluff / to see / pale ovals / face of a woman / open, painted lips / and /
stream of faces //
// afterwards / Redluff / to see / disappointed, pretty face / dancing couples //
// before / examination of passport / he / to see to it / that / people / not / to brush
against //
// after / examination of passport / to do him good / when / people / to brush
against //
Vergleichen Sie in dieser Weise weitere Eindrücke und Reaktionen Redluffs vor und nach der

Probe. Beziehen Sie sich dabei immer auf Ihre Antworten zu den A-Fragen und auf die Ausdrücke im Drill 3.

Wie unterscheiden sich seine Eindrücke **vorher** und **nachher?** Versuchen Sie, mit Modalverben, **werden, scheinen, haben** und **nicht brauchen** zu antworten.

3. Die Geschichte zeigt zwei Proben. Wie unterscheiden sie sich?

Was bemerkt Redluff vor dem Lokal und was vor der großen Halle?
// smell of beer, smoke, and food // whiff of perfume //
// to see / single figures / to hear / single footsteps // to notice / cars, newspaperboys, dancing couples //
Was geschieht in der Kneipe und was in der Halle? Beschreiben Sie in Ihren Worten die Paßkontrolle und die Gratulation.
Wie sind Redluffs Reaktionen in der Kneipe und wie in der Halle?
// to put out / cigarette // to be calm //
// to stand / as though / stunned //
Was antwortet er in der Kneipe und was in der Halle?
// to like / to be checked up on / like / criminal //
// to answer / with / real name //
Wie reagieren die Polizisten in der Kneipe und wie in der Halle?
// to leave (use: **aus . . . hinaus**) //
// barrier / policemen / to break up // to head toward him //
Warum besteht Redluff die erste, aber nicht die zweite Probe?

E. **C-Questions (Essay)**

Herbert Malecha charakterisiert die meisten Gefühle und Eindrücke seiner Hauptfigur mit Metaphern, die aus dem Bereich des Wassers genommen sind.

1. Welche Wassermetaphern haben Sie bemerkt?

2. Was, glauben Sie, will der Autor damit ausdrücken?

CHAPTER

GRAMMATICAL REVIEW

THE SUBJUNCTIVE

The subjunctive in German performs many more functions than does the subjunctive in English. In English the conditionals (*would + infinitive, would have + infinitive*), which are like the German conditionals (**würde**-forms), assume many of the functions of the German subjunctive.

1. The subjunctive is used in spoken and written German to express *irreality*, i.e., to refer to situations, conditions, wishes, or comparisons that are *contrary to fact*:

   (*a*) The subjunctive used to refer to a *hypothetical situation*:

Er bleibt zu Hause.	He stays at home.
Ich **bliebe** nicht zu Hause.	I *would* not *stay* at home.

   (*b*) The subjunctive used to express a *contrary-to-fact condition*:

Wenn er hier **wäre, könnten** wir anfangen.	If he *were* here, we *could* begin.

   (*c*) The subjunctive used to express an *unreal wish*:

Wenn er **doch** hier **wäre!**	If *only* he *were* here!

   (*d*) The subjunctive used in an *"as if" clause* to express an *unreal comparison*:

Er ist nicht Professor. Aber er tut, als ob er Professor **wäre.**	He is not a professor. But he acts as if he *were* a professor.

2. The subjunctive is used to express a *polite request*.

Könnte ich das Buch haben?	*Could* I have that book?

3. In contrast to English, the subjunctive is used in *indirect discourse* when the speaker or writer wishes to present *facts resting on the statement of another person* or on mere *hearsay*, or if he *quotes a source* showing *that the quotation does not necessarily express his own opinion or conviction*.

   (*a*) Direct quote:

   In der Zeitung steht: ,,Man trifft in der Stadt sanitäre Maßnahmen''.

(*b*) Indirect quote:

In der Zeitung steht, man **träfe (treffe)** in der Stadt sanitäre Maßnahmen. Or: In der Zeitung steht, daß man in der Stadt sanitäre Maßnahmen **träfe (treffe).**	The newspaper says that *they are taking* sanitary measures in the city.

I. THE SUBJUNCTIVE AS AN EXPRESSION OF IRREALITY

A. The Present Subjunctive

The forms of the *present subjunctive* are *derived from the indicative imperfect.*

All *subjunctive forms* have the *same endings* as those of the *imperfect indicative of regular verbs.*

Present indicative	Present subjunctive	Imperfect indicative
Ich **bin** Student.	Wenn ich Student **wäre,** . . .	Ich **war** Student.
Ich **habe** Bücher.	Wenn ich Bücher **hätte,** . . .	Ich **hatte** Bücher.
Ich **kann** Deutsch.	Wenn ich Deutsch **könnte,** . . .	Ich **konnte** Deutsch.
Ich **gehe** bald **weg.**	Wenn ich bald **wegginge,** . . .	Ich **ging** bald **weg.**
Ich **komme** morgen.	Wenn ich morgen **käme,** . . .	Ich **kam** gestern.

1. Forms of irregular verbs

The *subjunctive forms* of *irregular verbs* are *umlauted* if the *stem vowel* of the *indicative imperfect forms* is *a, o,* or *u.*

Present indicative	Present subjunctive	Imperfect indicative
ich komm e	ich **käm** e	ich **kam**
du komm st	du **käm est**	du **kam** st
er komm t	er **käm** e	er **kam**
wir komm en	wir **käm en**	wir **kam** en
ihr komm t	ihr **käm et**	ihr **kam** t
sie komm en	sie **käm en**	sie **kam** en

2. Forms of regular verbs

The *subjunctive forms* of *regular verbs* are the *same* as the *indicative imperfect forms.* This means that they are *ambiguous* and can therefore *be used only in contexts* in which it is *clear* whether they are *present subjunctives* or *imperfect indicatives.*

Present indicative	Present subjunctive	Imperfect indicative
ich mach e	ich **mach t e**	ich mach t e
du mach st	du **mach t est**	du mach t est
er mach t	er **mach t e**	er mach t e
wir mach en	wir **mach t en**	wir mach t en
ihr mach t	ihr **mach t et**	ihr mach t et
sie mach en	sie **mach t en**	sie mach t en

B. The Past Subjunctive

There is *only one subjunctive form for the past!* It is *derived* from the *pluperfect indicative.*

Imperfect indicative, perfect indicative, pluperfect indicative	Past subjunctive	Pluperfect indicative
ich **machte** das ich **habe** das **gemacht** ich **hatte** das **gemacht**	ich **hätte** das **gemacht** I *would have done* it	ich **hatte** das **gemacht**
ich **kam** ich **bin gekommen** ich **war gekommen**	ich **wäre gekommen** I *would have come*	ich **war gekommen**

1. Forms of the past subjunctive

ich hätte das gemacht	ich wäre gekommen
du hättest das gemacht	du wärest gekommen
er hätte das gemacht	er wäre gekommen
wir hätten das gemacht	wir wären gekommen
ihr hättet das gemacht	ihr wäret gekommen
sie hätten das gemacht	sie wären gekommen

C. The würde-Form

There are *two possible forms* referring to *present* and *future time:* (*a*) The *subjunctive form* of the *verb* itself (ich **käme**); (*b*) The **würde**-form (**würde** + infinitive) (ich **würde kommen**).

Alle gehen in diese Ausstellung.   Everybody goes to this exhibition.
(*a*) Ich **ginge** nicht **hin.**
(*b*) Ich **würde** nicht **hingehen.**   I would not go.

In most cases the use of the subjunctive form of the verb (**ich käme**, etc.) or the würde-form (**ich würde kommen**, etc.) is a matter of style, not of grammar, because *both mean exactly the same thing*.

Generally clauses such as the following should be avoided:

Wenn er sich verletzen **würde, würde** man ihm einen Verband machen.

It is preferable to put **dann** between the two **würde**-forms or to use the subjunctive form of the verb in the **wenn**-clause:

Wenn er sich verletzen würde, **dann** würde man ihm einen Verband machen.
Wenn er sich **verletzte, würde** man ihm einen Verband **machen.**

However, the würde-form *must* be used when *neither the subjunctive form* of the verb *nor the context* shows the *subjunctive meaning* of the sentence. For example, the following sentence can have two meanings:

Wenn sie zu Hause **blieben, spielten** sie Karten.

Whenever they stayed at home they played cards.
Or:
If they stayed at home, they would play cards.

Therefore to indicate the *exact meaning* one *must* say:

Wenn sie zu Hause **blieben, würden** sie Karten **spielen.**

1. Verbs for which the würde-form is seldom used

The **würde**-form is *rarely used* with the auxiliary verbs **haben** and **sein,** and *hardly ever* with the *modal verbs*.

sein
Er **ist** nicht damit zufrieden.

Ich **wäre** damit zufrieden.
I *would be* satisfied with it.

haben
Er **hat** keine Geduld.

Ich **hätte** Geduld.
I *would have* patience.

können
Er **kann** das nicht.

Ich **könnte** das.
I *would be able to do* that.

mögen
Er **mag** nicht hierbleiben.

Ich **möchte** hierbleiben.
I *would like to* stay here.

dürfen

Er **darf** nicht mitarbeiten.

Ich **dürfte** mitarbeiten.
I *would be allowed to* cooperate.

müssen

Er **muß** eine Pause machen.

Ich **müßte** auch eine Pause machen.
I too *would have to* make a pause.

wollen

Er **will** nicht anfangen.

Wenn er **doch** anfangen **wollte.**
If *only* he *would want to* begin!

sollen

Er **soll** nach Hause gehen.

Ich **sollte** auch nach Hause gehen.
I *should* go home too.

The *subjunctive forms* of **können, mögen, dürfen,** and **müssen** take an *umlaut*. Note carefully the grammatical and phonetic *distinction* between the *imperfect indicative* and the *present subjunctive* of the following *modal verbs:*

Imperfect indicative

Er konnte kommen.
He could (was able to) come.

Er mochte nicht lesen.
He did not like to read.

Er durfte über die Brücke gehen.
He was allowed to cross the bridge.

Er mußte anfangen.
He had to begin.

Present subjunctive

Er könnte kommen.
He could (would be able to) come.

Er möchte nicht lesen.
He would not like to read.

Er dürfte über die Brücke gehen.
He would be allowed to cross the bridge.

Er müßte anfangen.
He would have to begin.

D. Irregular Subjunctive Forms

There are *some irregular subjunctive forms.* The following occur very often in spoken and written German:

wissen

ich **wüßte**   I would know

bringen

ich **brächte**   I would bring

denken

ich **dächte**   I would think

The following occur in literary style only:

brennen	*helfen*
es brennte it would burn	er hülfe he would help
kennen	*stehen*
er kennte he would know	er stünde he would stand
nennen	*sterben*
er nennte he would name	er stürbe he would die
rennen	*werfen*
er rennte he would run	er würfe he would throw
senden	*schwimmen*
er sendete he would send	er schwömme he would swim
wenden	
er wendete he would turn	

E.   The Subjunctive Used to Refer to a Hypothetical Situation

Present indicative	*Present subjunctive and* **würde-form**
Er **bleibt** hier. He *stays* here.	Ich **bliebe nicht** hier. Ich würde nicht hierbleiben. I *would not stay* here.
Er **kauft** das Buch. He *buys* the book.	Ich **würde** das Buch **nicht kaufen.** I *would not buy* the book.
Er **kann** das tun. He *can* do that.	Ich **könnte** das **nicht** tun. I *could not* do that.

Drill 1   *Preliminary Drill   Put the sentences into the imperfect indicative. Follow the example.*

Er **denkt** nicht daran.
Er **dachte** nicht daran.

Er kann die Frage nicht
    verstehen.
Er verrät den Verbrecher nicht.

Er muß sich davor hüten.
Er bekommt das Geld.
Er darf nicht fahren.
Er bittet um seinen Paß.
Er beginnt zu arbeiten.

Er entschließt sich sofort.
Er weiß die Antwort.
Er benimmt sich gut.
Er spricht nicht darüber.

Drill 2 *Now respond with the subjunctive. Follow the example.*

Er denkt nicht daran.
Aber **ich dächte** daran.

Er kann die Frage nicht
verstehen.
Er verrät den Verbrecher
nicht.

Er muß sich nicht davor
hüten.
Er bekommt das Geld nicht.
Er darf nicht fahren.
Er bittet nicht um den Paß.
Er beginnt nicht zu arbeiten.

Er entschließt sich nicht
sofort.
Er weiß die Antwort nicht.
Er benimmt sich nicht gut.
Er spricht nicht darüber.

Drill 3 *Respond by using the **würde**-form. Pay attention to the negation. Follow the example.*

Er sorgt für Ordnung.
Aber **ich würde nicht** für
Ordnung **sorgen**.

Er lernt den Unterschied.

Er braucht einen Orden.
Er zeigt ihr das Theater.
Er macht ihm einen Verband.

Er hört jetzt auf.
Er sorgt für die Zukunft.
Er glaubt an die Haifische.

Imperfect, perfect, pluperfect indicative

Er **blieb** hier.
Er **ist hiergeblieben.**
Er **war hiergeblieben.**

Er **kaufte** das Buch.
Er **hat** das Buch **gekauft.**
Er **hatte** das Buch **gekauft.**

Er **konnte** das **tun.**
Er **hat** das **tun können.**
Er **hatte** das **tun können.**

Past subjunctive

Ich **wäre nicht hiergeblieben.**
I *would not have stayed* here.

Ich **hätte** das Buch **nicht gekauft.**
I *would not have bought* the book.

Ich **hätte** das **nicht tun können.**
I *could not have done* that.
I *would not have been able to do* that.

Drill 4 *The Past Subjunctive* *Follow the examples.*

Er **hat** die Antwort **nicht gewußt.**
Aber **ich hätte** die Antwort **gewußt.**

Er **ist nicht** zu Hause **geblieben.**
Aber **ich wäre** zu Hause **geblieben.**

Er hat sich nicht darauf bezogen.
Er ist nicht weggefahren.

Er hat den Unterschied nicht gelernt.
Er hat nicht darüber gesprochen.
Er hat sich nicht an den Tisch gesetzt.
Er ist nicht aufgestanden.
Er hat sich nicht sofort entschlossen.
Er hat den Orden nicht gebraucht.

Drill 5 *The Past Subjunctive* *Follow the examples.*

Er fuhr nicht weg.
Aber **ich wäre weggefahren.**

Er sprach nicht darüber.
Aber **ich hätte** darüber
gesprochen.

Er wußte die Antwort nicht.
Er blieb nicht zu Hause.
Er bezog sich nicht darauf.

Er brauchte den Orden nicht.   Er stand nicht auf.   Er entschloß sich nicht sofort.
Er setzte sich nicht an den   Er lernte den Unterschied
  Tisch.   nicht.

Drill 6   *The Past Subjunctive of Modal and Auxiliary Verbs   Follow the examples.*

Er hat heute **kommen können.**   Er hat sich davor hüten müssen.
Aber **wir hätten** heute **nicht kommen können.**   Er ist nett zu ihr gewesen.
                                                 Er hat ein Beispiel gehabt.
Er hat Zeit **gehabt.**   Er hat sich entscheiden können.
Aber **wir hätten keine** Zeit **gehabt.**   Er hat kommen dürfen.

Er ist heute lustig **gewesen.**   Er ist zufrieden gewesen.
Aber **wir wären** heute **nicht** lustig gewesen.   Er hat das Geld gehabt.

Drill 7   *The Past Subjunctive of Modal and Auxiliary Verbs   Follow the examples.*

Er konnte sich entscheiden.   Er konnte heute kommen.
Aber **wir hätten uns nicht entscheiden können.**   Er hatte Zeit.
                                                  Er mußte sich davor hüten.
Er war zufrieden.   Er war heute lustig.
Aber **wir wären nicht** zufrieden **gewesen.**   Er durfte kommen.
                                                  Er hatte ein Beispiel.
Er hatte das Geld.   Er war nett zu ihr.
Aber **wir hätten** das Geld **nicht gehabt.**

F.   The Subjunctive in Contrary-to-Fact Conditions

1. The contrary-to-fact condition and its conclusion referring to present and future time:

Facts   *Contrary-to-fact condition and conclusion*

Es **gibt kein** Fest. Sie **sind nicht** lustig.   (Aber) **wenn es ein** Fest **gäbe, wären** sie lustig.
                                             (Aber) **wenn** es **ein** Fest **geben würde, wären**
                                               sie lustig.

2. The contrary-to-fact condition and its conclusion referring to past time:

Facts   *Contrary-to-fact condition and conclusion*

Es **gab kein** Fest. Sie **waren nicht** lustig.   (Aber) **wenn** es **ein** Fest **gegeben hätte, wären**
Es **hat kein** Fest gegeben. Sie **sind nicht**   sie lustig **gewesen.**
  lustig **gewesen.**
Es **hatte kein** Fest gegeben. Sie **waren icht**
  lustig gewesen.

3. The contrary-to-fact condition may either *precede* or *follow* the conclusion:

   Wenn die Haifische Menschen wären, gäbe es auch eine Kunst.
   Auch eine Religion gäbe es, **wenn die Haifische Menschen wären.**

4. **Wenn** may be *omitted* in contrary-to-fact conditions. In this case the contrary-to-fact condition has to *precede* the conclusion:

   Gäbe es Schulen, könnten sie Geographie lernen.
   Hätten sie Posten bekommen, hätten sie für Ordnung gesorgt.

5. In conclusions **dann** or **so** is often used to repeat the idea of the contrary-to-fact condition:

   Hätten sie eine Kunst, **dann** hätten sie auch eine Religion.
   Wären sie Lehrer, **so** würden sie lehren.

6. In the English contrary-to-fact condition the *if-clause* uses the *subjunctive* form of the verb and the conclusion uses the *would* + infinitive form.

   If he *had* the book, he *would read* it.
   If he *were* a student, he *would be* at the university.
   If he *lived* in Munich, he *would study* there.

   In German the **würde**-form may be used in *either clause,* in *both,* or in *neither* if the clauses are *not ambiguous.* However, the **würde**-form is more frequently found in the conclusion:

   Wenn ein Fischlein **sich verletzen würde,** dann **würde** man ihm sogleich einen Verband **machen lassen.**
   Wenn sie Gehorsam **lernen würden, wäre** ihre Zukunft **gesichert.**
   Wenn sie Posten **hätten, würden** sie für Ordnung **sorgen.**
   Wenn die Haifische Menschen **wären, gäbe** es eine Kultur im Meer.

Drill 8 *Contrary-to-Fact Conditions Referring to Present and Future Time   Respond with a contrary-to-fact condition and its conclusion using **wenn** and the subjunctive form of the verb only. Follow the example.*

Die Haifische **sind keine** Menschen. Sie **sind nicht** nett zu den kleinen Fischen.
Aber **wenn** die Haifische Menschen **wären, wären** sie nett zu den kleinen Fischen.

Die Haifische sind nicht nett. Sie treffen keine sanitären Maßnahmen.
Es gibt keine Wasserfeste. Die Fische sind nicht lustig.
Die Fische haben keine Schulen. Sie können nicht Geographie lernen.
Die Fische können nicht Gehorsam lernen. Ihre Zukunft ist nicht gesichert.
Die Haifische sind keine Menschen. Es gibt keine Kriege.
Die Haifische haben keine Kunst. Es gibt auch keine Religion.
Die Fische haben keine Posten. Sie können nicht für Ordnung sorgen.
Die Fische können nicht Offiziere werden. Es gibt keine Kultur im Meer.

Drill 9   *Now repeat Drill 8 by responding with a contrary-to-fact condition omitting* **wenn**. *Begin the conclusion with* **dann**. *Follow the example.*

Die Haifische **sind keine** Menschen. Sie **sind nicht** nett zu den kleinen Fischen.
Wären die Haifische Menschen, **dann wären** sie nett zu den kleinen Fischen.

Drill 10   *Contrary-to-Fact Conditions Referring to Past Time*   *Respond with a contrary-to-fact condition and its conclusion using* **wenn** *and the subjunctive form of the auxiliary verb only. Follow the example.*

Seine Familie **hielt** ihn. Er **blieb** in der Stadt.
Wenn seine Familie ihn **nicht gehalten hätte, wäre** er **nicht** in der Stadt **geblieben.**

Die Soldaten plünderten. Er verstecke sich im Hof.
Die Soldaten befanden sich im Hause eines Protestanten. Sie schlugen alles kurz und klein.
Die Frau rannte aus dem Hause. Das Kind blieb allein zurück.
Die Frau verleugnete ihr Kind. Die Magd ging in die Gerberei zurück.
Sie saß bei dem Kind. Sie nahm es mit.
Die Schwägerin war mißtrauisch. Die Magd log.
Die Schwägerin erkundigte sich nach dem Vater des Kindes. Der Bruder suchte einen Mann für die Magd.
Der Häusler war todkrank. Die Magd heiratete ihn.

G.   The Subjunctive Used to Express an Unreal Wish

Wishes in contradiction to the facts have the form of contrary-to-fact conditions used without their conclusions. Such **wenn**-clauses must contain a **nur**, a **doch**, or, if the wish is emphasized, a **doch nur**, similar to the English *only*. As in contrary-to-fact conditions, **wenn** may be omitted. The verb then takes the first position.

1. Referring to present and future time:

Fact	*Unreal wish*
Die Frau **ist nicht** freundlich.	**Wenn** die Frau **doch** freundlich **wäre!** **Wäre** die Frau **doch** freundlich!
Die Magd **kann nicht** auf dem Hof **bleiben.**	**Wenn** die Magd **nur** auf dem Hof **bleiben könnte!** **Könnte** die Magd **nur** auf dem Hof **bleiben!**

2. Referring to past time:

Fact	*Unreal wish*
Die Frau **hat** ihr Kind **verleugnet.**	**Wenn** die Frau ihr Kind **doch nicht verleugnet hätte!** **Hätte** die Frau ihr Kind **doch nicht verleugnet!**

Der Mann **ist** im Hause **geblieben.**

Wenn der Mann **nur nicht** im Hause **geblieben wäre!**

Wäre der Mann **nur nicht** im Hause **geblieben!**

Drill 11   *Unreal Wishes Referring to Present and Future Time*   *Respond with an unreal wish using* **wenn** *and the subjunctive form of the verb. Follow the example.*

Er **kann sich nicht entschließen.**
Wenn er **sich** *doch* **entschließen könnte!**

Sie zieht nicht in die Vorstadt.
Sie nimmt ihr Kind nicht mit.
Die Schwägerin ist nicht freundlich.

Die Magd kann nicht auf dem Hof bleiben.
Das Kind ist nicht gesund.
Das Kind hat keinen Namen.
Der Mann gefällt ihr nicht.

Drill 12   *Now repeat Drill 11 by responding with an unreal wish omitting* **wenn.** *This time use* **nur** *instead of* **doch.** *Follow the example.*

Er **kann sich nicht entschließen.**
Könnte er **sich** *nur* **entschließen!**

H.   The Subjunctive Used in "as if" Clauses to Express an Unreal Comparison

If the words **ob** or **wenn** are omitted the verb immediately follows **als.**

1. Present:

Fact

Er **weiß** die Wahrheit **nicht.**

Unreal comparison

Aber er **tut, als ob** er die Wahrheit **wüßte.**
Aber er **tut, als wenn** er die Wahrheit **wüßte.**
Aber er **tut, als wüßte** er die Wahrheit.

2. Past:

Fact

Er **wußte** die Wahrheit **nicht.**

Unreal comparison

Aber er **tat, als ob** er die Wahrheit **gewußt hätte.**
Aber er **tat, als wenn** er die Wahrheit **gewußt hätte.**
Aber er **tat, als hätte** er die Wahrheit **gewußt.**

Drill 13   *Unreal Comparisons in the Present*   *Use the subjunctive form of the verb only. Respond according to the example.*

Die Frau **sagt nicht** die Wahrheit.
Die Frau **tut, als ob** sie die Wahrheit **sagte.**

Der Richter glaubt ihr nicht.
Der Richter ist nicht ratlos.

Die Frau ist nicht gekränkt.
Der Richter ist nicht hilflos.
Die Frau liebt ihr Kind nicht.
Die Magd ist nicht die Mutter des Kindes.

II.   THE SUBJUNCTIVE AS A POLITE REQUEST

The *polite forms* are *limited* to the *modal verbs* and **hätte, wäre,** and **würde.** „Würden Sie mir bitte ein Buch geben?" *cannot be replaced* by „Gäben Sie mir bitte ein Buch?"

Hätten Sie heute Zeit?	Would you have time today?
Wären Sie damit zufrieden?	Would you be satisfied with it?
Könnten Sie mir **helfen?**	Could you help me?
Würden Sie mir **helfen?**	Would you help me?

III.   THE SUBJUNCTIVE IN INDIRECT DISCOURSE

A.   The Use of the Indicative

When we shift from direct to indirect discourse we change the verbatim quote to an indirect quote with or without **daß** and the form of the person as the situation requires, as we have already learned in Chapter 3. No quotation marks are used.

Direct quote

Der Junge **sagt:** „Ich **bin** nicht müde."

The boy *says,* "I *am* not tired."

Indirect quote

Der Junge **sagt,** er **ist** nicht müde.
Der Junge **sagt, daß** er nicht müde **ist.**

The boy *says* (that) he *is* not tired.

In German the *tense of the verb* in the *indirect quote depends on* the *tense of the original statement,* i.e., of the *direct quote.*

Direct quote

Der Junge **sagte:** „Ich **bin** müde."

The boy *said,* "I *am* tired."

Indirect quote

Der Junge **sagte,** er **ist** müde.
Der Junge **sagte, daß** er müde **ist.**

The boy *said* (that) he *was* tired.

The *indicative* may be used in indirect discourse when *indisputable facts, personal opinions, or convictions* are to be expressed.

Direct quote		*Indirect quote*	
Der Junge **sagt:**		Der Junge **sagt,**	
Der Junge **sagte:**	„Ich **bin** müde."	Der Junge **sagte,**	daß er müde **ist.**
Der Junge **hat gesagt:**		Der Junge **hat gesagt,**	
Der Junge **hatte gesagt:**		Der Junge **hatte gesagt,**	

B.   The Use of the Subjunctive and of the würde-Form

The *subjunctive* is used in *indirect discourse* to indicate that the quote rests on a *statement of another person,* on mere *hearsay,* or does *not represent one's own conviction.*

Der Junge **sagt,**	
Der Junge **sagte,**	daß er müde **wäre.**
Der Junge **hat gesagt,**	
Der Junge **hatte gesagt,**	

The **würde**-form is preferred if the original statement referred to the future.

Indirect quote	*Direct quote*
Der Mann sagte: „Ich gebe **bald** Bescheid."	Der Mann sagte, (er gäbe bald Bescheid).
	er **würde bald** Bescheid **geben.**

C.   The Quotative

Direct quote	*Indirect quote*
Der Mann sagte: „Ich **gebe** bald **Bescheid."**	Der Mann sagte, er **gäbe** bald **Bescheid.**
	er **würde** bald **Bescheid geben.**
	er **gebe** bald **Bescheid.**

Besides the subjunctive form of the verb (**er gäbe**) and the **würde**-form (**er würde . . . geben**) there is *another set of subjunctive forms* used *primarily* in *indirect discourse*. We call it the *quotative*. But *this* set is *not complete.* In modern German it occurs almost exclusively in the **er-, es-, sie-**form (except in the case of the auxiliary verb **sein**). The quotative is derived from the **stem** of the **verb.** The *ending* of the **er-, es-, sie-** form is **-e.**

Direct quotes	*Indirect quotes*	*Infinitive stem*
Er sagte: „Ich **komme** bald."	Er sagte, er **komme** bald.	**komm** en
Sie sagte: „Ich **weiß** alles."	Sie sagte, sie **wisse** alles.	**wiss** en
Er sagte: „Ich **habe** jetzt Zeit."	Er sagte, er **habe** jetzt Zeit.	**hab** en
Sie sagte: „Ich **nehme** das Kind mit.	Sie sagte, sie **nehme** das Kind mit.	mit **nehm** en

1. The quotative forms of sein

Unser Freund sagte zu mir, **ich sei** in Gefahr.
Unser Freund sagte zu dir, **du seist** in Gefahr.
Unser Freund sagte, **er sei** in Gefahr.
Unser Freund sagte zu uns, **wir seien** in Gefahr.

Unser Freund sagte zu euch, **ihr seiet** in Gefahr.
Unser Freund sagte zu ihnen, **sie seien** in Gefahr.

2. The subjunctive stays subjunctive

If the original quote is in the subjunctive, the indirect quote will also be in the subjunctive:

Sie sagte: ,,**Ich könnte** das Kind nicht im Stich lassen.''
Sie sagte, daß **sie** das Kind nicht im Stich lassen **könnte**.

3. The quotative and the subjunctive in formal indirect discourse

Direct quote	*Formal indirect quote*
Future	*Future*
Er sagte: ,,Ich werde kommen.''	Er sagte, **er werde** kommen.
Sie sagten: ,,Wir werden kommen.''	Sie sagten, *sie* **würden** kommen.
Present	*Present*
Er sagte: ,,Ich weiß alles.''	Er sagte, **er wisse** alles.
Sie sagten: ,,Wir wissen alles.''	Sie sagten, *sie* **wüßten alles.**
Imperfect *Past* (with **haben**) *Pluperfect*	*Past*
Er sagte: ,,Ich tat nichts.'' ,,Ich habe nichts getan.'' ,,Ich hatte nichts getan.''	Er sagte, **er habe** nichts **getan**
Sie sagten: ,,Wir taten nichts.'' ,,Wir haben nichts getan.'' ,,Wir hatten nichts getan.''	Sie sagten, *sie* **hätten** nichts **getan.**
Imperfect *Perfect* (with **sein**) *Pluperfect*	*Past*
Er sagte: ,,Ich ging weg.'' ,,Ich bin weggegangen.'' ,,Ich war weggegangen.''	Er sagte, **er sei weggegangen.**
Sie sagten: ,,Wir gingen weg.'' ,,Wir sind weggegangen.'' ,,Wir waren weggegangen.''	Sie sagten, *sie* **seien weggegangen.**

The *quotative* is *restricted to formal indirect discourse* in the er-, es-, sie-form (except with **sein**), as shown in the foregoing table.

In *informal speech all quotative forms may be replaced by subjunctive forms,* or even by the **würde**-form, especially when the quote refers to future time. The following three indirect quotes *differ in style but are identical in meaning:*

Der Mann sagte, er **gäbe** bald **Bescheid.**
       er **würde** bald **Bescheid geben.**
       er **gebe** bald **Bescheid.**

An indirect quote may be introduced by **daß** following the *subordinate clause pattern.* If **daß** is omitted, the indirect quote follows the *main clause pattern.*

Direct quote	*Indirect quote*
Er sagte: ,,Ich habe keine Zeit.''	Er sagte, **daß** er keine Zeit **habe (hätte).**
	Er sagte, **er habe (hätte)** keine Zeit.

An *opening verb or expression* like **er sagte, er berichtete, er dachte, ich habe gelesen, ich habe gehört, in der Zeitung steht,** etc., *must always precede an indirect quote.* When several quotes are connected the *repetition* of **er sagte,** etc., is *unnecessary:*

Er sagte, er gebe noch Bescheid und werde bald kommen. Er sei schon auf dem Wege.

(a) Statements in formal indirect discourse – present and future time

▶ *Remember:* The *quotative* is used with the **er-, es-, sie-**form. The *subjunctive* is used with the **sie** (they)-form except with **sein.**

Direct quote	*Indirect quote*
Der Mann sagte: ,,Ich bleibe in der Stadt.''	Der Mann sagte, **er bleibe** in der Stadt.
	daß er in der Stadt **bleibe.**
Die Leute sagten: ,,Wir bleiben in der Stadt.''	Die Leute sagten, *sie bleiben* in der Stadt.
	daß *sie* in der Stadt **blieben.**
Die Frau sagte: ,,Das ist mein Kind.''	Die Frau sagte, das **sei** ihr **Kind.**
	daß das ihr **Kind sei.**
Die Frauen sagten: ,,Das sind unsere Kinder.''	Die Frauen sagten, das **seien** ihre **Kinder.**
	daß das ihre **Kinder seien.**

Drill 14 *The er-, es-, sie-Form (a) in Formal and (b) in Informal Indirect Discourse – Present and Future* Follow the examples.

Der Häusler sagte: ,,**Ich gebe** bald **Bescheid.**''
Was sagte der Häusler?
(*a*) Er sagte, **er gebe** bald **Bescheid.**
(*b*) Er sagte, **er gäbe** bald **Bescheid.**

Die Magd sagte: ,,**Ich überlege mir** noch alles.''
Was sagte die Magd?
(*a*) Sie sagte, **sie überlege sich** noch alles.
(*b*) Sie sagte, **sie überlegte sich** noch alles.

Der Richter sagte: ,,Die Magd lügt wie gedruckt.''
Was sagte der Richter?

Der Richter erklärte: ,,Das Anwesen fällt an die Verwandten.''
Was erklärte der Richter?

Der Richter meinte: ,,Man erkennt die recht Mutter an ihrer Liebe zum Kind.''
Was meinte der Richter?

Der Richter sagte: ,,Am Samstag halte ich Gericht.''
Was sagte der Richter?

Der Bruder berichtete: ,,Die Magd befindet sich auf dem Weg der Besserung.''
Was berichtete der Bruder?

Der Onkel erklärte: ,,Ich habe mit dem Kind nichts zu schaffen.''
Was erklärte der Onkel?

Der Häusler sagte: ,,Ich komme bald.''
Was sagte der Häusler?

Der Richter erklärte: ,,Es geht um die Gerberei.''
Was erklärte der Richter?

Drill 15 *The* sie *(they)-Form (a) in Formal and (b) in Informal Indirect Discourse – Present and Future   Follow the example.*

Die beiden Häusler sagten: ,,**Wir geben** bald **Bescheid.**''
Was sagten die beiden Häusler?
(*a*) and (*b*) Sie sagten, **sie gäben bald Bescheid.**

Der Richter erklärte: ,,Beide lügen wie gedruckt.''
Was erklärte der Richter?

Der Richter meinte: ,,Die Verhandlungen fallen so kürzer aus.''
Was meinte der Richter?

Die Verwandten erklärten: ,,Wir haben mit dem Kind nichts zu schaffen.''
Was erklärten die Verwandten?

Der Richter sagte: ,,Die Verwandten bekommen das Anwesen.''
Was sagte der Richter?

Der Richter sagte: ,,Wir nehmen jetzt eine Probe vor.''
Was sagte der Richter?

Drill 16 *Combination Drill The* **er-, es-, sie**-*Form and the* **sie** *(they)-Form in Formal and in Informal Indirect Discourse – Present and Future*

Der Häusler sagte: ,,Ich gebe bald Bescheid.''
Was sagte der Häusler?

Die beiden Häusler sagten: ,,Wir geben bald Bescheid.''
Was sagten die beiden Häusler?

Der Onkel erklärte: ,,Ich habe mit dem Kind nichts zu schaffen.''
Was erklärte der Onkel?

Die Verwandten erklärten: ,,Wir haben mit dem Kind nichts zu schaffen.''
Was erklärten die Verwandten?

Der Richter erklärte: ,,Die Frau lügt wie gedruckt.''
Was erklärte der Richter?

Der Richter erklärte: ,,Beide lügen wie gedruckt.''
Was erklärte der Richter?

Der Richter sagte: ,,Das Kind bekommt das Anwesen.''
Was sagte der Richter?

Der Richter sagte: ,,Die Verwandten bekommen das Anwesen.''
Was sagte der Richter?

Der Richter erklärte: ,,Ich nehme jetzt eine Probe vor.''
Was erklärte der Richter?

Der Richter erklärte: ,,Wir nehmen jetzt eine Probe vor.''
Was erklärte der Richter?

Drill 17 *The* **er-, es-, sie**-*Form of* **sein, wissen,** *and the Modal Verbs (a) in Formal and (b) in Informal Indirect Discourse – Present and Future* *Follow the examples.*

Die Magd erklärte: ,,**Herr Zingli ist** tot.''
Was erklärte die Magd?
(*a*) Sie erklärte, **Herr Zingli sei** tot.
(*b*) Sie erklärte, Herr **Zingli wäre** tot.

Der Bruder meinte: ,,**Anna kann** auf dem Hof **bleiben.**''
Was meinte der Bruder?
(*a*) Er meinte, **Anna könne** auf dem Hof **bleiben.**
(*b*) Er meinte, **Anna könnte** auf dem Hof **bleiben.**

Die Bäuerin sagte: ,,Der Hof muß ins Gerede kommen.''
Was sagte die Bäuerin?

Der Bruder meinte: ,,Anna will den Hof verlassen.''
Was meinte der Bruder?

Der Häusler sagte: ,,Ich kann mich nicht entschließen.''
Was sagte der Häusler?

Der Bruder erklärte: ,,Ich weiß eine Lösung.''
Was erklärte der Bruder?

Der Richter meinte: ,,Blut ist dicker als Wasser.''
Was meinte der Richter?

Der Richter erklärte: ,,Man muß auch das Kind bedenken.''
Was erklärte der Richter?

Die Frau sagte: ,,Ich will mein Kind nicht im Stich lassen.''
Was sagte die Frau?

Der Richter erklärte: ,,Die Versammlung ist geschlossen.''
Was erklärte der Richter?

Drill 18   *The* sie *(they)-Form of* sein, wissen, *and the Modal Verbs (a) in Formal and (b) in Informal Indirect Discourse – Present and Future*   *Follow the examples.*

Die Bäuerin sagte: ,,**Anna und das Kind dürfen** nicht im Hause **bleiben.**''
Was sagte die Bäuerin?
(*a*) and (*b*) Sie sagte, **Anna und das Kind dürften** nicht im Hause **bleiben.**

Die Verwandten erklärten: ,,**Wir sind** aus der Schweiz.''
Was erklärten die Verwandten?
(*a*) Sie erklärten, **sie seien** aus der Schweiz.
(*b*) Sie erklärten, **sie wären** aus der Schweiz.

Der Bruder berichtete: ,,Die beiden Häusler können sich nicht entschließen.''
Was berichtete der Bruder?

Der Richter erklärte: ,,Alle Zeugen sind da.''
Was erklärte der Richter?

Der Richter sagte: ,,Die Zuschauer müssen stehen.''
Was sagte der Richter?

Die Verwandten erklärten: ,,Wir wissen nichts.''
Was erklärten die Verwandten?

Der Richter sagte: ,,Beide sollen eine Hand des Kindes fassen.''
Was sagte der Richter?

Drill 19   *Combination Drill*   *The* er-, es-, sie-*Form and the* sie *(they)-Form of* sein, wissen, *and the Modal Verbs in Formal and Informal Indirect Discourse – Present and Future*

Der Bruder berichtete: ,,Die beiden Häusler können sich nicht entschließen.''
Was berichtete der Bruder?

Der Häusler sagte: „Ich kann mich nicht entschließen."
Was sagte der Häusler?

Der Richter sagte: „Blut ist dicker als Wasser."
Was sagte der Richter?

Die Verwandten erklärten: „Wir sind aus der Schweiz."
Was erklärten die Verwandten?

Der Richter sagte: „Man muß auch das Kind bedenken."
Was sagte der Richter?

Der Richter erklärte: „Die Zuschauer müssen stehen."
Was erklärte der Richter?

Die Verwandten sagten: „Wir wissen nichts."
Was sagten die Verwandten?

Der Bruder erklärte: „Ich weiß eine Lösung."
Was erklärte der Bruder?

Der Richter sagte: „Beide sollen in den Kreis treten."
Was sagte der Richter?

Der Richter erklärte: „Die Versammlung ist geschlossen."
Was erklärte der Richter?

(b) Statements in formal indirect discourse – past time

Direct quote	*Indirect quote*
Der Häusler sagte: „Eine Frau holte das Kind."	Der Häusler sagte, **eine Frau habe** das Kind **geholt.**
„Eine Frau hat das Kind geholt."	daß **eine Frau** das Kind **geholt habe.**
„Eine Frau hatte das Kind geholt."	
Die Magd berichtet: „Die Soldaten schlugen alles kurz und klein."	Die Magd berichtete, **die Soldaten hätten** alles kurz und klein **geschlagen.**
„Die Soldaten haben alles kurz und klein geschlagen."	daß **die Soldaten** alles kurz und klein **geschlagen hätten.**
„Die Soldaten hatten alles kurz und klein geschlagen."	

Die Magd sagte:	„Ich kehrte nicht in die Gerberei zurück."	Die Magd sagte,	**sie sei** nicht in die Gerberei **zurückgekehrt.**
	„Ich bin nicht in die Gerberei zurückgekehrt."		**daß sie** nicht in die Gerberei **zurückgekehrt sei.**
	„Ich war nicht in die Gerberei zurückgekehrt."		
Die Magd sagte:	„Die Soldaten kamen ins Haus."	Die Magd sagte,	**die Soldaten seien** ins Haus **gekommen.**
	„Die Soldaten sind ins Haus gekommen."		**daß die Soldaten** ins Haus **gekommen seien.**
	„Die Soldaten waren ins Haus gekommen."		

Drill 20 *The* er-, es-, sie-*Form and the* sie (they)-*Form of* sein *(a) in Formal and (b) in Informal Indirect Discourse – Past   Follow the examples.*

Die Magd sagte: „**Die Frau ist** in die Vorstadt **gezogen.**"
Was sagte die Magd?
(*a*) Sie sagte, **die Frau sei** in die Vorstadt **gezogen.**
(*b*) Sie sagte, **die Frau wäre** in die Vorstadt **gezogen.**

Die Leute berichteten: „**Die Magd und das Kind sind** in der Gerberei **geblieben.**"
Was berichteten die Leute?
(*a*) Die Leute berichteten, **die Magd und das Kind seien** in der Gerberei **geblieben.**
(*b*) Die Leute berichteten, **die Magd und das Kind wären** in der Gerberei **geblieben.**

Die Magd sagte: „Das Kind ist in seiner Wiege gewesen."
Was sagte die Magd?

Der Schwager sagte: „Die Magd ist nicht einmal anständig behandelt worden."
Was sagte der Schwager?

Die Magd sagte: „Betrunkene Soldaten sind ins Haus gekommen."
Was sagte die Magd?

Der Bruder sagte: „Die beiden Häusler sind noch zu keinem Entschluß gekommen."
Was sagte der Bruder?

Die Magd sagte: „Ich bin nicht in die Gerberei zurückgekehrt."
Was sagte die Magd?

Der Häusler berichtete: „Eine feingekleidete Frau ist vorgefahren."
Was berichtete der Häusler?

Drill 21   *The* er-, es-, sie-*Form and the* sie *(they)-Form of* haben *(a) in Formal and (b) in Informal Indirect Discourse – Past   Follow the examples.*

Die Magd sagte: ,,**Ich habe** Angst **gehabt.**''
Was sagte die Magd?
(*a*) Sie sagte, **sie habe** Angst **gehabt.**
(*b*) Sie sagte, **sie hätte** Angst **gehabt.**

Die Magd erzählte: ,,**Die Soldaten haben** alles kurz und klein **geschlagen.**''
Was erzählte die Magd?
(*a*) and (*b*) Sie erzählte, **die Soldaten hätten** alles kurz und klein **geschlagen.**

Die Nachbarn sagten: ,,Der Mann hat sich nicht entschließen können.''
Was sagten die Nachbarn?

Der Häusler sagte: ,,Ich habe mir alles überlegt.''
Was sagte der Häusler?

Der Bruder sagte: ,,Ich habe eine Lösung gefunden.''
Was sagte der Bruder?

Die Zuschauer sagten: ,,Die Verwandten haben sehr unfreundlich von der Frau gesprochen.''
Was sagten die Zuschauer?

Der Häusler berichtete: ,,Eine feingekleidete Frau hat das Kind geholt.''
Was berichtete der Häusler?

Die Bauern erzählten: ,,Der Richter hat mit den Augen gezwinkert.''
Was erzählten die Bauern?

Drill 22   *Combination Drill   The* er-, es-, sie-*Form and the* sie *(they)-Form of* sein *and* haben *in Formal and Informal Indirect Discourse – Past*

Die Leute berichteten: ,,Die Magd und das Kind sind in der Gerberei geblieben.''
Was berichteten die Leute?

Die Magd sagte: ,,Die Soldaten haben alles kurz und klein geschlagen.''
Was sagte die Magd?

Die Magd sagte: ,,Betrunkene Soldaten sind ins Haus gekommen.''
Was sagte die Magd?

Die Nachbarn sagten: ,,Der Mann hat sich nicht entschließen können.''
Was sagten die Nachbarn?

Die Magd sagte: ,,Ich bin nicht in die Gerberei zurückgekehrt.''
Was sagte die Magd?

Die Magd erklärte: ,,Ich habe Angst gehabt.''
Was erklärte die Magd?

Der Bruder meinte: „Die beiden Häusler sind noch zu keinem Entschluß gekommen."
Was meinte der Bruder?

Die Zuschauer berichteten: „Die Verwandten haben sehr unfreundlich von der Frau gesprochen."
Was berichteten die Verwandten?

Der Häusler sagte: „Ich habe mir alles überlegt."
Was sagte der Häusler?

Die Magd sagte: „Das Kind ist in seiner Wiege gewesen."
Was sagte die Magd?

Drill 23   *Express the sentences given below in the formal indirect discourse using, whenever possible, the quotative. Begin the first paragraph with* **Wir lesen, . . .** , *the second with* **Der Richter sagte, . . .** , *and the third with* **Der Richter verkündete, ...**

1. Page 269–271: – „Die Diele füllte sich . . . und erschlagen."
2. Page 295: – „Es ist nicht festgestellt worden . . . wer die rechte Mutter des Kindes ist."
3. Page 297: – „Diese Probe, die . . . in diesen Kreidekreis."

4. The command in indirect discourse

The command in an indirect quote is expressed with the help of the modal verbs **sollen** or **mögen**. The modals may take either the quotative or the subjunctive form. Indirect commands are usually expressed by **sollen** + infinitive. **Mögen** + infinitive is used if the command is a *polite request.*

Direct commands	*Indirect commands*
Der Richter befahl der Magd: „**Stell dich** in den Kreidekreis!"	Der Richter befahl der Magd, **sie solle (sollte) sich** in den Kreidekreis **stellen.**
	Der Richter sagte zu der Magd, **sie möge (möchte) sich** in den Kreidekreis **stellen.**
Der Richter befahl der Frau: „**Fassen Sie** eine Hand des Kindes!"	Der Richter befahl der Frau, **sie solle (sollte)** eine Hand des Kindes **fassen.**
	Der Richter sagte zu der Frau, **sie möge (möchte)** eine Hand des Kindes **fassen.**
Der Richter befahl beiden: „**Tretet** in den Kreis!" „**Treten Sie** in den Kreis!"	Der Richter befahl beiden, **sie sollten** in den Kreis **treten.**
Der Richter sagte zu beiden: „**Tretet** in den Kreis!" „**Treten Sie** in den Kreis!"	Der Richter sagte zu beiden, **sie möchten** in den Kreis **treten.**

Drill 24 *The Indirect Command* *Use (a) the quotative and (b) the subjunctive of* **sollen**. *Follow the example.*

Der Richter sagte zu der Magd: ,,Tritt ans Fenster!''
Was sagte der Richter zu der Magd?
(a) Er sagte, **sie solle** ans Fenster **treten.**
(b) Er sagte, **sie sollte** ans Fenster **treten.**

Der Richter sagte zu der Magd: ,,Bilde dir nichts ein!''
Was sagte der Richter zu der Magd?

Er sagte zum Gerichtsdiener: ,,Bring das Kind!''
Was sagte er zum Gerichtsdiener?

Er sagte zu der Magd: ,,Mach schnell!''
Was sagte er zu der Magd?

Er sagte zum Gerichtsdiener: ,,Zieh mit der Kreide einen Kreis!''
Was sagte er zum Gerichtsdiener?

Er sagte zum Gerichtsdiener: ,,Stell das Kind in den Kreis!''
Was sagte er zum Gerichtsdiener?

Drill 25 *The Indirect Command* *Use the subjunctive of* **sollen**. *Follow the example.*

Der Richter sagte zu den beiden: ,,**Stellt euch** in den Kreis!''
Was sagte der Richter zu den beiden?
Er sagte, **sie sollten sich** in den Kreis **stellen.**

Er sagte zu den Leuten: ,,Seid ruhig!''
Was sagte er zu den Leuten?

Er sagte zu den beiden: ,,Faßt eine Hand des Kindes!''
Was sagte er zu den beiden?

Er sagte zu den beiden: ,,Bemüht euch, das Kind aus dem Kreis zu ziehen!''
Was sagte er zu den beiden?

Er sagte zu den Leuten: ,,Nehmt der Schlampe das Kind weg!''
Was sagte er zu den Leuten?

Er sagte zu den beiden: ,,Sagt die Wahrheit!''
Was sagte er zu den beiden?

Drill 26 *Combination Drill* *Use the quotative and the subjunctive in the indirect commands. Use the modal verb* **sollen**.

Der Richter sagte zum Gerichtsdiener: ,,Bring das Kind!''
Was sagte der Richter zum Gerichtsdiener?

Er sagte zu der Magd: ,,Tritt ans Fenster!''
Was sagte er zu der Magd?

Er sagte zu den beiden: ,,Stellt euch in den Kreis!''
Was sagte er zu den beiden?

Er sagte zum Gerichtsdiener: ,,Zieh mit der Kreide einen Kreis!''
Was sagte er zum Gerichtsdiener?

Er sagte zu den beiden: ,,Bemüht euch, das Kind aus dem Kreis zu ziehen!''
Was sagte er zu den beiden?

Er sagte zu den Leuten: ,,Nehmt der Schlampe das Kind weg!''
Was sagte er zu den Leuten?

Er sagte zu den beiden: ,,Sagt die Wahrheit!''
Was sagte er zu den beiden?

5. The indirect question

The indirect question takes the subjuntive, the **würde**-form, or the quotative according to the rules given in the beginning of this chapter. The word order changes according to the rules given in Chapter 3:

Direct question	*Indirect question*
Er fragte: ,,Kann ich kommen?''	Er fragte, **ob er kommen könne (könnte).**
Er fragte: ,,Wann kann ich kommen?''	Er fragte, **wann er kommen könne (könnte).**

6. Other usages of the quotative

There are some other usages of the quotative which closely resemble English usages.

Special wishes and commands

Mögest du Erfolg haben!	May you be successful!
So **sei** es!	So be it!
Lang **lebe** die Freiheit	Long live freedom!

Exclamations

| Gott **sei** Dank! | Thank God! |

Recipes

| Man **nehme** eine Tasse Milch. | Take a cup of milk. |

The expression sei(en) . . . , sei(en) . . .

| **Sei** es gut, **sei** es schlecht, wir haben nichts damit zu tun. | Whether it be good or bad, we do not have anything to do with it. |
| **Sei** es, daß seine kleine Familie ihn hielt, **sei** es, daß er seine Gerberei nicht im Stiche lassen wollte, er konnte sich jedenfalls nicht entschließen, beizeiten wegzureisen. | Whether it was that his small family kept him back or he did not want to abandon his tannery, at any rate he could not decide to leave in time. |

THE PASSIVE VOICE

I. THE ACTIONAL PASSIVE

As in English, the passive voice is used in German *to emphasize the action* in a sentence rather than the person who performs it.

A. Forms of the Actional Passive

Werden + *perfect participle*

Present	Das Buch **wird** gelesen
Imperfect	Das Buch **wurde** gelesen
Perfect	Das Buch **ist** gelesen **worden**
Pluperfect	Das Buch **war** gelesen **worden**
Active sentence	Man liest täglich die Zeitung.
	One reads the newspaper daily.
Passive sentence	Die Zeitung **wird** täglich **gelesen.**
	The newspaper *is read* daily.
	Or:
Active sentence	Man liest die Zeitung.
	One is reading the newspaper.
Passive sentence	Die Zeitung **wird gelesen.**
	The newspaper *is being read.*

Indication of the agent is usually *omitted* if the agent performing the action is insignificant or unknown.

Active sentence	*Passive sentence*
Die Leute lesen täglich die Zeitung.	Die Zeitung wird täglich (*naturally:* von den Leuten) gelesen.

B. The Passive with Verbs + an Object in the Accusative

Active sentence	*Passive sentence*
Man liest **den Roman.**	**Der Roman** wird gelesen.

The *accusative object* of the *active sentence* becomes the *subject* of the *passive sentence.* This *subject* then *determines* the *form of the verb* in the passive sentence.

Der Roman wird gelesen.	*The novel is* (being) read.
Die Romane werden gelesen.	*The novels are* (being) read.

Drill 27 *Passive Sentences with Verbs + an Object in the Accusative* *Follow the examples.*

Man **fällt das Urteil** heute.
Das Urteil wird heute **gefällt.**

Man **fällt die Urteile** heute.
Die Urteile werden heute **gefällt.**

Man bewahrt die Farbe im Hof auf.
Man bewahrt die Farben im Hof auf.
Man zieht den Kreis mit der Kreide.

Man zieht die Kreise mit Kreide.
Man bringt das Kind herein.
Man fragt die Verwandten.
Man nimmt die Probe jetzt vor.
Man singt die Moritat oft.
Man plündert die Häuser.
Man ruft den Gerichtsdiener.

C. The Passive with Verbs + an Object in the Dative

The *dative object* of the *active sentence remains* the *dative object* of the *passive sentence.* Thus the dative object *does not determine* the verb form. In passive sentences with a dative object *the verb* **werden** *is always in the singular form.*

Active sentence	Man hilft **den Kindern.**
Passive sentence	**Den Kindern wird** geholfen.
Present	**Den Kindern wird** geholfen.
Imperfect	**Den Kindern wurde** geholfen.
Perfect	**Den Kindern ist** geholfen **worden.**
Pluperfect	**Den Kindern war** geholfen **worden.**

Compare the English and the German:

Active sentence

Man **hilft dem Kind.**
One *helps* the *child.*

Man **hilft den Kindern.**
One *helps the children.*

Passive sentence

Dem Kind wird geholfen.
The child is helped.

Den Kindern wird geholfen.
The children are helped.

Drill 28 *Passive Sentences with Verbs + an Object in the Dative* *Follow the examples.*

Man **dankt dem Arzt** herzlich.
Dem Arzt wird herzlich **gedankt.**

Man **dankt den Ärzten** herzlich.
Den Ärzten wird herzlich **gedankt.**

Man glaubt dieser Frau nicht.
Man glaubt diesen Frauen nicht.
Man hilft dem Kind endlich.

Man hilft den Kindern endlich.
Man antwortet dem Richter sofort.
Man antwortet den Zeugen sofort.
Man gratuliert den Kindern herzlich.
Man glaubt der Magd alles.
Man glaubt den Leuten alles.
Man hilft den alten Leuten immer.
Man dankt dem Richter öffentlich.

Drill 29 *Combination Drill   Passive Sentences with Verbs + an Object in the Accusative and Verbs + an Object in the Dative*

Man fragt die Verwandten.
Man glaubt den Leuten alles.
Man fällt das Urteil heute.
Man hilft den Kindern endlich.
Man glaubt der Magd alles.
Man bewahrt die Farben im Hof auf.

Man zieht den Kreis mit Kreide.
Man dankt dem Arzt herzlich.
Man singt die Moritat oft.
Man antwortet den Zeugen sofort.
Man antwortet dem Richter sofort.
Man plündert die Häuser.

D.   The Passive with Verbs without an Object

Passive sentences with verbs that have no object do not exist in English. In such sentences the verb **werden** is *always in the singular form.*

Active sentence	Sonntags arbeitet man nicht.
	One does not work on Sundays.
Passive sentence	Sonntags **wird** nicht **gearbeitet.**
	(There is no work on Sundays.)
	(People do not work on Sundays.)
Present	Sonntags **wird** nicht gearbeitet.
Imperfect	Sonntags **wurde** nicht gearbeitet.
Perfect	Sonntags **ist** nicht gearbeitet **worden.**
Pluperfect	Sonntags **war** nicht gearbeitet **worden.**

Drill 30 *Passive Sentences with Verbs without an Object*   *Follow the example.*

Auf dem Bauernhof arbeitet man hart.
Auf dem Bauernhof **wird** hart **gearbeitet.**

Hier macht man nicht auf.
Jetzt handelt man schnell.
Am Abend plündert man.
Hier bezahlt man gleich.

In diesem Fall urteilt man richtig.
Hier redet man zu viel.
Jetzt ruft man laut.
Hier lügt man wie gedruckt.
Im Gasthaus erzählt man viel.

Drill 31 *Combination Drill   Passive Sentences with Verbs with an Accusative Object, with a Dative Object, and without an Object*

Man fragt die Verwandten.
Man glaubt diesen Leuten alles.
Jetzt handelt man schnell.
Auf dem Bauernhof arbeitet man hart.
Man glaubt dieser Frau nicht.
Man plündert die Häuser.

Hier lügt man wie gedruckt.
Man fällt die Urteile heute.
Man antwortet dem Richter sofort.
Man bewahrt die Farben im Hof auf.
Man nimmt die Probe jetzt vor.
Man glaubt den Leuten alles.

Drill 32   *Passive Sentences in the Imperfect, Perfect, and Pluperfect*   *Follow the examples.*

Man brachte das Kind **herein.**
Das Kind **wurde hereingebracht.**

Man hat das Kind **hereingebracht.**
Das Kind **ist hereingebracht worden.**

Man hatte das Kind **hereingebracht.**
Das Kind **war hereingebracht worden.**

Man fragte die Verwandten.

Man hat dem Richter sofort geantwortet.
Man hatte den Frauen nichts geglaubt.
Man hat die Urteile heute gefällt.
Man hatte die Probe vorgenommen.
Man dankte den Ärzten herzlich.
Man hatte den Gerichtsdiener gerufen.
Am Abend plünderte man.
Auf dem Bauernhof hat man hart gearbeitet.

E.   The Impersonal es in the Vorfeld of Passive Sentences

We have already learned that for stylistic reasons the impersonal **es** can be used as a filler in any Vorfeld if the subject of the sentence is not a personal pronoun itself.

Vorfeld	P1	Satzfeld	P2
30 Studenten	sind	jetzt	im Kurs.
Es	sind	jetzt **30 Studenten**	im Kurs.
Viele Leute	kommen	heute.	
Es	kommen	heute **viele Leute.**	

This stylistic feature may be used in passive sentences too.

Vorfeld	P1	Satzfeld	P2
Zeitungen	werden	täglich	gelesen.
Es	werden	täglich **Zeitungen**	gelesen.
Den Kindern	wird	endlich	geholfen.
Es	wird	**den Kindern** endlich	geholfen.
Am Sonntag	wird	nicht	gearbeitet.
Es	wird	**am Sonntag** nicht	gearbeitet.

This impersonal **es** *disappears* as soon as the *subject* of the sentence or *another element is put into the Vorfeld.*

F.   The Agent in Passive Sentences

The agent may, of course, be indicated in passive sentences.

Active sentence

Das Volk besang den Richter in einer langen Moritat.

Passive sentence

Der Richter wurde **vom Volk** in einer langen Moritat besungen.

In English such sentences are used more often.

If *incidents* rather than persons, institutions, mechanisms, etc., *perform* or *bring about* the *action,* the preposition **durch** is used instead of **von.**

Der Mann wurde (von einem Mörder) **durch einen Schuß** getötet.
Der Mann wurde **durch Zufall** gerettet.

The *word order* in the *passive sentence* usually *follows* the *word order* in the *active sentence.*

Active sentence	*Passive sentence*
Der Richter fällte das Urteil am Freitag im Goldenen Saal.	Das Urteil wurde vom Richter am Freitag im Goldenen Saal gefällt.

Drill 33 *Passive Sentences in the Imperfect, Perfect, and Pluperfect   This time state the agent. Follow the example.*

Das Volk besang den Richter in einer langen Moritat.
Der Richter wurde vom Volk in einer langen Moritat **besungen.**

Die kaiserlichen Truppen haben die Stadt gestürmt.
Die Soldaten warfen Beutestücke auf die Straße.
Panik ergriff die Magd.
Die Soldaten hatten den Hausherrn erschlagen.
Die Bäuerin empfing die Magd nicht schlecht.
Die Leute hatten die Magd nicht einmal anständig behandelt.
Die Bauern brachten die Magd auf einen Hof.

II. THE STATAL PASSIVE

At times you will encounter sentences in which the auxiliary verb **sein** stands with a perfect participle:

Das Manuskript **ist** schon **geschrieben.**
Der Eingang **ist** zwei Stunden **geöffnet.**

In these examples *the perfect participle* used with **sein** describes a *state* or *condition,* and *the perfect participle* has the *meaning* and *function* of an *adjective.*

Das Manuskript **ist** schon **geschrieben.**	Der Eingang **ist** zwei Stunden **geöffnet.**
Or:	Or:
Das Manuskript **ist** schon **fertig.**	Der Eingang **ist** zwei Stunden **offen.**

This is perhaps more apparent in the perfect tense:

Das Manuskript **ist** schon **geschrieben gewesen.**	Der Eingang **ist** zwei Stunden **geöffnet gewesen.**
Or:	Or:
Das Manuskript **ist** schon **fertig gewesen.**	Der Eingang **ist** zwei Stunden **offen gewesen.**

III. THE MODAL VERBS IN PASSIVE SENTENCES

As in English, modal verbs can appear in passive sentences. The *modal* verb *keeps* the *active form*. Only the *infinitive* takes the *passive form*. In passive, as in active sentences, modal verbs can take all tenses.

Active sentence	Das **muß** man **machen.**
	One *must do* that.
Passive sentence	Das **muß gemacht werden.**
	That *must be done.*
Present	Das **muß gemacht werden.**
Imperfect	Das **mußte gemacht werden.**
Perfect	Das **hat gemacht werden müssen.**
Pluperfect	Das **hatte gemacht werden müssen.**

Drill 34 *Passive Sentences with the Modal Verb* müssen *in the Present and Imperfect*   *Follow the examples.*

Auf dem Bauernhof **wird** hart **gearbeitet.**
Auf dem Bauernhof **muß** hart **gearbeitet werden.**

Auf dem Bauernhof **wurde** hart **gearbeitet.**
Auf dem Bauernhof **mußte** hart **gearbeitet werden.**

Hier wird schnell gehandelt.
Hier wurde schnell gehandelt.

Dort wird richtig geurteilt.
Dort wurde richtig geurteilt.

Hier wird laut gerufen.
Hier wurde laut gerufen.

Dem Richter wird sofort geantwortet.
Dem Richter wurde sofort geantwortet.

Drill 35 *Passive Sentences with Modal Verbs in the Present*   *Follow the example.*

Die Verwandten **muß** man **fragen.**
Die Verwandten **müssen gefragt werden.**

Diesem Kind kann man helfen.
Dieser Magd darf man alles glauben.

Die Probe kann man jetzt vornehmen.
Den Kreis soll man mit Kreide ziehen.
Das Urteil muß man heute fällen.

Drill 36 *Passive Sentences with Modal Verbs in the Perfect*   *Follow the example.*

Das **kann gemacht werden.**
Das **hat gemacht werden können.**

Das muß gesagt werden.
Das Urteil kann gefällt werden.

Das muß erzählt werden.
Hier darf nicht geplündert werden.
Das muß geschrieben werden.

IV. SUBSTITUTE CONSTRUCTIONS FOR THE PASSIVE

Instead of the following passive sentences you may sometimes encounter the following active sentences which have almost the same meaning:

Das **kann** besser **gemacht werden.**	Das **läßt sich** besser **machen.**
Das **kann** besser **gemacht werden.**	Das **ist** besser **zu machen.**
Das Problem **wird geklärt.**	Das Problem **klärt sich.**
Die Tür **wird geöffnet.**	Die Tür **öffnet sich.**
Der Vorhang **wird geschlossen.**	Der Vorhang **schließt sich.**
Uns wird die Post **nachgeschickt.**	**Wir bekommen** die Post **nachgeschickt.**
Mir wird das Buch **zugeschickt.**	**Ich erhalte** das Buch **zugeschickt.**

der **Papierfabrikant, —en** paper manufacturer

bedeutend significant; **zugleich** at the same time; **umstritten** controversial

die **Naturwissenschaft, —en** science; **verwirklichen** *here:* to carry out; **ein·ziehen, o, o** to draft; **holen** to fetch; **der Regisseur, —e** (stage) director; **die zwanziger Jahre** the twenties; **die Trommel, —n** drum

die **herrschende bürgerliche Klasse** the ruling bourgeois class

Er stand politisch links He was on the political left; **Er hat sich zum Marxismus bekannt** He was a professed Marxist

selbstverständlich *here:* obvious **die Flucht** flight, escape

erst *here:* It was not before

die **Alliierten** the allies; **die Einreise, —n** entry; **verweigern** to refuse; **die Einladung, —n** invitation

Bertolt Brecht

Biographie   Bertolt Brecht ist eine der bedeutendsten und zugleich umstrittensten Gestalten der deutschen Literatur des zwanzigsten Jahrhunderts.

Er wurde 1898 in Augsburg als Sohn eines Papierfabrikanten geboren. Nachdem er 1917 das Abitur gemacht hatte, wollte er Medizin und Naturwissenschaften studieren. Aber bevor er diese Pläne verwirklichen konnte, zog ihn die Armee ein. Er verbrachte das letzte Jahr des Ersten Weltkriegs als Sanitäter im Kriegslazarett. 1919 begann er sein Studium, doch nun interessierten ihn die Literatur und das Theater mehr als die Wissenschaft. 1922 holte ihn der große Regisseur der zwanziger Jahre, Max Reinhardt, an das Deutsche Theater in Berlin. Ein Jahr später erhielt Brecht seinen ersten Literaturpreis für das Heimkehrerdrama *Trommeln in der Nacht*.

Schon als Schüler des Augsburger Gymnasiums hatte Brecht politisch links gestanden. Die Erfahrungen im Kriegslazarett hatten seine Kritik an der ,,herrschenden bürgerlichen Klasse'' und ihrer Moral noch verschärft. Doch Kritik allein genügte ihm, dem schöpferischen Menschen, nicht. Jahrelang suchte er eine geistige Orientierung. Er fand sie 1928–1929 in der Lehre des dialektischen Materialismus, in der Lehre von Karl Marx. Bis zu seinem Tode, 1956, hat Brecht sich zum Marxismus bekannt.

So ist es nur selbstverständlich, daß er 1933 aus Deutschland emigrieren mußte. Österreich, die Schweiz, Frankreich, Dänemark, Schweden und Finnland waren die Stationen seiner Flucht. 1941 ging er in die Sowjetunion, aber nicht, um dort zu bleiben, sondern um von dort in die U.S.A. zu emigrieren.

Erst 1947 kehrte er nach Europa zurück. Da ihm die Alliierten die Einreise nach Westdeutschland verweigerten, nahm er die Einladung der Ostdeutschen Regierung an und ging nach Ost-

gründen to found

sog. = **sogenannt** so-called; **die Dreigroschenoper**
Three Penny Opera; **unverkennbar** unmistakable

verlegen *here:* to shift

die Wirtin, –nen landlady; **allerhand** *here:* all sorts
of; **die Pflanze, –n** plant; **das Tierzeug** animal matter; **sogleich** immediately; **ab und zu** from time to
time; **faul** lazy; **irgendwo** somewhere; **unterrichten**
to teach

der Haifisch, –e shark; **nett** nice; **gewaltig** enormous;
der Kasten, ⸚ box; **die Nahrung** food, nourishment;
sorgen to see to it, to take care of; **Maßnahmen
treffen, a, o** to take measures; **die Flosse, –n** fin;
verletzen to injure; **der Verband, –e** bandage; **weg·
sterben, a, o** = **sterben** to die; **vor der Zeit** *here:*
prematurely; **trübsinnig** melancholy, sad; **das Fest,
–e** festival; **lustig** happy, gay; **der Rachen, –** maw;
die Hauptsache, –n chief concern; **die Ausbildung, –en**
education, training

Berlin. 1949 gründete er, zusammen mit seiner Frau, Helene Weigel, das „Berliner Ensemble" im Theater am Schiffbauerdamm. Es wurde Brechts Modelltheater und damit eines der besten Theater der Welt.

Brecht ist nicht nur ein bedeutender Theaterregisseur, Lyriker, Erzähler, und Dramatiker, der sich seine eigene Form des Theaters, das sog. „Epische Theater", geschaffen hat. Er ist ebenso bedeutend als Theoretiker. Von seinen Werken wurde die *Dreigroschenoper*, mit der Musik von Kurt Weill, ein Welterfolg. Der Einfluß seiner theoretischen Schriften auf das gesamte moderne Theater ist unverkennbar.

Die Parabel „Wenn die Haifische Menschen wären" steht in den *Geschichten von Herrn Keuner*, die Erzählung „Der Augsburger Kreidekreis" ist aus den *Kalendergeschichten*. Er dramatisierte sie 1944–1945, verlegte den Schauplatz ins südliche Rußland und nannte das Stück *Der kaukasische Kreidekreis*.

WENN DIE HAIFISCHE MENSCHEN WÄREN

Wenn die Haifische Menschen wären", fragte Herrn K. die kleine Tochter seiner Wirtin, „wären sie dann netter zu den kleinen Fischen?" „Sicher", sagte er. „Wenn die Haifische Menschen wären, würden sie im Meer für die kleinen Fische gewaltige Kästen bauen lassen, mit allerhand Nahrung drin, sowohl Pflanzen als auch Tierzeug. Sie würden sorgen, daß die Kästen immer frisches Wasser hätten, und sie würden überhaupt allerhand sanitäre Maßnahmen treffen. Wenn zum Beispiel ein Fischlein sich die Flosse verletzen würde, dann würde ihm sogleich ein Verband gemacht, damit es den Haifischen nicht wegstürbe vor der Zeit. Damit die Fischlein nicht trübsinnig würden, gäbe es ab und zu große Wasserfeste; denn lustige Fischlein schmecken besser als trübsinnige. Es gäbe natürlich auch Schulen in den großen Kästen. In diesen Schulen würden die Fischlein lernen, wie man in den Rachen der Haifische schwimmt. Sie würden zum Beispiel Geographie brauchen, damit sie die großen Haifische, die faul irgendwo liegen, finden könnten. Die Hauptsache wäre natürlich die moralische Ausbildung der Fischlein. Sie würden unterrichtet werden, daß

die **Zukunft** future; **bei·bringen, a, a,** to teach, to impress upon; **gesichert** assured, guaranteed; **untereinander** among each other; **verkünden** to proclaim; **der Seetang** seaweed; **an·heften** to pin on **tummeln** to romp; **der Klang, ⁻e** strain; **die Kapelle, ⁻n** band; **voran** in front; **träumerisch** dreamily; **allerangenehmst** most pleasant, delightful; **ein·lullen** to lull in; **übrigens** moreover; **usw. = und so weiter** etc.; **Es gäbe überhaupt erst eine Kultur im Meer, . . .** The sea would only begin to be civilized . . . ; **die Kultur, ⁻en** culture, civilization

sich auf·opfern to sacrifice oneself; **der Gehorsam** obedience; **niedrig** base; **die Neigung, ⁻en** tendency, inclination; **sich hüten vor** (+ *dat.*) to guard against; **verraten, ie, a** *here:* to reveal, to disclose; **Krieg führen** to wage war; **fremd** *here:* foreign; **erobern** to conquer; **der Unterschied, ⁻e** difference; **bestehen, a, a** to be, to exist; **riesig** huge, giant; **stumm** mute; **schweigen, ie, ie** to be silent; **bekanntlich** as is well known; **feindlich** hostile; **töten** to kill; **der Orden, ⁻** medal; **der Held, ⁻en** (MII) hero; **einen Titel verleihen, ie, ie** to award a title **die Kunst, ⁻e** art; **der Zahn, ⁻e** tooth; **prächtig** glorious; **die Farbe, ⁻n** color; **der Lustgarten, ⁻** garden of pleasure; **dar·stellen** to present, to show; **heldenmütig** heroic; **begeistert** enthusiastic; **strömen** to stream; **der Bauch, ⁻e** belly; **Es würde auf·hören** *here:* It would cease to be the case; **gleich** equal; **das Amt, ⁻er** official position; **auf·fressen, a, e** to eat up; **der Brocken, ⁻** morsel; **die Ordnung, ⁻en** order

es das Größte und Schönste sei, wenn ein Fischlein sich freudig aufopfert, und daß sie alle an die Haifische glauben müßten, vor allem, wenn sie sagten, sie würden für eine schöne Zukunft sorgen. Man würde den Fischlein beibringen, daß diese Zukunft nur gesichert sei, wenn sie Gehorsam lernten. Vor allen niedrigen, materialistischen und egoistischen Neigungen müßten sich die Fischlein hüten und es sofort den Haifischen melden, wenn eines von ihnen solche Neigungen verriete. Wenn die Haifische Menschen wären, würden sie natürlich auch untereinander Kriege führen, um fremde Fischkästen und fremde Fischlein zu erobern. Die Kriege würden sie von ihren eigenen Fischlein führen lassen. Sie würden die Fischlein lehren, daß zwischen ihnen und den Fischlein der andern Haifische ein riesiger Unterschied bestehe. Die Fischlein, würden sie verkünden, sind bekanntlich stumm, aber sie schweigen in ganz verschiedenen Sprachen und können einander daher unmöglich verstehen. Jedem Fischlein, das im Krieg ein paar andere Fischlein, feindliche, in anderer Sprache schweigende Fischlein tötete, würden sie einen kleinen Orden aus Seetang anheften und den Titel Held verleihen. Wenn die Haifische Menschen wären, gäbe es bei ihnen natürlich auch eine Kunst. Es gäbe schöne Bilder, auf denen die Zähne der Haifische in prächtigen Farben, ihre Rachen als reine Lustgärten, in denen es sich prächtig tummeln läßt, dargestellt wären. Die Theater auf dem Meeresgrund würden zeigen, wie heldenmütige Fischlein begeistert in die Haifischrachen schwimmen, und die Musik wäre so schön, daß die Fischlein unter ihren Klängen, die Kapelle voran, träumerisch, und in allerangenehmste Gedanken eingelullt, in die Haifischrachen strömten. Auch eine Religion gäbe es ja, wenn die Haifische Menschen wären. Sie würde lehren, daß die Fischlein erst im Bauch der Haifische richtig zu leben begännen. Übrigens würde es auch aufhören, wenn die Haifische Menschen wären, daß alle Fischlein, wie es jetzt ist, gleich sind. Einige von ihnen würden Ämter bekommen und über die andern gesetzt werden. Die ein wenig größeren dürften sogar die kleineren auffressen. Das wäre für die Haifische nur angenehm, da sie dann selber öfter größere Brocken zu fressen bekämen. Und die größeren, Posten habenden Fischlein würden für die Ordnung unter den Fischlein sorgen, Lehrer, Offiziere, Ingenieure im Kastenbau usw. werden. Kurz, es gäbe überhaupt erst eine Kultur im Meer, wenn die Haifische Menschen wären."

I. QUESTIONNAIRE

A.   A-Questions

Answer with complete sentences in the tense of the story.

1. Was würde sich zunächst im Meer ändern, wenn die Haifische Menschen wären?

    Welche **Frage stellte** *das kleine Mädchen* **Herrn K.?** // whether / sharks / to be / nicer / little fish / if / sharks / to be / people //
    Herr K. antwortete: „Sicher". Was, sagte er, **würden die Haifische** *zunächst* **für die kleinen Fische** tun? // to have enormous boxes built //
    Was wäre *darin?* // food //
    Wofür würden *die Haifische* **sorgen?** // that / boxes / to have / always / fresh water //
    Was würden *sie* überhaupt tun? // to take / sanitary measures //
    Wann würde *man* einem Fischlein einen Verband machen? // when / it / to injure / fin //
    Warum würden sich *die Haifische* **um das verletzte Fischlein kümmern?** // in order that / it / not / to die / prematurely //
    Warum gäbe es *ab und zu* **große Wasserfeste?** // in order that / little fish / not / to become / melancholy //
    Warum sollen *die Fischlein* **lustig sein?** // because / gay fish / to taste / better / than / melancholy fish //

2. Es gäbe natürlich auch Schulen in den großen Kästen. Was alles würden die Fischlein dort lernen?

    Was **würden sie** *zuerst* **lernen?** // how / to swim / maw / sharks //
    Warum **würden** *sie* Geographie brauchen? // in order to find / big sharks //
    Was wäre *die Hauptsache?* // moral training / little fish //
    Was, würden die Haifische sagen, **sei** *das Größte und Schönste?* // to sacrifice oneself / gladly //
    Was müßten die Fischlein *vor allem?* // to believe in / sharks //
    Was würden *die Haifische* ihnen sagen? // that / they / to care for / beautiful future //
    Wann, würden die Haifische sagen, **sei** *diese Zukunft* **nur gesichert?** // when / little fish / to learn / obedience //
    Wovor müßten sich *die Fischlein* **hüten?** // all base, materialistic and egoistic tendencies //
    Was **sollten** *die Fischlein* **sofort** machen, wenn eines von ihnen solche Neigungen verriete? // to report / it / sharks //

3. Wenn die Haifische Menschen wären, gäbe es natürlich auch Kriege. Wie wäre die Kriegführung?

    Warum **würden** *die Haifische* Kriege **führen?** // in order to conquer / foreign boxes / foreign fish //
    Wie **würden** *sie* die Kriege führen? // own fish / to let / wage war //
    Was würden *sie* die Fischlein lehren? // that / to exist / giant difference / between them / other fish //
    Was würden *sie* verkünden? // that / fish / to be / as is well known / mute // that / fish / to be silent / different languages //

Was **können** *die Fischlein* deswegen nicht? // to understand each other //
Was **würden** *die Haifische* einem Fischlein verleihen, wenn es ein paar feindliche Fischlein tötete? // medal / and / title hero //

4. Was gäbe es alles auf dem Gebiete der Kunst?

Wie **wären** *die Zähne der Haifische* dargestellt? // glorious colors //
Wie **sähen** *die Rachen* aus? // like / pure gardens of pleasure //
Was **würden** *die Theater* zeigen? // how / heroic fish / to swim / enthusiastically / maws / sharks //
Warum **würden** *die Fischlein* träumerisch in die Haifischrachen strömen? // because / music / to be / so beautiful //
Was **würde** *die Religion* lehren? // that / little fish / to begin / to really live / belly / sharks //

5. Wie wäre die politische Ordnung im Meer?

Was **würde** aufhören? // that / all fish / to be equal //
Was geschähe **mit** *einigen Fischlein*? // to get / official positions //
Was **dürften** *andere*? // to eat up / smaller ones //
Warum **wäre** *das* für die Haifische nur angenehm? // since / they themselves / then / to get / bigger morsels //
Was **würden** *die großen Fische* tun? // to see to / order / among fish //
Was **könnten** *sie* werden? // teachers / officers / engineers //
Wie schließt Herr K. seine Geschichte? // sea / to begin to be civilized / if / sharks / to be / people //

B.   B-Questions

1. Wer sind in der Perspektive Brechts die Haifische, und wer sind die Fischlein?

2. Was, glauben Sie, will Brecht mit dieser Parabel sagen?

3. Bezieht sich diese Parabel nur auf Verhältnisse in der bürgerlichen Gesellschaft?

namens by the name of; **die Augsburgerin, –nen** Augsburg woman; **sei es, daß, . . .** whether it was that . . . ; **jedenfalls** at any rate

der Kreidekreis, –e chalk circle; **der Dreißigjährige Krieg** Thirty Years War; **besitzen, a, e** to own; **die Gerberei, –en** tannery; **die Lederhandlung, –en** leather business; **die freie Reichsstadt** free imperial city; **der Lech** Lech river; **verheiratet sein mit** (+ *dat.*) to be married to; **zur Flucht raten, ie, a** to advise to flee; **dringend** urgently; **im Stich lassen, ie, a** to abandon; **beizeiten** in time; **weg·reisen** to leave, to depart

die kaiserlichen Truppen imperial troops; **das Kleid, –er** dress; **der Schmuck** jewelry; **von einem Fenster des ersten Stockes aus** from a window on the second floor

(sich) verstecken to hide; **der Hof, ⁻e** courtyard, yard; **die Farbe, –n** *here:* dye; **auf·bewahren** to store; **der Verwandte** (*perf. part.*) relative; **die Vorstadt, ⁻e** suburbs, outskirts; **ziehen, o, o** *here:* to move; **Sie hielt sich zu lange damit auf, ihre Sachen zu packen** She spent too much time packing her things; **die Rotte, –n** squad; **dringen, a, u** to force one's way; **außer sich vor Schrecken** beside herself with fear; **Sie ließ alles stehen und liegen** She dropped everything; **das Anwesen, –** premises

die Diele, –n hallway; **die Wiege, –n** cradle; **die Schnur, ⁻e** string; **die Decke, –n** ceiling

stürzen *here:* to dart, rush; **das Geräusch, –e** sound

die Magd, ⁻e servant girl, maid; **hantieren** to tinker around; **das Kupferzeug** copperware, copper pots and pans; **der Lärm** noise; **von der Gasse her** from the alley; **allerhand Beutestücke** all kinds of loot; **der Schlag, ⁻e** blow; **eichen** oaken; **die Haustür, –en** front door; **von Panik ergriffen** seized with panic; **die Treppe hinauf·fliegen, o, o** to flee up the stairs

das Wunder, – miracle

sich füllen to become filled; **kurz und klein schlagen, u, a** to smash to pieces; **die Durchsuchung, –en** search; **unentdeckt** undiscovered

DER AUGSBURGER KREIDEKREIS

Zu der Zeit des Dreißigjährigen Krieges besaß ein Schweizer Protestant namens Zingli eine große Gerberei mit einer Lederhandlung in der freien Reichsstadt Augsburg am Lech. Er war mit einer Augsburgerin verheiratet und hatte ein Kind von ihr. Als die Katholischen auf die Stadt zu marschierten, rieten ihm seine Freunde dringend zur Flucht, aber, sei es, daß seine kleine Familie ihn hielt, sei es, daß er seine Gerberei nicht im Stich lassen wollte, er konnte sich jedenfalls nicht entschließen, beizeiten wegzureisen.

So war er noch in der Stadt, als die kaiserlichen Truppen sie stürmten, und als am Abend geplündert wurde, versteckte er sich in einer Grube im Hof, wo die Farben aufbewahrt wurden. Seine Frau sollte mit dem Kind zu ihren Verwandten in die Vorstadt ziehen, aber sie hielt sich zu lange damit auf, ihre Sachen, Kleider, Schmuck und Betten zu packen, und so sah sie plötzlich, von einem Fenster des ersten Stockes aus, eine Rotte kaiserlicher Soldaten in den Hof dringen. Außer sich vor Schrekken ließ sie alles stehen und liegen und rannte durch eine Hintertür aus dem Anwesen.

So blieb das Kind im Hause zurück. Es lag in der großen Diele in seiner Wiege und spielte mit einem Holzball, der an einer Schnur von der Decke hing.

Nur eine junge Magd war noch im Hause. Sie hantierte in der Küche mit dem Kupferzeug, als sie Lärm von der Gasse her hörte. Ans Fenster stürzend, sah sie, wie aus dem ersten Stock des Hauses gegenüber von Soldaten allerhand Beutestücke auf die Gasse geworfen wurden. Sie lief in die Diele und wollte eben das Kind aus der Wiege nehmen, als sie das Geräusch schwerer Schläge gegen die eichene Haustür hörte. Sie wurde von Panik ergriffen und flog die Treppe hinauf.

Die Diele füllte sich mit betrunkenen Soldaten, die alles kurz und klein schlugen, Sie wußten, daß sie sich im Hause eines Protestanten befanden. Wie durch ein Wunder blieb bei der Durchsuchung und Plünderung Anna, die Magd, unentdeckt.

heraus·klettern to climb out; **erhellen** to light up; **entsetzt** horrified; **erblicken** = **sehen** to see

sich verziehen, o, o to disappear, to vanish; **der Schrank,** ⁼**e** closet, wardrobe; **unversehrt** unharmed; **Sie nahm es hastig an sich** She snatched it up hastily; **schleichen, i, i** to steal away, to sneak; **die übel zugerichtete Leiche** the badly battered corpse; **erschlagen, u, a** to slay

schweren Herzens with a heavy heart; **wiegen** to rock; **das Getümmel** turmoil; **den Sieg feiern** to celebrate victory; **mächtig** huge, great; **sich öffnen to** open; **geraume Zeit** quite a long while; **atemlos** breathless; **die Überzeugung gewinnen** to gain the conviction

Gefahr laufen, ie, au to be in danger; **auf·greifen, i, i** to catch; **sich drängen** to force one's way; **begleitet** accompanied; **auf·suchen** to seek out; **heraus·stecken** to stick out; **berichten** to relate, to report; **tot** dead; **aus fischigen Augen** with fishlike eyes; **die Nichte, –n** niece; **nichts zu schaffen haben mit** (+ *dat.*) to have nothing to do with; **der Bankert** bastard; **der Schwager, –** brother-in-law; **der Vorhang,** ⁼**e** curtain; **sich schämen** to be ashamed; **anscheinend** apparently; **verleugnen** to repudiate

eine Zeitlang for a while; **ordentlich** conventional, respectable; **erschrocken** dismayed, shocked

erklären to declare, to explain; **aus·reden** to talk out of; **anständig** decent; **behandeln** to treat

fehlen (+ *dat.*) to lack

versprechen, a, o to promise; **unvernünftig** unreasonable, rash; **schauen** to look; **. . . , ob dem Kind nichts fehlte . . . . . .** whether the child needed anything

Die Rotte verzog sich, und aus dem Schrank herauskletternd, in dem sie gestanden war, fand Anna auch das Kind in der Diele unversehrt. Sie nahm es hastig an sich und schlich mit ihm auf den Hof hinaus. Es war inzwischen Nacht geworden, aber der rote Schein eines in der Nähe brennenden Hauses erhellte den Hof, und entsetzt erblickte sie die übel zugerichtete Leiche des Hausherrn. Die Soldaten hatten ihn aus seiner Grube gezogen und erschlagen.

Erst jetzt wurde der Magd klar, welche Gefahr sie lief, wenn sie mit dem Kind des Protestanten auf der Straße aufgegriffen wurde. Sie legte es schweren Herzens in die Wiege zurück, gab ihm etwas Milch zu trinken, wiegte es in Schlaf und machte sich auf den Weg in den Stadtteil, wo ihre verheiratete Schwester wohnte. Gegen zehn Uhr nachts drängte sie sich, begleitet vom Mann ihrer Schwester, durch das Getümmel der ihren Sieg feiernden Soldaten, um in der Vorstadt Frau Zingli, die Mutter des Kindes, aufzusuchen. Sie klopften an die Tür eines mächtigen Hauses, die sich nach geraumer Zeit auch ein wenig öffnete. Ein kleiner alter Mann, Frau Zinglis Onkel, steckte den Kopf heraus. Anna berichtete atemlos, daß Herr Zingli tot, das Kind aber unversehrt im Hause sei. Der Alte sah sie kalt aus fischigen Augen an und sagte, seine Nichte sei nicht mehr da, und er selber habe mit dem Protestantenbankert nichts zu schaffen. Damit machte er die Tür wieder zu. Im Weggehen sah Annas Schwager, wie sich ein Vorhang in einem der Fenster bewegte, und gewann die Überzeugung, daß Frau Zingli da war. Sie schämte sich anscheinend nicht, ihr Kind zu verleugnen.

Eine Zeitlang gingen Anna und ihr Schwager schweigend nebeneinander her. Dann erklärte sie ihm, daß sie in die Gerberei zurück und das Kind holen wollte. Der Schwager, ein ruhiger, ordentlicher Mann, hörte sie erschrocken an und suchte ihr die gefährliche Idee auszureden. Was hatte sie mit diesen Leuten zu tun? Sie war nicht einmal anständig behandelt worden.

Anna hörte ihm still zu und versprach ihm, nichts Unvernünftiges zu tun. Jedoch wollte sie unbedingt noch schnell in die Gerberei schauen, ob dem Kind nichts fehle. Und sie wollte allein gehen.

wagen to dare; **das Licht, –er** *here:* candle; **an·zünden** to light; **hüllen** to wrap; **die Leinendecke, –n** linen cover, blanket

Sie setzte ihren Willen durch She got her own way; **müde** tired; **betrachten** to look, to gaze at; **winzig** tiny; **der Leberfleck, –en** mole; **das Hälschen** *here:* little throat; **atmen** to breathe; **die Faust, ⁻e** fist; **saugen** to suck; **schwerfällig** heavily; **scheu** shy; **das Gewissen, –** conscience; **die Diebin, –nen** thief

die Beratung, –en consultation; **zu Gesicht bekommen, a, o** to set eyes on

darauf, after that; **das Dorf, ⁻er** village; **der Bauer, -** peasant, farmer; **der Bauernhof, ⁻e** farm; **ein·heiraten** to marry into; **Es war ausgemacht worden** It had been agreed; **auf·nehmen, a, o** to receive

das Gesinde farmhands; **empfangen, i, a** to receive; **der Blick, –e** glance; **veranlassen** to induce, to lead; **sogleich** immediately; **auf·tauen** to thaw; **gebührend** duly; **bewundern** to admire

vor·stellen to represent, to introduce; **die Mühle, –n** mill; **erwarten** to expect

das Gehölz wood; **sammeln** to gather; **seiner Frau gegenüber** in front of his wife; **großzügig** generous; **die Haltung, –en** attitude

Sie schenkte ihm reinen Wein ein She told him the whole truth; **Ihm war nicht wohl in seiner Haut** He felt ill at ease; **gefestigt** secure; **loben** to praise; **den Mund halten, ie, a** to hold one's tongue

Sie setzte ihren Willen durch. Mitten in der zerstörten Halle lag das Kind ruhig in seiner Wiege und schlief. Anna setzte sich müde zu ihm und betrachtete es. Sie hatte nicht gewagt, ein Licht anzuzünden, aber das Haus in der Nähe brannte immer noch, und bei diesem Licht konnte sie das Kind ganz gut sehen. Es hatte einen winzigen Leberfleck am Hälschen. Als die Magd einige Zeit, vielleicht eine Stunde, zugesehen hatte, wie das Kind atmete und an seiner kleinen Faust saugte, erkannte sie, daß sie zu lange gesessen und zu viel gesehen hatte, um noch ohne das Kind weggehen zu können. Sie stand schwerfällig auf, und mit langsamen Bewegungen hüllte sie es in die Leinendecke, hob es auf den Arm und verließ mit ihm den Hof, sich scheu umschauend, wie eine Person mit schlechtem Gewissen, eine Diebin.

Sie brachte das Kind, nach langen Beratungen mit Schwester und Schwager, zwei Wochen darauf aufs Land in das Dorf Großaitingen, wo ihr älterer Bruder Bauer war. Der Bauernhof gehörte der Frau, er hatte nur eingeheiratet. Es war ausgemacht worden, daß sie vielleicht nur dem Bruder sagen sollte, wer das Kind war, denn sie hatten die junge Bäuerin nie zu Gesicht bekommen und wußten nicht, wie sie einen so gefährlichen kleinen Gast aufnehmen würde.

Anna kam gegen Mittag im Dorf an. Ihr Bruder, seine Frau und das Gesinde saßen beim Mittagessen. Sie wurde nicht schlecht empfangen, aber ein Blick auf ihre neue Schwägerin veranlaßte sie, das Kind sogleich als ihr eigenes vorzustellen. Erst nachdem sie erzählt hatte, daß ihr Mann in einem entfernten Dorf eine Stellung in einer Mühle hatte und sie dort mit dem Kind in ein paar Wochen erwartete, taute die Bäuerin auf, und das Kind wurde gebührend bewundert.

Nachmittags begleitete sie ihren Bruder ins Gehölz, Holz sammeln. Sie setzten sich auf Baumstümpfe, und Anna schenkte ihm reinen Wein ein. Sie konnte sehen, daß ihm nicht wohl in seiner Haut war. Seine Stellung auf dem Hof war noch nicht gefestigt, und er lobte Anna sehr, daß sie seiner Frau gegenüber den Mund gehalten hatte. Es war klar, daß er seiner jungen Frau keine besonders großzügige Haltung gegenüber dem Pro-

zu·trauen to credit with

auf die Länge in the long run

die Ernte, –n harvest; **pflegen** to nurse, to take care of; **zwischendurch** between times; **sich aus·ruhen** to rest; **sich erkundigen nach** (+ *dat*.) to make inquiries about

Es sprach nichts dagegen, daß Anna blieb There was nothing against Anna's remaining; **nützlich** useful

an·spannen to harness; **heißen, ie, ei** = **befehlen** to order; **das Kalb, ⁻er** calf; **ab·holen** to pick up; **rattern** to clatter; **der Fahrweg, –e** road; **mit·teilen** to tell; **ausgemergelt** emaciated; **schmierig** smeary, greasy; **das Laken, –** sheet; **niedrig** low; **die Hütte, –n** hut, hovel

das Kopfende head; **das Lager, –** bed; **gelbhäutig** yellow-skinned; **das Entgelt** reward, compensation; **der Dienst, –e** service; **erweisen, ie, ie** to render

ein Geschäft aus·handeln to conclude a deal; **erstehen, a, a,** = **kaufen** to buy; **der Pfarrer, –** priest; **die Trauungsformel** marriage service; **der glasige Blick** lifeless stare

die Täuschung, –en deception; **aufrechterhalten, ie, a** to keep up

gedeihen, ie, ie to thrive

schlimm bad; **ins Gerede kommen, a, o** to get gossiped about

totkrank dying; **der Häusler, –** cottager

ehelichen = **heiraten** to marry

die Verehelichung = **die Hochzeit** wedding; **zweifeln** to doubt; **der Totenschein, –e** death certificate; **irgendwo** somewhere; **die Witwe, –n** widow

testantenkind zutraute. Er wollte, daß die Täuschung aufrechterhalten wurde.

Das war nun auf die Länge nicht leicht.

Anna arbeitete bei der Ernte mit und pflegte „ihr" Kind,
zwischendurch immer wieder vom Feld nach Hause laufend,
wenn die andern ausruhten. Der Kleine gedieh und wurde sogar
dick, lachte, so oft er Anna sah, und suchte kräftig den Kopf
zu heben. Aber dann kam der Winter, und die Schwägerin begann sich nach Annas Mann zu erkundigen.

Es sprach nichts dagegen, daß Anna auf dem Hof blieb, sie
konnte sich nützlich machen. Das Schlimme war, daß die Nachbarn sich über den Vater von Annas Jungen wunderten, weil
der nie kam, nach ihm zu sehen. Wenn sie keinen Vater für das
Kind zeigen konnte, mußte der Hof bald ins Gerede kommen.

An einem Sonntagmorgen spannte der Bauer an und hieß Anna
laut mitkommen, ein Kalb in einem Nachbardorf abzuholen.
Auf dem ratternden Fahrweg teilte er ihr mit, daß er für sie
einen Mann gesucht und gefunden hätte. Es war ein todkranker
Häusler, der kaum den ausgemergelten Kopf vom schmierigen
Laken heben konnte, als die beiden in seiner niedrigen Hütte
standen.

Er war willig, Anna zu ehelichen. Am Kopfende des Lagers
stand eine gelbhäutige Alte, seine Mutter. Sie sollte ein Entgelt
für den Dienst, der Anna erwiesen wurde, bekommen.

Das Geschäft war in zehn Minuten ausgehandelt, und Anna und
ihr Bruder konnten weiterfahren und ihr Kalb erstehen. Die
Verehelichung fand Ende derselben Woche statt. Während der
Pfarrer die Trauungsformel murmelte, wandte der Kranke nicht
ein einziges Mal den glasigen Blick auf Anna. Ihr Bruder
zweifelte nicht, daß sie den Totenschein in wenigen Tagen
haben würden. Dann war Annas Mann und Kindsvater auf dem
Weg zu ihr in einem Dorf bei Augsburg irgendwo gestorben,
und niemand würde sich wundern, wenn die Witwe im Haus
ihres Bruders bleiben würde.

seltsam strange; **die Kirchenglocke, –n** church bell; **die Blechmusik** brass band; **die Jungfer, –en** *here:* bridesmaid; **der Hochzeitsschmaus** wedding banquet; **die Scheibe, –n** slice; **der Speck** bacon; **die Speise-kammer, –n** pantry; **die Kiste, –n** wooden box; **stopfen** *here:* to tuck in; **fest** tightly

verzehren = essen to eat, to consume

allerdings indeed; **auf sich warten lassen, ie, a** to take its time

nunmehr now; **beschwerlich** difficult, troublesome; **vergehen, i, a** to pass (time)

der Bescheid word; **ernstlich beunruhigt** seriously perturbed

das Fuhrwerk, –e wagon, carriage; **knarren** to creak; **aus·spannen** to unharness; **sich zusammen·krampfen** to be convulsed

der Todgeweihte (*perf. part.*) doomed man; **mit beiden Backen kauen** to chew with both cheeks full

üble Nachricht bad news; **vor·finden, a, u** to find; **der Hemdsärmel, –** shirt sleeve; **gesunden** to recover health

übrigens by the way; **jedoch** however; **jammern** to lament; **auf dem Hals haben** to be saddled with; **zum Schweigen verweisen, ie, ie** to command to be silent; **bedächtig** with deliberation; **die Käsespeise, –n** cheese dish

die Wendung, –en turn of events; **ebenfalls** likewise; **überrascht** surprised; **unangenehm** unpleasant; **der Eindruck, ⸚e** impression; **fremd** *here:* someone else's

der Spinnrocken, – distaff; **los·lassen, ie, a** to let go

bekümmert troubled

Anna kam froh von ihrer seltsamen Hochzeit zurück, auf der es weder Kirchenglocken noch Blechmusik, weder Jungfern noch Gäste gegeben hatte. Sie verzehrte als Hochzeitsschmaus ein Stück Brot mit einer Scheibe Speck in der Speisekammer und trat mit ihrem Bruder dann vor die Kiste, in der das Kind lag, das jetzt einen Namen hatte. Sie stopfte das Laken fester und lachte ihren Bruder an.

Der Totenschein ließ allerdings auf sich warten.

Es kam weder die nächste noch die übernächste Woche Bescheid von der Alten. Anna hatte auf dem Hof erzählt, daß ihr Mann nun auf dem Weg zu ihr sei. Sie sagte nunmehr, wenn man sie fragte, wo er bliebe, der tiefe Schnee mache wohl die Reise beschwerlich. Aber nachdem weitere drei Wochen vergangen waren, fuhr ihr Bruder doch, ernstlich beunruhigt, in das Dorf bei Augsburg.

Er kam spät in der Nacht zurück. Anna war noch auf und lief zur Tür, als sie das Fuhrwerk auf dem Hof knarren hörte. Sie sah, wie langsam der Bauer ausspannte, und ihr Herz krampfte sich zusammen.

Er brachte üble Nachricht. In die Hütte tretend hatte er den Todgeweihten beim Abendessen am Tisch sitzend vorgefunden, in Hemdsärmeln, mit beiden Backen kauend. Er war wieder völlig gesundet.

Der Bauer sah Anna nicht ins Gesicht, als er weiter berichtete. Der Häusler, er hieß übrigens Otterer, und seine Mutter schienen über die Wendung ebenfalls überrascht und waren wohl noch zu keinem Entschluß gekommen, was zu geschehen hätte. Otterer habe keinen unangenehmen Eindruck gemacht. Er hatte wenig gesprochen, jedoch einmal seine Mutter, als sie darüber jammern wollte, daß er nun ein ungewünschtes Weib und ein fremdes Kind auf dem Hals habe, zum Schweigen verwiesen. Er aß bedächtig seine Käsespeise weiter während der Unterhaltung und aß noch, als der Bauer wegging.

Die nächsten Tage war Anna natürlich sehr bekümmert. Zwischen ihrer Hausarbeit lehrte sie den Jungen gehen. Wenn er den Spinnrocken losließ und mit ausgestreckten Ärmchen auf

wackeln to totter; **unterdrücken** to suppress; **umklam-**
mern to clasp; **auf·fangen, e, a** to catch

schluchzen to sob

die Kerze, –n candle

ein **abgearbeiteter Fünfziger** a man in his fifties,
worn out by work; **halt so** just

ein **großer Aufwand an Heimlichkeit** a great show of
secrecy; **ab·gehen, i, a** *here:* to branch off; **die**
Verehelichten = die Eheleute married people

der **Hausierer, –** peddler; **aus·richten** to give a message; **antik** ancient; **der Feldherr, –en** (MII) commander, general; **die Schlachtreihe, –n** battle line;
auf·fordern to invite

der **Schafspelz, –e** sheepskin coat; **der Händler, –**
trader; **Er möchte ihr durch einen Schlächter aus-**
richten lassen He should have a butcher give her a
message; **vor ihrer Schwägerin** in the presence of her
sister-in-law

der **Zahn, ⸚e** tooth; **überlegen** to think over; **erkrankt**
sein to be taken sick

auf·bringen, a, a *here:* to exasperate

die Botschaft, –en message; **mit dem Gedanken um·**
gehen, i, a to be thinking of, to contemplate

der Aufenthalt, –e stay

sie zugewackelt kam, unterdrückte sie ein trockenes Schluchzen und umklammerte ihn fest, wenn sie ihn auffing.

Einmal fragte sie ihren Bruder: Was ist er für einer? Sie hatte ihn nur auf dem Sterbebett gesehen und nur abends, beim Schein einer schwachen Kerze. Jetzt erfuhr sie, daß ihr Mann ein abgearbeiteter Fünfziger sei, halt so, wie ein Häusler ist.

Bald darauf sah sie ihn. Ein Hausierer hatte ihr mit einem großen Aufwand an Heimlichkeit ausgerichtet, daß „ein gewisser Bekannter" sie an dem und dem Tag zu der und der Stunde bei dem und dem Dorf, da wo der Fußweg nach Landsberg abgeht, treffen wolle. So begegneten die Verehelichten sich zwischen ihren Dörfern wie die antiken Feldherren zwischen ihren Schlachtreihen, im offenen Gelände, das vom Schnee bedeckt war.

Der Mann gefiel Anna nicht.

Er hatte kleine graue Zähne, sah sie von oben bis unten an, obwohl sie in einem dicken Schafspelz steckte und nicht viel zu sehen war, und gebrauchte dann die Wörter „Sakrament der Ehe". Sie sagte ihm kurz, sie müsse sich alles noch überlegen und er möchte ihr durch irgendeinen Händler oder Schlächter, der durch Großaitingen kam, vor ihrer Schwägerin ausrichten lassen, er werde jetzt bald kommen und sei nur auf dem Weg erkrankt.

Otterer nickte in seiner bedächtigen Weise. Er war über einen Kopf größer als sie und blickte immer auf ihre linke Halsseite beim Reden, was sie aufbrachte.

Die Botschaft kam aber nicht, und Anna ging mit dem Gedanken um, mit dem Kind einfach vom Hof zu gehen und weiter südwärts, etwa in Kempten oder Sonthofen, eine Stellung zu suchen. Nur die Unsicherheit der Landstraßen, über die viel geredet wurde, und daß es mitten im Winter war, hielt sie zurück.

Der Aufenthalt auf dem Hof wurde aber jetzt schwierig. Die Schwägerin stellte am Mittagstisch vor allem Gesinde mißtraui-

das Mitleid compassion, pity; „armes Wurm" *here:* poor thing

hochrot flushed; **trüb** clouded; **wachen über** (+ *dat.*) to watch over; **die Hoffnung, –en** hope; **die Besserung, –en** recovery

seinerseits for his part

sich verstellen to pretend, to feign; **äußern** to disclose; **erwähnen** to mention

böse angry; **wenn auch** although; **unterdrückt** *here:* subdued; **nichts als** nothing but

brabbeln to gurgle

flüchtig fleetingly; **Das nahm Anna noch mehr gegen ihn ein** This turned Anna against him even more

fallen lassen, ie, a to drop; **die Redensart, –en** remarks; **Bei ihm ist Schmalhans Küchenmeister** There is no fuss about cooking at his place (*idiom.*) *lit.* at his house Jack Spratt is the cook; **nachlässig** careless; **vor·täuschen** to pretend; **einsilbig** monosyllabic

neugierig curious, inquisitive; **laden, u, a = einladen** to invite; **gleich = sogleich** immediately

vermeiden, ie, ie to avoid; **Holz hacken** to chop wood; **auf·fordern** to invite

sche Fragen nach ihrem Mann. Als sie einmal sogar, mit falschem Mitleid auf das Kind sehend, laut „armes Wurm" sagte, beschloß Anna, doch zu gehen, aber da wurde das Kind krank.

Es lag unruhig mit hochrotem Kopf und trüben Augen in seiner Kiste, und Anna wachte ganze Nächte über ihm in Angst und Hoffnung. Als es sich wieder auf dem Weg zur Besserung befand und sein Lächeln zurückgefunden hatte, klopfte es eines Vormittags an die Tür, und herein trat Otterer.

Es war niemand außer Anna und dem Kind in der Stube, so daß sie sich nicht verstellen mußte, was ihr bei ihrem Schrecken auch wohl unmöglich gewesen wäre. Sie standen eine gute Weile wortlos, dann äußerte Otterer, er habe die Sache seinerseits überlegt und sei gekommen, sie zu holen. Er erwähnte wieder das Sakrament der Ehe.

Anna wurde böse. Mit fester, wenn auch unterdrückter Stimme sagte sie dem Mann, sie denke nicht daran, mit ihm zu leben, sie sei die Ehe nur eingegangen ihres Kindes wegen und wolle von ihm nichts, als daß er ihr und dem Kind seinen Namen gebe.

Otterer blickte, als sie von dem Kind sprach, flüchtig nach der Richtung der Kiste, in der es lag und brabbelte, trat aber nicht hinzu. Das nahm Anna noch mehr gegen ihn ein.

Er ließ ein paar Redensarten fallen; sie solle sich alles noch einmal überlegen, bei ihm sei Schmalhans Küchenmeister, und seine Mutter könne in der Küche schlafen. Dann kam die Bäuerin herein, begrüßte ihn neugierig und lud ihn zum Mittagessen. Den Bauern begrüßte er, schon am Teller sitzend, mit einem nachlässigen Kopfnicken, weder vortäuschend, er kenne ihn nicht, noch verratend, daß er ihn kannte. Auf die Fragen der Bäuerin antwortete er einsilbig, seine Blicke nicht vom Teller hebend, er habe in Mering eine Stelle gefunden, und Anna könne zu ihm ziehen. Jedoch sagte er nichts mehr davon, daß dies gleich sein müsse.

Am Nachmittag vermied er die Gesellschaft des Bauern und hackte hinter dem Haus Holz, wozu ihn niemand aufgefordert

übernachten to spend the night; an·rühren to touch

das Deckbett, –en feather bed; merkwürdigerweise strangely enough; abwesend absentminded

teilnahmslos apathetic; nach·lassen, ie, a to abate, to ease up; kriechen, o, o to crawl; die Decke zurecht·stopfen to fix the covers

vor·fahren, u, a to drive up; der Leiterwagen, – farm wagon

wieder zu Kräften kommen, a, o to regain strength; dünn thin; schmutzig dirty

empfangen, i, a here: to welcome; wachsen, u, a to grow; auf·patschen to clap; der Holzzuber, – wooden tub; die Zuversicht confidence, optimism

behaupten to maintain, to declare; die Geschwindigkeit, –en speed; der Schrei, –e scream; aus·stoßen, ie, o to emit, utter

freilich indeed; wickeln to wrap

aus·halten, ie, a to put up with, to stand

schwach auf den Beinen weak in the knees; die Schneeschmelze thaw; geizig stingy; der Straßengraben, ̈ ditch; bangen um (+ acc.) to worry about, fear for

vor·haben to intend; sich den Fuß verstauchen to sprain one's foot

hatte. Nach dem Abendessen, an dem er wieder schweigend teilnahm, trug die Bäuerin selber ein Deckbett in Annas Kammer, damit er dort übernachten konnte, aber da stand er merkwürdigerweise schwerfällig auf und murmelte, daß er noch am selben Abend zurück müsse. Bevor er ging, starrte er mit abwesendem Blick in die Kiste mit dem Kind, sagte aber nichts und rührte es nicht an.

In der Nacht wurde Anna krank und verfiel in ein Fieber, das wochenlang dauerte. Die meiste Zeit lag sie teilnahmslos, nur ein paarmal gegen Mittag, wenn das Fieber etwas nachließ, kroch sie zu der Kiste mit dem Kind und stopfte die Decke zurecht.

In der vierten Woche ihrer Krankheit fuhr Otterer mit einem Leiterwagen auf dem Hof vor und holte sie und das Kind ab. Sie ließ es wortlos geschehen.

Nur sehr langsam kam sie wieder zu Kräften, kein Wunder bei den dünnen Suppen der Häuslerhütte. Aber eines Morgens sah sie, wie schmutzig das Kind gehalten war, und stand entschlossen auf.

Der Kleine empfing sie mit seinem freundlichen Lächeln, von dem ihr Bruder immer behauptet hatte, er habe es von ihr. Er war gewachsen und kroch mit unglaublicher Geschwindigkeit in der Kammer herum, mit den Händen aufpatschend und kleine Schreie ausstoßend, wenn er auf das Gesicht niederfiel. Sie wusch ihn in einem Holzzuber und gewann ihre Zuversicht zurück.

Wenige Tage später freilich konnte sie das Leben in der Hütte nicht mehr aushalten. Sie wickelte den Kleinen in ein paar Decken, steckte ein Brot und etwas Käse ein und lief weg.

Sie hatte vor, nach Sonthofen zu kommen, kam aber nicht weit. Sie war noch recht schwach auf den Beinen, die Landstraße lag unter der Schneeschmelze, und die Leute in den Dörfern waren durch den Krieg sehr mißtrauisch und geizig geworden. Am dritten Tag ihrer Wanderung verstauchte sie sich den Fuß in einem Straßengraben und wurde nach vielen Stunden, in denen sie um das Kind bangte, auf einen Hof gebracht, wo sie

der **Stall,** ⁼e stable; die **Kuh,** ⁼e cow; **auf·schreien,
ie, ie** to cry out

der **Acker,** ⁼ field; **satt werden** to get enough to eat;
mitunter occasionally; der **Färber,** – dyer; **Es steht
ihm gut** It looks good on him

der **Fluchtversuch,** –e attempt to escape; **Sie nahm
ihr Los hin** She accepted her lot; **heraus·holen aus**
(+ *dat.*) to get out; die **Wirtschaft,** –en *here:* farm;
in Gang halten, ie, a to keep going; **ein Röcklein
ein·färben** to dye a little coat

Sie wurde zufrieden gestimmt She became quite contented; die **Erziehung** education

die **Kutsche,** –n carriage; **ein Bündel mit Eßbarem** a
bundle of food

Sie taumelte an die Wand vor Entsetzen She reeled
against the wall in horror

ihr erster Gang her first visit (she first went . . .)

vor·lassen, ie, a to admit

vergebens in vain; **Trost zu·reden** to console

die **Behörde,** –n authorities; **an·deuten** to insinuate,
to hint; **daraufhin** whereupon; **Jetzt herrschten
andere Zeiten** Times had changed; **Frieden schließen,
o, o** to make peace

Sie hätte kaum etwas ausgerichtet She would hardly
have accomplished anything

ein besonderer Glücksumstand an unusually fortunate circumstance; die **Rechtssache,** –n lawsuit;
besonder(s) unusual; der **Richter,** – judge; **verweisen,
ie, ie an** (+ *acc.*) to refer to

im Stall liegen mußte. Der Kleine kroch zwischen den Beinen der Kühe herum und lachte nur, wenn sie ängstlich aufschrie. Am Ende mußte sie den Leuten des Hofs den Namen ihres Mannes sagen, und er holte sie wieder nach Mering.

Von nun an machte sie keinen Fluchtversuch mehr und nahm ihr Los hin. Sie arbeitete hart. Es war schwer, aus dem kleinen Acker etwas herauszuholen und die winzige Wirtschaft in Gang zu halten. Jedoch war der Mann nicht unfreundlich zu ihr, und der Kleine wurde satt. Auch kam ihr Bruder mitunter herüber und brachte dies und jenes als Präsent, und einmal konnte sie dem Kleinen sogar ein Röcklein rot einfärben lassen. Das, dachte sie, mußte dem Kind eines Färbers gut stehen.

Mit der Zeit wurde sie ganz zufrieden gestimmt und erlebte viele Freude bei der Erziehung des Kleinen. So vergingen mehrere Jahre.

Aber eines Tages ging sie ins Dorf Sirup holen, und als sie zurückkehrte, war das Kind nicht in der Hütte, und ihr Mann berichtete ihr, daß eine feingekleidete Frau in einer Kutsche vorgefahren sei und das Kind geholt habe. Sie taumelte an die Wand vor Entsetzen, und am selben Abend noch machte sie sich, nur ein Bündel mit Eßbarem tragend, auf den Weg nach Augsburg.

Ihr erster Gang in der Reichsstadt war zur Gerberei. Sie wurde nicht vorgelassen und bekam das Kind nicht zu sehen.

Schwester und Schwager versuchten vergebens, ihr Trost zuzureden. Sie lief zu den Behörden und schrie außer sich, man habe ihr Kind gestohlen. Sie ging so weit, anzudeuten, daß Protestanten ihr Kind gestohlen hätten. Sie erfuhr daraufhin, daß jetzt andere Zeiten herrschten, und zwischen Katholiken und Protestanten Friede geschlossen worden sei.

Sie hätte kaum etwas ausgerichtet, wenn ihr nicht ein besonderer Glücksumstand zur Hilfe gekommen wäre. Ihre Rechtssache wurde an einen Richter verwiesen, der ein ganz besonderer Mann war.

taufen to christen, to baptize; *here:* to call

Schwaben Swabia; berühmt famous; die Grobheit rudeness; die Gelehrsamkeit erudition, learning; der Kurfürst von Bayern Elector of Bavaria; einen Rechtsstreit aus·tragen, u, a to settle a dispute; „dieser lateinische Mistbauer" "this Latin clodhopper"; die Moritat, –en folk ballad; besingen, a u to celebrate in song

kahl bare; das Blatt, ⁻er piece of paper; brummen to growl; treten, a, e to step

ungemein fleischig extraordinarily corpulent; die Stube, –n room; Stöße von Pergamenten piles of documents; an·hören (+ *acc.*) = zu·hören (+ *dat.*) to listen to; dirigieren *here:* to direct; die Stelle, n spot; weg·winken to wave aside; der Stoßseufzer, – snort

die Schwelle, –n threshold

der Gerichtsdiener, – constable, beadle, bailiff; . . . daß es (Anna) um eine Gerberei geht . . . . . . that a tannery is at stake . . . ; pfundig grand, sizable

verstockt doggedly

Bild dir nicht ein, . . . Don't imagine . . . ; schnappen to snap up; Das Anwesen fällt an die Verwandten The property goes to the relatives

bellen to bark

husten to cough; ordnen to straighten

der Knirps, –e little chap, brat; die Ziege, –n she-goat; *here:* hag; der Seidenrock, ⁻e silk skirt

Es war der Richter Ignaz Dollinger, in ganz Schwaben berühmt wegen seiner Grobheit und Gelehrsamkeit, vom Kurfürsten von Bayern, mit dem er einen Rechtsstreit der freien Reichsstadt ausgetragen hatte, „dieser lateinische Mistbauer'' getauft, vom niedrigen Volk aber in einer langen Moritat löblich besungen.

Von Schwester und Schwager begleitet kam Anna vor ihn. Der kurze aber ungemein fleischige alte Mann saß in einer winzigen kahlen Stube zwischen Stößen von Pergamenten und hörte sie nur ganz kurz an. Dann schrieb er etwas auf ein Blatt, brummte: „Tritt dorthin, aber mach schnell!'' und dirigierte sie mit seiner kleinen plumpen Hand an eine Stelle des Raums, auf die durch das schmale Fenster das Licht fiel. Für einige Minuten sah er genau ihr Gesicht an, dann winkte er sie mit einem Stoßseufzer weg.

Am nächsten Tag ließ er sie durch einen Gerichtsdiener holen und schrie sie, als sie noch auf der Schwelle stand, an: „Warum hast du keinen Ton davon gesagt, daß es um eine Gerberei mit einem pfundigen Anwesen geht?''

Anna sagte verstockt, daß es ihr um das Kind gehe.

„Bild dir nicht ein, daß du die Gerberei schnappen kannst'', schrie der Richter. „Wenn der Bankert wirklich deiner ist, fällt das Anwesen an die Verwandten von dem Zingli.''

Anna nickte, ohne ihn anzuschauen. Dann sagte sie: „Er braucht die Gerberei nicht''.

„Ist er deiner?'' bellte der Richter.

„Ja'', sagte sie leise. „Wenn ich ihn nur so lange behalten dürfte, bis er alle Wörter kann. Er weiß erst sieben''.

Der Richter hustete und ordnete die Pergamente auf seinem Tisch. Dann sagte er ruhiger, aber immer noch in ärgerlichem Ton:

„Du willst den Knirps, und die Ziege da mit ihren fünf Seidenröcken will ihn. Aber er braucht die rechte Mutter''.

„Ja'', sagte Anna und sah den Richter an.

der **Perlachturm** tower of the Town Hall; **sonderbar** strange; **der Fall,** ⸚**e** case; **Aufsehen erregen** to attract attention; **weit und breit** far and wide; **beliebt** popular; **der Plärrer** Augsburg fair; **die Kirchweih** church fair

Verschwind! *here:* Get along with you!; **Gericht halten, ie, a** to hold court; **dem Prozeß beiwohnen** to attend the trial; **die Wirtschaft, –en** *here:* tavern; **streiten, i, i über** (+ *acc.*) to argue about; **echt** real; **volkstümlich** folksy; **bissig** biting; **die Redensart, –en** turn of phrase; **der Weisheitsspruch,** ⸚**e** wise saying; **die Verhandlung, –en** trial

sich stauen to throng

der Markttag, –e market day; **die Umgegend** surrounding countryside, vicinity; **die Erwartung, –en** expectation; **übernachten** to stay overnight

die Säule, –n column, pillar; **die Decke, –n** ceiling; **an Ketten aufgehängt** suspended from chains; **der Dachfirst, –e** rafters

der Saal, ⸚**e** hall; **verhandeln** to try cases; **die Größe** size, magnitude

das Erztor, –e bronze gate; **die Längswand,** ⸚**e** side wall; **der Zuhörer,** – *here:* spectator; **eine Anordnung treffen, a, o** to make an arrangement; **Er hielt viel von Aufmachung** He thought highly of trappings

gewöhnlich ordinary; **das Seil, –e** rope; **ab·trennen** to separate; **auf ebenem Boden** on the level floor (i.e., not on a podium)

der Raum, ⸚**e** space; **zugereist** newly arrived; **würdig** dignified; **wohlbestallt** well established

anwesend present; **abgeseilt** roped off; **verstorben** late; **der Kaufmann, –leute** merchant; **die Amme, –n** nursemaid

der Beteiligte (*perf. part*) participant

Parteien und Zeugen litigants and witnesses; **Er pflegte zu sagen** He was in the habit of saying; **Die Verhandlungen fallen . . . aus** The proceedings turn out; **Sie verdeckten ihn vor dem Publikum** They screened him from the audience

,,Verschwind", brummte er. ,,Am Samstag halt ich Gericht". An diesem Samstag war die Hauptstraße und der Platz vor dem Rathaus am Perlachturm schwarz von Menschen, die dem Prozeß um das Protestantenkind beiwohnen wollten. Der sonderbare Fall hatte von Anfang an viel Aufsehen erregt, und in Wohnungen und Wirtschaften wurde darüber gestritten, wer die echte und wer die falsche Mutter war. Auch war der alte Dollinger weit und breit berühmt wegen seiner volkstümlichen Prozesse mit ihren bissigen Redensarten und Weisheitssprüchen. Seine Verhandlungen waren beliebter als Plärrer und Kirchweih.

So stauten sich vor dem Rathaus nicht nur viele Augsburger; auch nicht wenige Bauersleute der Umgegend waren da. Freitag war Markttag, und sie hatten in Erwartung des Prozesses in der Stadt übernachtet.

Der Saal, in dem der Richter Dollinger verhandelte, war der sogenannte Goldene Saal. Er war berühmt als einziger Saal von dieser Größe in ganz Deutschland, der keine Säulen hatte; die Decke war an Ketten im Dachfirst aufgehängt.

Der Richter Dollinger saß, ein kleiner runder Fleischberg, vor dem geschlossenen Erztor der einen Längswand. Ein gewöhnliches Seil trennte die Zuhörer ab. Aber der Richter saß auf ebenem Boden und hatte keinen Tisch vor sich. Er hatte selber vor Jahren diese Anordnung getroffen; er hielt viel von Aufmachung.

Anwesend innerhalb des abgeseilten Raums waren Frau Zingli mit ihren Eltern, die zugereisten Schweizer Verwandten des verstorbenen Herrn Zingli, zwei gutgekleidete würdige Männer, aussehend wie wohlbestallte Kaufleute, und Anna Otterer mit ihrer Schwester. Neben Frau Zingli sah man eine Amme mit dem Kind.

Alle, Parteien und Zeugen, standen. Der Richter Dollinger pflegte zu sagen, daß die Verhandlungen kürzer ausfielen, wenn die Beteiligten stehen mußten. Aber vielleicht ließ er sie auch nur stehen, damit sie ihn vor dem Publikum verdeckten,

sich auf die Fußzehen stellen to stand on tiptoe; sich den Hals aus·renken to crane one's neck

trampeln to kick, to struggle; heftig violently; brüllen to howl

Es kam zu einem Zwischenfall An incident occurred; erblicken to catch sight of; einen Schrei aus·stoßen, ie, o to utter a cry; vor·treten, a, e to step forward

auf·rufen, ie, u to call up

Sie kam vorgerauscht She came rustling forward; das Sacktüchlein, – handkerchief; lüften here: to raise; wahrscheinlich probably; die Köchin, –nen cook (fem.); deuten auf (+ acc.) to point to; sich bemächtigen (+ gen.) to get hold of, to seize; irgendwie somehow; über kurz oder lang sooner or later; die Forderung, –en demand; zuvor = vorher beforehand; ab·nehmen, a, o =weg·nehmen to take away

schildern, to describe, to depict; entreißen, i, i to snatch away, to tear away; das Trinkgeld, –er tip; an·nehmen, a, o to assume; Geld erpressen to extort money

sich erkundigen nach (+ dat.) to inquire about

in guter Hut sein to be in good hands

aus·sagen to state, to declare; an·vertrauen to entrust; allerdings to be sure; verloren·gehen, i, a to be lost

die Aussage, –n statement

der Überfall, ⸚e attack, raid; im Stich lassen, ie, a to abandon

blaß pale; wie verwundert astonished

so daß man ihn nur sah, wenn man sich auf die Fußzehen stellte und den Hals ausrenkte.

Zu Beginn der Verhandlung kam es zu einem Zwischenfall. Als Anna das Kind erblickte, stieß sie einen Schrei aus und trat vor, und das Kind wollte zu ihr, strampelte heftig in den Armen der Amme und fing an zu brüllen. Der Richter ließ es aus dem Saal bringen.

Dann rief er Frau Zingli auf.

Sie kam vorgerauscht und schilderte, ab und zu ein Sacktüchlein an die Augen lüftend, wie bei der Plünderung die kaiserlichen Soldaten ihr das Kind entrissen hätten. Noch in derselben Nacht war die Magd in das Haus ihres Vaters gekommen und hatte berichtet, das Kind sei noch im Haus, wahrscheinlich in Erwartung eines Trinkgelds. Eine Köchin ihres Vaters habe jedoch das Kind, in die Gerberei geschickt, nicht vorgefunden, und sie nehme an, die Person (sie deutete auf Anna) habe sich seiner bemächtigt, um irgendwie Geld erpressen zu können. Sie wäre auch wohl über kurz oder lang mit solchen Forderungen hervorgekommen, wenn man ihr nicht zuvor das Kind abgenommen hätte.

Der Richter Dollinger rief die beiden Verwandten des Herrn Zingli auf und fragte sie, ob sie sich damals nach Herrn Zingli erkundigt hätten und was ihnen von Frau Zingli erzählt worden sei.

Sie sagten aus, Frau Zingli habe sie wissen lassen, ihr Mann sei erschlagen worden, und das Kind habe sie einer Magd anvertraut, bei der es in guter Hut sei. Sie sprachen sehr unfreundlich von ihr, was allerdings kein Wunder war, denn das Anwesen fiel an sie, wenn der Prozeß für Frau Zingli verlorenging.

Nach ihrer Aussage wandte sich der Richter wieder an Frau Zingli und wollte von ihr wissen, ob sie nicht einfach bei dem Überfall damals den Kopf verloren und das Kind im Stich gelassen habe.

Frau Zingli sah ihn mit ihren blassen blauen Augen wie ver-

sich räuspern to clear one's throat

gleichgültig regardless

früher former; **die Voruntersuchung, –en** preliminary inquiry, investigation; **zugleich** at the same time; **horchen** to listen

unter·bringen, a, a to place, to house

unterbrechen, a, o to interrupt; **schnappen** *here:* to snap; **andererseits** on the other hand; **Es heißt im Volksmund** . . . The popular saying goes . . . ; **das Gesetz, –e** law; **streng** strict; **das Eigentum** property, possessions; **lügen, o, o** to lie; **ebenfalls** = **auch** also

gerkränkt hurt, offended

der Hintern, – rear, behind; **verhauen** to beat soundly, to thrash

zwar it is true, to be sure; **ein lediges Kind** an illegitimate child

grob coarse, rude; **zumindest** at least; **verspüren** = **spüren, fühlen** to feel; **fest·stellen** to establish a (fact), to settle; **beweisen, ie, ie** to prove; **die Vernunft** sense, reason; **der Zeuge, –n** (MII) witness; **die Zeugin, –nen** witness; **eine Lektion halten, ie, a** to give a lecture; **derb** blunt; **die Abgefeimtheit** cunning; **an·schwindeln** to lie to; **der Abstecher, –** digression; **unschuldig** innocent

wundert an und sagte gekränkt, sie habe ihr Kind nicht im Stich gelassen.

Der Richter Dollinger räusperte sich und fragte sie interessiert, ob sie glaube, daß keine Mutter ihr Kind im Stich lassen könnte.

Ja, das glaube sie, sagte sie fest.

Ob sie dann glaube, fragte der Richter weiter, daß einer Mutter, die es doch tue, der Hintern verhauen werden müßte, gleichgültig, wie viele Röcke sie darüber trage?

Frau Zingli gab keine Antwort, und der Richter rief die frühere Magd Anna auf. Sie trat schnell vor und sagte mit leiser Stimme, was sie schon bei der Voruntersuchung gesagt hatte. Sie redete aber, als ob sie zugleich horchte, und ab und zu blickte sie nach der großen Tür, hinter die man das Kind gebracht hatte, als fürchtete sie, daß es immer noch schreie.

Sie sagte aus, sie sei zwar in jener Nacht zum Haus von Frau Zinglis Onkel gegangen, dann aber nicht in die Gerberei zurückgekehrt, aus Furcht vor den Kaiserlichen und weil sie Sorgen um ihr eigenes, lediges Kind gehabt habe, das bei guten Leuten im Nachbarort Lechhausen untergebracht gewesen sei.

Der alte Dollinger unterbrach sie grob und schnappte, es habe also zumindest eine Person in der Stadt gegeben, die so etwas wie Furcht verspürt habe. Er freue sich, das feststellen zu können, denn es beweise, daß eben zumindest eine Person damals einige Vernunft besessen habe. Schön sei es allerdings von der Zeugin nicht gewesen, daß sie sich nur um ihr eigenes Kind gekümmert habe, andererseits aber heiße es ja im Volksmund, Blut sei dicker als Wasser, und was eine rechte Mutter sei, die gehe auch stehlen für ihr Kind, das sei aber vom Gesetz streng verboten, denn Eigentum sei Eigentum, und wer stehle, der lüge auch, und lügen sei ebenfalls vom Gesetz verboten. Und dann hielt er eine seiner weisen und derben Lektionen über die Abgefeimtheit der Menschen, die das Gericht anschwindelten, bis sie blau im Gesicht seien, und nach einem kleinen Abstecher über die Bauern, die die Milch unschuldiger Kühe

die **Zeugenaussage schließen, o, o** to end the examination of witnesses

verpantschen to adulterate; **die Marktsteuer, –n** market taxes; **verkündigen** to announce; **ergeben, a, e** to result in, to produce

das Anzeichen = das Zeichen sign; **die Ratlosigkeit** helplessness, perplexity; **der Vorschlag, ⁻e** suggestion

recken to crane; **erwischen** to catch

verblüfft dumbfounded

das Wort ergreifen, i, i to begin to speak; **seufzen** to sigh

sich drücken to shirk one's duty; **der Schuft, –e** rogue; **der Gerichtshof, ⁻e** court; **verdienen** to deserve, to earn; **geschlagene fünf Minuten** exactly five minutes; **gedruckt** printed; **Ohne auf bloßes Geschwätz einzugehen . . .** Without submitting to mere chatter . . .

Das Kind ist zu bedauern The child is to be pitied; **sich melden** *here:* to come forward; **gleich** at the same time; **zu der Überzeugung gelangen** to become convinced; **Beide lügen wie gedruckt** Both lie like a book; **Das Kind ist zu bedenken** The child is to be considered

der Fußboden, ⁻ floor; **an·weisen, ie, ie** to direct, to instruct

einen Kreis ziehen, o, o to draw a circle

mit Wasser verpantschten, und den Magistrat der Stadt, der zu hohe Marksteuern von den Bauern nehme, der überhaupt nichts mit dem Prozeß zu tun hatte, verkündigte er, daß die Zeugenaussage geschlossen sei und nichts ergeben habe.

Dann machte er eine lange Pause und zeigte alle Anzeichen der Ratlosigkeit, sich umblickend, als erwarte er von irgendeiner Seite her einen Vorschlag, wie man zu einem Schluß kommen könnte.

Die Leute sahen sich verblüfft an, und einige reckten die Hälse, um einen Blick auf den hilflosen Richter zu erwischen. Es blieb aber sehr still im Saal, nur von der Straße herauf konnte man die Menge hören.

Dann ergriff der Richter wieder seufzend das Wort.

„Es ist nicht festgestellt worden, wer die rechte Mutter ist", sagte er. „Das Kind ist zu bedauern. Man hat schon gehört, daß die Väter sich oft drücken und nicht die Väter sein wollen, die Schufte, aber hier melden sich gleich zwei Mütter. Der Gerichtshof hat ihnen so lange zugehört, wie sie es verdienen, nämlich einer jeden geschlagene fünf Minuten, und der Gerichtshof ist zu der Überzeugung gelangt, daß beide wie gedruckt lügen. Nun ist aber, wie gesagt, auch noch das Kind zu bedenken, das eine Mutter haben muß. Man muß also, ohne auf bloßes Geschwätz einzugehen, feststellen, wer die rechte Mutter des Kindes ist".

Und mit ärgerlicher Stimme rief er den Gerichtsdiener und befahl ihm, eine Kreide zu holen.

Der Gerichtsdiener ging und brachte ein Stück Kreide.

„Zieh mit der Kreide da auf dem Fußboden einen Kreis, in dem drei Personen stehen können", wies ihn der Richter an. Der Gerichtsdiener kniete nieder und zog mit der Kreide den gewünschten Kreis.

„Jetzt bring das Kind", befahl der Richter.

heulen to cry out loud; **das Geplärr** crying; **die Ansprache, –n** address

eine Probe vor·nehmen, a, o to undertake a test

Die Probe gilt als recht gut The test is considered very good; **der Grundgedanke, –n** basic idea; **erkennen an** (+ *dat.*) to recognize by; **erproben** to test; **die Stärke** strength

fort·fahren, u, a to continue, to go on

fassen *here:* to take; **los** go; **sich bemühen** to try; **ziehen, o, o** to pull; **die Kraft, ⸚e** strength

sich streiten, i, i to quarrel

unruhig restless

ahnen to sense, to suspect

totenstill dead silent; **verstummen** to become silent; **tränenüberströmt** tear-stained; **empor·wenden zu** (+ *dat.*) to turn up to

heftig violent; **der Ruck, –e** jerk; **reißen, i, i** to tear; **verstört** bewildered, disturbed; **ungläubig** incredulous; **Schaden erleiden, i, i** to suffer harm; **zugleich** at once; **die Richtung, –en** direction; **sogleich** immediately; **los·lassen, ie, a** to let go

somit thus

die Schlampe, –n slut; **kalten Herzens** in cold blood

Das Kind wurde hereingebracht. Es fing wieder an zu heulen und wollte zu Anna. Der alte Dollinger kümmerte sich nicht um das Geplärr und hielt seine Ansprache nur in etwas lauterem Ton.

,,Diese Probe, die jetzt vorgenommen werden wird", verkündete er, ,,habe ich in einem alten Buch gefunden, und sie gilt als recht gut. Der einfache Grundgedanke der Probe mit dem Kreidekreis ist, daß die echte Mutter an ihrer Liebe zum Kind erkannt wird. Also muß die Stärke dieser Liebe erprobt werden. Gerichtsdiener, stell das Kind in diesen Kreidekreis".

Der Gerichtsdiener nahm das plärrende Kind von der Hand der Amme und führte es in den Kreis. Der Richter fuhr fort, sich an Frau Zingli und Anna wendend.

,,Stellt auch ihr euch in den Kreidekreis, faßt jede eine Hand des Kindes, und wenn ich ,los' sage, dann bemüht euch, das Kind aus dem Kreis zu ziehen. Die von euch die stärkere Liebe hat, wird auch mit der größeren Kraft ziehen und so das Kind auf ihre Seite bringen."

Im Saal war es unruhig geworden. Die Zuschauer stellten sich auf die Fußspitzen und stritten sich mit den vor ihnen Stehenden.

Es wurde aber wieder totenstill, als die beiden Frauen in den Kreis traten und jede eine Hand des Kindes faßte. Auch das Kind war verstummt, als ahnte es, um was es ging. Es hielt sein tränenüberströmtes Gesichtchen zu Anna emporgewendet. Dann kommandierte der Richter ,,los".

Und mit einem einzigen heftigen Ruck riß Frau Zingli das Kind aus dem Kreidekreis. Verstört und ungläubig sah Anna ihm nach. Aus Furcht, es könne Schaden erleiden, wenn es an beiden Ärmchen zugleich in zwei Richtungen gezogen würde, hatte sie es sogleich losgelassen.

Der alte Dollinger stand auf.

,,Und somit wissen wir", sagte er laut, ,,wer die rechte Mutter ist. Nehmt der Schlampe das Kind weg. Sie würde es kalten

zu·nicken to nod to

in Stücke reißen, i, i to tear to pieces

Sie waren nicht auf den Kopf gefallen They were no
fools

das Kind zu·sprechen, a, o (+ *dat.*) to award the
child to; mit den Augen zwinkern to wink

Herzens in Stücke reißen". Und er nickte Anna zu und ging schnell aus dem Saal, zu seinem Frühstück.

Und in den nächsten Wochen erzählten sich die Bauern der Umgebung, die nicht auf den Kopf gefallen waren, daß der Richter, als er der Frau aus Mering das Kind zusprach, mit den Augen gezwinkert habe.

II.   QUESTIONNAIRE

A.   Exercises for the A-Questions

Study the following expressions.

1. Er **war mit einer** Augsburgerin **verheiratet.**
   He was married to an Augsburg woman.
2. Er **versteckte sich** in einer Grube im Hof.
   He hid in a pit in the courtyard.
3. Die Diele **füllte sich** mit betrunkenen Soldaten.
   The hallway was filled with drunk soldiers.
4. Sie **nahm** das Kind hastig **an sich.**
   She snatched up the child hastily.
5. Sie **schämte sich** nicht, ihr Kind zu verleugnen.
   She was not ashamed to repudiate her child.
6. Sie setzte ihren Willen durch.
   She got her own way.
7. Sie schenkte ihm reinen Wein ein.
   She told him the whole truth.
8. Ihm war nicht wohl in seiner Haut.
   He felt ill at ease.
9. Der Hof mußte bald ins Gerede kommen.
   The farm would soon get gossiped about.
10. Sie **überlegt sich** noch alles.
    She will think everything over.
11. Sie mußte **sich** nicht **verstellen.**
    She did not have to pretend.
12. Sie nahm ihr Los hin.
    She accepted her fate.
13. Die Rechtssache **wurde an einen** Richter **verwiesen.**
    The lawsuit was referred to a judge.
14. Das Anwesen **fällt an die** Verwandten von Zingli.
    The property goes to Zingli's relatives.
15. Die Probe **gilt als** recht gut.
    The test is considered quite good.
16. Man **erkennt** die echte Mutter **an ihrer** Liebe zum Kind.
    One recognizes the real mother by her love for the child.

B.   A-Questions

Change the direct quotes to indirect quotes by using the subjunctive or quotative, if not otherwise indicated.

Bertolt Brecht gibt uns zunächst eine genaue Beschreibung der Anfangssituation und der Personen in dieser Situation.

1. Was alles erfahren wir über die Situation zu Anfang der Geschichte, und wie charakterisiert Brecht Herrn Zingli?

   Wann **spielt** *die Geschichte?* // time / Thirty Years War //
   Wer **ist** *Herr Zingli?* // Swiss Protestant / who / to own / tannery / and / leather business //
   Wo **hat** *er seinen Besitz?* // free imperial city Augsburg / Lech //
   Was erfahren wir über seine Familie? // he / to be married to / Augsburg / woman / and / to have / child //
   Was hat sich ereignet? // Catholics / to have marched / on / city //
   Was **haben** ihm *seine Freunde geraten?* // to flee //
   Aber was **hat** *er nicht gekonnt?* // to decide / to leave / in time //
   Welche Gründe mag er gehabt haben? // perhaps / small family / to have held back // perhaps / he / not / to have wanted / to abandon / tannery //
   Was tut **er,** *wenn die kaiserlichen Truppen die Stadt stürmen?* // to hide / pit / courtyard / where / dyes / to be stored //

2. Wie charakterisiert Brecht Frau Zingli, und was erfahren wir über das Kind?

   Was **hat** *Frau Zingli* tun sollen? // to move / with / child / relatives / suburbs //
   Was aber tut **sie** *stattdessen?* // to spend / too much time / to pack / things //
   Was **sieht** *sie plötzlich?* // squad of imperial soldiers / to force one's way / courtyard //
   Wie reagiert **sie?** // to drop / everything / and / to run / premises //
   Was geschieht mit dem **Kind?** // to remain / house //
   Wo befindet **es** sich? // to lie / large hall / cradle //
   Was tut **es?** // to play / wooden ball / which / to hang / on / string / from / ceiling //

3. Wie charakterisiert Brecht die Magd Anna?

   Womit beschäftigt **sie** sich im Hause? // to tinker around / copperware //
   Was **hört sie** *plötzlich?* // noise / alley //
   Was **sieht** sie, *wenn sie ans Fenster stürzt?* // how / from / house opposite / soldiers / to throw / all kinds of loot / alley //
   Was tut **sie** *sofort?* // to run / large hallway / and / to want / to take / child / cradle //
   Was aber **hört sie** *plötzlich?* // heavy blows / oaken front door //
   Wie reagiert **sie?** // to be seized / by / panic / and / to flee / up / stairs //

Bertolt Brecht beschreibt nun die für die Erzählung entscheidende Szene in genauen Details.

4. Was geschieht in der Diele?

   Wie verhalten sich die Soldaten? // large hallway / to be filled / with / drunk soldiers / who / to smash to pieces / everything //
   Was **wissen** *die Soldaten?* // that / they / to be / Protestant's house //
   Was **ist** *ein Wunder?* // that / Anna / to remain / undiscovered //
   Was macht **die Rotte Soldaten** *schließlich?* // to withdraw //

5. Wie verhält sich Anna, nachdem die Soldaten das Haus verlassen haben?

Wo **hat sie** *bei der Plünderung des Hauses* **gestanden?** // closet //
Wie **findet** *sie* **das Kind?** // large hallway / unharmed //
Was macht *sie* sofort? // to snatch up / hastily / and / to steal / courtyard //
Was **erblickt sie** *beim Schein eines in der Nähe brennenden Hauses?* // badly battered corpse / master //
Was ist mit Herrn Zingli geschehen? // soldiers / to have pulled out of pit / and / to slay //
Was **wird** *Anna* jetzt klar? // which danger / to be in //
Worin besteht *diese Gefahr?* // to be caught / with / Protestant's child / on / street // (*inf.*)
Wozu **entschließt** *sie* sich? // to put back / child / cradle //
Wohin geht *sie* zunächst? // to set out for / part of the city / where / sister / to live //

6. Wozu entschließt sich Anna gegen zehn Uhr nachts?

Wohin geht *sie?* // to force one's way / soldiers / suburbs //
Von wem **wird** *sie* **begleitet?** // sister's husband //
Warum **geht** *sie* in die Vorstadt? // in order to seek out / Mrs. Zingli //
Sie klopft an die Tür eines mächtigen Hauses. Was sieht sie, wenn die Tür sich öffnet? // Mrs. Zingli's uncle / to stick out / head //
Was **berichtet** *Anna?* / (*a*) / that / Mr. Zingli / to be dead / (*b*) / that / child / to be unharmed / house //
Wie reagiert *der Alte?* // to look at / Anna / coldly / fishlike eyes //
Was **sagt er?** / (*a*) / that / niece / to be no longer there / (*b*) / that / he himself / to have nothing to do / Protestant bastard //
Der Alte macht die Tür wieder zu. Was sieht *Annas Schwager* im Weggehen? // how / curtain / to move / at one of the windows //
Wovon ist *er* überzeugt? // that / Mrs. Zingli / to be there //
Was **denkt er?** // that / Mrs. Zingli / apparently / not / to be ashamed / to repudiate / child //

7. Was erfahren wir aus dem Gespräch zwischen Anna und ihrem Schwager?

Was **erklärt** *Anna* nach einiger Zeit? // that / she / to want / to go back / tannery / and / to fetch / child //
Wie reagiert *der Schwager?* // to try / to talk her out of / dangerous idea //
Was **fragt** *er?* // what / she / to have to do / these people //
Was **stellt** *er* **fest?** // that / Anna / to have been treated / not even decently //
Anna hört ihrem Schwager still zu. Was **verspricht** *sie* ihm? // to do nothing unreasonable //
Was aber **will** *sie* unbedingt noch schnell tun? // to look / tannery / whether / child / to need / anything //
Worauf besteht *sie?* // to go alone //
Und was tut *sie?* // to get her own way //

8. Zu welcher entscheidenden Tat entschließt sich Anna, nachdem sie über eine Stunde bei dem Kind gesessen hat?

Was **sieht sie** *mitten in der zerstörten Halle?* // child / to lie / quietly / cradle //
Was tut *sie zunächst?* // to sit down / tired / and / to gaze at / child //
Beim Schein des in der Nähe brennenden Hauses kann sie das Kind gut sehen. Was **sieht sie?** // how / child / to breathe / and / to suck / little fist //
Was **erkennt sie?** // that / to have sat / too long / in order to be able / to go away / without / child //
Was tut *sie* darauf? // to stand up / heavily / and / to lift / child / arm //
Wie verläßt *sie* den Hof? // to look back / shy / like / person / bad conscience / like / thief //

9. Was geschieht mit dem Kind nach langen Beratungen mit Schwester und Schwager?

Wohin **bringt Anna das Kind?** // to the country / to the village Großaitingen / where / elder brother / to be / peasant //
Wie ist die Situation des Bruders auf dem Hof? // farm / to belong to / wife // he / to have married into //
Was **ist ausgemacht worden?** // that / Anna / to tell / only / brother / who / to be / child //
Was **weiß Anna nicht?** // how / brother's wife / to receive / dangerous guest //
Anna kommt im Dorf an und wird nicht schlecht empfangen. Wozu veranlaßt *sie* ein Blick auf ihre Schwägerin? // to represent / child / as her own //
Was **erzählt Anna der Schwägerin?** / (a) / that / husband / to have / job / mill / distant village / (b) / that / he / to expect / her / and / child / few weeks //

10. Was ist der Inhalt des Gesprächs zwischen Anna und ihrem Bruder?

Anna kann ihren Bruder nicht belügen. Was tut *sie?* // "to tell the whole truth" //
Was **kann sie sehen?** // that / he / to feel ill at ease //
Wie **ist seine Stellung auf dem Hof?** // not yet secure //
Wofür **lobt er Anna sehr?** // that / she / to hold her tongue / in front of / wife //
Was **will er?** // that / deception / to be kept up //

11. Welches Problem entsteht auf dem Hof?

Wie geht es dem *Kind?* // to grow fat / and / to laugh / when / to see / Anna //
Wie verhält sich **die Schwägerin?** // to begin / to make inquiries about / Anna's husband //
Was **ist schlimm?** // that / neighbors / to be surprised about / father / because / he / not / to come //
Welche Gefahr besteht, **wenn Anna keinen Vater für das Kind zeigen kann?** // farm / to get gossiped about //
Was **teilt der Bruder Anna an einem Sonntagmorgen mit?** // that / he / to have sought and found / husband //
Wen **hat er gefunden?** // dying cottager //

12. Wie versucht Annas Bruder das Problem zu lösen?

Wozu **ist** *der Häusler* **bereit?** // to marry / Anna //
Wann **findet** *die Hochzeit* **statt?** // end / same week //
Woran **zweifelt** *Annas Bruder* **nicht?** // that / they / to have / death certificate / few days //
Was für eine Geschichte **würden** *sie* **dann erzählen?** // that / Anna's husband / father of the child / to have died / somewhere / on the way //
Wor**über** **würde sich** *niemand* **wundern?** // that / widow / to stay / brother's house //
Warum **lacht** *Anna* ihren Bruder **an?** // because / child / to have / name / now //
Warum **ist** *Annas Bruder* **ernstlich beunruhigt?** // because / death certificate / to take its time //
Was **kommt** *weder die nächste noch die übernächste Woche?* // word //

13. Was alles berichtet der Bruder Anna, und wie reagiert sie?

Was für eine Nachricht **bringt** *er* **mit?** // bad news //
Wie **hat** *er* den Häusler **vorgefunden?** // completely recovered //
Was **berichtet** *der Bruder* **weiter?** // that / name / to be / Otterer / and / that / he / and / mother / to seem surprised about / turn of events / likewise //
Welchen Eindruck **hat** *Otterer* auf den Bruder **gemacht?** // not an unpleasant impression //
Wie **reagiert** *Anna* auf diese Nachricht? // to be troubled / very much //
Was **tut** *sie* zwischen *ihrer Hausarbeit?* // to teach / boy / to walk //
Warum **fragt** *sie* ihren Bruder einmal, was für ein Mann Otterer **ist?** // because / she / to have seen / him / only / deathbed //
Was **erfährt** *sie* **jetzt?** // that / husband / to be / man in his fifties / worn out by work //

14. Wie ist die Begegnung Otterers mit Anna?

Was **geschieht** *bald darauf?* // Anna / to see / him //
Was **hat** ihr ein *Hausierer* **ausgerichtet?** // that / certain acquaintance / to want / to meet / her //
Wie **begegnen sich** *die Eheleute?* // like / ancient generals / between / battle lines / open terrain //
Welchen Eindruck macht Otterer auf *Anna?* // not / to like / man //
Warum? // he / to have / little grey teeth //
Welche **Wörter gebraucht** *Otterer?* // sacrament of marriage //
Was **erwidert** *Anna?* // that / she / to have to think over / everything //
Was **soll** *er* ihr ausrichten **lassen?** // that / he / to come / soon / and / only / to be taken sick / way //
Wie **reagiert** *Otterer?* // to nod / and / always / to look at / left side of her throat //

15. Was ereignet sich auf dem Hof?

Was **kommt nicht?** // message //
Mit welchem **Gedanken geht** *Anna* **um?** // to leave / farm / with / child / and / to look / for / job / further south //

Was **hält sie zurück?** // uncertainty / routes / and that / to be / middle of winter //

Warum **wird** *der Aufenthalt auf dem Hof* jetzt **schwierig?** // because / sister-in-law / to ask / distrustful questions / husband //

Anna beschließt wegzugehen. Aber warum **kann** *sie* **nicht weg?** // because / child / to fall sick //

Was geschieht *eines Vormittags?* // to knock / door / and / to enter / Otterer //

Was **ist Anna unmöglich?** // to pretend //

Was **äußert Otterer?** / (*a*) / that / he / to have thought matter over / (*b*) / that / he / to have come / to fetch / her //

Was **erwähnt** *er* **wieder?** // sacrament of marriage //

Wie reagiert *Anna?* // to become angry //

Was **will** *sie von ihm* **nur?** // that / he / to give / child / name //

Was nimmt Anna noch mehr gegen *Otterer* ein? // to look / fleetingly / box / but / not / to go up to //

Was **sagt** *er zu* **Anna?** // that / she / should / think over / everything / again //

16. Wie verhält sich Otterer Annas Bruder und Schwägerin gegenüber?

    Wie **begrüßt ihn** *die Bäuerin?* // curious / and / to invite for / dinner //

    Wie begrüßt *Otterer* den Bruder Annas? // to act / as if / he / not / to know / him //

    Was **antwortet** *er* **auf die Fragen der Bäuerin?** // that / he / to have found / position / Mering / and / that / Anna / to be able / to move to / his house //

    Wovon sagt *er* **nichts?** // that / this / to have to be / immediately //

    Was **tut** *die Bäuerin nach dem Abendessen?* // to carry / feather bed / Anna's room //

    Aber was **sagt** *Otterer* da **merkwürdigerweise?** // that / he / to have go back / same evening //

17. Wie kommt Anna in die Häuslerhütte?

    Was geschieht, *nachdem Otterer wieder abgefahren ist?* // Anna / to fall sick / for weeks //

    Was **tut Otterer** *in der vierten Woche ihrer Krankheit?* // to drive up / farm / and / to pick up / Anna / child //

    Wie reagiert *Anna?* // to let it happen / without a word //

    Warum **kommt** *sie nur sehr langsam wieder zu Kräften?* // because of / thin soups / cottage //

    Warum **steht** *sie eines Morgens entschlossen* **auf?** // because / she / to see / how dirty / child / to be kept //

    Was **hat** *Annas Bruder* immer **behauptet?** // that / child / to have / Anna's smile //

    Was **kann Anna** *wenige Tage später* nicht mehr? // to stand / life / cottage //

    Was tut *sie?* // to run away / with / child //

18. Wie endet Annas Fluchtversuch und wie ist das Leben in der Häuslerhütte?

    Was **hat** *Anna* **vor?** // to reach / Sonthofen //

    Was passiert *am dritten Tag ihrer Wanderung?* // she / to sprain / foot / and / to be brought / farm //

Was **muß sie am Ende?** // to tell / people / name / husband //
Was tut **Otterer?** // to fetch / Anna / again / Mering //
Wie verhält sich **Anna von nun an?** // to make / no attempt / to escape // to accept / fate //
Sie arbeitet hart. Was **ist schwer?** // to get something out / little field // to keep going / tiny farm //
Wie **ist Otterer zu ihr?** // not unfriendly //
Wie geht es dem **Kind?** // to get enough to eat //
Was tut **der Bruder** mitunter? // to come / and / to bring / present //
Was **kann Anna sogar?** // to have a little coat dyed red //
Wie entwickelt sich ihre Situation **mit der Zeit?** // she / to become quite contented / and / to experience / much joy / education / child //

19. Wie ändert sich Annas Situation?

Anna kommt eines Tages vom Dorf zurück. Was **berichtet ihr Otterer?** // that / well-dressed lady / to have driven up / and / to have fetched / child //
Wie reagiert **sie?** // to reel / against / wall / horror // to set out for / Augsburg //
Wohin **geht sie** in der Reichsstadt **zuerst?** // tannery //
Was erlebt **sie** dort? // not / to be admitted // not / to get to see / child //
Was ist ihr nächster Schritt? // she / to run / authorities / and / to scream / that / one / to have stolen / child / from her //
Was aber **erfährt sie daraufhin?** // (a) / that / times / to have changed / (b) / that / peace / to be concluded //
Welcher besondere Glücksumstand aber kommt ihr zu Hilfe? // her case / to be referred to / judge / who / to be / unusual man //

20. Wie charakterisiert Brecht den Richter Dollinger, und wie ist Annas erste Begegnung mit ihm?

Weswegen **ist der Richter Dollinger** in ganz Schwaben **berühmt?** // because of / rudeness / and / erudition //
Was **hat er** mit dem Kurfürsten von Bayern **ausgetragen?** //dispute / free imperial city //
Wie **hat ihn der Kurfürst** genannt? // this Latin clodhopper //
Wie ist sein Verhältnis zum niedrigen Volk? // he / to have been celebrated / **folk** ballad //
Wie behandelt **er** Anna? // to listen to / a very short time // then / to direct / her / spot / room / on which / to fall / light //
Was tut **er für einige Minuten?** // to look at / her / carefully // then / to wave her aside //

21. Wie ist die zweite Begegnung Annas mit Dollinger?

Was geschieht am nächsten Tag? // Dollinger / to have Anna fetched / by / bailiff //
Der Richter schreit sie an. Was **fragt er sie?** // why / she / not / to have said / that / tannery / to be at stake //
Was **antwortet Anna?** // that / child / to be at stake //
Aber was, sagt der Richter, **soll sich Anna nicht einbilden?** // that / she / can / snap up / tannery //

Was geschieht, *wenn der Junge wirklich Annas Kind ist?* // property / to go to / relatives //

Was **entgegnet Anna?** // that / she / not / to need / tannery //

Was **fragt der Richter?** // whether / child / to be / hers //

Was sagt Anna da leise? // if / to be allowed / to keep / him / so long / until / he / to know / all words // he / to know / only seven // (*direct quote*)

Der Richter hustet. Was **sagt er dann?** // (*a*) / that / Anna / to want / little fellow / (*b*) / that / hag / five silk skirts / to want / him / (*c*) / that / child / to need / right mother //

Was **sagt er zum Schluß?** // that / he / Saturday / to hold court //

22. Was erfahren wir über den Prozeß zunächst?

Worüber hat man *in Wohnungen und Wirtschaften* **gestritten?** // who / to be / real / and / who / false / mother //

Weswegen ist *der alte Dollinger* **berühmt?** // folksy trials // biting turns of phrase / and / wise sayings //

Warum **sind** *viele Bauersleute der Umgegend* da? // because / Friday / to be / market day / and / they / to have stayed overnight / city //

Wo **verhandelt der Richter?** // Golden Hall //

Wo befindet **er** sich? // to sit / closed bronze gate / level floor / and / to have / no table / in front of //

Wer ist *innerhalb des abgeseilten Raums* anwesend? // to be / Mrs. Zingli / parents / Swiss relatives of late Mr. Zingli / Anna Otterer / sister / nursemaid / child //

Warum müssen alle Parteien und Zeugen stehen? // judge / to be in the habit of saying (*imperf. tense*) / that / proceedings / this way / to end more quickly //

Welchen Grund gibt es noch dafür? // they / to screen him from / audience //

23. Wie beginnt der Prozeß?

Was geschieht *zu Beginn der Verhandlung?* // incident / to occur //

Was tut **Anna,** *wenn sie das Kind erblickt?* // to utter / cry / and / to step forward //

Wie reagiert *das Kind?* // to want / (to go) to her //

Wozu **entschließt sich der Richter?** // to have him taken out / hall //

Wie beginnt **er** die Verhandlung? // to call up / Mrs. Zingli //

Frau Zingli kommt vorgerauscht. Was **schildert sie?** // how / imperial soldiers / to have snatched away / child / from her //

Was **berichtet sie von Anna?** // that / maid / to have come / father's house //

Was, sagt *sie,* habe die Magd berichtet? // that / child / to be / still / house //

Was **nimmt** *Frau Zingli* an? // that / Anna / somehow / to want (*imperf. tense*) / to extort / money //

24. Was erfahren wir während der Verhandlung über die Verwandten und über Frau Zingli?

Was **fragt** *der Richter* die Verwandten? // whether / to have inquired about / Mr. Zingli / at that time //

Was sagen die Verwandten aus? // Mrs. Zingli / to have let them know / that / Mr. Zingli / to have been slain //

Was **hat** *Frau Zingli* den Verwandten noch erzählt? // that / she / to have entrusted / child / maid //

Warum **sprechen** *die Verwandten* sehr unfreundlich von Frau Zingli? // because / property / to go to / them / if / trial / to be lost / for / Mrs. Zingli //

Was **will** *der Richter* jetzt von Frau Zingli wissen? // whether / she / to have lost / head / at that time / and / whether / she / to have abandoned / child //

Wie reagiert *Frau Zingli?* // to say / offended / that / she / not / to have abandoned / child //

Was **fragt** *der Richter* weiter? // whether / she / to believe / that / no mother / to be able / to abandon / child //

Was **antwortet** *Frau Zingli?* // yes / she / to believe / that //

25. Wie ist Annas Zeugenaussage?

Warum **blickt** *Anna* ab und zu nach der großen Tür? // as if / to fear / that / child / still / to scream //

Was **sagt** *Anna* aus? // she / to have gone / that night / house of Mrs. Zingli's uncle / but not / to have returned / tannery //

Warum **sei** *sie* nicht zurückgegangen? // fear / imperial soldiers / and / because / to have worried about / own illegitimate child //

Was, sagt der Richter, *sei nicht schön von Anna gewesen?* // that / to have cared about / own child only //

Aber was **sagt** *der Volksmund?* // that / blood / to be thicker / water //

Was, sagt Dollinger, tue *eine rechte Mutter?* // to go / steal / child //

26. Wie verhält sich der Richter schließlich?

Was für **eine Lektion hält** *Dollinger* dann? // wise and blunt lecture / cunning / people //

Was für **einen Abstecher macht** *er?* // about / peasants / who / to adulterate / milk / innocent cows //

Was **sagt** *er* über den Magistrat? // that / to take / too high market taxes / peasants //

Wie ist *dieser ganze Abstecher?* // to have nothing to do with / trial //

Was **verkündet** *der Richter* plötzlich? // that / examination of witnesses / to be ended / and / to have resulted in / nothing //

Der Richter macht eine Pause. Was **zeigt er?** // all signs / helplessness //

Wie **blickt** *er* um sich? // as if / to expect / suggestion //

Wie reagieren *die Leute?* // to look at one another / dumbfounded //

27. Zu welchen Feststellungen kommt der Richter?

Was, sagt er, *sei nicht festgestellt worden?* // who / to be / real mother //

Was sagt er über *das Kind?* // to be pitied //

Was, sagt er, habe *man* schon gehört? // that / fathers / not / to want / to be fathers //

Aber wie sei die Situation *hier?* // to come forward / two mothers / at the same time //

Zu welcher Überzeugung sei *der Gerichtshof* gelangt? // that / both / to lie like a book //

Was aber **sei** noch zu bedenken? // child / who / to have to have / mother //

Was **müsse** *man* feststellen? // who / to be / child's real mother //

28. Wie erklärt der Richter die Probe, die er vornehmen will?

Was **befiehlt er dem Gerichtsdiener?** // to fetch / piece of chalk //

Was **weist er ihn an?** // to draw / circle / floor / in which / three persons / to be able / to stand //

Was **befiehlt er ihm** *dann*? // to bring / child //

Wie verhält sich *das Kind*? // to begin / to cry out loud / again / and / to want (to go to) / Anna //

Was **sagt** *Dollinger* **über die Probe,** die er vornehmen wird? // (*a*) / that / to have found / it / old book / (*b*) / that / test / to be considered / very good //

Was **sei** *der einfache Grundgedanke der Probe?* // that / real mother / to be recognized by / love / child //

Was **müsse also erprobt werden?** // strength / love //

29. Wie beginnt die Probe?

Was tut *der Gerichtsdiener* jetzt? // to take / child / and / to lead / him / circle //

Was **sollen** *Anna und Frau Zingli?* // (*a*) / to go and stand / circle / (*b*) / each / to take / one hand / child //

Worum sollen *sie sich bemühen,* wenn der Richter ,,los" sagt? // to pull / child / circle //

Wer **werde das Kind auf ihre Seite bringen?** // whoever / to have / stronger love //

Im Saal wird es unruhig. Wann **wird es wieder totenstill?** // when / both women / to enter / circle //

Was tut *jede?* // to take / one hand / child //

Warum **ist** *das Kind* verstummt? // as if / to sense / what / to be at stake //

Wie steht **es** im Kreidekreis? // to turn to // Anna / tear-stained little face //

30. Wie endet die Probe und damit der Prozeß?

Was geschieht, *wenn der Richter ,,los" sagt?* // Mrs. Zingli / to tear / child / violent jerk / circle //

Wie **sieht** *Anna* ihm nach? // disturbed / and / incredulous //

Warum **hat** *sie* sogleich losgelassen? // fear / child / could suffer harm //

Was **sagt** *Dollinger?* // that / one / thus / to know / who / to be / real mother //

Was **befiehlt** *er?* // to take away / child / from slut //

Was **würde** *sie* tun? // to tear him to pieces / in cold blood //

Wie geht *Dollinger* aus dem Saal? // to nod to / Anna //

Was **erzählen sich später** *die Bauern, die nicht auf den Kopf gefallen sind?* // that / judge / to have winked / when / to have awarded / child / to woman from Mering //

C.   Exercises for the B-Questions

Drill 1   *Give the German equivalents.*

He is married to an Augsburg woman.
He hides in a pit in the courtyard.
The hallway is filled with drunk soldiers.
She snatches up the child hastily.

She is not ashamed to repudiate her child.
She gets her own way.
She tells him the whole truth.
He feels ill at ease.

The farm would soon get gossiped about.
She will think everything over.
She does not have to pretend.
She accepts her fate.
The lawsuit is referred to a judge.

The estate goes to Zingli's relatives.
The test is considered quite good.
One recognizes the real mother by her love for her child.

D. B-Questions

Quote indirectly where possible.

1. Bertolt Brecht gibt uns eine detaillierte Einführung in seine Erzählung.

   (a) Was erfahren wir zu Anfang der Geschichte über die Zeit, den Ort und die Personen der Handlung (Herr und Frau Zingli, Anna, das Kind)?
   (b) Was geschieht in der Gerberei und worin zeigt sich der Charakter Frau Zinglis?

2. Die Handlung der Erzählung entwickelt sich aus verschiedenen Entschlüssen, die Anna faßt, und aus einer Reihe von Ereignissen und Situationen, die niemand vorhersehen konnte.

   (a) Was alles bringt Anna zu ihrem ersten Entschluß, das Kind mitzunehmen und auf den Hof ihres Bruders zu bringen?
   (b) Was erfahren wir über Annas Bruder und ihre Schwägerin, die Bäuerin?
   (c) Wie ist Annas Situation auf dem Bauernhof, und was bringt sie zu ihrem zweiten Entschluß? Was tut Anna?
   (d) Was alles hat Anna nicht vorhergesehen, und wie kommt sie endlich in die Häuslerhütte?
   (e) Was bringt Anna zu ihrem Entschluß, die Häuslerhütte zu verlassen?
   (f) Wie endet ihr Fluchtversuch, und wie lebt sie von da ab bei Otterer?
   (g) Welches Ereignis bringt Anna zu ihrem letzten Entschluß? Was tut sie?

3. Der Streit um das Kind wird durch eine Probe entschieden.

   (a) Was für ein Mann ist der Richter Dollinger?
   (b) Was alles weiß er nach der zweiten Begegnung mit Anna? Was will Anna, und was will sie nicht?
   (c) Welches sind die wichtigen Punkte der Zeugenaussage?
   (d) Zu welchem Schluß kommt der Richter?
   (e) Beschreiben Sie die Probe.
   (f) Warum hat der Richter Anna am Ende zugezwinkert?

E. C-Questions (Essay)

1. Für welche Figur der Erzählung interessieren Sie sich am meisten? Warum?

2. Was ist der Hauptunterschied zwischen Brechts Erzählung und der Parabel der Bibel? Was ist Brechts Grundgedanke?

3. Was halten Sie von dem Urteil Dollingers? Was spricht dafür und was dagegen?

CHAPTER

7

kaum scarcely; **aus·üben** to exercise; **sprichwörtlich** proverbial; **der Gemeinplatz, ⸚e** cliché, commonplace; **auf·wachsen, u, a** to grow up

geschäftstüchtig efficient, able; **drängen** to trust

die Anerkennung, –en recognition; **ringen, a, u um** (+ *acc.*) to struggle for; **verhängnisvoll** fatal; **bestimmen** to determine; **die Macht, ⸚e** power

der juristische Doktorgrad doctor of law; **die Arbeiter-Unfall-Versicherungsanstalt** Accident insurance company for working men; **der Mangel, ⸚** want, lack; **gegenseitig** mutual

das Verhältnis, –se relationship; **der Jude, –n** (MII) Jew; **die Feindeligkeit, –en** hostility; **ausgesetzt sein** (+ *dat.*) to be exposed to; **der Angehörige** (*adj.*) *here:* member; **der Angestellte** (*adj.*) employee

sich nähern to approach; **eigenartig** peculiar; **unzugänglich** unapproachable

LITERATURE

PARABELN
Franz Kafka

Biographie   Franz Kafka (1883–1924) ist eine der ungewöhn-
lichsten und bedeutendsten Gestalten der Weltliteratur des 20.
Jahrhunderts. Kaum ein anderer Schriftsteller hat mit seinem
Werk einen solchen Einfluß auf die moderne Literatur ausgeübt
wie er. Sein Stil wurde sprichwörtlich und das Adjektiv „kaf-
kaesque" ein Gemeinplatz der literarischen Diskussion unserer
Zeit.

Geboren im damals österreichischen Prag, wuchs er im Kreise
seiner Geschwister in einer deutsch-jüdischen Familie auf.
Schon früh fühlte er sich in den Schatten eines geschäftstüch-
tigen und erfolgreichen Vaters gedrängt, um dessen Anerkennung er sein Leben lang rang und dessen vitale Simplizität der
geistig komplizierte, der suchende und träumende Kafka als
tyrannische, sein Leben verhängnisvoll bestimmende Macht
erlebte.

Kafkas unglückliches Verhältnis zu seinem Vater, seine Situation als deutschsprachiger Jude in Prag, wo er sowohl der
Feindseligkeit der slawischen Nationalisten wie dem Antisemitis-
mus der Deutsch-Österreicher ausgesetzt war, und die Tatsache,
daß er, der Angehörige der bürgerlichen Klasse, der Akademiker
mit dem juristischen Doktorgrad, jahrelang nichts anderes war
als Angestellter in einer Arbeiter-Unfall-Versicherungsanstalt,
– all das mag dazu beigetragen haben, jenes Gefühl der Ver-
lorenheit, der Fremdheit, der Unsicherheit und des Mangels an
gegenseitigem Verständnis zu entwickeln, das Kafka so meister-
haft in seinem Werk beschreibt.

Dem Leser, der sich Kafkas Werk zum ersten Mal nähert,
erscheinen die Erzählungen und Romane zunächst eigenartig
fremd und unzugänglich. Fremd und unzugänglich stehen sie

der **Alptraum,** ⁻e nightmare; **gemeinsam haben** to have in common; **der Ort,** –e location; **rätselhaft** enigmatic

unbeholfen clumsy; **die Verwandlung,** –en metamorphosis; **das Ungeziefer,** – vermin; **der Käfer,** – beetle, bug

der **Vergleich,** –e comparison; **der Prinz,** –en (MII) prince; **der Frosch,** ⁻e frog; **die Stiefmutter,** ⁻ stepmother; **die Hexe,** –n witch; **wie** *here:* like, can be compared with; **als** *here:* as; **die Ewigkeit,** –en eternity; **die Unendlichkeit,** –en infinity; **„Eine Kaiserliche Botschaft"** "An Imperial Message"; **der Palast,** ⁻e palace; **die Wohnstätte,** –n dwelling place, residence; **der Bote,** –n (MII) messenger; **unüberwindlich** invincible

erschließen, o, o to find access

Es ist uns überlassen It is left to us; **umgekehrt** *here:* opposite

das Bruchstückhafte (*adj.*) the fragmentlike

die Formulierung, –en formulation; **hinaus·gehen, i, a über** (+ *acc.*) to go beyond; **übermitteln** to convey; **die sittliche Lehre** ethical precepts; **das Moralgebot,** –e moral precept; **durch·dringen, a, u** to penetrate; **das Zeitalter,** – age

vor uns wie Träume, manche dieser Geschichten wie Alpträume. Denn mit Träumen und auch mit den Märchen haben sie gemeinsam, daß Raum und Zeit sich auflösen, daß Figuren, Orte und Szenen sich plötzlich verwandeln, und daß Ursachen und Motive von Handlungen und Entscheidungen oft rätselhaft bleiben.

So könnten Märchen und Traum uns zumindest eine Tür zum Verständnis der Kafkaschen Erzähltechnik öffnen. Wie das Märchen einige menschliche Figuren nicht mit Metaphern oder Vergleichen charakterisiert, also nicht sagt, daß der unbeholfene Prinz wie ein Frosch und die böse Mutter wie eine Stiefmutter oder gar Hexe sei, sondern den Prinzen als Frosch und die böse Mutter als Stiefmutter oder Hexe darstellt, so charakterisiert auch Kafka z.B. die Hauptfigur in seiner Erzählung Die Verwandlung nicht mit Hilfe eines Vergleichs, und sagt nicht, sie sei wie ein Ungeziefer, sondern er stellt sie als Ungeziefer, als Käfer dar. Ähnlich arbeitet der Traum. Minuten erscheinen in manchen Träumen nicht wie Ewigkeiten und kurze Distanzen nicht wie Unendlichkeiten. Sie sind im Traum Ewigkeiten und Unendlichkeiten, so wie in Kafkas Parabel Eine Kaiserliche Botschaft die Paläste und Wohnstätten für den Boten endlos und unüberwindlich sind.

Gibt uns der realistische Dichter die Welt so, wie er glaubt, daß sie ist, und überläßt er es uns, die symbolische Bedeutung der Dinge zu erschließen, so geht Kafka den umgekehrten Weg: Wie das Märchen und der Traum gibt er uns eine symbolische Welt, und es ist uns überlassen, ihre letzte existenzielle Bedeutung für unsere eigene Welt, für die Wirklichkeit der Dinge, zu suchen.

Alle Romane und Erzählungen Kafkas sind somit Parabeln. Sie sind Parabeln in dem Sinne, daß sie symbolische Formulierungen existenzieller Fragen sind. „Dabei geht Kafka nie über die Formulierung von Fragen hinaus. Seine Parabeln zeigen, daß sich nichts zeigen läßt. Sie übermitteln nicht sittliche Lehren und Moralgebote, sondern das Bruchstückhafte, das Unbestimmte und Dunkle als letzten (aber nicht absoluten) Sinn, zu dem wir überhaupt durchdringen können. Damit drücken sie die tiefste Wahrheit eines Zeitalters aus, das eins

das **Wesen** *here:* essence

beiseite treten, i, e to step aside; **locken** to tempt, to allure; **Wenn es dich so lockt . . .** If you are so tempted . . .

das **Gesetz,** – the law; der **Türhüter,** – doorkeeper; **gewähren** to grant, to allow; das **Tor, –e** gate; das **Verbot, –e** prohibition; **trotz meines Verbotes** against my will; **mächtig** powerful; den **Anblick ertragen, u, a** to stand the sight

Er entschließt sich, doch lieber zu warten He decides that he had better wait; **aus·fragen über** (+ *acc.*) to question about; **Und sei es noch so wertvoll . . .** No matter how valuable . . . ; **zwar** to be sure

erwarten to expect; **zugänglich sein** (+ *dat.*) to be accessible to; der **Pelzmantel,** ⸚ fur coat; **genauer an·sehen, a, e** (+ *acc.*) to look more closely at; die **Spitznase, –n** pointed nose; der **tatarische Bart,** ⸚e Tartar beard; der **Schemel,** – stool; **seitwärts von der Tür** beside the gate; **sich nieder·setzen** to sit down; der **Versuch, –e** attempt, trial; die **Bitte, –n** request; **ermüden** to tire, to weary; **öfters** from time to time; **Verhöre an·stellen** to make investigations; **teilnahmslos** impersonal; **zum Schluß** at the end; **sich aus·rüsten** to equip oneself; **verwenden** to use, to employ; **bestechen, a, o** to bribe; **an·nehmen, a, o** to accept; **versäumen** to omit, to neglect

beobachten to watch, to study; **ununterbrochen** uninterruptedly; das **Hindernis, –se** obstacle, hindrance; **verfluchen** to curse

gelernt hat: Das Wesen jeder Antwort ist das Stellen neuer
Fragen.''

VOR DEM GESETZ

Vor dem Gesetz steht ein Türhüter. Zu diesem Türhüter kommt
ein Mann vom Lande und bittet um Eintritt in das Gesetz. Aber
der Türhüter sagt, daß er ihm jetzt den Eintritt nicht gewähren
könne. Der Mann überlegt und fragt dann, ob er also später
werde eintreten dürfen. ,,Es ist möglich'', sagt der Türhüter,
,,jetzt aber nicht.'' Da das Tor zum Gesetz offensteht wie immer
und der Türhüter beiseite tritt, bückt sich der Mann, um durch
das Tor in das Innere zu sehn. Als der Türhüter das merkt,
lacht er und sagt: ,,Wenn es dich so lockt, versuche es doch,
trotz meines Verbotes hineinzugehn. Merke aber: Ich bin mächtig. Und ich bin nur der unterste Türhüter. Von Saal zu Saal
stehn aber Türhüter, einer mächtiger als der andere. Schon
den Anblick des dritten kann nicht einmal ich mehr ertragen.''
Solche Schwierigkeiten hat der Mann vom Lande nicht erwartet;
das Gesetz soll doch jedem und immer zugänglich sein, denkt
er, aber als er jetzt den Türhüter in seinem Pelzmantel genauer
ansieht, seine große Spitznase, den langen, dünnen, schwarzen
tatarischen Bart, entschließt er sich, doch lieber zu warten, bis
er die Erlaubnis zum Eintritt bekommt. Der Türhüter gibt ihm
einen Schemel und läßt ihn seitwärts von der Tür sich nieder-
setzen. Dort sitzt er Tage und Jahre. Er macht viele Versuche,
eingelassen zu werden, und ermüdet den Türhüter durch seine
Bitten. Der Türhüter stellt öfters kleine Verhöre mit ihm an,
fragt ihn über seine Heimat aus und nach vielem andern, es
sind aber teilnahmslose Fragen, wie sie große Herren stellen,
und zum Schluß sagt er immer wieder, daß er ihn noch nicht
einlassen könne. Der Mann, der sich für seine Reise mit vielem
ausgerüstet hat, verwendet alles, und sei es noch so wertvoll,
um den Türhüter zu bestechen. Dieser nimmt zwar alles an,
aber sagt dabei: ,,Ich nehme es nur an, damit du nicht glaubst,
etwas versäumt zu haben.'' Während der vielen Jahre beobachtet der Mann den Türhüter fast ununterbrochen. Er vergißt
die andern Türhüter, und dieser erste scheint ihm das einzige
Hindernis für den Eintritt in das Gesetz. Er verflucht den un-

kindlich childlike

der **Zufall,** ⸚e accident, coincidence; **rücksichtslos** recklessly; **vor sich hinbrummen** to mutter, to grumble to oneself; **kindisch** childish; **der Floh,** ⸚e flea; **jemand um·stimmen** to bring someone around, to make someone change his mind; **das Augenlicht** eyesight; **täuschen** to deceive; **unverlöschlich** unextinguishably; **der Glanz** radiance; **brechen, a, o aus** (+ *dat.*) *here:* to stream out of

erstarren to stiffen; **zugunsten** to the advantage

sich sammeln zu (+ *dat.*) to condense into; **bisher** until now; **zu·winken** (+ *dat.*) to beckon, to nod to; **der Größenunterschied, –e** difference in size; **zuungunsten** to the disadvantage; **sich hinunter·neigen** to bend down; **streben nach** (+ *dat.*) to strive for; **unersättlich** insatiable; **Wieso kommt es?** How come? Why is it?; **verlangen** to demand, to require; **vergehen, i, a** to die away; **das Gehör** hearing; **an·brüllen** to bellow at, to roar; **erhalten, ie, a** to receive, to get; **bestimmt sein für** (+ *acc.*) to be intended for

der Nachlaß posthumous writings; **überlaufen, ie, au** to pass by; **nachträglich** subsequently; **erschrecken, a, o** to be frightened; **der Wächter, –** watchman; **abgewendet sein** *here:* to be off guard; **Er sah vor sich hin** He dropped his gaze

die Turmuhr, –en tower clock

glücklichen Zufall, in den ersten Jahren rücksichtslos und laut, später, als er alt wird, brummt er nur noch vor sich hin. Er wird kindisch, und, da er in dem jahrelangen Studium des Türhüters auch die Flöhe in seinem Pelzkragen erkannt hat, bittet er auch die Flöhe, ihm zu helfen und den Türhüter umzustimmen. Schließlich wird sein Augenlicht schwach, und er weiß nicht, ob es um ihn wirklich dunkler wird, oder ob ihn nur seine Augen täuschen. Wohl aber erkennt er jetzt im Dunkel einen Glanz, der unverlöschlich aus der Türe des Gesetzes bricht. Nun lebt er nicht mehr lange. Vor seinem Tode sammeln sich in seinem Kopfe alle Erfahrungen der ganzen Zeit zu einer Frage, die er bisher an den Türhürter noch nicht gestellt hat. Er winkt ihm zu, da er seinen erstarrenden Körper nicht mehr aufrichten kann. Der Türhüter muß sich tief zu ihm hinunterneigen, denn der Größenunterschied hat sich sehr zuungunsten des Mannes verändert. ,,Was willst du denn jetzt noch wissen?" fragt der Türhüter, ,,du bist unersättlich." ,,Alle streben doch nach dem Gesetz", sagt der Mann, ,,wieso kommt es, daß in den vielen Jahren niemand außer mir Einlaß verlangt hat?" Der Türhüter erkennt, daß der Mann schon an seinem Ende ist, und, um sein vergehendes Gehör noch zu erreichen, brüllt er ihn an: ,,Hier konnte niemand sonst Einlaß erhalten, denn dieser Eingang war nur für dich bestimmt. Ich gehe jetzt und schließe ihn."

AUS DEM NACHLASS

I

Ich überlief den ersten Wächter. Nachträglich erschrak ich, lief wieder zurück und sagte dem Wächter: ,,Ich bin hier durchgelaufen, während du abgewendet warst." Der Wächter sah vor sich hin und schwieg. ,,Ich hätte es wohl nicht tun sollen", sagte ich. Der Wächter schwieg noch immer. ,,Bedeutet dein Schweigen die Erlaubnis zu passieren?"

II

Es war sehr früh am Morgen, die Straßen rein und leer, ich ging zum Bahnhof. Als ich eine Turmuhr mit meiner Uhr verglich,

Der Schrecken über diese Entdeckung ließ mich im Wege unsicher werden The fright over this discovery made me uncertain as to my direction; **Ich kannte mich in dieser Stadt noch nicht sehr gut aus** I did not yet know my way around this city very well; **Er wandte sich mit einem großen Schwunge ab** He turned away from me emphatically (with great impetus)

sich beeilen to hurry, to hasten; **glücklicherweise** fortunately; **der Schutzmann, –leute** policeman; **in der Nähe** nearby; **atemlos** breathless; **auf·geben, a, e** to give up

sah ich, daß es schon viel später war, als ich geglaubt hatte, ich mußte mich sehr beeilen, der Schrecken über diese Entdeckung ließ mich im Wege unsicher werden, ich kannte mich in dieser Stadt noch nicht sehr gut aus, glücklicherweise war ein Schutzmann in der Nähe, ich lief zu ihm und fragte atemlos nach dem Weg. Er lächelte und sagte: „Von mir willst du den Weg erfahren?" „Ja", sagte ich, „da ich ihn selbst nicht finden kann." „Gibs auf, gibs auf", sagte er und wandte sich mit einem großen Schwunge ab, so wie Leute, die mit ihrem Lachen allein sein wollen.

I. QUESTIONNAIRE

A. Exercises for the A-Questions

Study the following expressions.

1. Er **ermüdete** ihn **durch** Fragen.	He wearied him with questions.
2. Er schien ihm das einzige **Hindernis für** den Eintritt.	He seemed to him the only obstacle to entering.
3. Er **murmelte vor sich hin.**	He muttered to himself.
4. Er mußte **sich hinunterbeugen.**	He had to bend down.
5. Er **sah vor sich hin.**	He dropped his gaze.
6. Alle **streben nach** dem Gesetz.	Everyone strives for the law.
7. Er mußte **sich beeilen.**	He had to hurry.
8. die **Furcht vor** dieser Entdeckung	the fright over this discovery

B. A-Questions

Change the direct quotes to indirect quotes using the subjunctive or quotative, if not otherwise indicated.

1. Mit was für einer Situation beginnt Kafka die Erzählung?

   Wie ist die Situation *vor dem Gesetz?* // to stand / doorkeeper // man from the country / to ask for / admittance //
   Was **antwortet** *der Türhüter?* // that / he / now / not to be able / to allow / him / entrance //
   Was erfahren wir über *das Tor zum Gesetz?* // to stand open / as always //

Was tut **der Mann vom Lande,** *als der Türhüter beiseite tritt?* // to bend down / in order to see into / interior //
Wie reagiert *der Türhüter, als er das merkt?* // to laugh //
Was **sagt er?** // that / man / should try / to enter / against / will //
Was aber, **sagt er, solle der Mann sich merken?** // (*a*) / that / he / to be powerful / (*b*) / that / he / to be / only / lowest one / (*c*) / that / one / to be / more powerful / than / the other //
Was, **sagt der Türhüter, könne nicht einmal er?** // stand / sight / third one //

2. Wir haben bisher die Situation des Mannes vor dem Gesetz aus der Perspektive des Türhüters gesehen. Im Folgenden sehen wir diese Situation und den Türhüter mit den Augen des Mannes vom Lande.

Wie sieht *der Türhüter* aus? // to have / fur coat / pointed nose / and / long, thin, black Tartar beard //
Wie behandelt *der Türhüter* den Mann vom Lande? // to give / stool / and / to let him sit down / beside / gate //
Was **stellt er öfters** an? // little investigations / with / man from the country //
Aber wie **sind seine Fragen?** // impersonal //
Was **sagt er** *zum Schluß* immer wieder? // that / he / not yet / to be able / to let him in //
Wie lange **sitzt der Mann** vor dem Tor zum Gesetz? // days / and / years //

3. Welche Versuche macht der Mann, um eingelassen zu werden?

Was tut **er?** // (*a*) / to weary / doorkeeper / questions / (*b*) / to observe / doorkeeper / uninterruptedly //
Was **versucht er?** // everything / to bribe / doorkeeper //
Wie reagiert *der Türhüter?* // to accept / everything //
Warum? // man / to be supposed / not / to believe / to have neglected / anything //
Was **verflucht der Mann?** // unfortunate coincidence / recklessly //
Aber was tut **er** *später nur noch?* // to mutter to himself //
Was passiert? // man / to grow old / and / to become childish //
Was macht **er** *schließlich?* // to ask / fleas / doorkeeper's fur / to help him //
Was geschieht *endlich?* // eyesight / to become weak //

4. Fragen zu den zwei Parabeln aus dem Nachlaß.

Was tut **der Erzähler** in der ersten Parabel? // to pass by / first watchman / and / to run back / again //
Was **sagt er** *zu dem Wächter?* // that / he / to have passed / while / he / to have been off guard //
Was sagt der Erzähler noch? // presumably, I should not have done it (*direct quote*) //
Wie reagiert *der Wächter?* // to drop / gaze / and / to remain silent //

Wohin **geht** *der Erzähler* in der zweiten Parabel? // station //
Was tut **er** *auf dem Wege*? // to compare / tower clock / his watch //
Was **entdeckt er?** // that / it / to be much later / than / he / to have thought //
Was **muß er?** // to hurry //
Zu wem **läuft er?** // policeman / who / to be / near by //
Wonach fragt er ihn? // way //
Wie reagiert *der Schutzmann?* // to smile //

In den Fragen 1—4 haben wir die äußere Situation des Mannes vom Lande und des Erzählers in der ersten und zweiten Parabel aus dem Nachlaß dargestellt. Wir beziehen uns jetzt auf ihre innere Situation, auf ihre Gedanken, Erwartungen und Hoffnungen.

5. Wie ist die innere Situation des Mannes vom Lande?

   Der Türhüter sagt, daß er dem Mann den Eintritt jetzt nicht gewähren könne. Wie reagiert *der Mann?* // to consider / and / to ask / whether / he / to be allowed / to enter / later //
   Das Tor zum Gesetz steht wie immer offen. Aber was **hat der Mann vom Lande** nicht erwartet? // such difficulties //
   Was **denkt er?** // that / Law / to be accessible to / everyone / and / always //
   Was tut **er schließlich**, nachdem er den Türhüter genauer angesehen hat? // to decide / to wait / until / he / to receive / permission / to enter //
   Wie lange **wartet er nach diesem Entschluß** // days / and / years //
   Was geschieht *schließlich?* // eyesight / to become weak //
   Aber was **weiß er nicht?** // whether / it / really / to become darker / or / whether / eyes / to deceive / him //
   Was **erkennt er?** // radiance / which / unextinguishably / to stream out of / gate / Law //

6. Wie ist die innere Situation des Erzählers in der ersten Parabel aus dem Nachlaß?

   Wie reagiert *der Erzähler,* als er den ersten Wächter überläuft? // to be frightened / and / to run back //
   Der Wächter schweigt, als der Erzähler ihn anredet. Wie reagiert *der Erzähler* auf dieses Schweigen? // to ask / whether / silence / to mean / permission / to pass //

7. Wie ist die innere Situation des Erzählers in der zweiten Parabel aus dem Nachlaß?

   Was **sieht er plötzlich** *auf dem Wege zum Bahnhof?* // that / it / to be much later / than / to have thought //
   Was **läßt ihn** plötzlich **im Wege unsicher werden?** // fright / over / discovery //
   Was **hält** *der Erzähler* **für ein Glück?** // that / policeman / to be / near by //
   Was **fragt** *der Schutzmann?* // whether / he / to want / to learn / way / from him //

Warum **antwortet** *der Erzähler* mit ja? // because / he himself / to be unable / to find / it //

8. Wie endet die Erzählung Vor dem Gesetz?

Der Mann lebt nun nicht mehr lange. Was tut **er** *am Ende?* // to ask / question / which / he / until now / not yet / to have asked //
Warum **winkt** *er* dem Türhüter zu? // since / he / not any more / to be able / to straighten up //
Wie reagiert *der Türhüter?* // to have to bend down //
Was **glaubt** *der Mann vom Lande?* // that / all people / to strive for / law //
Was **fragt** er deshalb? // why is it / that no one else / to have demanded / admittance (*direct quote*) //
Was **erkennt** *der Türhüter?* // that / man / to be / near / end //
Was **brüllt** er? // that / here / no one else / could get / admittance //
Was **sagt** er über den Eingang? // that / this entrance / to be intended / only for him //
Was tut **er?** // to go / and / to close / it //

9. Wie endet die erste Parabel aus dem Nachlaß?

Was tut *der Wächter?* // to drop / gaze / and / to be silent //
Was **will** *der Erzähler* wissen? //whether / silence / to mean / permission / to pass //

10. Wie endet die zweite Parabel aus dem Nachlaß?

Warum **fragt** *der Erzähler* den Schutzmann nach dem Weg? // because / he himself / to be unable / to find / it //
Was **sagt** ihm *der Schutzmann?* // to give up (*direct quote*) //
Was tut **er?** // to turn away / like / people / who / to want / to be alone / with / laughter //

C. B-Questions

1. Vergleichen Sie die äußere und die innere Situation des Mannes vom Lande und des Erzählers in der ersten und in der zweiten Parabel aus dem Nachlaß.
Wo sehen Sie Parallelen und wo sehen Sie Unterschiede?
Welche Widersprüche erkennen Sie zwischen den Gedanken und Erwartungen und der äußeren Situation des Mannes vom Lande und des Erzählers?

2. Welches Grundgefühl haben der Mann vom Lande und der Erzähler?
Warum haben sie dieses Grundgefühl?

3. Der Mann vom Lande und der Erzähler in beiden Parabeln sind „auf dem Wege". Kafka beschreibt diesen Weg konkret.
Welche allgemeine, welche symbolische Bedeutung mag dieser Weg haben?

4. Vergleichen Sie den Schluß der Erzählung mit dem Schluß der Parabeln.
Was scheint der Irrtum des Mannes vom Lande und des Erzählers gewesen zu sein?
Oder mit andern Worten: Was könnten die Widersprüche zwischen den Gedanken und Erwar-
tungen und der wahren, äußeren Situation des Mannes und des Erzählers mit dem Ende der
Erzählung und der Parabeln zu tun haben?

so heißt es it is said; gerade dir just to you; So sehr war ihm an der Botschaft gelegen, daß er sich sie noch ins Ohr wiedersagen ließ He cared so much about the message that he had it repeated in his ear; das Kopfnicken nodding; bestätigen to confirm; die Zuschauerschaft audience; sich schwingen, a, u to sweep; die Freitreppe, –n open-air stairway; ab·fertigen to dispatch

die Botschaft, en message; der Kaiser, – emperor; der Einzelne *(adj.)* individual; jämmerlich pitiful, miserable; der Untertan, –en (MII) subject; die fernste Ferne, –n the most remote distance; flüchten vor (+ *dat.*) to flee from; der Bote, –n (MII) messenger; nieder·knien to kneel down; nieder·brechen, a, o to tear down; der Ring, –e *here:* circle; die Großen des Reichs the dignitaries of the realm

vor·strecken to stretch forward; vorwärts forward

kräftig strong; unermüdlich untiring; Er schafft sich durch die Menge Bahn He forces his way through the crowd; das Zeichen, – sign; vorwärts·kommen, a, o to advance, to progress; Die Wohnstätten nehmen kein Ende The residences are endless; herrlich glorious

das innerste Gemach, ⸚er the innermost chamber; Die Treppen hinab müßte er sich kämpfen He would have to fight his way down the stairs; umschließen, o, o to enclose; stürzen *here:* to rush, tumble; äußerst *here:* outermost; hochgeschüttet heaped high; der Bodensatz sediment, dregs

statt dessen instead; nutzlos uselessly, in vain; sich ab·mühen to exert oneself, to labor; überwinden, a, u to overcome; Gelänge ihm dies, nichts wäre gewonnen Even if he succeeded in this, nothing would be won; durchmessen, a, e to cross; und wieder Treppen and more steps; das Jahrtausend, –e millennium; die Residenzstadt, ⸚e imperial capital; durch·dringen, a, u to penetrate; gar much less; träumen to dream; sich etwas erträumen to conjure up something

EINE KAISERLICHE BOTSCHAFT

Der Kaiser — so heißt es — hat dir, dem Einzelnen, dem jämmerlichen Untertanen, dem winzig vor der kaiserlichen Sonne in die fernste Ferne geflüchteten Schatten, gerade dir hat der Kaiser von seinem Sterbebett aus eine Botschaft gesendet. Den Boten hat er beim Bett niederknien lassen und ihm die Botschaft ins Ohr geflüstert; so sehr war ihm an ihr gelegen, daß er sich sie noch ins Ohr wiedersagen ließ. Durch Kopfnicken hat er die Richtigkeit des Gesagten bestätigt. Und vor der ganzen Zuschauerschaft seines Todes — alle hindernden Wände werden niedergebrochen und auf den weit und hoch sich schwingenden Freitreppen stehen im Ring die Großen des Reichs — vor allen diesen hat er den Boten abgefertigt. Der Bote hat sich gleich auf den Weg gemacht; ein kräftiger, ein unermüdlicher Mann; einmal diesen, einmal den andern Arm vorstreckend schafft er sich Bahn durch die Menge; findet er Widerstand, zeigt er auf die Brust, wo das Zeichen der Sonne ist; er kommt auch leicht vorwärts, wie kein anderer. Aber die Menge ist so groß; ihre Wohnstätten nehmen kein Ende. Öffnete sich freies Feld, wie würde er fliegen und bald wohl hörtest du das herrliche Schlagen seiner Fäuste an deiner Tür. Aber statt dessen, wie nutzlos müht er sich ab; immer noch zwängt er sich durch die Gemächer des innersten Palastes; niemals wird er sie überwinden; und gelänge ihm dies, nichts wäre gewonnen; die Treppen hinab müßte er sich kämpfen; und gelänge ihm dies, nichts wäre gewonnen; die Höfe wären zu durchmessen; und nach den Höfen der zweite umschließende Palast; und wieder Treppen und Höfe; und wieder ein Palast; und so weiter durch Jahrtausende; und stürzte er endlich aus dem äußersten Tor — aber niemals, niemals kann es geschehen —, liegt erst die Residenzstadt vor ihm, die Mitte der Welt, hochgeschüttet voll ihres Bodensatzes. Niemand dringt hier durch und gar mit der Botschaft eines Toten. — Du aber sitzt an deinem Fenster und erträumst sie dir, wenn der Abend kommt.

II. QUESTIONNAIRE

A. Exercises for the A-Questions

Study the following expressions.

1. Er **ist vor** der Sonne **geflüchtet.**	He has fled from the sun.
2. Er **schafft sich** durch die Menge **Bahn.**	He forces his way through the crowd.
3. Die Wohnstätten **nehmen kein Ende.**	The residences are endless.
4. Er **müht sich** nutzlos **ab.**	He exerts himself in vain.
5. Er müßte **sich** die Treppen **hinab kämpfen.**	He would have to fight his way down the stairs.
6. Er **erträumt sich** die Botschaft.	He conjures up the message.

B. A-Questions

1. Der erste Satz dieser Parabel enthält die Worte: Der Kaiser – so heißt es – hat eine Botschaft gesendet.

   Wem – so wird berichtet – **hat der Kaiser eine Botschaft gesendet?** // to you / individual / miserable subject //
   Wie charakterisiert Kafka den Einzelnen, **das Du** noch? // to be / tiny shadow / who / to have fled / from / sun / most remote distance //
   Wie charakterisiert Kafka dagegen den **Kaiser?** // to be / sun //
   In welchem Zustand befindet sich **der Kaiser?** // to lie / on / deathbed //

2. Was erfahren wir über die Botschaft und den Boten?

   Woher wissen wir, daß die Botschaft sehr wichtig ist? // emperor / to have messenger kneel down // to have him repeat message //
   Wie ist die Situation, in der **er den Boten abfertigt?** // in front of / dignitaries / empire //
   Was tut **der Bote** sogleich? // to set out for //
   Wie charakterisiert Kafka den **Boten?** // to be / strong / and / untiring / man //
   Wie beginnt **der Bote** seinen Weg? // (a) / to force / way / through / crowd / (b) / to advance / easily //
   Was tut **er, wenn er Widerstand findet?** // to point to / chest / where / sign of the sun / to be //

3. Aber wie entwickelt sich die Situation? Was wäre möglich, aber was ist unmöglich?

   Was hindert den Boten zunächst? // crowd / to be / big // residences / to be / endless //
   Was **würde der Bote** tun, **wenn sich freies Feld öffnete?** // to fly //
   Was **würde der Untertan, das Du, hören?** // soon / glorious beating / fists / against / door //
   Aber was geschieht **statt dessen?** // messenger / to exert oneself / in vain //
   Warum? // he / never / to overcome (future tense) / chambers / innermost palace //
   Warum wäre nichts gewonnen, **selbst wenn ihm dies gelänge?**// he / to have to cross (*subj.*) / courtyards / and / second palace //

Was alles **hätte *er*** noch **zu überwinden?** // more stairs / and courtyards / another palace //
Wie **ginge *sein Weg*** weiter? // through / millennia //
Was **liegt erst vor ihm, *wenn er endlich aus dem äußersten Tor stürzte?*** // imperial capital / center / world //
Was **kann *niemand?*** // to penetrate / here / much less / message / dead man //

4. Was aber tut während aller dieser vergeblichen Bemühungen des Boten **der Untertan, das Du?**

// to sit / window / and / to conjure up / message //

C. B-Questions

1. Vergleichen Sie die Bemühungen des Boten, dem Untertanen die Botschaft zu bringen, mit den „Bemühungen" des Untertanen, sie zu erhalten.
Was alles tut der Bote, und was „tut" der Untertan?
Welchen Widerspruch sehen Sie?

D. C-Questions (Essay)

1. Was charakterisiert die Personen in den Erzählungen und Parabeln, die wir bisher gelesen haben?

2. In was für einem menschlichen und sozialen Verhältnis stehen diese Personen zueinander? Was könnten die Personen repräsentieren?

3. Was wird in den Erzählungen und Parabeln nie erreicht?
Könnte das etwas mit dem immer gleichen Verhältnis der Personen zueinander zu tun haben?

4. Kafka beginnt die Erzählungen „Vor dem Gesetz" und „Eine Kaiserliche Botschaft" mit einer konkreten, realistisch beschriebenen Situation. Mit welchen Sätzen werden auch diese beiden Erzählungen zu abstrakten Parabeln, d.h. wo verlieren Raum und Zeit jede Bedeutung?
Was, glauben Sie, möchte Kafka damit sagen, wenn er eine konkrete Erzählung an einer bestimmten Stelle zu einer abstrakten Parabel macht, die wie das Märchen und der Traum weder Raum noch Zeit kennt?

sich wenden to turn; gleich *here:* just, immediately

der Schlag, ⸚e knock, blow; das Hoftor, –e *here:* manor gate, gate to manorial estate; vorüber·kommen, a, o an (+ *dat.*) to pass; der Mutwille (MII) mischief; die Zerstreutheit absence of mind; drohen to threaten; nur *here:* merely; erschrecken, a, o to be frightened; gebückt vor Schrecken cowed with terror (fright); jemanden erinnern an (+ *acc.*) to remind somebody of; der Besitzer, – proprietor, owner; verklagen to sue, to charge; die Untersuchung, –en investigation, interrogation

begreiflich machen to make clear; sich des Urteils enthalten, ie, a to refrain from judgment; verhüllen to conceal; die Spitze, –n tip, point; die Lanze, –n lance, spear; die Truppe, –n troop; verschwinden, a, u to disappear; das Pferd, –e horse

beruhigen to calm; wahrscheinlich probably; deswegen on account of that; nirgends nowhere; einen Beweis führen to furnish proof; an·klagen to accuse, to sue; die Rauchwolke, –n cloud of smoke; der Reiter, – horseman; sich erheben, o, o to rise

das Kleid, –er dress; treten, a, e to step; noch von den Pferden herab before dismounting, still on horseback (*speaking down to them*); lebhaft lively; der Gehilfe (MII) helper, assistant

fort·drängen to urge to leave; etwas ins Reine bringen, a, a to straighten out something; (sich) weigern to refuse; sich um·kleiden to change (clothes); die Herren *here:* masters, lords; folgen *here:* to obey; augenblicklich at the moment; gleichgiltig = gleichgültig indifferent; auf·nehmen, a, o *here:* to record, to receive; auf·fordern to ask, to command; die Bauernstube, –n livingroom of a farmhouse

DER SCHLAG ANS HOFTOR

Es war im Sommer, ein heißer Tag. Ich kam auf dem Nach-
hauseweg mit meiner Schwester an einem Hoftor vorüber. Ich
weiß nicht, schlug sie aus Mutwillen ans Tor oder aus Zerstreutheit oder drohte sie nur mit der Faust und schlug gar nicht.
Hundert Schritte weiter an der nach links sich wendenden
Landstraße begann das Dorf. Wir kannten es nicht, aber gleich
nach dem ersten Haus kamen Leute hervor und winkten uns,
freundschaftlich oder warnend, selbst erschrocken, gebückt vor
Schrecken. Sie zeigten nach dem Hof, an dem wir vorüberge-
kommen waren, und erinnerten uns an den Schlag ans Tor. Die
Hofbesitzer werden uns verklagen, gleich werde die Untersuchung beginnen. Ich war sehr ruhig und beruhigte auch
meine Schwester. Sie hatte den Schlag wahrscheinlich gar nicht
getan, und hätte sie ihn getan, so wird deswegen nirgends auf
der Welt ein Beweis geführt. Ich suchte das auch den Leuten
um uns begreiflich zu machen, sie hörten mich an, enthielten
sich aber eines Urteils. Später sagten sie, nicht nur meine
Schwester, auch ich, als Bruder werde angeklagt werden. Ich
nickte lächelnd. Alle blickten wir zum Hofe zurück, wie man
eine ferne Rauchwolke beobachtet und auf die Flamme wartet.
Und wirklich, bald sahen wir Reiter ins weit offene Hoftor
einreiten. Staub erhob sich, verhüllte alles, nur die Spitzen der
hohen Lanzen blinkten. Und kaum war die Truppe im Hof verschwunden, schien sie gleich die Pferde gewendet zu haben und
war auf dem Wege zu uns. Ich drängte meine Schwester fort,
ich werde alles allein ins Reine bringen. Sie weigerte sich, mich
allein zu lassen. Ich sagte, sie solle sich aber wenigstens um-
kleiden, um in einem besseren Kleid vor die Herren zu treten.
Endlich folgte sie und machte sich auf den langen Weg nach
Hause. Schon waren die Reiter bei uns, noch von den Pferden
herab fragten sie nach meiner Schwester. Sie ist augenblicklich
nicht hier, wurde ängstlich geantwortet, werde aber später
kommen. Die Antwort wurde fast gleichgiltig aufgenommen;
wichtig schien vor allem, daß sie mich gefunden hatten. Es
waren hauptsächlich zwei Herren, der Richter, ein junger leb-
hafter Mann und sein stiller Gehilfe, der Aßmann genannt
wurde. Ich wurde aufgefordert in die Bauernstube einzutreten.

den Kopf wiegend wagging his head; der Hosenträger, – suspender; rücken to move, adjust; an den Hosenträgern rückend hitching up the trousers; unter den scharfen Blicken under the intensive glances; Noch glaubte ich fast . . . I still half believed . . . ; sogar noch unter Ehren even honorably; die Schwelle, –n threshold; überschreiten, i, i to step over; vor·springen, a, u to jump forward, to hasten to the front; über allem Zweifel beyond all doubt; die Steinfliese, –n flagstone

sich in Gang setzen to begin to move; genügen to suffice; der Städter, – city man; Dieser Mann tut mir leid I feel sorry for this man; gegenwärtig present; der Zustand, ⸚e state; ähnlich sehen, a e (+ dat.) to resemble; die Gefängniszelle, –n prison cell; kahl bare; eingemauert embedded, immured; die Pritsche, –n prison cot

schmecken to taste; vielmehr rather; Aussicht auf Entlassung prospect of release

Langsam, den Kopf wiegend, an den Hosenträgern rückend, setzte ich mich unter den scharfen Blicken der Herren in Gang. Noch glaubte ich fast, ein Wort werde genügen, um mich, den Städter, sogar noch unter Ehren, aus diesem Bauernvolk zu befreien. Aber als ich die Schwelle der Stube überschritten hatte, sagte der Richter, der vorgesprungen war und mich schon erwartete: „Dieser Mann tut mir leid." Es war aber über allem Zweifel, daß er damit nicht meinen gegenwärtigen Zustand meinte, sondern das, was mit mir geschehen würde. Die Stube sah einer Gefängniszelle ähnlicher als einer Bauernstube. Große Steinfliesen, dunkel, ganz kahle Wand, irgendwo eingemauert ein eiserner Ring, in der Mitte etwas, das halb Pritsche, halb Operationstisch war.

Könnte ich noch andere Luft schmecken als die des Gefängnisses? Das ist die große Frage oder vielmehr, sie wäre es, wenn ich noch Aussicht auf Entlassung hätte.

III.   QUESTIONNAIRE

A.   Exercises for the A-Questions

Study the following expressions.

1. Sie **kamen an** einem Hoftor **vorüber.**	They passed a manor gate.
2. **gebückt vor** Schrecken	cowed with terror (fright)
3. Sie **weigerte sich,** ihn allein zu lassen.	She refused to leave him by himself.
4. Er sagte, sie solle **sich** wenigstens **umziehen.**	He said she should at least change (clothes).
5. Dieser Mann tut mir leid.	I feel sorry for this man.
6. Er wird alles allein ins Reine bringen.	He will straighten out everything by himself.
7. die **Aussicht auf** Entlassung	the prospect of release

B.   A-Questions

Change the direct quotes to indirect quotes using the subjunctive or quotative, if not otherwise indicated.

1. Wie ist die Ausgangssituation (initial situation) der Parabel?

   Wo befinden sich *der Bruder und die Schwester*? // way / home // they / to pass / manor gate //

Was **weiß** *der Bruder* nicht? // whether / sister / to have knocked / gate / mischief / or / absence of mind //

Was **weiß** *er nicht einmal?* // whether / sister / merely / to have threatened / fist / and / not / to have knocked / at all //

Was **kennt** *der Bruder* auch nicht? // village / which / to begin / on / road //

2. Wie ändert sich die Situation?

Gleich nach dem ersten Haus kommen Leute hervor. Wie **winken** *die Leute* dem Bruder und der Schwester? // friendly / warning / frightened / cowed with terror //

Was tun *sie?* // to point / toward / manor house / and / to remind / them / of / knock / on / gate //

Was **sagen** *sie?* // (a) / that / proprietors / manor / to sue (*future tense*) / them / (b) / that / interrogation / immediately / to begin (*future tense*) //

Was **sagen** sie *später?* // that / not only / sister / but also / brother / to be sued (würde-form) //

Wie **blicken** *alle* zum Hof zurück? // as / one / to watch / distant smoke cloud / and to wait for / flame //

3. Wie ändert sich die Situation weiter?

Was **sehen** *sie?* // horseman / to ride in / through / wide-open gate //

Was tun **die Reiter** *sogleich?* // to turn / horses / and / to be / on / way / to brother / and / sister //

Was **möchte** *der Bruder?* // (that) / sister / to leave him by himself //

Wie reagiert **die Schwester** *zunächst?* // to refuse //

Welchen **Vorschlag macht** *der Bruder* da? // sister / should / at least / change / in order to step / before / "masters" / better clothes //

Was tut **die Schwester** *endlich?* // to obey / and / to set out for / home //

Schon sind die Reiter da. Was tun **sie** *noch von den Pferden herab?* // to ask for / sister //

Was **wird** *ängstlich* geantwortet? // that / she / not / to be / there / at the moment // that / she / to come (*future tense*) / later //

Wie **wird** *diese Antwort* aufgenommen? // indifferently //

Was **scheint** *vor allem* wichtig? // that / they / to have found / brother //

4. Wie hat sich die Situation am Ende der Parabel verändert?

Wem **steht** *der Bruder* jetzt gegenüber? // judge / and / silent assistant //

Wozu **wird** *der Bruder* aufgefordert? // to enter / living room / farmhouse //

Wie reagiert *er?* // slowly / to begin / to move //

Was **sagt** der Richter, *als der Bruder die Schwelle überschritten hat?* // that / he / to feel sorry / for / this man //

Was *ist* **über allem** Zweifel? // that / he / by this / not / to mean / present state / but (that) / what / to happen (würde-form) / to him //

Wie sieht **die Stube** aus? // to resemble / prison cell //

Was **befindet** sich *in der Stube?* // embedded iron ring / and / something / that / to be / half a prison cot / half an operation table //

5. Wir haben in den ersten vier Fragen die Veränderung der äußeren Situation des Bruders dargestellt. Wie ändert sich die Haltung (attitude) des Bruders, während sich seine Situation verändert?

Wie reagiert *der Bruder* auf die Leute aus dem Dorf, als sie ihm sagen, daß die Hofbesitzer ihn und seine Schwester verklagen werden? // to be calm / and / to calm / sister //
Was **glaubt er?** // that / she / probably / not / to have knocked / gate //
Was **versucht er den Leuten begreiflich zu machen?** // that / nowhere / in / world / proof / to be furnished / on account of that //
Die Leute enthalten sich eines Urteils. Wie reagiert *der Bruder,* als die Leute ihm sagen, daß auch er angeklagt werden würde? // to nod / smiling //
Was *aber* tut **er, als er die Reiter kommen sieht?** // to urge / sister / to leave //
Was **sagt er ihr?** // that / he / to straighten out / everything / by himself //
Was **glaubt *der Bruder* immer noch,** als er aufgefordert wird, in die Bauernstube einzutreten? // that / one word / to be enough / in order to free / him / city man / from / peasant folk //
Was **ist *die große Frage*** am Ende der Parabel? // whether / he / still / to be able / to taste / any other air / than / air / prison //
Aber ist das wirklich die große Frage? // it would be / great question / if / he / still / to have (*subj.*) / prospect / release //

C.   B-Questions

1. Was weiß und was kennt der Bruder am Anfang der Parabel nicht?
Was glaubt er deshalb?
Sind Sie der Meinung, daß es wichtig ist, ob die Schwester den Schlag ans Hoftor wirklich getan hat oder nicht? – Warum?

2. Wie beschreibt Kafka die Leute aus dem Dorf?
Was wissen und behaupten sie?
Wer sieht die wahre Situation von Anfang an, der Bruder oder die Leute?
Was bedeutet das für den Bruder?

3. Welcher Satz der Parabel zeigt uns, daß der Bruder zu ahnen beginnt, in welcher Situation er sich in Wahrheit befindet?
Und in welchen Sätzen zeigt Kafka, wie der Bruder beginnt, seine Haltung zu ändern? Was aber glaubt der Bruder immer noch?

4. Vergleichen Sie den Anfang und den Schluß der Parabel. Wie sieht der Bruder seine Situation am Ende? Wie stellt er sich zu dieser Situation?

hochgewachsen lanky; **Er strich sich mit der Hand über die Augen** He passed his hands over his eyes; **schwach** *here:* dim; **weichen, i, i** to give way, to yield; **der Stab, ⁔e** *here:* spoke

der Steuermann helmsman; **verscheuchen** *here:* to banish; **das Steuer** helm, steering wheel; **beiseite schieben, o, o** to push aside; **die Brust** chest; **nieder·treten, a, e** to trample down; **herum·reißen, i, i** *here:* to turn all the way

fassen to grasp; **die Luke, –n** hatch; **vertreiben, ie, ie** to drive away; **auf·steigen, ie, ie aus** (+ *dat.*) to emerge from, to ascend, to rise; **die Schiffstreppe, –n** hatchway; **mächtig** *here:* massive, huge; **die Gestalt, –en** figure, shape; **der Halbkreis, –e** semi-circle

etwas in Ordnung bringen, a, a to put it right; **weg·stoßen, ie, o** to shove away; **Ich besann mich** I came to my senses, I collected myself; **die Mannschaft, –en** crew; **schwanken** to stagger; **müde** tired; **Blicke hatten sie nur für den Fremden** They had eyes only for the stranger; **befehlen, a, o** to order, to command; **stören** to bother, to disturb; **sich sammeln** *here:* to gather, to assemble; **hinab·ziehen, o, o** *here:* to move down; **schlurfen** to shuffle

die Sünde, –n sin; **das Leid, –en** sorrow; **der wahre Weg, –e** the true path

die Betrachtung, –en view, consideration; **auf·lösen** to dissolve; **schwach** *here:* weak; **fest** *here:* solid; **schamhaft** ashamed; **zerschmettern** to shatter, to crush; **wagen** to dare

DER STEUERMANN

Bin ich nicht Steuermann?" rief ich. „Du?" fragte ein dunkler hochgewachsener Mann und strich sich mit der Hand über die Augen, als verscheuche er einen Traum. Ich war am Steuer gestanden in der dunklen Nacht, die schwachbrennende Laterne über meinem Kopf, und nun war dieser Mann gekommen und wollte mich beiseite schieben. Und da ich nicht wich, setzte er mir den Fuß auf die Brust und trat mich langsam nieder, während ich noch immer an den Stäben des Steuerrades hing und beim Niederfallen es ganz herumriß. Da aber faßte es der Mann, brachte es in Ordnung, mich aber stieß er weg. Doch ich besann mich bald, lief zur Luke, die in den Mannschaftsraum führte und rief: „Mannschaft! Kameraden! Kommt schnell! Ein Fremder hat mich vom Steuer vertrieben!" Langsam kamen sie, stiegen auf aus der Schiffstreppe, schwankende müde mächtige Gestalten. „Bin ich der Steuermann?" fragte ich. Sie nickten, aber Blicke hatten sie nur für den Fremden, im Halbkreis standen sie um ihn herum und, als er befehlend sagte: „Stört mich nicht," sammelten sie sich, nickten mir zu und zogen wieder die Schiffstreppe hinab. Was ist das für ein Volk! Denken sie auch oder schlurfen sie nur sinnlos über die Erde?

BETRACHTUNGEN ÜBER SÜNDE, LEID, HOFFNUNG UND DEN WAHREN WEG

Mit stärkstem Licht kann man die Welt auflösen. Vor schwachen Augen wird sie fest, vor noch schwächeren bekommt sie Fäuste, vor noch schwächeren wird sie schamhaft und zerschmettert den, der sie anzuschauen wagt.

IV. QUESTIONNAIRE

A. Exercises for the A-Questions

Study the following expressions.

1. Er brachte es in Ordnung. He put it right.
2. Er **besinnt sich** bald. He comes to his senses soon.
3. Sie **stiegen aus** der Schiffstreppe **auf.** They emerged from the hatchway.
4. Blicke hatten sie nur für den Fremden. They had eyes only for the stranger.

B.   A-Questions

1. Wie ist die Situation zu Beginn der Parabel?

Was erfahren wir über den *Erzähler?* // to have stood / ship's wheel //
Wer **ist gekommen?** // this man / who / to want / to push aside / him //
Was tut **der Mann,** *da der Erzähler nicht weicht?* // to put / foot / on / his chest / and / to trample down / slowly //
Was geschieht, **während der Erzähler niederfällt?** // he / to turn / ship's wheel / all the way //
Wie reagiert *der Mann?* // to put it right / and / to shove him away //

2. Wie ist die Situation am Ende der Parabel?

Was tut **der Erzähler?** // to come to his senses //
Wen **ruft er um Hilfe?** // crew / comrades //
Wie beschreibt Kafka **die Leute?** // (a) / to come / slowly / and / staggering / (b) / to be / tired
Was tun **sie,** *als er sie fragt, ob er der Steuermann sei?* // to nod / but / to stand / around / stranger //
Was **sagt** *der Fremde* da **befehlend?** // that / they / should / not / disturb / him //
Wie reagieren **die Leute?** // to nod to / narrator / and / to walk down / again / hatchway //

3. Die Parabel beginnt und endet mit Fragen.

Wie lautet die erste Frage? // narrator / to ask / whether / he / to be / not / helmsman //
Wie reagiert *der Fremde?* // to answer / with / question / Du? //
Dabei streicht er sich mit der Hand über die Augen. Wie **ist** *diese Bewegung?* // as if / he / to banish / dream //
Wann **wiederholt** *der Erzähler* seine Frage, diesmal ohne das „nicht"? // when / he / to call / crew //
Wie reagieren **die Leute?** // to nod / but / to have eyes / only / for / stranger //
Welche **Fragen stellt der Erzähler** *am Ende der Parabel?* // (a) / what kind of people / they / to be / (b) / whether / they / also / to think / or / whether / they / to shuffle along / only senselessly / over / earth //

C.   B-Questions

1. Vergleichen Sie die Haltung des Fremden mit der des Erzählers.
Wie spricht und was sagt der Fremde, als er am Steuer steht?
Von wem macht der Erzähler es abhängig, ob er der Steuermann ist oder nicht?

2. Welche Wirkung hat die Haltung des Erzählers auf die Mannschaft, und welche Wirkung die Haltung des Fremden?
Was, glauben Sie, repräsentieren diese Haltungen?

D.   C-Questions (Essay)

1. Was könnte uns Kafkas Betrachtung über die Bedeutung der Parabeln ,,Der Steuermann'' und ,,Der Schlag ans Hoftor'' sagen?

den **Kopf senken** to bend one's head; **ringsum** all around; **fest** *here:* firm, safe, secure; **aus·strecken** to stretch out; **geduckt** cowering, cringing; **unübersehbar** innumerable; **das Heer, –e** *here:* host, large number; **die Stirn, –en** forehead; **drücken** to press; **gegen . . . hin** toward; **atmen** to breathe; **durch Schwenken** by swinging; **der Reisighaufen, –** (MII) pile of brushwood

versunken submerged; **die Schauspielerei, –en** acting; **unschuldig** innocent; **die Selbsttäuschung, –en** self-deception; **die Matratze, –n** mattress; **das Tuch, ⸚er** sheet; **sich zusammen·finden, a, u** to gather; **wüst** waste, desolate; **die Gegend, –en** region; **das Lager, –** camp; **im Freien** in the open; **wachen** to guard

NACHTS

Versunken in die Nacht. So wie man manchmal den Kopf senkt, um nachzudenken, so ganz versunken sein in die Nacht. Ringsum schlafen die Menschen. Eine kleine Schauspielerei, eine unschuldige Selbsttäuschung, daß sie in Häusern schlafen, in festen Betten, unter festem Dach, ausgestreckt oder geduckt auf Matratzen, in Tüchern, unter Decken, in Wirklichkeit haben sie sich zusammengefunden wie damals einmal und wie später in wüster Gegend, ein Lager im Freien, eine unübersehbare Zahl von Menschen, ein Heer, ein Volk, unter kaltem Himmel auf kalter Erde, hingeworfen wo man früher stand, die Stirn auf den Arm gedrückt, das Gesicht gegen den Boden hin, ruhig atmend. Und du wachst, bist einer der Wächter, findest den nächsten durch Schwenken des brennenden Holzes aus dem Reisighaufen neben dir. Warum wachst du? Einer muß wachen, heißt es. Einer muß da sein.

V.   QUESTIONNAIRE

A.   A-Questions

1. In welchem Zustand befindet sich *das Du*? // to be submerged / night / in order to ponder //

Was tun dagegen *die Menschen ringsum*? // to sleep //
Was *ist eine unschuldige Selbsttäuschung*? // that / they / to sleep / houses / beds / roof / mattresses / sheets //
Was aber **ist *die Wirklichkeit*?** // they / to have gathered / in / waste area / in the open / under / cold skies / in / cold soil / thrown down / face / toward / earth //
Was **ist dagegen *die Aufgabe des Du*?** // (*a*) / to guard // (*b*) / to be / one of / guardsmen //
Warum **wacht *das Du*?** // because / it / to be said / that / one / to have to guard / that / one / to have to be / there //

B.   B-Questions

1. Was hält der Erzähler, der, in die Nacht versunken, nachdenkt, für die Selbsttäuschung, für die Wirklichkeit und für die Aufgabe der Menschen?

C.   C-Questions (Essay)

Betrachten wir die Parabeln Kafkas, die wir gelesen haben:

1. Welches menschliche Verhältnis ist überall dominierend?
   Welches fehlt vollkommen?

2. In welchem Widerspruch befinden sich die Hauptfiguren, und was ist ihr Irrtum?

3. Wie ist die „Welt" dieser Parabeln? Woraus besteht sie und was fehlt darin? (Situationen, Personen, Verhältnisse, Gedanken und Gefühle.)

APPENDIX

I. PRINCIPAL PARTS OF STRONG AND IRREGULAR VERBS

Infinitive	3rd sing. pres.	Imperfect	Perf. part.	Meaning
backen	bäckt	buk or backte	gebacken	to bake
befehlen	befiehlt	befahl	befohlen	to order, command
beginnen		begann	begonnen	to begin, start
beißen		biß	gebissen	to bite
bergen	birgt	barg	geborgen	to shelter, house
bersten	birst	barst	ist geborsten	to burst
bewegen		bewog	bewogen	to induce
biegen		bog	gebogen	to bend
bieten		bot	geboten	to offer
binden		band	gebunden	to bind
bitten		bat	gebeten	to request
blasen	bläst	blies	geblasen	to blow
bleiben		blieb	ist geblieben	to remain
braten	brät	briet	gebraten	to fry, roast
brechen	bricht	brach	hat, ist gebrochen	to break
brennen		brannte	gebrannt	to burn
bringen		brachte	gebracht	to bring
denken		dachte	gedacht	to think
dingen		dingte or dang	gedungen	to hire, engage
dreschen	drischt	drosch	gedroschen	to thresh
dringen	dringt	drang	gedrungen	to urge, press, penetrate
dünken	(es) dünkt (mich)	deuchte	gedeucht	to seem, appear
dürfen	darf	durfte	gedurft	to be allowed
empfehlen	empfiehlt	empfahl	empfohlen	to recommend
erbleichen		erblich	ist erblichen	to grow pale
erlöschen	erlischt	erlosch	ist erloschen	to go out (said of a light)
erschrecken	erschrickt	erschrak	ist erschrocken	to become frightened
erwägen		erwog	erwogen	to consider
essen	ißt	aß	gegessen	to eat (said of people)
fahren	fährt	fuhr	hat, ist gefahren	to drive
fallen	fällt	fiel	ist gefallen	to fall
fangen	fängt	fing	gefangen	to catch
fechten	ficht	focht	gefochten	to fence, fight
finden		fand	gefunden	to find
flechten	flicht	flocht	geflochten	to braid

I. PRINCIPAL PARTS OF STRONG AND IRREGULAR VERBS *(continued)*

Infinitive	*3rd sing. pres.*	*Imperfect*	*Perf. part.*	*Meaning*
fliegen		floh	ist geflohen	to flee
fließen		floß	ist geflossen	to flow
fressen	frißt	fraß	gefressen	to eat (said of animals)
frieren		fror	gefroren	to freeze
gären		gor	gegoren	to ferment
gebären	gebiert	gebar	geboren	to give birth
geben	gibt	gab	gegeben	to give
gedeihen		gedieh	ist gediehen	to thrive
gehen		ging	ist gegangen	to go, walk
gelingen	(es) gelingt	gelang	ist gelungen	to succeed
gelten	gilt	galt	gegolten	to be valid
genesen		genas	ist genesen	to regain health, recover
genießen		genoß	genossen	to enjoy
geschehen	geschieht	geschah	ist geschehen	to happen
gewinnen		gewann	gewonnen	to win
gießen		goß	gegossen	to pour
gleichen		glich	geglichen	to resemble
gleiten		glitt	ist geglitten	to glide
glimmen		glomm or glimmte	geglommen or geglimmt	to glimmer
graben	gräbt	grub	gegraben	to dig
greifen		griff	gegrifften	to seize
haben	hat	hatte	gehabt	to have
halten	hält	hielt	gehalten	to hold
hängen		hing	gehangen	to hang
hauen		hieb (haute)	gehauen	to hit, strike
heben		hob	gehoben	to lift
heißen		hieß	geheißen	to be called
helfen	hilft	half	geholfen	to help
kennen		kannte	gekannt	to know
klimmen		klomm	ist geklommen	to climb
klingen		klang	ist geklungen	to sound
kneifen		kniff	gekniffen	to pinch
kommen		kam	ist gekommen	to come
können	kann	konnte	gekonnt	to be able, can
kriechen		kroch	ist gekrochen	to crawl, creep
laden	lädt	lud	geladen	to load
(ein)laden	lädt or ladet (ein)	lud (ein)	(ein)geladen	to invite
lassen	läßt	ließ	gelassen	to leave, let
laufen	läuft	lief	ist gelaufen	to run

Infinitive	3rd sing. pres.	Imperfect	Perf. part.	Meaning
leiden		litt	gelitten	to suffer
leihen		lieh	geliehen	to lend
lesen		las	gelesen	to read
liegen		lag	gelegen	to lie (flat), be situated
lügen		log	gelogen	to (tell a) lie
mahlen		mahlte	gemahlen	to grind
meiden		mied	gemieden	to avoid
melken		melkte or molk	gemelkt or gemolken	to milk
messen	mißt	maß	gemessen	to measure
mögen	mag	mochte	gemocht	to like; may
müssen	muß	mußte	gemußt	to have to, must
nehmen	nimmt	nahm	genommen	to take
nennen		nannte	genannt	to name
pfeifen		pfiff	gepfiffen	to whistle
preisen		pries	gepriesen	to praise
quellen	quillt	quoll	ist gequollen	to gush
raten	rät	riet	geraten	to advise
reiben		rieb	gerieben	to rub
reißen		riß	hat, ist gerissen	to rip
reiten		ritt	hat, ist geritten	to ride
rennen		rannte	ist gerannt	to run
riechen		roch	gerochen	to smell
ringen		rang	gerungen	to wrestle, struggle
rinnen		rann	ist geronnen	to run, flow, leak
rufen		rief	gerufen	to call
salzen		salzte	gesalzen	to salt
saufen	säuft	soff	gesoffen	to drink (of animals)
saugen		sog	gesogen	to suck
schaffen		schuf	geschaffen	to create
schallen		scholl	ist geschollen	to sound, peal
scheiden		schied	geschieden	to separate
scheinen		schien	geschienen	to shine, seem
schelten	schilt	schalt	gescholten	to scold
scheren		schor	geschoren	to shear, trim
schieben		schob	geschoben	to push, shove
schießen		schoß	geschossen	to shoot
schlafen	schläft	schlief	geschlafen	to sleep
schlagen	schlägt	schlug	geschlagen	to beat, strike
schleichen		schlich	ist geschlichen	to sneak
schleifen		schliff	geschliffen	to grind, sharpen

I. PRINCIPAL PARTS OF STRONG AND IRREGULAR VERBS *(continued)*

Infinitive	3rd sing. pres.	Imperfect	Perf. part.	Meaning
schließen		schloß	geschlossen	to close
schlingen		schlang	geschlungen	to tie, twist
schmeißen		schmiß	geschmissen	to throw, fling
schmelzen	schmilzt	schmolz	hat, ist geschmolzen	to melt
schreiben		schrieb	geschrieben	to write
schreien		schrie	geschrien	to cry, yell
schreiten		schritt	ist geschritten	to stride, step
schweigen		schwieg	geschwiegen	to be silent
schwellen	schwillt	schwoll	ist geschwollen	to swell
schwimmen		schwamm	hat, ist geschwommen	to swim
schwinden		schwand	ist geschwunden	to disappear
schwingen		schwang	geschwungen	to swing
schwören		schwor, schwur	geschworen	to swear
sehen	sieht	sah	gesehen	to see
sein	ist	war	ist gewesen	to be
senden		sandte	gesandt	to send
sieden		sott	gesotten	to seethe, boil
singen		sang	gesungen	to sing
sinken		sank	ist gesunken	to sink
sinnen		sann	gesonnen	to think, meditate
sitzen		saß	gesessen	to sit
sollen	soll	sollte	gesollt	to be (supposed) to, shall
spalten	spaltet	spaltete	gespalten	to split
speien		spann	gesponnen	to spin
sprechen	spricht	sprach	gesprochen	to speak
sprießen		sproß	ist gesprossen	to sprout
springen		sprang	ist gesprungen	to spring
stechen	sticht	stach	gestochen	to prick
stehen		stand	gestanden	to stand
stehlen	stiehlt	stahl	gestohlen	to steal
steigen		stieg	ist gestiegen	to climb, ascend
sterben	stirbt	starb	ist gestorben	to die
stinken		stank	gestunken	to smell bad, stink
stoßen	stößt	stieß	gestoßen	to push, hit
streichen		strich	gestrichen	to stroke
streiten		stritt	gestritten	to argue, fight
tragen	trägt	trug	getragen	to carry
treffen	trifft	traf	getroffen	to meet
treiben		trieb	getrieben	to drive
treten	tritt	trat	hat, ist getreten	to step

Infinitive	3rd sing. pres.	Imperfect	Perf. part.	Meaning
trinken		trank	getrunken	to drink
trügen		trog	getrogen	to deceive
tun		tat	getan	to do
verderben	verdirbt	verdarb	hat, ist verdorben	to spoil
verdrießen	(es) verdrießt (mich)	verdroß	verdrossen	to annoy
vergessen	vergißt	vergaß	vergessen	to forget
verlieren		verlor	verloren	to lose
verzeihen		verzieh	verziehen	to pardon
wachsen	wächst	wuchs	ist gewachsen	to grow
waschen	wäscht	wusch	gewaschen	to wash
weben		wob	gewoben	to weave
weichen		wich	ist gewichen	to give way, yield
weisen		wies	gewiesen	to indicate, show
wenden		wandte or wendete	gewandt or gewendet	to turn
werben	wirbt	warb	geworben	to woo, recruit
werden	wird	wurde	ist geworden	to become
werfen	wirft	warf	geworfen	to throw
wiegen		wog	gewogen	to weigh
winden		wand	gewunden	to wind, roll, wreathe
wissen	weiß	wußte	gewußt	to know
wollen	will	wollte	gewollt	to want, will
ziehen		zog	hat, ist gezogen	to pull, move
zwingen		zwang	gezwungen	to force

II. COMPOUNDS WITH SEPARABLE AND INSEPARABLE PREFIXES

ab-	abspringen	to jump off
abwärts-	abwärtsfahren	to drive down
an-	annehmen	to assume, accept
auf-	aufgeben	to give up
aufwärts-	aufwärtssteigen	to climb up
aus-	ausziehen	to pull out, move, undress
be-	bekennen	to confess
bei-	beitragen	to contribute to
da-	dableiben	to stay (there)
durch-	durchfallen	to fall through, fail (an exam)
ein-	eindringen	to intrude
emp-	empfangen	to receive
empor-	emporsteigen	to mount

II. COMPOUNDS WITH SEPARABLE AND INSEPARABLE PREFIXES *(continued)*

ent-	entfliehen	to escape, flee
entgegen-	entgegenhalten	to contrast with
entlang-	entlanglaufen	to run along
er-	erfinden	to invent
fort-	fortfahren	to depart, continue
ge-	geraten	to get into
gegenüber-	gegenüberstehen	to face
her-	herkommen	to come here
hin-	hingehen	to go there
hinter-	hinterlassen	to bequeath, leave behind
los-	loslassen	to let go
miß-	mißverstehen	to misunderstand
mit-	mitbringen	to bring (along)
nach-	nachdenken	to reflect, meditate
nahe-	nahestehen	to be closely connected with
über-	überladen	to overload
um-	umringen	to surround
unter-	unterwerfen	to subject
ver-	verstehen	to understand
voll-	vollbringen	to accomplish
vor-	vorziehen	to prefer
weg-	weglaufen	to run away
wider-	widersprechen	to contradict
wieder-	wiedersehen	to see or meet again
zer-	zerreißen	to rip to pieces
zu-	zufrieren	to freeze over
zurück-	zurücktreten	to step back
zusammen-	zusammenfallen	to collapse

VOCABULARY

A

ab – off

ab und zu from time to time

ab·biegen, o, o to turn off

der Abend, –e evening

    heute abend tonight

    gestern abend last night

die Abendausgabe, –n evening edition

das Abendessen supper

abendländisch occidental, western

aber but, however

ab·fahren, u, a (fährt ab) (ist) to depart, to leave

ab·fertigen to dispatch

abgearbeitet worn out by work

ab·geben, a, e (gibt ab) to deliver

abgedämpft stifled

die Abgefeimtheit cunning, infamy

ab·gehen, i, a (ist) to branch off

abgeseilt roped off

abgestoßen pushed aside, repelled

abgewendet sein to be off guard

ab·hängen von to depend on

ab·holen to pick up

das Abitur German high school diploma

    Er machte das Abitur He received the high school diploma

sich ab·mühen to exert oneself, to labor

ab·nehmen, a, o (nimmt ab) to take, to take off, to remove, to reduce

die Abneigung, –en aversion, dislike

ab·reiben, ie, ie to rub down

die Abreise, –n departure

abreißen, i, i to tear off

ab·schließen, o, o to lock

der Abschnitt, –e section, part

ab·schreiben, ie, ie to copy

die Abschrift, –en copy

ab·setzen to set down

die Absicht, –en intention

der Abstecher, – digression

ab·trennen to separate

sich ab·wenden, a, a von (+ dat.) to turn away from

abwesend absent-minded

achten auf (acc.) to pay attention to

der Acker, ⁓ soil, land

ahnen to sense, to suspect

ahnungslos unsuspecting, unconscious

der Akzent, –e accent

all – all

    alle drei Wochen every three weeks

die Allee, –n avenue

allerangenehmst most pleasant, delightful

allerdings of course, to be sure, indeed

allerhand all sorts of

alles everything, all

die Alliierten the Allies

der Alptraum, ⁓e nightmare

als as, when, than

    als ob ... (+ subj.) as if ...

    nichts als nothing but

also thus, so, therefore

alt old

die Amme, –n nursemaid

das Amt, ⁓er office, position

    das Statistische Amt Bureau of Statistics

an at, to, on

die Analyse, –n analysis

an·bieten, o, o to offer

der Anblick, –e sight, view

an·brüllen to bellow at, to roar

ander– other

ändern to change

anders different

die Änderung, –en change, alteration

an·deuten to insinuate, hint

andrerseits on the other hand

die Anerkennung, –en recognition

an·fahren, u, a (ist) to start

der Anfang, ⁓e beginning

an·fangen, i, a (fängt an) to begin

die Anfangssituation, –en situation at the beginning

an·fassen an (+ dat.) to take hold of by

an·fragen to inquire

an·geben, a, e (gibt an) to declare

angefahren hit (by a car)

an·gehören (+ dat.) to belong to

der Angehörige, –n (adj.) member

angelsächsisch Anglo-Saxon

angenehm pleasant

der Angestellte, –n (*adj.*) employee

die Anglistik study of English language and
    literature

die Angst, ⸚e fear

  Angst haben vor (+ *dat.*) to be afraid of

ängstlich nervous, anxious

an·hängen, to attach, label

an·heften to pin on

an·hören (+ *acc.*) = zuhören (+ *dat.*) to listen to

an·klagen to accuse, sue

an·kommen, a, o (ist) to arrive

  darauf kommt es an that's what matters

  es kommt drauf an it depends

die Ankunft, ⸚e arrival

an·lachen to laugh at

die Annahme, –n assumption

an·nehmen, a, o to adopt, assume, accept

die Anordnung, –en arrangement

an·passen to adapt

  sich an·passen (*dat.*) to conform to

die Anpassung, –en adaptation

an·reden to speak to

an·rühren to touch

an·schauen to look at, to consider

anscheinend apparently

die Anschlagsäule, –n advertisement pillar, billboard

an·schreien, ie, ie to shout at

an·schwindeln to swindle, to cheat

an·sehen, a, e (sieht an) to look at

  sich etwas an·sehen to have a (close) look at
    something

an·spannen to harness

die Ansprache, –n address

anständig decent

anstatt instead of

an·stecken to light up

  eine Zigarette an·stecken to light a cigarette

an·stellen to place; to hire

an·stoßen, ie, o (stößt an) to push

an·strengen to exert

antik ancient

die Antwort, –en answer

antworten (+ *dat.*) to answer

  antworten auf (+ *acc.*) to answer to

an·vertrauen to entrust

an·weisen, ie, ie to direct, to instruct

das Anwesen, – premises, estate

anwesend present

das Anzeichen, – = das Zeichen sign

an·ziehen, o, o to attract, put on

  sich anziehen to get dressed

der Anzug, ⸚e suit

an·zünden to light, to kindle

der Apfel, ⸚ apple

die Apotheke, –n pharmacy

applaudieren to applaud

die Arbeit, –en work

  bei der Arbeit at work

arbeiten to work

die Arbeiter-Unfall-Versicherungsanstalt accident
    insurance company for workers

der Arbeitsdienst, –e premilitary labor service

ärgerlich angry

arm poor

das Ärmchen, – little arm

ärmlich poor, shabby

die Art, –en kind, sort

der Arzt, ⸚e physician

atemlos breathless

atmen to breathe

auf einmal all at once

der Aufbau building up, erection

auf·bauen to build up

auf·bewahren to store

auf·bringen, a, a to exasperate

der Aufenthalt, –e stay

auf·fahren, u, a (fährt auf) to drive up

auf·fangen, i, a (fängt auf) to catch

auf·fordern to ask, to request, to command

auf·fressen, a, e (frißt auf) to eat, to gobble up

die Aufführung, –en performance

die Aufgabe, –n job, task, lesson

auf·geben, a, e (gibt auf) to give up

auf·gehen, i, a (ist) to open, rise

aufgeregt excited

aufgetakelt rigged up

auf·greifen, i, i to catch

auf·halten, ie, a (hält auf) to stop, to detain

  sich aufhalten mit to spend time (on)

auf·hängen, i, a to hang up, to suspend

auf·hören to stop

auf·leuchten to become bright

auf·lösen to dissolve

  sich auf·lösen to disperse, to split up

die Aufmachung, –en display, show

auf·nehmen, a, o (nimmt auf) to receive to record

(sich) auf·opfern to sacrifice (oneself)

auf·passen to watch, to look out for, be careful,
    to stand guard

  auf·passen auf (+ *acc.*) to stand guard over,
    to watch out for

auf·patschen to slap, to clap

aufrecht·erhalten, ie, a (erhält aufrecht) to keep up,
    to maintain

auf·regen to excite

auf·richten to straighten up
    sich auf·richten to raise oneself up
auf·rufen, ie, u to call
auf·schauen to look up
auf·schlagen, u, a (schlägt auf) to break open,
    to strike
    Mein Herz schlägt auf My heart leaps with joy
auf·schreien, ie, ie to cry out
auf·setzen to put on (a hat)
auf·stehen, a, a to stand up, to get up
auf·steigen, ie, ie (ist) to arise
    auf·steigen, ie, ie aus (+ dat.) to emerge from,
    to ascend, to rise
auf·suchen to go and see
auf·summen to hum
auf·tauen to thaw
auf·wachsen, u, a (ist) – (wächst auf) to grow up
der Aufwand an (+ dat.) display, expenditure of
das Auge, –n eye
    aus fischigen Augen with fishlike eyes
der Augenblick, –e moment, instant
augenblicklich at the moment
das Augenlicht eyesight
die Ausbildung, –en education
aus·bleiben, ie, ie (ist) to fail to appear
aus·brechen, a, o (ist) to break out, to escape
der Ausdruck, ⁻e expression
aus·drücken to express, to put out
ausdrücklich explicit
aus·fallen, i, a (ist) to turn out
    Die Verhandlungen fallen so kürzer aus The
    proceedings end more quickly this way
aus·fragen über (+ acc.) to question about
ausgebombt bombed out
aus·gehen, i, a (ist) to go out
ausgemergelt emaciated
ausgesetzt sein (+ dat.) to be exposed to
aus·halten, ie, a (hält aus) to stand, to endure
aus·handeln to conclude (a deal)
sich aus·kennen, a, a to know where one is,
    to be at home with, to be well versed in
aus·machen to agree upon
aus·rechnen to calculate, to figure out
aus·reden to talk out of
aus·richten to give a message, to accomplish
sich aus·ruhen to rest
sich aus·rüsten to equip oneself
die Aussage, –n statement
aus·sagen to state, to declare
aus·schicken to send out
aus·sehen, a, e (sieht aus) to look, to appear
äußer– outer, external
außerhalb outside of

äußern to disclose
äußerst exceeding (ly), outermost
die Äußerung, –en remark
aus·setzen to pause, to discontinue
    Sein Herz setzt aus His heart skips a beat
Aussicht auf (+ acc.) prospect of
aus·spannen to unharness
die Ausstellung, –en exhibition
aus·stoßen, ie, o to emit, to utter, to dispel
aus·strecken to stretch out
aus·suchen to select, to choose
aus·tragen, u, a (trägt aus) to carry out
    einen Rechtsstreit austragen to settle a dispute
aus·üben to exercise, to practice, to exert
die Auswahl selection
aus·wählen to select, to choose
der Ausweis, –e identification
das Auto, –s automobile
der Automat, –en (MII) automat, vending machine
der Autor, –en author

B

die Backe, –n cheek
der Bahnhof, ⁻e train station
die Bahre, –n stretcher, bier
bald soon
bangen um (+ acc.) to worry about, to fear for
die Bank, ⁻e bench
der Bankert, –e bastard
die Bar, –s bar
der Bart, ⁻e beard
die Basis, –en basis, foundation
der Bataillonskommandeur, –e batallion commander
der Bauarbeiter, – construction worker
der Bauch, ⁻e belly, stomach
bauen to build
der Bauer, –n peasant, farmer
der Bauernhof, ⁻e farm
die Bauernstube, –n living room of a farmhouse
die Bauersleute (pl.) farm people
der Baumstumpf, ⁻e tree stump
beantragen to petition, to solicit, to propose
bearbeiten to work on
der Becher, – mug, cup, goblet
bedächtig with deliberation
bedauern to pity
bedenken, a, a to consider
bedeuten to mean, to signify
bedeutend significant
bedingen to stipulate, to set as a condition

die **Bedingung**, –en condition
sich **beeilen** to hurry, to hasten
beenden to finish, to end
der **Befehl**, –e order
befehlen, a, o to order, to command
sich **befinden**, a, u to be (located)
befragen to interrogate
befriedigt satisfied, content
begegnen (+ *dat.*) to encounter, to meet
die **Begegnung**, –en meeting, encounter
begeistert enthusiastic
begleiten to accompany
die **Begleitung** accompaniment
begnadigen to pardon
begreifen, i, i to grasp, to comprehend
begreiflich machen to make clear
der **Begriff**, –e concept
begrüßen to greet
behandeln to treat
behaupten to maintain, to declare
die **Behörde**, –n authority
behost trousered
bei at, near, in connection with, at the home of
bei·bringen, a, a to teach, to impress upon
beide(s) both
das **Bein**, –e leg
   krumme Beine bow legs
   schwach auf den Beinen weak in the knees
beinah almost
das **Beispiel**, –e example
   zum Beispiel, z.B. for example
der **Beitritt**, –e joining (of)
bei·wohnen (+ *dat.*) to attend
beizeiten in time
bekannt familiar, well known
   bekannt machen mit to acquaint with
der **Bekannte**, –n (*adj.*) acquaintance, friend
bekanntlich as is well known, notoriously
sich **bekennen**, a, a zu to embrace, to take up the cause, to avow loyalty to
bekommen, a, o to receive, to get
   zu Gesicht bekommen to set eyes on
bekümmert troubled
belebt busy
belegen to authenticate, to prove
beliebt popular
bellen to bark
die **Belohnung**, –en reward
belügen to lie to
sich **bemächtigen** (+ *gen.*) to get hold of, seize
bemalt painted
sich **bemühen** to try
sich **benehmen**, a, o to behave

benommen dizzy
beobachten to watch, to study
die **Beratung**, –en consultation
sich **berauschen an** (+ *dat.*) to become intoxicated with
die **Berechnung**, –en calculation
der **Bereich**, –e area, sphere
bereit ready
   bereits already
der **Berg**, –e mountain
der **Bericht**, –e report
berichten to relate, to report
bersten, a, o (birst) to burst
beruhigen to calm
berühmt famous
berühren to touch
sich **beschäftigen mit** to busy oneself with
der **Bescheid** word, information
beschlagen fogged up
beschließen, o, o to decide
beschreiben, ie, ie to describe
sich **beschweren** to complain
beschwerlich difficult, troublesome
besingen, a, u to celebrate
sich **besinnen**, a, o to come to one's senses, to collect oneself
   ohne Besinnung unconscious
besitzen, a, e to own, to possess
der **Besitzer**, – proprietor, owner
besonder– special, specific
   besonders especially
besprechen, a, o (bespricht) to discuss
die **Besprechung**, –en discussion
die **Besserung**, –en recovery
bestätigen to confirm
bestechen, a, o (besticht) to bribe
bestehen, a, a to exist, to subsist, to last, to continue
bestehen aus to consist of
bestehen auf (+ *dat.*) to insist upon
bestellen to order
bestimmen to determine
   bestimmt definite, certain
   bestimmt sein für to be intended for
der **Besuch**, –e visit, attendance
der **Besucher**, – visitor
betäubt stupefied, benumbed, stunned
der **Beteiligte**, –n (*adj.*) participant
betrachten to look, to gaze at
die **Betrachtung**, –en view, consideration
betreten, a, e (betritt) to enter
betrunken drunk
das **Bett**, –en bed
beugen to bend

beunruhigen to perturb
die **Beute** loot
die **Bevölkerung, –en** population
bewegen to move
die **Bewegung, –en** movement, motion
der **Beweis, –e** proof
beweisen, ie, ie to prove
bewundern to admire
das **Bewußtsein** consciousness
   in dem Bewußtsein with the knowledge
bezahlen to pay
bezeichnen to designate
die **Bezeichnung, –en** designation
sich **beziehen o, o auf** (+ *acc.*) to refer to
die **Bibel, –n** bible
die **Bibliothek, –en** library
der **Bibliothekar, –e** librarian
die **Biederkeit** honesty
das **Bier, –e** beer
das **Bild, –er** picture
der **Bildhauer, –** sculptor
die **Bildung** education, training
die **Bildungswelt** educated world, world of education
billig cheap
bis until, up to, as far as, by
bisher until now
ein **bißchen** a little
bissig biting
die **Bitte, –n** request
bitten, a, e to beg
   bitten um to ask for
blank shiny
blaß pale
das **Blatt, ⸚er** piece of paper, leaf, newspaper
blättern in (+ *dat.*) to leaf through
das **Blech** tin
die **Blechmusik** brass band
die **Blechschachtel, –n** tin box
bleiben, ie, ie (ist) to stay, to remain
der **Blick, –e** glance, sight
   Blicke haben für to have eyes for
blicken to look, to glance
   blicken auf (+ *acc.*) to look on, to glance at
blind blind
blinken to blink, to gleam
blinzeln to blink
blitzen to flash
bloß bare, mere
das **Blut** blood
bluten to bleed
der **Boden, ⸚** floor, attic
   auf ebenem Boden on the bare floor
der **Bodensatz** sediment, dregs

der **Bodensee** Lake Constance
die **Bombe, –n** bomb
das **Boot, –e** boat
böse angry, bad, evil
   böse sein (+ *dat.*) to be angry with (someone)
der **Bote, –n** (*MII*) messenger
die **Botschaft, –en** message
brabbeln to gurgle
brackig brackish
brauchen to need, to use
brechen, a, o (ist) (hat) to break, to stem
breit broad, wide
die **Bremse, –n** brake
brennen, a, a to burn
das **Brett, –er** board
der **Brief, –e** letter
die **Briefadresse, –n** letter address
die **Brille, –n** glasses
bringen, a, a to bring
   etwas in Ordnung bringen to put something right
   etwas ins Reine bringen to straighten something out
der **Brocken, –** morsel
das **Brot, –e** bread, loaf of bread
das **Bruchstückhafte** (*adj.*) the fragmentlike
die **Brücke, –n** bridge
brüllen to scream, to roar
brummen to growl
   vor sich hin·brummen to mutter, to grumble to oneself
brüsk brusk, curt, blunt
die **Brust** chest
die **Buchhandlung, –en** bookshop
der **Buchstabe, –n** (*MII*) letter of the alphabet
   große Buchstaben capital letters
   kleine Buchstaben lowercase letters
buchstabieren to spell
sich **bücken** to bend down
   sich vor Schrecken bücken to cower in terror
bumsen to bump
das **Bündel, –** bundle
bunt multicolored, colorful
bürgerlich bourgeois
der **Bursche, –n** (*MII*) fellow

C

das **Café, –s** café, coffeehouse
charakterisieren to characterize
der **Chef, –s** boss

der Cherfarzt, ⸚e medical superintendent
christlich christian

D

da since, because; there, here, then
dabei besides, moreover, considering, and yet
der Dachfirst, –e rafter
daher in that way, from there, thus
damalig of that time
damals at that time
damit in order that; with it
der Dank thanks
    vielen Dank many thanks, thank you very much
dankbar thankful
danken (+ *dat.*) to thank
dann then
daraufhin whereupon
dar·stellen to present, to show
das Datum, Daten date
dauern to take (time), to last
davon·stolpern to stumble away
das Deckbett, –en feather bed
die Decke, –n blanket, cover, ceiling
defilieren (*milit.*) to march past
denken, a, a to think
    denken an (+ *acc.*) to think of, about
    sich denken to imagine
denkwürdig noteworthy
denn for (*conj.*)
denunzieren to denounce
derb blunt
deswegen on account of that
detailiert detailed
deuten auf to point to
das geteilte Deutschland divided Germany
die Deutung, –en interpretation
dialektisch dialectical
dicht close
der Dichter, – poet
dick fat, thick
der Dieb, –e thief
die Diele, –n large hall
der Dienst, –e service
die Diktatur, –en dictatorship
das Ding, –e thing, matter
dirigieren to conduct, to indicate
dividieren to divide
doch anyway, nonetheless
der juristische Doktorgrad doctor of law
die Donau Danube River

Donnerwetter, ja! Good Heavens! You're right!
doppelt double, twofold
das Dorf, ⸚er village
der Dorsch, –e cod fish
dösen to doze
das Drama, Dramen drama
der Dramatiker, – dramatist
drängen to thrust
    sich drängen to crowd and shove, to force
    one's way
draußen outside, outdoors, out there
drehen to turn
    Zigaretten drehen to roll cigarettes
dreimal thrice, three times
dreißigjährig thirty-year-old
dringen, a, u (ist) to force one's way, penetrate
dringend strongly, urgent
drohen to threaten
dröhnen to thunder, to boom
drüben over there
drücken to press
    sich drücken to beat it (*slang*)
das Dunkel the dark
dünn thin
der Dunst, ⸚e smell
    der Dunst nach smell of
durchdringen, a, u (ist) to penetrate
durchfahren, u, a (ist) (fährt durch) to drive or
    pass through
    es durchfuhr ihn he shuddered
durch·halten, ie, a (hält durch) to endure, to hold
    out
durch·kommen, a, o (ist) to get through, to get
    away with (*slang*)
durchlaufen, ie, au (ist) (durchläuft) to run through
durchmessen, a, e (durchmißt) to cross
der Durchschnitt, –e average
sich durch·setzen to prevail
    durch·setzen to carry through, to put into effect
durchsuchen to search
die Durchsuchung, –en search
dürfen, u, u (darf) to be permitted to, to be
    allowed to
das Dutzend dozen

E

eben just, even
    auf ebenem Boden on the bare floor
ebenfalls likewise, also
echt real, genuine

die Ecke, −n corner
egal all the same; equal
    egal sein (+ *dat*.) not to matter to (someone)
egoistisch egoistical
ehelichen to marry
eher sooner, earlier
die Ehre, −n honor
    sogar noch unter Ehren even honorably
eichen oaken
eigenartig peculiar
eigensinnig stubborn
eigentlich actual(ly), real(ly)
das Eigentum, ⸚er personal property
ein · biegen, o, o (ist) in (+ *acc*.) to turn into
sich ein · bilden to imagine, to fancy
die Einbildung, −en imagination, illusion
der Eindruck, ⸚e impression
einfach simple
ein · färben to dye
einfarbig of one color
der Einfluß, ⸚e (auf) (+ *acc*.) influence (on)
ein · führen to introduce
die Einführung, −en introduction
der Eingang, ⸚e entrance
ein · gehen, i, a (ist) to go into, to enter
    ein · gehen auf (+ *acc*.) to enter into, to agree to
eingemauert imbedded, immured
eingezogen werden, u, o (ist) (wird eingezogen) to be
    drafted
ein · heiraten to marry into
einige several, some
ein · kaufen to shop
ein · laden, u, a (lädt ein) to invite
die Einladung, −en invitation
der Einlaß, ⸚e entrance
ein · lassen, ie, a (läßt ein) to let in; to admit
die Einleitung, −en introduction
ein · lullen to lull in
einmal once
    auf einmal all at once
ein · nehmen, a, o gegen (nimmt ein) to prejudice
    against
ein · packen to pack up
die Einreise, −n entry
einsam lonely
die Einsamkeit loneliness
ein · schenken to pour in
    reinen Wein ein · schenken (+ *dat*.) to tell someone
    the whole truth
einschließlich including
der Einschnitt, −e cut, gap
ein · setzen to start up
ein · stecken to stick in; to pocket

ein · tauchen to immerse
ein · treten, a, e (ist) (tritt ein) to enter, to step into
der Eintritt, −e entry, admission
der Einundzwanzigjährige, −n (*adj*.) the twenty-one-
    year-old
einzeln separate, individual, single
    der Einzelne, −n (*adj*.) individual
die Einzelzelle, −n solitary confinement
ein · ziehen, o, o to draft
die Eisdiele, −n ice-cream parlor
das Elend misery
der Ellbogen, − elbow
die Eltern (*pl*.) parents
die Emigration, −en emigration
emigrieren to emigrate
empfangen, i, a (empfängt) to receive
empfinden, a, u to feel, to experience
die Empfindung, −en perception, sensation, feeling
empor · wenden zu to turn up to
das Ende, −n end
enden to end
die Entdeckung, −en discovery, disclosure
sich entfärben to lose color, to pale
entfernt far away, far off
entgegen · kommen, a, o (ist) (+ *dat*.) to come toward
entgegnen (*dat*.) to counter, to reply
das Entgelt, −e reward, compensation
enthalten, ie, a (enthält) to contain
    sich enthalten (+ *gen*.) to refrain from
entlang along
die Entlausungsanstalt, −en delousing station
entreißen, i, i to snatch away, to tear away
entscheiden, ie, ie to decide
entscheidend decisive
die Entscheidung, −en decision
sich entschließen, o, o to decide
entschlossen determined
der Entschluß, ⸚e decision
entschuldigen to excuse
das Entsetzen horror, shock
    vor Entsetzen in horror
entsetzt horrified
entstehen, a, a, (ist) to arise, to originate
enttäuscht disappointed
(sich) entwickeln to develop
die Epik, −en epic poetry
das Epos, Epen epic (poem)
erblicken to see, to catch sight of
die Erde ground, earth
sich ereignen to happen
das Ereignis, −se event
erfahren, u, a (erfährt) to learn, to find out
    erfahren über (+ *acc*.) to learn about

die **Erfahrung**, –en experience
der **Erfolg**, –e success
erfolglos without success
erfolgreich successful
ergeben, a, e **(ergibt)** to yield, to result in
das **Ergebnis**, –se result
sich **ergießen**, o, o to pour
ergreifen, i, i to seize
erhalten, ie, a **(erhält)** to receive
sich **erheben**, o, o to rise
erhellen to light up
erinnern to remind
  sich **erinnern an** (+ *acc.*) to remember
  erinnern an (+ *acc.*) to remind (someone) of
erkennen, a, a to recognize, to realize
  erkennen an (+ *dat.*) to recognize by
erklären to declare, to explain
erkrankt sein to be taken sick
sich **erkundigen (nach)** to inquire (about)
die **Erlaubnis**, –se permission
erleben to experience
erleiden, i, i to suffer
ermüden to tire, to weary
ernstlich serious
die **Ernte**, –n harvest
erobern to conquer
erpressen to extort
erproben to test
erregen to excite
  Aufsehen erregen to attract attention
erreichen to reach
erscheinen, ie, ie **(ist)** to appear
erschlagen, u, a **(erschlägt)** to beat to death
erschließen, o, o to open, to open up, to develop
erschrecken, to frighten
  (sich) erschrecken a, o **(erschrickt) (ist)** to be frightened
erschrocken dismayed, shocked
erst first, not until, only, not before
erstarren to stiffen
erstehen, a, a to buy
ertragen, u, a **(erträgt)** to stand, to endure
sich etwas **erträumen** to conjure up something
erwachsen adult
erwähnen to mention
erwarten to expect
die **Erwartung**, –en expectation
erwecken to arouse, to awaken
erweisen, ie, ie to render
erwidern (+ *dat.*) to reply
erwischen to catch
erzählen to tell, to narrate
der **Erzähler**, – narrator

der **Erzählerwettbewerb** contest for writers
die **Erzählform**, –en narrative form
die **Erzählung**, –en narration, story
erziehen, o, o to educate, to train
die **Erziehung** education
das **Erztor**, –e bronze gate
eßbar edible
das **Essen**, – meal
essen, a, e **(ißt)** to eat
etwas something; some, somewhat, rather
europäisch european
ewig for ever, eternal
die **Ewigkeit**, –en eternity
das **Examen**, –mina exam, test
das **Exil**, –e exile

F

der **Fabrikarbeiter**, – factory worker
der **Fachmann**, **Fachleute** expert
fähig (zu) able, capable (of)
die **Fähigkeit**, –en ability
fahl pale
fahren, u, a **(ist) (fährt)** to drive, to go
der **Fahrer**, – driver
der **Fahrweg**, –e road
der **Fall**, ⁔e case
  im Falle (+ *gen.*) in case of
fallen, ie, a **(ist)** to fall
  auf den Kopf gefallen sein to be a fool
  fallen lassen to drop
falls in case
falsch false, wrong
die **Falte**, –n fold, wrinkle
die **Farbe**, –n color, dye
der **Färber**, – dyer
farbig colored
die **Fassade**, –n front side, front, facade
fassen to take, to grasp
fast almost, half
faul lazy
die **Faust**, ⁔e fist
fehlen (+ *dat.*) to lack, to be in need of
feiern to celebrate
feig(e) cowardly
fein fine
der **Feindeinsatz**, ⁔e combat
feindlich hostile
die **Feindseligkeit**, –en hostility
feingekleidet well dressed
der **Feldherr**, –en (*MII*) commander, general
das **Fenster**, – window

die Ferien (*pl.*) vacation
fern distant
die Ferne, –n distance
fertig ready, finished
    fertig werden mit to manage
fest tight(ly), solid, firm, safe, secure
das Fest, –e festival
fest·halten, ie, a (hält fest) to hold tightly
fest·stellen to establish (fact), to ascertain
die Feststellung, –en statement, assertion
fett fat; in bold print
der Fetzen, – rag, shred
das Feuer, – light, fire
das Fieber, – fever
fieberhaft feverish
die Figur, –en figure
finden, a, u to find
fingern to finger
der Fingernagel, ⸚ fingernail
die Fingerspitze, –n fingertip
fischig fishlike
der Fischkasten, ⸚ fish box
fix clever
flau slack
das Fleckfieber spotted fever, typhus
der Fleckfieberverdacht suspicion of typhus
der Fleischberg, –e a "mountain of flesh"
fleischig fleshy, corpulent
fleißig diligent
flicken to patch
fliegen, o, o (ist) to fly
fließen, o, o (ist) to flow
flimmern to glimmer, to flicker
der Floh, ⸚e flea
die Flosse, –n fin
die Flucht flight, escape
flüchten vor (+ *dat.*) to flee from
flüchtig fleeting, hasty
der Flüchtling, –e refugee
der Fluchtversuch, –e attempt to escape
der Fluß, ⸚sse river, stream
flüstern to whisper
fluten to flood
flutend surging
die Folge, –n result, consequence
folgen (+ *dat.*) to follow, to obey
folgendermaßen in the following way, as follows,
    thus
die Forderung, –en demand
die Form, –en form
formen to form, mold
förmlich veritably, literally
die Formulierung, –en formulation

fort·drängen to urge to leave
fort·fahren, u, a (ist) (fährt fort) to continue,
    to go on
das Foto, –s photograph, photo
der Fotoblitz, –e flashbulb
die Frage, –n question
    eine Frage stellen to ask a question
fragen to ask
    fragen nach to inquire into
das Fragezeichen, – question mark
fragwürdig questionable
die Frau, –en woman, wife
die Frauenstimme, –n lady's voice
das Fräulein, – miss, young lady
frei free
    im Freien in the open
die Freiheit, –en freedom
freilich indeed
frei·machen to set free, to clear
    sich frei·machen to free onself
die Freitreppe, –n open-air stairway
die Freizeit, –en leisure time
fremd strange, foreign
fressen, a, e (frißt) to eat (said of animals), to gorge
die Freude, –n joy, pleasure
    Freude machen to give joy
die Freudigkeit, –en joyfulness, cheerfulness
    vor innerer Freudigkeit from sheer joy
freuen to please
    sich freuen über (+ *acc.*) to be happy about
    sich freuen auf (+ *acc.*) to look forward to
der Freund, –e friend
freundlich friendly, pleasant
die Freundschaft, –en friendship
der Friede, –n (*MII*) peace
    Frieden schließen to make peace
frieren, o, o to freeze, to be cold
frisch fresh
froh happy, glad
fröhlich happy, merry
die Front, –en front (front line)
der Frosch, ⸚e frog
frösteln to feel chilly
früh early
    früher earlier, sooner, former(ly)
    frühestens at the earliest
der Frühling, –e spring
(sich) fühlen to feel
    fühlen nach to feel for
    sich nahe fühlen (+ *dat.*) to feel close to
führen to lead
    einen Beweis führen to furnish proof
der Führer, – leader

die **Führung,** –en guidance, direction, management
das **Fuhrwerk,** –e wagon, carriage
sich **füllen** to become filled
fünfstellig of five digits
der **Fünfziger,** – a man in his fifties
für und wider pro and con
die **Furcht** fear, fright
fürchten to fear
    sich **fürchten vor** (+ *dat.*) to be afraid of
der **Fuß,** ⸚e foot
    zu **Fuß** on foot
der **Fußboden,** ⸚ floor
die **Fußspitze,** –n tip of foot
der **Fußweg,** –e path
die **Fußzehen** (*pl.*) tiptoes
    sich **auf die Fußzehen stellen** to stand on tiptoe
füttern to feed
das **zweite Futur** future perfect

G

gaffen to gape
gähnen to yawn
der **Gang,** ⸚e motion, course, flow, walk, passage
    in **Gang halten** to keep going
ganz complete(ly), quite, very
    ganz **anders** completely different
    ganz **etwas anders** something quite different
gar much less
    gar **nicht** not at all
die **Gasse,** –n alley, narrow street
der **Gast,** ⸚e guest
der **Gastdozent,** –en guest lecturer
das **Gasthaus,** ⸚er inn, restaurant
geben, a, e (gibt) to give
    es **gibt** there is, there are
das **Gebiet,** –e area
gebieten, o, o to order, to command
das **Geblinzel** blink, peek
geboren (*perf. part.*) born
    er **wurde geboren** he was born
gebrauchen to use
gebührend duly
der **Gedanke,** –n (*MII*) thought, idea
    mit **dem Gedanken umgehen** to contemplate
gedeihen, ie, ie (ist) to thrive
das **Gedicht,** –e poem
das **Gedränge** mob, pushing crowd
geduckt cowering, cringed
die **Geduld** patience
die **Gefahr,** –en danger

außer Gefahr out of danger
gefährlich dangerous
gefallen, ie, a (gefällt) (+ *dat.*) to please
    er **gefällt mir** I like him
die **Gefangenschaft** captivity, imprisonment
    in **Gefangenschaft geraten** to be taken prisoner
das **Gefängnis,** –se prison
die **Gefängniszelle,** –n prison cell
gefestigt secure
das **Geflüster** whispering
gegen against, toward
    gegen **. . . hin** toward
die **Gegend,** –en region
der **Gegensatz,** ⸚e contrast, opposite
    im **Gegensatz zu** in contrast to
gegenseitig mutual
das **Gegenteil,** –e contrary, reverse
    im **Gegenteil** on the contrary
gegenüber opposite
die **Gegenwart** presence; present
gegenwärtig present
der **Gegner,** – opponent
gehen, i, a (ist) to go, to walk
    es **geht um** (+ *acc.*) it is a matter of
    es **geht mir gut** I am fine
der **Gehilfe,** –n (*MII*) helper, assistant
das **Gehirn,** –e brain
das **Gehölz** wood
das **Gehör** hearing
gehorchen (+ *dat.*) to obey
    gehören (+ *dat.*) to belong to
    gehören zu to be part of, to belong to
der **Gehorsam** obedience
der **Gehsteig,** –e sidewalk
der **Gehweg,** –e sidewalk
der **Geist,** –er spirit, intellect
geistig intellectual, mental, spiritual
geistlich religious, sacred
geizig stingy
gekränkt hurt, injured (of feelings)
das **Gelände** ground, area
gelangen (ist) to reach, to attain
    zu **der Überzeugung gelangen** to become convinced
gelbhäutig yellow skinned
das **Geld,** –er money
die **Gelehrsamkeit** erudition, learning
gelehrt learned, educated
die **Geliebte,** –n sweetheart
gelingen, a, u (ist) (+ *dat.*) to succeed
    es **gelingt mir** I succeed
gelten, a, o (gilt) to be valid, of value, to be
    considered (to be)
die **Geltung** validity, recognition

das **Gemach,** ¨er chamber
der **Gemeinplatz,** ¨e cliché, commonplace
gemeinsam haben to have in common
genau exact(ly)
   genau soviel exactly that many
der **General,** ¨e general
die **Generation, –en** generation
genug enough
genügen (+ *dat.*) to suffice
der **Geograph, –en** (*MII*) geographer
die **Geographie, –n** geography
geölt suave
das **Geplärr** crying
gerade just
geradewegs straight
geraten, ie, a (ist) (gerät) to come, to fall, to get
   (into)
geraum long
   nach geraumer Zeit after a long time
das **Geräusch, –e** sound
die **Gerberei, –en** tannery
das **Gerede** talk, gossip
   ins Gerede kommen to get talked about
das **Gericht, –e** court
   Gericht halten to hold court
der **Gerichtsdiener, –** constable, court attendant,
   bailiff
der **Gerichtshof,** ¨e court
geringschätzig contemptuous
die **Germanistik** study of German language and
   literature
gern(e) gladly
gerötet reddened
gerunzelt wrinkled
gesamt entire
geschäftstüchtig efficient (in business)
geschehen, a, e (ist) (geschieht) to happen
das **Geschenk, –e** present, gift
die **Geschichte, –n** story; history
geschichtlich historical
der **Geschmack,** ¨e taste, flavor
das **Geschwätz, –e** chatter, idle talk
die **Geschwindigkeit, –en** speed
die **Gesellschaft, –en** society, company
gesellschaftlich social
das **Gesetz, –e** law
gesichert assured
das **Gesicht, –er** face
   zu Gesicht bekommen to set eyes on
das **Gesinde** farm servants
das **Gespräch, –e** conversation
die **Gesprächsfetzen** (*pl.*) bits of conversation
die **Gestalt, –en** shape, form, figure

gestalten to form, to shape, to model
   ein Thema gestalten to develop a theme
gestern yesterday
gestrig yesterday, of yesterday
gesund healthy, wholesome
gesunden to become healthy, to recuperate
die **Gesundheit** health
das **Getümmel** turmoil
gewähren to grant, to allow
gewaltig enormous
gewinnen, a, o to gain, to win, to earn
das **Gewirr** confusion
gewiß certain
das **Gewissen, –** conscience
gewöhnlich ordinary
gewöhnt sein an (+ *acc.*) to be accustomed to
die **Gitarre, –n** guitar
der **Glanz** radiance
glänzend shiny, brilliant
das **Glas,** ¨er glass, lens
glasig glassy, lifeless
glatt smooth, flat(ly)
der **Glaube, –n** (*MII*) belief, faith
glauben (+ *dat.*) to believe
   glauben an (+ *acc.*) to believe in
gleich equal, same; at the same time, just,
   immediately, at once
   gleich darauf right after that
   gleich sein (+ *dat.*) to not matter to (someone)
gleichgültig indifferent(ly); regardless
gleißend glistening
das **Glück** good luck, success, happiness
glücklich happy
glücklicherweise fortunately
der **Glücksumstand,** ¨e fortunate circumstance
die **Glühlampe, –n** electric light
das **Glühwürmchen, –** glowworm
golden golden
der **Gott,** ¨er god
das **Grab,** ¨er grave
graben to dig
der **Grad, –e** degree
die **Gratulation, –en** congratulation
gratulieren to congratulate
grau grey
greifen, i, i an (+ *acc.*) to touch
grell gaudy, garish
der **Grenadier, –e** grenadier, infantryman
grinsen to grin
die **Grobheit, –en** rudeness
groß big, large, tall, great
der **Große, –n** (*adj.*) big man, dignitary
die **Größe, –n** greatness, size

der Größenunterschied, –e difference in size

die Großmutter, ⸚ grandmother

großzügig broadminded, generous

die Großzügigkeit generosity

die Grube, –n ditch

grün green

der Grund, ⸚e ground, reason, cause, foundation
  Grund haben to have reason

die Grundbedingung, –en basic condition

gründen to found, to establish

der Grundgedanke, –n basic idea

gründlich thorough, complete, careful

die Gruppe, –n group
  die Gruppe 47 an avant-garde group of democratic
    German writers formed in 1947

grüßen to greet

gutgekleidet well dressed

das Gymnasium, –ien public preparatory school

H

das Haar, –e hair

das Haargestrüpp, –e bush of hair

hacken to chop

der Hafen, ⸚ harbor

haften an (+ dat.) to be fixed upon

der Haifisch, –e shark

haken to hook
  Sie hakten ihn unter They took him by the arms

der Haken, – check mark, hook

halb half

der Halbkreis, –e semicircle

halblaut half loud, soft

die Halle, –n hall

der Hals, ⸚e neck, throat
  auf dem Hals haben to be saddled with
  sich den Hals ausrenken to crane one's neck

die Halsseite, –n side of the throat

halt so just

halten, ie, a (hält) to hold, to keep, to stop
  halten für to consider
  halten von to think of

die Haltung, –en attitude

hämmern to hammer, to make a monotonous sound

handeln to act, to trade
  handeln von to deal with
  es handelt sich um it is a question of

der Händler, – dealer

der Handschuh, –e glove

die Handtasche, –n pocketbook

hantieren to tinker around

hart hard

der Hase, –n (MII) rabbit, hare

häßlich ugly

hastig hasty

der Hauch, –e whiff

der Haufen, – pile
  über den Haufen werfen to upset, to cause great
    confusion

häufen to pile

häufig frequent

die Hauptfigur, –en main figure

der Hauptmann, –leute captain

die Hauptsache, –n main thing

die Hauptstadt, ⸚e capital

die Hauptstraße, –n main street

der Hauptunterschied, –e main difference

die Hausarbeit, –en housework

der Hausherr, –en master of the house, householder

der Hausierer, – peddler

der Häusler, – cottager

die Häuslerhütte, –n cottage hut

die Haustür, –e front door

die Haut, ⸚e skin

heben, o, o to lift

das Heer, –e host, large number

heftig violent

die Heimat, –en home, homeland

die Heimatstadt, ⸚e home town

die Heimkehr return home

heim·kehren to return home

der Heimkehrer, – homecomer

die Heimkehrergeschichte, –n story of somebody
    returning home

die Heimlichkeit, –en secrecy

heiraten to marry

heiß hot

heißen, ie, ei to order
  so heißt es it is said

heiter cheerful

der Held, –en (MII) hero

heldenmütig heroic

helfen, a, o (hilft) (+ dat.) to help

hell bright, light

der Hemdsärmel, – shirt sleeve

herab down, downward
  noch von den Pferden herab before dismounting,
    still on horseback

heran·gehen, i, a (ist) an (+ acc.) to go toward

heran·treten, i, e (ist) an (+ acc.) (tritt) to approach,
  to step up to

heraus·holen aus to get out

heraus·klettern (ist) to climb out

heraus·kommen, a, o (ist) aus to come out of

heraus·stecken to stick out

der Herbst, –e autumn, fall

herein·bringen, a, a to bring in

herein·treten, a, e (ist) (tritt herein) to walk in,
to step in

der Herr, –en (*MII*) Mr., gentleman, lord, master

herrlich splendid, glorious

herrschen to rule, to prevail

herum around

herum·fahren, u, a (ist) (fährt herum) um to travel
or drive around

herum·gehen, i, a (ist) um to go around

herum·kriechen, o, o (ist) to crawl around, to creep
around

herum·reißen, i, i to turn all the way, to jerk around

herum·schwirren to whirl around

herunter·sehen, a, e (sieht herunter) auf (+ *acc.*) to
look down on (at)

das Herz, –en (*gen.* des Herzens) heart

  kalten Herzens in cold blood

herzlich sincere

heulen to howl

heute today

heutig modern, of today

die Hexe, –n witch

hierher to this place

hilflos helpless

hilfreich helpful

hin und her back and forth

hinab·ziehen, o, o to move down, to pull down

hinauf·fahren, u, a (ist) (fährt hinauf) auf (+ *acc.*)
to travel or drive up to

hinauf·fliegen, o, o (ist) to fly up

hinauf·gehen, i, a (ist) auf (+ *acc.*) to go up

hinaus·gehen, i, a (ist) über (+ *acc.*) to go beyond

das Hindernis, –se obstacle, hindrance

hindurch·blinzeln to blink through

hindurch·gehen, i, a (ist) durch to go through

hindurch·sehen, a, e (sieht hindurch) durch to look
through

hindurch·scheinen, ie, ie durch to shine through

hinein·gehen, i, a (ist) to go into

hinein·laufen, ie, au (ist) (läuft hinein) in (+ *acc.*)
to run into

hin·legen to lay down

hin·nehmen, a, o (nimmt hin) to accept

hin·sehen, a, e (sieht hin) to look over at

hinter behind

der Hintergrund, ⁻e background

das Hinterhaus, ⁻er back building

hinterlassen, ie, a (hinterläßt) to leave behind

der Hintern rear, behind, rump

die Hintertür, –e back door

hinüber·fahren, u, a (ist) (fährt hinüber) über (+ *acc.*)
to travel over

hinüber· schielen to glance over

hinüber·schwimmen, a, o (ist) über (+ *acc.*) to swim
over

sich hinunter·beugen to bend down

sich hinunter·neigen to bend down

hinzu·zählen to add (to)

die Historie, –n history

historisch historical

die Hitlerjugend Hitler Youth

hoch high

hochgeschüttet heaped high

hochgewachsen lanky

hoch·halten, ie, a (hält hoch) to hold up

hoch·heben, o, o to lift up

hoch·nehmen, a, o (nimmt hoch) to lift

höchst most, highest

höchstens at the most

die Hochzeit, –en wedding

der Hochzeitsschmaus wedding breakfast

der Hof, ⁻e courtyard, yard

hoffen to hope

die Hoffnung, –en hope

höflich polite

das Hoftor, –e manor gate, gate to estate

hohl hollow

holen to fetch

höllisch hellish(ly), mighty, terrible

das Holz, ⁻er wood

der Holzball, ⁻e wooden ball

der Holzzuber, – wooden bucket

horchen to listen

das Hörspiel, –e radio play

die Hose, –n trousers, pants

das Hosenbein, –e trouser leg

  an den Hosenbeinen hoch up the trouser legs

der Hosenboden, ⁻ seat of the pants

der Hosenträger, – suspender

hübsch pretty, nice

hüllen to wrap

der Humor humor

humoristisch humorous

hundert hundred

hundertfach hundredfold

Hunger haben to be hungry

die Hungerjahre years of hunger

husten to cough

der Hut, ⁻e hat

die Hut care, charge

  in guter Hut sein to be in good hands

sich hüten vor (*dat.*) to guard against

die Hütte, –n hut, hovel

I

das Ideal, –e ideal
idealistisch idealistic
die Idee, –n idea
sich identifizieren to identify oneself
immerzu always, constantly
in in, into
indem while (*conj.*)
der Inder, – Indian
der Indianer, – American Indian
das Individuum, –duen individual
die Industrie, –n industry
der Infanterist, –en (*MII*) infantryman
der Ingenieur, –e engineer
der Inhalt, –e content
die Innentasche, –n inside pocket
inner inner, internal
   das Innere (*adj.*) inside, interior
innerhalb inside, within
insgeheim secretly
intelligent intelligent
interessant interesting
interessieren to interest
   sich interessieren für to be interested in
inzwischen meanwhile
irgendwie somehow
irgendwo somewhere
die Ironie irony
ironisch ironic
sich irren in (+ *dat.*) to be mistaken about
der Irrtum, ¨er error

J

das Jackett, –e coat (of a suit)
das Jahr, –e year
   zwölf Jahre lang for twelve years
   die zwanziger Jahre the twenties
das Jahrhundert, –e century
jährlich annual, yearly
das Jahrtausend, –e millennium
jämmerlich pitiful, miserable
jammern to lament
der Januar, –e January
jaulen to howl
jawohl yes, indeed, of course
je . . . desto (umso) the . . . the (with comparatives)
jedenfalls at any rate
jeder each, every
jedesmal every time

K

jedoch however
jemand someone
jener that
jetzt now
jubeln to rejoice, to shout for joy
jucken to itch
der Jude, –n (*MII*) Jew
der Juli July
jung young
der Junge, –n(s) (*MII*) boy
die Jungfer, –n maid, bridesmaid
der Juni June
juristisch juridical, legal

K

der Käfer, – beetle, bug
der Kaffee coffee
kahl bare
der Kaiser, – emperor
kaiserlich imperial
das Kalb, ¨er calf
Kalinin Russian city, 100 miles NW of Moscow
kalt cold
die Kälte cold, coldness
kämmen to comb
der Kandidat, –en (*MII*) candidate
das Kaninchen, – rabbit
das Kaninchenfutter rabbit feed
der Kaninchenstall, ¨e rabbit cage, hutch
die Kapelle, –n band
die Karte, –n card, ticket, map
der Käse cheese
die Käsespeise, –n cheese dish
die Kaskade, –n cascade
die Kasse, –n ticket office
der Kasten, ¨ box
die Katastrophe, –n catastrophe
der Katholik, –en (*MII*) Catholic
katholisch catholic
kauen to chew
kaufen to buy
der Kaufmann, –leute merchant
kaum hardly, scarcely
   kaum jemand hardly anybody
der Keller, – cellar
der Kellner, – waiter
kennen, a, a to know, to be acquainted with
kennenlernen to become acquainted with
die Kenntnis, –se knowledge

der **Kerl**, –e fellow, guy
  ein fixer **Kerl** a smart fellow
die **Kerze**, –n candle
die **Kette**, –n chain
der **Kilometer**, – kilometer
der **Kilometerzähler**, – mileage indicator
das **Kind**, –er child
kindisch childish
kindlich childlike
das **Kino**, –s movies
die **Kirche**, –n church
die **Kirchenglocke**, –n church bell
kirchlich ecclesiastical, clerical, religious
die **Kirchweih**, – church fair
die **Kiste**, –n crate, wooden box
das **Kistenbrett**, –er crate board
sich **klammern an** (+ *acc.*) to cling to
der **Klang**, ⁖e strain, sound
klar clear; sure
die **Klasse**, –n class
das **Kleid**, –er dress
klein little, small
klingeln to ring the bell
klopfen to knock, to pat
knabbern to nibble, to chew
knarren to rattle
der **Knäuel** throng
die **Kneipe**, –n bar, joint
knien to kneel
der **Knirps**, –e little chap, brat
der **Knöchel**, – knuckle
die **Köchin**, –nen cook
die **Kohle**, –n coal
kommandieren to command
kommen, a, o (ist) to come
  kommen aus to come from
die **Kompanie**, –n company (military)
der **Kompaniechef**, –s company commander
der **Kompanieführer**, – company commander
kompliziert complicated
der **Konflikt**, –e conflict
der **König**, –e king
der **Konjak** cognac
können, o, o to be able to, to know how to
der **Kontakt**, –e contact
  Kontakt aufnehmen to take up, to make contact
der **Kontrast**, –e contrast
die **Kontrolle**, –n check, control
kontrollieren to check
sich **konzentrieren auf** (+ *acc.*) to concentrate on
der **Kopf**, ⁖e head
das **Kopfende** head

das **Kopfnicken** nod, nodding
der **Kopfschuß**, ⁖e shot through the head
der **Korb**, ⁖e basket
der **Kordon** cordon, barrier
der **Kork**, –e cork
der **Körper**, – body
korrekt exact
die **Kraft**, ⁖e strength
  wieder zu Kräften kommen to regain strength
kräftig strong
der **Kragen**, – collar
die **Krähe**, –n crow
kramen to rummage
krank sick
das **Krankenhaus**, ⁖er hospital
der **Krankenträger**, – stretcher bearer
die **Krankheit**, –en sickness
die **Krawatte**, –n tie
die **Kreide**, –n chalk
der **Kreidekreis**, –e chalk circle
der **Kreis**, –e circle
  einen Kreis ziehen to draw a circle
kriechen, o, o (ist) to crawl
der **Krieg**, –e war
  Krieg führen to wage war
kriegen to get, to receive
die **Kriegsführung**, –en warfare
das **Kriegsgericht**, –e court-martial
das **Kriegslazarett**, –e field hospital
der **Kriegsverletzte**, –n (*adj.*) disabled veteran
das **Kriterium**, –rien criterion
die **Kritik**, –en criticism
kritisch critical
kritisieren to criticize
krumm crooked, bent
  krumme Beine bowlegs
die **Küche**, –n kitchen
die **Kuh**, ⁖e cow
die **Kuhle**, –n pit
die **Kultur**, –en culture, civilization
sich **kümmern um** to be concerned about
der **Kumpel**, – chum, buddy
die **Kunst**, ⁖e art
das **Kunstwerk**, –e work of art
das **Kupferzeug** copperware
der **Kurfürst von Bayern** Elector of Bavaria
der **Kurs**, –e course
kurz short
  über kurz oder lang sooner or later
die **Kurzgeschichte**, –n short story
kurzgeschoren shaved
die **Kutsche**, –n carriage

L

lächeln to smile
lachen to laugh
der Laden, ⸚ shop
das Lager, – bed, camp
das Laken, – sheet
das Lämpchen, – small lamp
das Land, ⸚er land, country
der Landarbeiter, – farmhand
der Landsmann, –leute fellow countryman
die Landstraße, –n highway
lang long
die Länge length
   auf die Länge in the long run
längs along
langsam slow
die Längswand, ⸚e side wall
langweilig boring
die Lanze, –n lance, spear
der Lärm, –e noise
lassen, ie, a (läßt) to let, to permit, to allow
lateinisch Latin
laufen, ie, au (ist) (läuft) to run
laut loud
lauter nothing but; lots of
der Lautsprecher, – loudspeaker
die Lautsprechermusik music from a loudspeaker
das Lazarett, –e military hospital
das Leben, – life
lebendig living, alive
der Leberfleck, –en mole
lebhaft lively
der Lech river Lech
die Lederhandlung, –en leather business
der Ledermantel, ⸚ leather coat
ledig unmarried; illigitimate (as child)
leer empty
legen to lay, to put, to place
   sich legen to lie down
lehnen to lean
die Lehre, –n teaching, lesson, precept
lehren to teach
der Lehrer, – teacher
   die Lehrerin, –nen female teacher
der Lehrling, –e apprentice
die Leiche, –n corpse
   die übel zugerichtete Leiche the badly butchered corpse
leicht easy, slight, light
   das Leichte light stuff, frivolous stuff, light-hearted stuff

das Leid, –en sorrow
   es tut mir leid I am sorry
die Leidenschaft, –en passion
leidenschaftlich passionate
die Leinendecke, –n linen cover, blanket
leise soft, gentle, quiet
die Leistung, –en achievement
der Leiterwagen, – farm wagon
die Lektion, –en lecture
   eine Lektion halten to give a lecture
der Lenz, –e spring (poetic)
   das ist ein Lenz that is a snap
lernen to learn
lesen, a, e (liest) to read
der Leser, – reader
letzt– last
letztens finally, last of all
der Leuchtturm, ⸚e lighthouse
die Leute (pl.) people
der Leutnant, –e lieutenant
das Licht, –er light
das Lichtband, ⸚er stream of light
lieb dear
   lieber rather
   am liebsten (to like) most of all
lieben to love
liegen, a, e to lie
der Likör, –e liquor, cordial
link- left-
   links to the left
die Lippe, –n lip
die Literatur, –en literature
der Literaturpreis, –e literary prize
loben to praise
löblich commendable, praiseworthy, laudable
das Loch, ⸚er hole
locken to tempt, to allure
das Lokal, –e restaurant
los! go!
das Los lot, fate
lösen to solve
loslassen, ie, a (läßt los) to let go
die Lösung, –en solution, answer
der Löwe, –n (MII) lion
lüften to raise
der Lufthauch, –e breath of air
lügen, o, o to lie
   wie gedruckt lügen to lie like a book
die Luke, –n hatch
der Lustgarten, ⸚ garden of pleasure
lustig happy, gay
der Lyriker, – writer of lyrics, lyricist

M

machen to make, to do, to put

    das macht nicht viel that does not matter much

    Hat es Ihnen etwas gemacht? Were you hurt (upset)?

die Macht, ⸚e power

mächtig huge, great, powerful, massive

machtlos powerless

das Mädchen, – girl

die Magd, ⸚e servant girl

der Magistrat, –e magistrate

der Mai May

der Major, –e major

das Mal, –e time

    mal times (as in three times)

    nicht (ein) mal not even

    einmal once

    zum erstenmal for the first time

malen to paint, to draw; to write slowly

man one (*impers. pron.*)

mancher many a

manchmal sometimes

der Mangel, ⸚ lack, want

der Mann, ⸚er man, husband

die Mannschaft, –en crew, team

der Mantel, ⸚ coat

die Manteltasche, –n coat pocket

das Märchen, – fairy tale

die Marktsteuer, –n market taxes

der Markttag, –e market day

marschieren to march

die Masche, –n mesh, stitch; trick

    das ist die Masche that's the ticket, that's pops (*slang*)

die Maschinerie, –n machinery

das Maß, –e measure, proportion

    in gleichem Maße in the same extent

die Maßnahme, –n measure, action

    Maßnahmen treffen to take measures

der Materialismus materialism

materialistisch materialistic

materiell material

die Matratze, –n mattress

die Mauer, –n wall

die Mauerreste remains of the wall

die Medizin, –en medicine

das Meer, –e ocean, sea

der Meeresgrund, ⸚e bottom of the sea

mehr more

mehrere several

meinen to mean, to say

die Meinung, –en opinion

die meisten most

meistens mostly

melden to announce, to report

    sich krank melden to call in sick, to go on sick call (military)

die Menge, –n crowd

der Mensch, –en man, human being

    der heutige Mensch man of our time

    der moderne Mensch überhaupt modern man in general

der Menschenstrom, ⸚e stream of people

die Menschenwürde man's dignity

merken to notice

    sich etwas merken to check, to keep in mind

merkwürdig strange

merkwürdigerweise strangely enough

das Messer, – knife

das Metall, –e metal

die Metapher, –n metaphor

die Mietskaserne, –n tenement

die Milch milk

das Militär military, army

die Million, –en million

die Minute, –n minute

mißlingen, a, u (ist) to fail

mißtrauen (+ dat.) to mistrust

mißtrauisch distrustful, suspicious

der Mistbauer, – clodhopper

mit with

mit·arbeiten to cooperate

mit·bringen, a, a to bring along

das Mitleid compassion, pity

mit·marschieren to march along

mit·nehmen, a, o (nimmt mit) to take along

mit·schwimmen, a, o (ist) to swim with

der Mittag, –e midday, noon

der Mittagstisch, –e midday meal (*lit.* midday table)

mit·teilen to report, make known, tell

mitten in the middle

die Mitternacht midnight

mitunter occasionally

das Modelltheater, – model theatre

modern modern

mögen, o, o (mag) to like, to be possible

möglich possible

die Möglichkeit, –en possibility

möglichst if at all possible

    möglichst schnell as fast as possible

der Monat, –e month

monatlich monthly

der Montag, –e Monday

die **Moral** morals
das **Moralgebot, –e** moral precept
moralisch moral
der **Morgen, –** morning
morgen tomorrow
   zu morgen for tomorrow
morgig of tomorrow
die **Moritat, –en** folk ballad
der **Motor, –en** motor
müde tired
die **Mühe, –n** trouble, effort
   Mühe machen (+ *dat.*) to be an effort for
    (someone)
die **Mühle, –n** mill
multiplizieren to multiply
der **Mund, ⸚er** mouth
   den Mund halten to hold one's tongue
murmeln to murmur, to mutter
   vor sich hin·murmeln to mutter to oneself
der **Musikautomat, –en** juke box
müssen, u, u (muß) to have to, must
der **Mut** courage
mutig courageous, brave
die **Mutter, ⸚** mother
der **Mutwille** (*MII*) mischief

N

na, na ja! well!
nach to, after, according to
der **Nachbar, –n** (*MI* and *MII*) neighbor (*masc.*)
   die **Nachbarin, –nen** neighbor (*fem.*)
das **Nachbardorf, ⸚er** neighboring village
der **Nachbarort, –e** neighboring locality
nachdem after (*conj.*)
nach·denken, a, a to ponder
nachher afterwards
der **Nachlaß** posthumous writings
nach·lassen, ie, a (läßt nach) to abate, to ease up,
   to lessen, to loosen
nachlässig careless
der **Nachmittag, –e** afternoon
die **Nachricht, –en** news
nach·sehen, a, e (sieht nach) (+ *dat.*) to look after
nächst next, nearest
nach·starren (+ *dat.*) to stare after
die **Nacht, ⸚e** night
   in der Nacht during the night
   Nächte durch throughout the nights
   nachts at night, during the night
nächtlich nocturnal, nightly

nachträglich subsequently
nah close, near
die **Nähe** nearness, proximity
   in der Nähe close by
sich nähern to approach
die **Nahrung, –en** food, nourishment
der **Name, –n** (*MII*) name
namens by the name of
nämlich namely
die **Nase, –n** nose
naß wet
nationalsozialistisch national socialistic, Nazi-
natürlich natural(ly)
die **Naturwissenschaft, –en** science
das **Nazi-Regime** the Nazi government, regime
die **Nebelkrähe, –n** hooded crow
neben next to, beside
   nebeneinander next to one another
nee (*slang*) no
der **Neger, –** Negro
nehmen, a, o (nimmt) to take, to seize
   an sich nehmen to get hold of, to snatch up
   ein Ende nehmen to come to an end
sich neigen to bend, to incline, to bow
die **Neigung, –en** tendency, inclination
nennen, a, a to name
nesteln an (+ *dat.*) to fuss with
nett nice
neu new
neugierig curious, inquisitive
neulich recently, the other day
die **Nichte, –n** niece
nichts nothing
   gar nichts nothing at all
   nichts als nothing but
   das **Nichts** nothingness, nonentity
nicken to nod
nie never
nieder·brechen, a, o (bricht nieder) to tear down
nieder·fallen, ie, a (fällt nieder) to fall down
nieder·knien to kneel down
die **Niederlande** (*pl.*) Netherlands
sich nieder·setzen to sit down
nieder·treten, a, e (tritt nieder) to trample down
niedrig base, low
niemals never
niemand no one
nirgends nowhere
noch still, yet
   noch (ein)mal again
   noch (et)was something else, something in
    addition
der **Norden** north

die Not distress, misery
notdürftig scanty, poor
die Notlüge, –n white lie
notwendig necessary
die Novelle, –n novella
novellistisch fictional
der November, – November
die Nummer, –n number
nun now
   nunmehr now
nur only, merely
   nicht nur . . . sondern auch not only . . . but also
nützen (+ *dat.*) to be of use
nützlich useful
nutzlos uselessly, in vain

O

ob whether, if
oben above, on top, upstairs
   oben drauf on it; on top of
   von oben from above
der Oberfeldarzt, ⁻e high-ranking military doctor
oberhalb above
der Oberstatistiker, – head statistician
obgleich although (*conj.*)
obschon although (*conj.*)
obwohl although (*conj.*)
oder so (etwas) or something like that
offen open
öffentlich public
der Offizier, –e officer
(sich) öffnen to open
öfters from time to time
ohne without
ohnmächtig helpless
das Ohr, –en ear
ölen to oil
   geölt oiled; suave
der Onkel, – uncle
der Orden, – medal
ordentlich respectable, decent
ordnen to straighten, to arrange
die Ordnung, –en order
die Orientierung, –en orientation
der Ort, –e location
ostdeutsch East German
der Osten east
an Ostern on Easter
Österreich Austria
der Österreicher, – Austrian
die Ostfront eastern front

P

das Paar, –e couple
   ein Paar a pair of
   ein paar several
das Paket, –e package
der Palast, ⁻e palace
das Papier, –e paper, document
der Papierfabrikant, –en (*MII*) paper manufacturer
die Parabel, –n parable
das Parfüm, –e perfume
der Park, –s park
die Partei, –en party, litigant
der Paß, ⁻e passport
passieren to happen, to pass by
die Paßkontrolle, –n passport check
pathetisch pathetic, overexpressive
der Pelzkragen, – fur collar
der Pelzmantel, ⁻ fur coat
pendeln to dangle
das Pergament, –e document
die Person, –en person
persönlich personal
die Perspektive, –n perspective
der Pessimismus pessimism
der Pfarrer, – priest, minister
die Pfeife, –n pipe
das Pferd, –e horse
der Pferdewagen, – cart, carriage
die Pflanze, –n plant
pflegen to tend, to take care of, to be in the habit of
pfundig grand, sizable
das Phänomen, –e phenomenon
die Phantasie, –n fantasy
der Philosoph, –en (*MII*) philosopher
physisch physical
plärren to bawl, to cry
der Plärrer Augsburg fair
der Platz, ⁻e square
der Platzregen, – shower
plötzlich sudden(ly)
plump plump
plündern to plunder, to loot
die Plünderung, –en raiding, plundering, pillaging
der Poet, –en (*MII*) poet
der Pole, –n (*MII*) Pole
politisch political
die Polizei police
der Polizist, –en (*MII*) policeman
poltern to thump
die Portiersuniform, –en porter's uniform
die Post post office, mail

der Posten, – post, position
prächtig glorious
das Präsent, –e present, gift
der Präsident, –en (MII) president
der Preis, –e price, prize
der Prinz, –en (MII) prince
das Prinzip, –ien principle
die Pritsche, –n prison cot
die Probe, –n test, trial
    eine Probe vor·nehmen to undertake a test
    die Probe bestehen to stand the test
das Problem, –e problem
der Professor, –en professor
das Programm, –e program
der Protestant, –en (MII) protestant
prozentual percentual
prozentualizieren to figure percentages
der Prozeß, –sse trial
die Psychologie psychology
psychologisch psychological
das Publikum public
der Puls, –e pulse
pulsieren to pulsate, to hum
der Punkt, –e point

Q

der Qualm, –e smoke
quer diagonal, across
quietschen to screech

R

der Rachen, – jaw
der Rahmen, – frame
    im engsten Rahmen within the closest possible
        framework
der Rand, ‒er rim, edge
rasch fast, quickly
raten, ie, a (rät) to advise, to guess
das Rathaus, ‒er city hall
ratlos helpless, perplexed
die Ratlosigkeit helplessness, perplexity
das Rätsel, – puzzle
rätselhaft enigmatic
die Ratte, –n rat
rattern to clatter
rauchen to smoke
rauchig smoky

die Rauchwolke, –n cloud of smoke
der Raum, ‒e room, space
raus = heraus out
sich räuspern to clear one's throat
reagieren auf (+ acc.) to react to
die Reaktion, –en reaction
rechnen to figure
    rechnen auf (+ acc.) to count on
recht right, proper, very, quite
    rechts to the right
    recht haben to be right
    recht sein (+ dat.) to be all right with someone
die Rechtssache, –n case, lawsuit
der Rechtsstreit, –e dispute (legal)
    einen Rechtsstreit aus·tragen to settle a dispute
recken to crane
reden to speak
    beim Reden while speaking
die Redensart, –en remark, expression
die Regel, –n rule
der Regen, – rain
die Regierung, –en government
der Regisseur, –e (stage) director
reich an (+ dat.) rich in
das Reich, –e realm, empire
die Reichsstadt, ‒e imperial city
der Reichtum, ‒er wealth
reifen to mature
die Reihe, –n line
die Reihenfolge, –n sequence
rein clean
die Reise, –n trip, travel
reisen to travel
der Reisighaufen, – pile of brushwood
reißen, i, i to tear, to snatch
reiten, i, i (hat, ist) to ride horseback
der Reiter, – horseman
das Reklamelicht, –er advertisement light
die Religion, –en religion
rennen, a, a (ist) to run
renoviert renovated
die Residenzstadt, ‒e imperial capital
das Resultat, –e result
der Rhythmus, –men rhythm
sich richten nach to conform to
    sich richten gegen to be directed against
der Richter, – judge
richtig right, correct
die Richtung, –en direction
riechen, o, o to smell
    riechen nach to smell like
der Riesenblumenstrauß, ‒e giant bouquet of flowers
riesig giant

der Ring, –e circle, ring
ringen, a, u um to struggle for
ringsum all around
das Rinnsal, –e rivulet, gutter
riskieren to risk
das Röcklein, – little coat
die Rolle, –n role
  eine Rolle spielen to play a role
der Roman, –e novel
rot red
die Rotte, –n squad
der Ruck, –e jerk
rücken to move, to adjust
  an den Hosenträgern rückend hitching up the
    trousers
rücksichtslos recklessly
rufen, ie, u to call
ruhig calm, quiet; safely, without worrying
das Ruinenhaus, ⁀er house in ruins
die Runde, –n round
der Russe, –n (MII) Russian
russisch Russian
(das) Rußland Russia
rutschen to slip, slide

S

der Saal, ⁀e room, hall
die Sache, –n thing, matter
das Sacktüchlein, – handkerchief
sagen to say, to tell
  sagen über (+ acc.) to say about
das Sakrament, –e sacrament
sammeln to gather
  sich sammeln to gather, to assemble
  sich sammeln zu to condense into
der Samstag, –e Saturday
samt together with
sanitär sanitary
der Sanitäter, – medical orderly
satt satiated
  satt werden to get enough to eat
der Satz, ⁀e sentence
sauber clean, neat
  schön sauber (coll.) nice and neat
sauer sour
saugen to suck
die Säule, –n column
schade what a shame! it's a shame! too bad!
schaden (+ dat.) to damage, to harm, to do harm

der Schaden, ⁀ harm, damage
  Schaden erleiden to suffer harm
schaffen to create; to make, to work
  sich Bahn schaffen to make, to force one's way
  nichts zu schaffen haben mit to have nothing to
    do with
der Schafpelz, –e sheepskin
der Schal, –s shawl, scarf
sich schämen (+ gen.) to be ashamed of
schamhaft ashamed
scharf sharp, intensive
der Scharfschütze, –n (MII) sharpshooter
der Schatten, – shadow
  Schattenmänner und Schattenfrauen phantoms
schätzen to esteem, value
schauen to look
der Schauplatz, ⁀e setting, scene
die Schauspielerei, –en acting
die Scheibe, –n slice
der Schein, –e appearance, gleam, glow
scheinen, ie, ie to seem, to shine
das Scheinwerferlicht, –er spot light
das Schema, –mata scheme
schematisch schematic
der Schemel, – stool
schenken to give (as a present), to bestow upon
scheren, o, o to shear, to shave
scheu shy
scheußlich dreadful
die Schicht, –e layer; shift
schicken to send
das Schicksal, –e fate
schieben, o, o to push, to slide
  beiseite schieben to push aside
schießen, o, o to shoot
  Da schoß es A shot rang out
das Schiff, –e boat, ship, vessel
  die Schiffstreppe, –n hatchway
das Schild, –er sign
schildern to describe, depict
der Schirm, –e lamp shade
die Schlacht, –en battle
der Schlächter, – butcher
die Schlachtreihe, –n battleline
der Schlaf sleep
schlafen, ie, a (schläft) to sleep
der Schlag, ⁀e blow, knock
schlagen, u, a (schlägt) an (+ acc.) to strike
  kurz und klein schlagen to smash to pieces
das Schlagwort, ⁀er catchword, cliché
die Schlagzeile, –n headline
die Schlampe, –n slut
schlecht bad, evil, rotten

schleichen, i, i (ist) to steal, to sneak

schließen, o, o to close

schließlich finally

schlimm bad

schluchzen to sob

schlurfen to shuffle, to scuff

der Schluß, ⸚sse end

schmal narrow, short

> **Bei ihm ist Schmalhans Küchenmeister** He has trouble making ends meet

schmalzen to ooze

schmecken to taste

> **es schmeckt mir** it tastes good to me

schmelzen, o, o (schmilzt) to melt

schmierig soiled; smeary, greasy

der Schmuck, –e jewelry

schmutzig dirty

schnappen to grab, to catch, to snap

der Schnee snow

die Schneeschmelze, –n thaw

schneidig snappy, dashing

schnell quick, fast

der Schnupfen, – cold

die Schnur, ⸚e string

schon already

schön beautiful, nice

> **schön sauber** nice and neat
> **schön warm** nice and warm

die Schönheit, –en beauty

schöpferisch creative

die Schornsteinreste (*pl.*) the remains of chimneys

der Schrank, ⸚e closet

der Schrecken fear, horror, terror

> **außer sich vor Schrecken** beside oneself with fear

der Schrei, –e scream

schreiben, ie, ie to write

> **schreiben von** to write about
> **schreiben an** (+ *acc.*) to write to

das Schreibheft, –e exercise book, notebook

die Schreibung, –en spelling

der Schreiner, – carpenter

die Schreinerei, –en carpenter's workshop

die Schrift, –en writing; letter; characters

schriftlich written, in writing

der Schriftsteller, – writer

schrill shrill, piercing

der Schritt, –e step

> **Seine Schritte schwangen weit aus** He strode along

der Schuft, –e rogue

die Schule, –n school

der Schulhof, ⸚e school yard

die Schulter, –n shoulder

der Schuß, ⸚sse shot

der Schutt rubble, debris

die Schuttwüste, –n desert of rubble

der Schutzmann, –leute policeman

Schwaben Swabia

Schwäbisch-Hall city in Württemberg

schwach weak, dim

die Schwäche, –n weakness

der Schwager, – brother-in-law

die Schwägerin, –nen sister-in-law

schwanken to sway, to stagger

schwarz black

schwarzgerändert bordered in black

schwatzen to chatter

schweigen, ie, ie to be silent

das Schweigen silence

> **zum Schweigen verweisen** to command to be silent

schweißig perspiring, sweaty

die Schweiz Switzerland

der Schweizer, – Swiss

die Schwelle, –n threshold

schwenken to swing

schwer difficult, heavy

schwerfällig heavily

die Schwester, –n sister, nurse

schwierig difficult

die Schwierigkeit, –en difficulty

(sich) schwingen, a, u to sweep

der Schwung, ⸚e swing, spring, bound

> **mit großen Schwung** with great vitality

der Seetang seaweed

sehen, a, e (sieht) to see

> **sehen auf** (+ *acc.*) to look at
> **ähnlich sehen** (+ *dat.*) to resemble (someone)
> **vor sich hin·sehen** to drop one's gaze

sehr very, very much

der Seidenrock, ⸚e silk skirt

das Seil, –e rope

sein, war, gewesen (ist) to be

> **ihm war, als . . .** it seemed to him as if . . .
> **ihm war wie nach Sekt** he felt as though he should have champagne

seinerseits for his part

seit since, for

> **seitdem** since
> **seither** since then

die Seite, –n side, page

die Seitenstraße, –n side street

seitwärts von beside

die Sekretärin, –nen secretary

der Sekt, –e champagne

selbst even; -self

die Selbstsucht egoism

die Selbsttäuschung, –en self-deception

selbstverständlich obvious
selten seldom
seltsam strange
das Semester, – semester, term
senden, a, a to broadcast
senken to sink, to lower
    den Kopf senken to bend one's head
setzen to set, to put
    sich setzen to sit down
    sich in Gang setzen to begin to move
die Seuche, –n epidemic
das Seuchenlazarett, –e isolation hospital
seufzen to sigh
sicher certain
die Sicherheit certainty, safety
der Sieg, –e victory
singen, a, u to sing
der Sinn, –e sense, meaning
sinnlos senseless
die Sinnlosigkeit senselessness
sittlich ethical
die Situation, –en situation
sitzen, a, e to sit
    es sitzt sich gut it is comfortable
so so, thus, as
sodaß in order that (*conj.*)
sofort immediately
der Sog, –e wake
sogar even
sogenannt (sog.) so-called
sogleich immediately
der Sohn, ⸚e son
solch- such a, such
der Soldat, –en (*MII*) soldier
sollen to ought to, to be (supposed) to, to be said to
somit thus
der Sommer, – summer
sonderbar strange
sondern but (on the contrary)
die Sonne, –n sun
der Sonntag, –e Sunday
sonst otherwise; formerly, any other time
die Sorge, –n worry
    sich Sorgen machen um to worry about, to be worried about
    sich sorgen to worry
sowas = so etwas that sort of thing
sowie as well as
    sowieso anyway
die Sowjetunion Soviet Union
sowohl as well as
die Spalte, –n newspaper column
die Spannung, –en tension

der Spaß, ⸚e joke, fun
    es macht ihnen Spaß they have fun
spät late
spazieren gehen, ging spazieren, (ist) spazieren gegangen to take a walk
der Speck bacon
die Speisekammer, –n pantry
die Spezialität, –en specialty
der Spiegel, – mirror
die Spiegelglasscheibe, –n plateglass window
spiegeln to shine, to reflect
die Spiegelung, –en reflection
spielen to play
das Spinnenbein, –e spider's leg
der Spinnrocken, – distaff
das Spital, ⸚er hospital
spitz sharp, pointed
die Spitze, –n tip, point
die Spitznase, –n pointed nose
sprechen, a, o (spricht) to speak
    sprechen von to talk about, to mention
sprichwörtlich proverbial
spröde rough, brittle; prudish
spüren to feel
der Staat, –en state
staatlich of the state, pertaining to the state
der Staatsbürger, – citizen (of a country)
das Staatsexamen, –mina university diploma for high school teachers
der Stab, ⸚e spoke
die Stadt, ⸚e city, town
der Städter, – city man
städtisch urban; municipal
der Stadtteil, –e section of the city
der Stall, ⸚e stable
der Stammvater, ⸚ father
stark strong
die Stärke, –n strength
starren to stare
die Station, –en station
die Statistik, –en statistics
statt (anstatt) instead of
stattdessen instead of this
statt·finden, a, u to take place
das Staubgewölk, –e clouds of dust
sich stauen to throng, to converge
stehen, a, a to stand
    gut stehen (+ *dat.*) to suit
    stehen bleiben to stand still
    alles stehen und liegen lassen to drop everything
    es steht darauf it says
stehlen, a, o (stiehlt) to steal
steigen, ie, ie (ist) to climb

steil steep

    steilgereckt erect

der Stein, –e stone, rock

die Steinfliese, –n flagstone

die Stelle, –n spot

stellen to put

    sich stellen to place oneself, to go and stand

    eine Frage stellen to ask a question

die Stellung, –en position, job

das Sterbebett, –en deathbed

sterben, a, o (ist) (stirbt) to die

das Steuer, – helm, steering wheel

der Steuermann, ⸚er helmsman

der Stich, –e stitch, prick

    im Stich lassen to abandon

die Stiefmutter, ⸚ stepmother

der Stil, –e style

das Stilexperiment, –e experiment in style

das Stilmittel, – technique

die Stimme, –n voice

stimmen to tune, to be correct

die Stimmung, –en atmosphere

der Stint, –e smelt (fish)

die Stirn, –en forehead

der Stock, ⸚e stick; floor

stockend haltingly

stockig stiff, stocky

der Stoff, –e material

stolz auf (+ *acc.*) proud of

stopfen to tuck

stören to bother, to disturb

der Stoß, ⸚e push, kick

    Stöße von Pergamenten piles of documents

stoßen, ie, o (stößt) to push, to kick

der Stoßseufzer, – snort

strahlen to beam, to shine

strampeln to kick, to struggle

die Straße, –n street

die Straßenbahn, –en streetcar

der Straßengraben, ⸚ ditch

streben nach to strive for

streichen, i, i to stroke, to rub gently (with the hand)

    sich über die Augen streichen to pass the hand over the eyes

das Streichholz, ⸚er match

streifen to brush

der Streit, –e quarrel, fight

sich streiten, i, i über (+ *acc.*) to argue about

streng strict

der Strom, ⸚e stream

die Stube, –n room

das Stück, –e piece, stretch, play

der Student, –en (*MII*) student

studieren to study

das Studium, –en study

die Stufe, –n step

der Stuhl, ⸚e chair

stumm silent, mute, dumb

stumpf blunt

die Stunde, –n hour

das Stundenergebnis, –se result(s) of an hour

der Sturm, ⸚e storm

stürmen to storm, to assault

stürzen to dart, to rush, to tumble

suchen to look for, to seek

die Sucht mania, passion

(das) Süddeutschland Southern Germany

der Süden South

südlich southern

südwärts toward the south

die Sünde, –n sin

die Suppe, –n soup

süß sweet

symbolisch symbolic

T

die Tafel, –n blackboard, table

der Tag, –e day

tagelang for days

täglich daily

das Talent, –e talent

tartarisch Tartar

die Tasche, –n bag, pocket

die Tat, –en deed, act

die Tatsache, –n fact

die Taube, –n dove

taufen to christen, to baptize, to call

taumelig staggering

taumeln to reel

täuschen to deceive

die Täuschung, –en deception

der Teil, –e part

    zu einem großen Teil for the most part

teilen to separate, to divide

    teilen in (+ *acc.*) to divide into

teilnahmslos apathetic

teil·nehmen, a, o (nimmt teil) to participate

    teil·nehmen an (+ *dat.*) to participate in, to take part in

telefonieren to telephone

der Teller, – plate

die Temperatur, –en temperature

der Teppich, –e rug
teuer expensive
das Theater, – theater
der Theaterregisseur, –e theater director
die Theke, –n bar, counter
das Thema, –en theme, topic
der Theoretiker, – theorist
theoretisch theoretical
das Ticken, – ticking
tief deep
das Tierzeug animal matter
der Tisch, –e table
   die Tischkante, –n edge of the table
der Titel, – title
die Todesstrafe, –n death penalty
der Todgeweihte, –n (adj.) doomed man
der Todkranke, –n (adj.) a fatally sick person
der Ton, –e sound, tone
das Tor, –e gate
tot dead
total total, totalitarian
der Tote, –n (adj.) dead person
töten to kill
der Totenschein, –e death certificate
totenstill dead silent
totkrank dying
die Tradition, –en tradition
traditionell traditional
tragen, u, a (trägt) to wear, to carry
der Träger, – carrier, bearer
tränenüberströmt tear-stained
das Transparent, –e poster, billing
transportieren to transport, to convey
träumen to dream
träumerisch dreamily
traurig sad
die Trauungsformel, –n marriage vows
treffen, a, o (trifft) to meet, to encounter; to hit
  (sich) treffen to meet
  eine Anordnung treffen to make an arrangement
trennen to separate
die Treppe, –n stair; stairs
   die Treppen hinab down the stairs
treten, a, e (tritt) to step
  beiseite treten to step aside
treu devoted, faithful
der Trinkbecher, – drinking mug
trinken, a, u to drink
das Trinkgeld, –er tip
der Triumph, –e triumph
triumphierend triumphantly
trocken dry
Troja Troy

der Trojanische Krieg Trojan War
die Trommel, –n drum
der Trost comfort, consolation
  Trost zureden (+ dat.) to console
trotz despite, in spite of
trotzdem nevertheless
trüb clouded
trübsinnig melancholy, sad
die Trümmer (pl.) ruins
die Truppe, –n troop
der Tscheche, –n (MII) Czech
die Tschechoslowakei Czechoslovakia
das Tuch, –er cloth, sheet
die Tüchtigkeit efficiency, competence
tummeln to romp
tun, a, a to do
die Tür, –en door
der Türhüter, – doorkeeper
die Türkei Turkey
türlich = natürlich naturally
die Turmuhr, –en tower clock
typisch typical
der Typus, Typen type

U

übel bad
die Übelkeit, –en sickness, nausea
üben to practice
über over, across, about
überein·stimmen to agree
der Überfall, –e attack, raid
übergießen, o, o to flood
überhaupt at all
überlassen, ie, a (überläßt) to leave (a thing to a
   person)
über·laufen, ie, au (hat) (läuft über) to pass by
überleben to survive
überlegen to consider
  sich überlegen to think over
übermitteln to convey
übernächst the one after
übernachten to spend the night, to stay overnight
überrascht surprised
überschreiten, i, i to step over
überwinden, a, u to overcome
überzeugen to convince
die Überzeugung, –en conviction
  zu der Überzeugung gelangen to become convinced
übrigens moreover, by the way
die Uhr, –en clock, watch

das **Uhrwerk,** –e clockwork
um around, about
   um . . . zu in order to
sich **um · blicken** to glance around
(sich) um · drehen to turn around
die **Umgebung,** –en surroundings, environment
die **Umgegend,** –e surrounding countryside, vicinity
umgehen, i, a (ist) to go around
umgekehrt opposite
umklammern to clasp
(sich) um · kleiden to change (clothes)
sich **umschauen** to look around
umschließen, o, o to enclose
umschreiben, ie, ie to paraphrase
um · stimmen (+ *acc.*) to bring someone around,
   to make someone change his mind
umstritten controversial
unangenehm unpleasant
unauffällig inconspicuous
unbedingt absolute, unconditional
unbeholfen clumsy
undeutlich indistinct, blurred
die **Unendlichkeit,** –en infinity
unentdeckt undiscovered
unermüdlich untiring
unersättlich insatiable
unfreundlich unfriendly
ungeheuer appalling, immense, monstrous
ungemein uncommon(ly)
das **Ungenügen** dissatisfaction
ungewünscht unwanted, not wished for
ungezählt uncounted
das **Ungeziefer,** – vermin
ungläubig unbelieving
unglaublich unbelievable
unglücklich unlucky, unhappy
unheilbar incurable
die **Universität,** –en university
die **Unmenschlichkeit,** –en inhumanity
unruhig restless
unschuldig innocent
unsicher uncertain
die **Unsicherheit,** –en danger; uncertainty
der **Unsinn** nonsense
unten down below, downstairs
unter under, beneath, among
der **Unterarzt,** ⁻e low-ranking military doctor
das **Unterbewußte** (*adj.*) subconscious
unterbleiben, ie, ie (ist) not to take place
unterbrechen, a, o (unterbricht) to interrupt
unter · bringen, a, a to place, to house
unterdrücken to suppress
untereinander among each other

unter · haken to take by the arm
unterhalb below
unterhalten, ie, a (unterhält) to entertain
   sich **gut unterhalten** to have a good time
   sich **unterhalten** to converse
die **Unterhaltung,** –en conversation
unterrichten to teach
sich **unterscheiden, ie, ie** to differ from
der **Unterschied,** –e difference
unterschlagen, u, a (unterschlägt) to suppress
die **Untersuchung,** –en investigation, interrogation
der **Untertan,** –en (*MII*) subject (to a king)
unübersehbar innumerable
unüberwindlich invincible
ununterbrochen uninterrupted
unverdächtig above suspicion
unverkennbar unmistakable
unverlöschlich unextinguishable
unvernünftig unreasonable, rash
unversehrt unharmed
unwiderstehlich irresistible
unwillkürlich involuntary
unzugänglich unapproachable
unzuverlässig unreliable, inaccurate
die **Uraufführung,** –en opening night, premiere
die **Ursache,** –n cause
das **Urteil,** –e judgment, verdict
urteilen to judge
usw. = und so weiter etc.

V

der **Vater,** ⁻ father
das **Vaterland** fatherland, mother country
väterlich paternal, fatherly
verachten to despise, to scorn
verächtlich scornful
die **Verachtung** contempt, scorn
(sich) verändern to change
veranlassen, ie, a (veranläßt) to induce, lead
verantwortlich responsible
die **Verantwortung,** –en responsibility
der **Verband,** ⁻e bandage
verblüfft dumbfounded
das **Verbot,** –e prohibition, restriction
   trotz meines Verbotes against my will
verboten forbidden
der **Verbrecher,** – criminal
verbringen, a, a to spend (time)
der **Verdacht** suspicion
verdächtig suspicious

verdammt dammed
verdecken vor to hide something or someone from
verdienen to deserve, to earn
die Verehelichten married people
die Verehelichung, –en wedding
die Vereinigten Staaten (pl.) United States
vereinsamen to become lonely
vereinsamt deserted
verenden to perish (miserably)
verfallen, ie, a (verfällt) (ist) to fall into decline, to decay
sich verfärben to change colors
der Verfasser, – author
verfluchen to curse
die Vergangenheit, –en past
vergebens in vain
sich vergegenwärtigen to visualize
vergehen, i, a (ist) to pass (time); to die
vergessen, a, e (vergißt) to forget
der Vergleich, –e comparison
vergleichen, i, i to compare
das Verhalten, – behavior
sich verhalten, ie, a (verhält) to behave
das Verhältnis, –se relationship, condition
verhandeln to negotiate, to deliberate; to try cases
die Verhandlung, –en proceeding, conference
verhängnisvoll fatal
verhauen to beat soundly, whack
verheiratet sein mit to be married to
das Verhör, –e examination, investigation
    Verhöre an·stellen to make investigations
verhüllen to conceal
verklagen to sue, to charge
sich verkriechen, o, o to crawl into a hole
verkünden to proclaim
verkündigen to announce
verlangen to demand, to require
verlassen, ie, a (verläßt) to leave
    sich verlassen auf (+ acc.) to rely on
verlegen to shift
verleihen, ie, ie to award
verletzen to injure, to hurt
die Verletzung, –en hurt, injury
verleugnen to repudiate
verloren·gehen, i, a (ist) to be lost
vermeiden, ie, ie to avoid
vermuten to assume, to suppose, to guess, to suspect
die Vermutung, –en assumption
die Vernunft sense, reason
veröffentlichen to publish
die Veröffentlichung, –en publication
verpantschen to adulterate
die Verpflichtung, –en obligation

der Verrat betrayal, treason
verraten, ie, a (verrät) to betray, to reveal, to disclose, to give something away
verrückt crazy
die Versammlung, –en meeting, assembly
versäumen to omit, neglect
verschärfen to increase, to intensify, to sharpen
verscheuchen to banish
verschieden different
der Verschleiß wear and tear; loss
verschließen, o, o to lock
verschweigen, ie, ie to suppress, to keep secret
verschwinden, a, u (ist) to disappear
das Versehen, – mistake, oversight, error
versetzen to transfer, to shift
versprechen, a, o (verspricht) to promise
verspüren to feel, to perceive
verstauchen to sprain
(sich) verstecken to hide
verstehen, a, a to understand
sich verstellen to dissemble
verstockt doggedly
verstorben late, deceased
verstört bewildered, disturbed
verstrecken to stretch forward
verströmen to stream forth, to flow
verstummen to become silent
der Versuch, –e attempt, try
versuchen to try
versunken submerged
sich vertiefen to deepen
    sich vertiefen in (+ acc.) to plunge into
vertrauen (+ dat.) to trust
vertreiben, ie, ie to drive away
der Vertreter, – representative, traveling salesman
die Vertretung, –en representation
verwandeln to convert
die Verwandlung, –en metamorphosis
der Verwandte, –n (adj.) relative
verweigern to deny
verweisen, ie, ie an (+ acc.) to command, to refer to
verwenden to use, to employ
verwirklichen to carry out
verwundert surprised, astonished
verwundet wounded, hurt
sich verzählen (um) to miscount (by)
verzehren to eat, to consume
verziehen, o, o to distort
    sich verziehen to disappear, to vanish
viel much, many
vielleicht maybe, perhaps
vielmehr rather
das Volk, ¨er people

der Volksmund vernacular
  es heißt im Volksmund the popular saying goes
volkstümlich popular
der Volkszähler, – census taker
voll full
völlig complete
vollkommen complete
von of, from, by
vor before, ago, in front of
  vor allem above all
vorbei·gehen, i, a (ist) an (+ *dat.*) to go past
vorbei·kommen, a, o (ist) to pass (by)
vorbei·schrammen to graze past
das Vorbild, –er example, standard
vorbildlich exemplary, model, ideal
der Vordergrund foreground
vor·fahren, u, a (ist) to drive up
vor·finden, a, u to find, to come upon
vor·haben to intend
der Vorhang, ⸗e curtain
vorher before that
vorig last
vor·kommen, a o (ist) to occur
vor·lassen, ie, a (läßt vor) to be admitted
der Vormittag, –e forenoon
  eines Vormittags one forenoon
vor·rauschen to rustle by
der Vorschlag, ⸗e suggestion
vor·schlagen, u, a (schlägt vor) to suggest
die Vorsicht caution, care
vorsichtig careful
vor·springen, a, u (ist) to jump forward, to hasten
  in front
die Vorstadt, ⸗e suburbs, outskirts
vor·stellen to introduce
  sich vor·stellen to imagine
vor·täuschen to pretend
vorüber·kommen, a, o (ist) an (+ *dat.*) to pass
die Voruntersuchung, –en preliminary inquiry,
  investigation
das Vorurteil, –e prejudice
vorwärts onward, forward
vorwärts·kommen, a, o (ist) to advance, progress

W

wachen to guard
  wachen über (+ *dat.*) to watch over
wachsen, u, a (ist) (wächst) to grow
der Wächter, – watchman
wackeln to totter
wagen to dare

der Wagen, – car, wagon
die Wagentür, –en car door
wählen to choose
wahr true
während during, while
die Wahrheit, –en truth
wahrscheinlich probable
die Währungsreform currency reform (1948)
der Wald, ⸗er wood, forest
die Wand, ⸗e wall
die Wanderung, –en walking tour, hike
wann when (*interr.*)
warm warm
die Wärme warmth
warnen to warn
warten auf (+ *acc.*) to wait for
  auf sich warten lassen to take one's time
warum why (*interr.*)
was für ein what kind of
waschen, u, a (wäscht) to wash
wechseln to change
wechselnd flashing, changing
wedeln to wag
weder . . . noch neither . . . nor
weg away, gone
der Weg, –e path, way
  sich auf den Weg machen nach to set out for
wegen on account of, because of
weg·gehen, i, a (ist) to go away
weg·laufen, ie, au (ist) (läuft weg) to run away
weg·nehmen, a, o (nimmt weg) to take away
weg·reisen to leave, to depart
weg·sterben, a, o (ist) (stirbt weg) to die
weg·stoßen, ie, o (stößt weg) to shove away
weg·werfen, a, o (wirft weg) to throw away
weg·winken to wave aside
der Wehrdienst military service
weich soft
weichen, i, i (ist) to give way, to yield
sich weigern to refuse
die Weihnacht, –en Christmas
die Weile while; space of time
der Wein, –e wine
weise wise
die Weise, –n manner, way
der Weisheitsspruch, ⸗e wise saying
weiß white
weißgrau whitish gray
weit far
  weit und breit far and wide
weiter·fahren, u, a (fährt weiter) to travel on
weiter·laufen, ie, au (ist) (läuft weiter) to run on
weiter·treiben, ie, ie to drive on

die Welle, –n wave
die Welt, –en world
die Weltanschauung, –en philosophy of life
der Welterfolg, –e success of the world, world success
die Weltliteratur world literature
wenden, a, a to turn
   sich wenden an (+ *acc*.) to turn to
der Wendepunkt, –en turning point
die Wendung, –en turn, change
wenig little, few
wenigstens at least
wenn when, if, whenever
   wenn auch although
wer who, whoever (*interr*.)
werden, u, o (ist) (wird) to become, get
werfen, a, o (wirft) to throw
   über den Haufen werfen to upset, to cause great
     confusion
das Werk, –e work
die Werkstatt, ⁻e workshop
wert worthy, honorable
wertvoll valuable
das Wesen, – essence, nature
   nichtige Wesen nonentities
wesentlich essential
die Wespe, –n wasp
Westdeutschland West Germany
der Westen west
die Westfront, –en western front
westlich west, western, in a western direction
weswegen on what account, why (*interr*.)
das Wetter weather
wichtig important
wickeln to wrap
wider against
wider·spiegeln to mirror
widersprechen, a, o (widerspricht) (+ *dat*.) to
   contradict
der Widerspruch, ⁻e contradiction
der Widerstand resistance movement
widerstehen, a, a (+ *dat*.) to resist, to oppose
wie how (*interr*.); how, like, as, what, just as, can
   be compared with
   wie nie zuvor like never before
wieder again; more
der Wiederaufbau rebuilding, reconstruction
wiederauf·bauen to rebuild
wiederholen to repeat
die Wiege, –n cradle
wiegen to rock, wag
wild wild
der Wille, –n (*MII*) will
willig willing

willkommen welcome
der Wind, –e wind
der Winkel, – corner
die Winterschlacht, –en winter battle
winzig tiny
wirklich real, actual
die Wirklichkeit, –en reality
die Wirtin, –nen landlady
die Wirtschaft, –en economy, farm, tavern
das Wirtschaftswunder economic miracle
wischen to wipe
wissen, u, u (weiß) to know
   wissen von to know about
die Wissenschaft, –en science
die Witwe, –n widow
der Witz, –e joke
wo where
die Woche, –n week
   vorige Woche last week
das Wochenende, –n weekend
wochenlang for weeks
die Wochenzeitung, –en weekly newspaper
wohin where(to)
wohl well, good, probably
wohlbestallt well established
der Wohlstand well-being, prosperity, wealth
wohnen to live, to dwell
die Wohnstätte, –n dwelling place, residence
die Wohnung, –en dwelling
das Wohnviertel, – residential district
wollen (will) to want to; to claim
woran at what, about what, how, why (*interr*.)
woraus out of what, from what (*interr*.)
das Wort, ⁻er (–e) word, phrase
   das Wort ergreifen, i, i to begin to speak
wortlos speechless, wordless
wovon about what, from what (*interr*.)
wozu for what, what for, why (*interr*.)
wulstig thick
die Wunde, –n wound
das Wunder, – miracle, wonder
wundern to surprise
   sich wundern über (+ *acc*.) to be surprised, to be
     astonished
der Wunsch, ⁻e wish
wünschen to wish
die Würde, –n dignity
würdig dignified, worthy
der Wurm, ⁻er worm
   armes Wurm poor thing
wüst waste, desolate
die Wüste, –n desert, wilderness
wütend furious, angry

Z

zaghaft shy, irresolute
die Zaghaftigkeit shyness, wavering
die Zahl, –en number
zählen to count
zahm tame
der Zahn, ⸚e tooth
zart delicate
zehnmal ten times
das Zeichen, – sign
der Zeigefinger, – index finger, trigger finger
zeigen to show
    zeigen auf (+ acc.) to point at
die Zeit, –en time
    vor der Zeit untimely, prematurely
    geraume Zeit quite a long time
das Zeitalter, – age
eine Zeitlang for a while
die Zeitschrift, –en periodical
die Zeitung, –en newspaper
der Zeitungsverkäufer, – newspaper seller
die Zelle, –n cell
zerbröckeln to crumble
zerfallen, ie, a (ist) (zerfällt) to fall to pieces, to separate
zerschmettern to shatter, to crush
zerstören to destroy
die Zerstörung, –en destruction
die Zerstreutheit absence of mind
der Zeuge, –n die Zeugin, –nen witness
die Zeugenaussage, –n examination of witnesses
die Ziege, –n she-goat; hag
ziehen, o, o to pull, to move, draw, to pluck
ziemlich rather
die Ziffer, –n figure, cipher
die Zigarette, –n cigarette
das Zimmer, – room
zögern to hesitate
zucken to flash
zuerst (at) first
der Zufall, ⸚e coincidence
zu·fallen, ie, a (ist) (fällt zu) to shut (of a door)
zufrieden content
der Zug, ⸚e train; feature; trait; puff, draw
zugänglich sein (+ dat.) to be accessible to
zu·gehen, i, a (ist) to close (of a door)
zugereist newly arrived
zugleich at the same time, at once
zugunsten to the advantage
zu·haben to keep (have) shut, closed
der Zuhörer, – listener, member of the audience
zu·klappen to close, to snap shut

zu·kommen, a, o (ist) auf (+ acc.) to come up to
die Zukunft future
zu·laufen, ie, au (läuft zu) (+ acc.) to run toward, to run up to
zu·machen to close
zumindest at least
zunächst at first
zu·nehmen, a, o (nimmt zu) to increase
die Zunge, –n tongue
die Zungenspitze, –n tip of the tongue
zu·nicken (+ dat.) to nod to
zu·reden to urge, to encourage
    Trost zureden to console
zurück·blicken to look back
    zurückblicken auf (+ acc.) to look back on
zurück·finden, a, u to find one's way back
zurück·geben, a, e (gibt zurück) to give back
zurück·gewinnen, a, o to win back
zurück·halten, ie, a (hält zurück) to hold back
zurück·kehren (ist) to return
zurück·kommen, a, o (ist) to return, to come back
zurück·legen to put back
sich zurück·lehnen to lean back
zusammen·brechen, a, o (bricht zusammen) to break down, to collapse
der Zusammenbruch, ⸚e collapse
sich zusammen·finden, a, u to gather
der Zusammenhang, ⸚e relationship, connection
sich zusammen·krampfen to be seized by a cramp
zusammen·sacken to collapse
die Zuschauer (pl.) public, audience
die Zuschauerschaft audience
zu·sehen, a, e (sieht zu) to watch, to see to it that
zu·sprechen, a, o (spricht zu) to award
der Zustand, ⸚e state
zu·steuern auf (+ acc.) to head for
zu·trauen to credit with
zuungunsten to the disadvantage
zuverlässig reliable
die Zuversicht confidence, optimism
zuvor beforehand, previously
zu·wackeln to stagger to, to wobble to
zu·winken (+ dat.) to beckon, to nod to
(sich) zwängen to squeeze
zwar to be sure
der Zweifel, – doubt
    über allem Zweifel beyond all doubt
zweifeln an (+ dat.) to doubt
zwinkern to wink
zwischen between
zwischendurch between times
der Zwischenfall, ⸚e incident, event

INDEX

INDEX